BOLAN

THE RISE AND FALL OF A 20TH CENTURY SUPERSTAR

MARK PAYTRESS

OMNIBUS PRESS

London/New York/Paris/Sydney/Copenhagen/Madrid/Tokyo

Cover designed by Fresh Lemon
Picture research by Steve Behan & Mark Paytress

ISBN: 1-84609-147-0
Order No: OP 51227

Exclusive Distributors:
Music Sales Limited,
8/9 Frith Street,
London W1D 3JB, UK.

Music Sales Corporation,
257 Park Avenue South,
New York, NY 10010, USA.

Macmillan Distribution Services,
53 Park West Drive,
Derrimut, Vic 3030,
Australia.

To the Music Trade only:
Music Sales Limited,
8/9 Frith Street,
London W1D 3JB, UK.

All lyrics used by kind permission.

Every effort has been made to trace the copyright holders of the photographs in this book but one or two were unreachable. We would be grateful if the photographers concerned would contact us.

Printed by Gutenberg Press Ltd, Malta.

A catalogue record for this book is available from the British Library.

www.omnibuspress.com

Contents

Prelude   vii

1   Sweet Little Rock'n'Roller   1

2   You Can't Catch Me   17

3   Little Queenie   33

4   Let It Rock   68

5   Beautiful Delilah   90

6   No Particular Place To Go   126

7   Almost Grown   152

8   Let It Rock   171

9   Superstar   202

10   Reelin' And Rockin'   236

11   Too Pooped To Pop   265

12   Go, Johnny Go   292

Epilogue   "If I Could Have Grown . . ."   328

Whatever happened to . . .?   335

Discography   339

Acknowledgements   353

Source Notes & Bibliography   356

Index   361

Prelude

"Light emanated from him. He had the most charisma of all the stars I've met or worked with."

– Tony Visconti, producer

"He had a wonderful life and he lived life to the full."

– Gloria Jones, partner

When I convinced Chris Charlesworth at Omnibus Press that my 1992 Marc Bolan biography ought to be back in print again, we envisaged little more than a handful of minor changes: weeding out inaccuracies, working in details that had come to light since then and, perhaps, a quick stylistic once-over. Four months later, having dedicated virtually every available waking hour to the project, the result is an entirely different book – 50% bigger and, I hope, rather more authoritative.

A day spent at the National Sound Archive prompted a complete over-haul of my research materials; within a month, I had amassed a huge, 30,000-word document that I intended to work into the original text. Then, I turned to the original biography. Now a decade old, *Twentieth Century Boy: The Marc Bolan Story* seemed convoluted and tired. I had no alternative but to consign huge chunks to the wastebasket, and use the basic information, the musical critiques and the cultural contexts as notes for what I now regarded as a completely different book. Marc Bolan's life story was no longer going to be 'remastered'; it was having to be rebuilt again from scratch – and with a new title, too.

Having bitten the bullet, I then approached a couple of key interviewees missing from the original book. I was delighted when Marc's partner, and mother of his son, Gloria Jones agreed to come on board. Insisting that I only wanted to pursue the truth, that a cosy, crowd-pleasing version of events does no one any favours, she nevertheless opened up with remarkable generosity during a short series of lengthy, long-distance telephone conversations. I hope that her trust in me has been vindicated. Mick Gray, who was Marc's personal assistant and executive tour manager between 1971 and 1976 and who spent as much time with him during those years as anyone did, has also given me many new insights. As a consequence, the latter half of the book – which was certainly the weaker part back in 1992 – is now virtually unrecognisable.

Quite a few people offered their condolences when I told them I was about to revisit an old book project. They needn't have done, for despite the time limitations, the formidable task turned out to be an often exhilarating experience.

That's partly because the Marc Bolan I have discovered this time round is an immensely more complicated person than the 1992 model. His life spans one of the most vibrant eras in British culture. There is an even greater wealth of sources – on record and tape, in private papers and commercial magazines – than ever before, and many potential interviewees all eager to tell me how he touched their lives. Bolan was a pop idol in the sense that, like Jimi Hendrix and Elvis Presley, he was simply one of those characters that was a star almost by nature. The fame was simply a by-product that came later.

Bolan was rich in extremes and contradictions. He was fascinatingly flawed and a fearless interviewee; deadly ambitious and, beneath that flashy exterior, painfully vulnerable. He could be both creative and crass, a peacenik with a streak of viciousness. Often brilliant, sometimes bland, he made some great records and more than a few lousy ones. In public, he could be an ego monster; at home, he became a crushed little Mark Feld who'd tell his cassette recorder just how lonely he was.

Marc Bolan relished change. Restless and impatient, he was forever in search of something. In my search for Marc Bolan, I too have incorporated many changes. Often, they're minor ones, such as my different take on 'Solid Gold Easy Action'. Essentially, though, the canvas has been wiped clean to allow a more accurate and hopefully entertaining portrait to emerge. I've finished the book firm in the belief that the life and work of Marc Bolan holds more fascination for me now than it's ever done. I hope you find something of that in the book, too.

Mark Paytress, London, May 2002.

1

Sweet Little Rock'n'Roller

"When I was younger I certainly thought I was a superior sort of being. And I didn't feel related to other human beings . . . I created a world where I was king of my neighbourhood."

– Marc Bolan (1972)

"The Greek artists, the tragedians for example, poetised in order to conquer; their whole art cannot be thought of apart from contest . . . ambition gave their genius its wings."

– Friedrich Nietzsche, *Human, All Too Human* (1878)

"At nine years old I became Elvis Presley."

– Marc Bolan (1972)

When Marc Bolan exploded so spectacularly all over the front pages during 1971 and 1972, huge chunks of his immediate past were virtually erased from history. The T. Rex Superstar as a bongos-in-the-dirt merchant performing to indifferent festival goers as Tyrannosaurus Rex? It was messy and low achieving, and besides, the truth could be easily corroborated. Bolan preferred to skip these years of hippie humility and instead let his keenly developed imaginative talents loose on the darker continent of his distant past. For an audience barely able to recall The Beatles without beards, Bolan's yarns provided a thrilling portrait of life as a permanent revolution of the self, each costume change bringing with it an entirely new world.

Cynics looked at the credentials of this supposed Superstar – a bare handful of chords, a clown's wardrobe and more front than Jayne Mansfield – and roared. Bolan had effected the most shameful volte-face since the Soviet Union signed a pact with Nazi Germany in 1939, they claimed. Even better, for a rock press reduced to interminable profiles of 'Supersessionmen', this apparent charlatan of the most insincere kind was photogenic, popular and eminently quotable.

The creation of Marc Bolan: Superstar was as crucial to the health of the pop press as it was to a teenage audience desperate for someone to encourage and inspire their fantasies. Despite spending much of his life gazing up at the stars, the reality of Superstardom stunned Bolan too – even though he'd been playing the part since the late Fifties as if it had been his God-given right.

The life and death of Marc Bolan is a gutter-to-glitter opus rich in all the pleasures, and many of the pitfalls, that life can offer – art and ambition, excess and hubris, mythology and, finally, tragedy. Notoriously economical with the truth, Bolan took great delight in obscuring the details of his tortuous path to fame with a repertoire of preposterous stories and golden one-liners, all grist to the illusion that Superstardom – and nothing less than Superstardom – was his destiny. "I was always a star even if it was only being the star of three streets in Hackney," he'd boast proudly on many occasions.

That much, at least, is true: Marc Bolan was working class and enjoyed premonitions of grandeur from an early age. But did he really play skiffle with Helen Shapiro? Roadie for Eddie Cochran? Audition at the 2I's while still in short trousers? Was he really London's sharpest Mod at 14? Or commanding four-figure fees for modelling assignments a year later? By the age of 17, he was practising the black arts with a cannibalistic wizard in Paris – or so he claimed. How did that tally with those heavy hints of French ancestry? Born To Boogie? Well, maybe. He certainly wasn't born Marc Bolan. According to official records, Marc was born Mark Feld in Hackney, east London, the second and younger son of a lorry driver and his market-stallholder wife.

While revealing no obvious French connection, The Feld family records do disclose a genuine continental link, albeit one devoid of the connotations of Gallic sophistication that Bolan later coveted. Mark's paternal grandfather was Henry Feld, born in Whitechapel on March 21, 1894 and of known Polish-Russian descent. His parents – Mark Feld's great grandparents – were almost certainly among the thousands of Jewish émigrés from eastern Europe who resettled in east London after the pogroms unleashed on their communities in the wake of the assassination of Tsar Alexander II in 1881.

Traditionally excluded from many professions, London's Jewish settlers often turned to the rag trade, particularly tailoring and millinery. However, Henry Feld applied his hands somewhat less delicately. By day a porter in Smithfield's busy meat market, he supplemented his income with regular bouts of bare-knuckle fighting, an illegal though not uncommon sideline for the more fearless among east London's meat-packers. Henry would occasionally get his tasks confused: when a horse once had the temerity to stand on his foot, he punched the animal between the eyes and watched it fall to the ground.*

On December 3, 1913, the 19-year-old Henry Feld met and married a local girl, Betsie Ruffell, also 19, a redhead of Irish descent, at the United Synagogue of London. Settling in nearby Stepney, the pair later made the short move to 9 Reeds Mansions in Gosset Street, Bethnal Green. It was while living there that 'Bessie' (as she preferred to be known) gave birth to a son, Simeon, on August 22, 1920.

Simeon Feld inherited his mother's fair colouring but not his father's stocky stature. Nevertheless he continued the family's meat trade associations, starting his working life at Blooms, the noted kosher butchers. It didn't last long. On September 3, 1939, Britain declared war on Nazi Germany and 19-year-old Simeon was conscripted to join the army. Six weeks later he was back on civvy street on account of his poor eyesight. Determined to play his part, Sid (as he was better known) joined the Dutch merchant navy, and spent much of the wartime period as a steward on a munitions ship that journeyed between Liverpool, New York and the West Indies.

Back in London, teenager Phyllis Winifred Atkins was one of millions of women who staffed the factories in support of the war effort. Born on August 23, 1927, Phyllis lived at 32 Kinnoul Road in north-east Fulham from where her father, Henry Leonard Atkins, ran a small, unprofitable greengrocery business. During the early Thirties, in order to make ends meet, Henry's wife Elsie (mother to three other daughters as well) undertook early morning cleaning jobs for the idle ladies of South Kensington. By the early Forties, Phyllis was a breadwinner too, making the short daily trip to the Earl's Court Exhibition Centre that had been requisitioned as a munitions factory. There, she helped make tarpaulin decoy lorries for the Ministry of Supply. Meanwhile, Henry's business had ceased trading and he'd become a dust destructor, operating the incinerator at the end of the refuse collecting process.

Sometime during 1944, Sid Feld returned home from sea and joined the

---

* Animal justice was meted out years later when Henry got slapped in the head by a side of beef, an unlikely event that forced him into early retirement.

Ministry of Supply's payroll as a porter at the Earl's Court building. That's where he met and – spinning tales of his high seas exploits – wooed young Phyllis Atkins. Blissfully oblivious to the seven-year age difference the pair became sweethearts, and by the end of the year, the 17-year-old had become pregnant. This far from unusual occurrence demanded a similarly routine response: on January 31, 1945, Sid and Phyllis were married at Fulham Registry Office, and headed eastwards, renting the upper rooms of a three-storey house in Stoke Newington for 15 shillings per week. The newlyweds were soon separated, though, when Phyllis was evacuated to Walton Hall, a stately residence on the outskirts of Wakefield in Yorkshire. She returned to London in the summer; with her was the couple's first child, Harry Leonard Feld, born on June 25, 1945.

With a wife and baby to support, Sid – who had obtained his driving licence before the war – found a job with a local road haulage firm. Long-distance lorry driving from his firm's base in Islington was hardly an ideal occupation for a man who preferred his own bed to the notorious hospitality of the English guesthouse, but excepting one brief interlude hawking hairbrushes in 1947, Sid spent much of his life on the road. The Felds' marriage survived the disruption, though it did mean that Phyllis played a more significant role in the upbringing of her sons than was usual.

When Sid Feld made it home, which he endeavoured to do as often as he could, it was to 25 Stoke Newington Common, a large, late Victorian terrace house owned by a Mr. Ambrose who occupied the middle floor. The Felds' living-quarters consisted of four shared rooms split over two levels. At the top of a long flight of stairs was a kitchen, fitted with a gas stove and a coal fire, and a cold-water bathroom; a few steps up was a back bedroom and a living room that looked out across the common. Actually no bigger than a small football pitch, the common – like the railway linking the suburb with Liverpool Street station and the West End-bound number 73 bus – helped alleviate any feelings of inner city claustrophobia.

One distinctive feature of the row of houses that skirted the common were the stone columns at every entrance, each topped with ornamental Corinthian capitals. Among the Gothic moulds that adorned number 25 and its immediate neighbours was a bird of prey with wings outstretched, an Old Father Time figure, and a distinctive, long-necked swan – more cream than white.

* * *

While we await the arrival of the Mark Feld who is the subject of this book, we must pause briefly to meet another Mark Feld, whose fate provides a cautionary note to the moral back-slapping that resounded throughout the Allied territories in the immediate post-war euphoria. Unlike his brother Simeon, this Mark – the youngest of the four Feld boys – was a physical lad who wasn't averse to getting into the occasional scrap. Having served in the army during the war, he was posted to the Burton Dassett camp in Warwickshire. It was a poorly disciplined establishment where indiscriminate gunfire and soldiers going AWOL were not uncommon.

This indiscipline reached a horrific climax on the night of August 19, 1946 when Mark Feld, asleep in his billet, was struck a fatal blow to the head with a truncheon. Apparently, following an earlier incident, 35-year-old Patrick Francis Lyons of the camp military police, together with the acting company Sergeant Major, Sgt. Henry Storey Crampsie, ended a night's drinking by paying Feld a surprise visit. It was alleged in court that Lyons had told Crampsie that he intended to "do Feld up" and that Feld was a bad soldier who "would fit only one place and that was Belsen". Lyons claimed that his only intention was to frighten his victim.

"When I was about a yard from the foot of his bed," he told the court, "Feld jumped up and came for me. I struck out with my truncheon and aimed what I thought to be a light blow at his shoulder." That blow, which was indelicate enough to fracture Mark Feld's skull, earned Lyons a conviction for manslaughter. Sentencing Lyons to 10 years' penal servitude, the judge told him that he was as nearly convicted of murder as possible.

Private Mark Feld 14709755, a Jew who didn't need to go to Belsen to meet a tragic end, received two posthumous tributes: the Under-Secretary of State for War belatedly sent a service medal to his mother Bessie Feld; his elder brother Simeon named his second son in his memory.

★   ★   ★

The baby boom peaked in 1947 at 20.5 per thousand of the population, an inevitable consequence of demobilisation. Liberated from the hardships of war, the nation rejected Winston Churchill at the polls, and instead turned to the Labour Party which had fought the 1945 election on a platform of economic and social regeneration based on state socialist principles. Promising mass nationalisation of the country's industrial infrastructure, the party's egalitarian instinct chimed with the camaraderie and optimism that victory in war had given.

On September 30, 1947, while the nation gazed idly into a future that promised economic prosperity and perhaps even that much-vaunted classless society, a second Mark Feld gave his first yelp to a tiny audience in Hackney Hospital. Phyllis and Sid's delight was soon tempered by the arrival of one of the coldest winters of the last century. In a flat with no hot water or proper heating, where the walls were held up by thick layers of wallpaper and which occasionally entertained a stray mouse, Mark's first experience of life was the snug protection of a mound of heavy blankets.

The widespread belief that 'things can only get better' filled young families like the Felds with aspirations for their children. Mark, an outgoing, endearingly precocious boy with a cute smile, became the focus of these hopes from a young age. At the height of his fame, in 1972, he recalled how Phyllis' mother Elsie would flatter him and insist that he would be famous one day. He was four at the time.

For Harry, the arrival of a younger brother gave him the opportunity to exercise some sibling authority – if he could keep up with him. "We always played together when we were young, but because I was that bit older I had to look after him, which wasn't easy because he was always running. He was like a little bullet. He had this peculiar way of pushing his feet out sideways as he ran."

One day, Harry did catch up with him – and gave Mark his first taste of public exhibitionism. "It was one winter, around 1951 or 1952, when there was a heavy snow – the only time I can ever recall six-foot mounds of snow in the streets. I dressed Mark up in my bright red school blazer and my mum's fur boots, and I took him out into the street. Everyone laughed at him."

More typically, the neighbours would see the infant Mark on the porch at number 25, pushing his Dinky cars through the flowerbeds and gazing out at the common across the road. Indoors, Mark spent much of his time in the family living-room – the largest room in the flat – which had been converted into a bedroom for the boys who slept in twin beds separated by a wooden cabinet. With television still a luxury, Mark and Harry's main contact with the wider world during the Fifties was the radio. "One of the highlights of our week was to take the radio – an early portable from Radio Rentals – up to our room at bedtime, put it on the cabinet and lie in bed listening to *Saturday Night Theatre*," Harry remembers. Ghost stories were a particular hit with the boys.

According to Harry, Mark adored anything that "stoked up his imagination" – comics, fairytales and the Biblical tales that Phyllis would read to them at night. "It wasn't a religious exercise," he says. "We were too young to understand Biblical language anyway, so she used to put the stories into plain English, so we could enjoy the adventures of David and Goliath or Daniel and the Lion's Den." Tales from bygone days fascinated the Feld boys – and the stranger the better. Inevitably, they seized upon the prehistoric, dinosaur-dominated world with boyish awe. "I think Mark liked the idea that such huge creatures walked the earth, but weren't here any more," Harry muses.

The dinosaurs had been obliterated, Hitler had been humbled, and still panic-prone post-war Britain trembled. This time, the enemy was more insidious: American mass culture. The seductive spectre of what cultural critic Richard Hoggart called its "shiny barbarism" united voices from both sides of the political spectrum. For Hoggart and the intellectual left, a vibrant, 'authentic' working-class culture, typified by stoicism and cycling clubs, would become corrupted by capitalism central's promised land, a "candy-floss world" of instant gratification and Disneyland aesthetics. The establishment, ever desperate to preserve their own interests, was similarly terror-stricken. As custodians and dispensers of high culture, any 'triumph of mediocrity' scenario would further undermine their *raison d'être*.

What Hoggart underestimated in *The Uses Of Literacy*, his magisterial work on popular culture, was the pleasure principle. Though brilliant and well meaning, his book romanticised the culture of Hoggart's youth; when workingmen's clubs were apparently debating societies with beer and 'Don't Dilly-Dally On The Way' was top of the pre-war pops.

Mark Feld was both vibrant and authentically working class, but that didn't stop him rejoicing in the ultra-brite surfaces that illuminated post-war Britain. Mark, like many among his generation, seized upon anything that promised liberation from the puritan restraint of the traditional working-class lifestyle. And nowhere was this promise more seductive than in the cinema, that cathedral of dreams where alternative lives could be watched, worshipped and aspired to.

Phyllis Feld regularly took her two sons to the ABC cinema along Lower Clapton Road and the Regent (later the Odeon) in Stamford Hill. "The cinema really fired Mark's imagination," says Harry, who recalls his brother's almost unnatural desire to live life through a succession of on-screen heroes. It was, Harry suggests, as much about self-protection as it was fantasy. "If ever Mark was unsure of a situation, he'd become one of the characters he'd seen or read about as a way of shielding himself. That way he could never get hurt. That way, he could cope with anything."

Audie Murphy, the most decorated war hero in Hollywood, provided an obvious shell for young Mark to inhabit. But his first and most relished piece of theatrical armour was Mighty Joe Young, a name many would later assume was that of a little known bluesman from Chicago's South Side. In fact Mighty Joe Young was a fictional gorilla, a King Kong for kids who in the 1949 movie that bears his name is transported from the African jungle into an American household. All goes smoothly until a sip of alcohol sends him berserk. While his classmates fought to assume the identity of Apache legend Geronimo, Mark preferred to masquerade as something significantly less human. Oddly enough, the film's kitschy compound of the strange and the sentimental neatly anticipated the future course that Marc Bolan's creative life would take.

★   ★   ★

Today, Stoke Newington has succumbed to bourgeoisification, especially around the restaurant-strewn Church Street, although areas of high deprivation still exist behind the fashionable façade. The High Street, once home to department stores and thriving small businesses, has been sacrificed to a one-way traffic system. The housing estates, built to replace war-damaged properties and alleviate poverty, have brought their own problems. What has remained, though, is a strong nonconformist presence. The Angry Brigade, a group of anarchists who exploded two bombs at the house of Home Secretary Robert Carr in 1971, were based here, while the occasional Class War slogan can still be spotted between the ubiquitous To Let and For Sale signs.

The district has long been a haven for immigrants and the marginalised. Religious dissenters established a thriving community here in the 18th century, while the Victorian era saw the emergence of a small Jewish community, which grew dramatically during the 20th century. Simeon's parents Henry and Bessie Feld, who brought up their four sons and two daughters in accordance with the Jewish faith, were among those who migrated northwards towards the end of the Thirties ending up at 38 Carlton Mansions, Holmleigh Road in nearby Stamford Hill. But with Simeon marrying a Gentile, and Harry and Mark given a secular upbringing, contact between the two Feld families was confined to weddings and funerals.

"We were a very self-contained family," Harry remembers. Independently minded, too. "There were never any restrictions," Mark proudly proclaimed years later. The Felds sent their sons to the nearby Northwold

Road Primary, a state school where religious content was restricted to a daily hymn followed by a recital of the Lord's Prayer. The headmaster Mr. Kershaw was Jewish, and the school was situated at the heart of the Jewish community on the Stoke Newington/Clapton borders, but the prevailing ethos was always education over faith.

Mark, who began his schooling in September 1952, was a popular and happy pupil at Northwold Primary, liked by his teachers and surrounded by a wide circle of friends. At first, Phyllis would pick him up and take him home for lunch, but he soon settled in and was forced to eat school dinners like everyone else.

Even at this early age, it was obvious that gap-toothed Mark Feld was destined for diminutiveness. This pint-sized propensity, which he shared with Napoleon and Adolf Hitler, has – as psychologists constantly remind us – always demanded a trade-off and, typically, Mark grew bigger in other ways. Harry remembers his brother's boldness, at least in public, where – with or without a little help from Mighty Joe Young – he'd often play the tough guy. His bravura also started to show in his appetite for horror films, sparked by a thrill-packed encounter with *Phantom Of The Opera* starring Claude Rains as the disguised, disfigured organist. But once indoors, and with no audience to play to, Mark was barely able to climb the stairs in the dark without quivering in fear. Instead, he'd conquer his fear of darkness by summoning one of his expanding roster of (anti)heroes and swagger to the rooms at the top as if Mark Feld didn't have a care in the world.

These protective masks suggest that fantasy loomed large in Mark's life from a young age. While his schoolmates left their alter egos in the playground, Mark Feld took his everywhere, his flight from self hastened by cinema, stories and, increasingly, his imagination. In common with Roger 'Syd' Barrett, avidly listening with mother in middle-class Cambridge around the same time, Mark's wide-eyed thirst for life tended to blur the boundary between reality and fantasy. Syd never did grow to accept the rules of adulthood, though Mark was sufficiently versed in survival techniques to make a more successful transition.

That was largely down to his mother, from whom he inherited his dark colouring and a lifelong passion for reading. Phyllis Feld firmly instilled in her boys a traditional sense of right and wrong, even administering the occasional slap, but she never babied them, preferring instead a healthy, almost adult dialogue when difficulties arose within the Feld household.

Although the Felds weren't great socialisers, they had the occasional night out, confident that Harry and Mark would gorge on the lemonade and crisps they left on the table and leave everything else in the flat intact. As a precautionary measure, Phyllis would ask the neighbours to listen for signs of trouble. The keenest pair of ears belonged to Frances Perrone, who had moved into 25 Stoke Newington Common at the end of the Forties, occupying the rooms on the middle floor.

"They were ordinary, working-class people," she remembers. "Phyllis wore the trousers. She was nice and friendly, a real Cockney. I got on very well with her, and they weren't bad tenants at all. They were a happy family; they didn't quarrel a lot." Mrs. Perrone can recall only one occasion when a party at the Felds' got out of hand, and that, as Harry now admits, was down to him and his mates.

The brothers were just two years apart, and maintained a remarkably peaceful co-existence in their shared bedroom. But in almost every other way they were polar opposites. "Harry was quiet like his father; he wasn't like Mark at all," remembers their neighbour. "Mark took after his mum. He was strong-willed, and much more sociable and jolly." Harry, fair like his father and stocky like his mother (the inverse of Mark's genetic inheritance), concurs. "We were 100 per cent different. I realised that from an early age and it became more apparent as time went on. Even my friends were more rough and ready."

Harry was boisterous but content. Mark demanded attention. As the younger son, he felt compelled to keep up with Harry and his friends, a task made doubly difficult by the fact that he looked young for his age. Swaggering around in his treasured Davy Crockett hat and suit worked for a while, but the novelty wore off and Mark was soon searching for new ways to project and exaggerate his individuality.

Speaking in 1972, his father remembered the eight- or nine-year-old Mark as ". . . well, sort of different. He had a head full of ideas." Initially, these took the form of school-sanctioned pursuits, like experiments in plasticene and painting in a style that anticipated "all this contemporary lark". But the moment Mark Feld heard Elvis Presley, a singing, dancing demigod whose very name sounded ultra-modern and deliciously deviant, his life changed forever. Goodbye Mighty Joe Young, Davy Crockett, Audie Murphy and Geronimo. Hail! Hail! Rock'n'Roll . . .

★ ★ ★

Presleymania had been sending British teenagers wild for months. As the embodiment of rock'n'roll, Elvis incited Teddy Boys to riot and big-skirted girls to swoon. It was September 1956 and, still several days shy of his ninth birthday, Mark Feld was similarly mesmerised. Elvis Presley had it all. The animal grace of his movements; the way he cradled his guitar, curled his lip, raised his heels and swivelled his hips; the ghostly tone of his voice, bathed in echo as if from Mars; and that drive-in lyricism rammed home with magnificent insolence. Mark Feld was too young to appreciate fully the latent aggression and sexuality in Presley's performances, but he understood that as a sensationalist of the strange, Elvis was without peer.

The close-knit Feld family were not in the habit of defying convention. Even Simeon's estrangement from his own family was tempered by the fact that he spent every Sunday helping his father assemble trellis and cover units for the stallholders at Petticoat Lane market. One particular Sunday early in September 1956, as Sid lent a philanthropic hand in a bustling East End market, as 'Hound Dog', the fourth Elvis Presley single, was about to hit the shops, and as a potential crisis over the Suez Canal simmered ominously, Phyllis Feld and her two sons were on the number 73 bus making their way across central London towards South Kensington. On arrival, they picked up a number 30 that took them all the way to Phyllis' family home in Fulham. Mark and Harry always enjoyed the trip especially if, by some quirk of timing, they glimpsed the Changing of the Guard as the 73 passed The Mall.

On this particular autumn day, Mark glimpsed something of rather more consequence on the back page of Phyllis' *Sunday Pictorial* newspaper. It was one of those 'Buy Now, Pay Later' warehouse advertisements, the kind that offered relatively expensive goods at affordable hire purchase rates. Mark's finger wagged furiously at the line drawing of a six-string acoustic guitar, but Phyllis knew that at £9, the cost would be more than twice Sid's weekly wage. But the HP facility made the price manageable and besides, she was now earning too, helping out on a friend's fruit and vegetable stall in Soho's Berwick Street market. On September 30, 1956, with 'Hound Dog' neatly installed in the British Top five, nine-year-old Mark Feld unwrapped the best present he'd had in his life. It was, as he said years later, time to become Elvis Presley.

Of course, this ambitious rock'n'roll juvenile couldn't play a note, but who cared when he could now impress his invisible bedroom audiences with real conviction. "I had a guitar as a kid, but I used to just look in the mirror and wiggle about," he recalled in 1972. Out went the home-made contraption his father had fashioned out of orange boxes and elastic bands. The snare drum he'd been given even before discovering rock'n'roll gathered dust in a corner. And as for that soap-box car he later sung about on 'Thunderwing' . . .

Mark Feld's musical education had advanced significantly since the start of the year when his father picked up a copy of Bill Hayes' 'Ballad Of Davy Crockett' in Petticoat Lane market. Mark had been so pleased with it that Sid went out and bought him another Hayes record. Or so he thought. "I looked at the cover," Bolan remembered many years later, "and there was this guy jumping around with a guitar. I said, 'Dad, this isn't Bill Hayes, this is Bill Haley.' " Disappointment soon turned to delight when Mark spun the record, a 1956 EP that included two of Haley's biggest hits, 'Rock Around The Clock' and 'See You Later Alligator'. "Just one play of that and I chucked Bill Hayes out of the window," he recalled. "Haley was much more exciting." Well, until Elvis came along.

In a diary entry dated May 7, 1966, Mark recounts the story of how his prized, 78rpm copy of Presley's 'Blue Suede Shoes' was smashed into smithereens by a stoned associate called Freddy. "I used to, when about 9, dig that very record, sitting real close to the speakers and be washed and resouled by that fantastic 'Oh-a-hum – one for the money' bit," he remembered. Considerably less enamoured of Presley's music, which would boom out of a monstrously sized radiogram, was Frances Perrone, whose living room was directly beneath the boys' bedroom.

"Noisy? When you came in that front door and he had that radiogram on, you could hear him down three flights of stairs," she exclaims. "He'd sit up there in front of his player in that big room with all his records on full blast. Sometimes I had to go up there and tell him to pack it in." Harry also remembers Mark's one-man rock'n'roll parties. "The music used to sound so loud because that large room acted like an echo chamber." Rock'n'roll was, in the words of Frank Sinatra "a rancid-smelling aphrodisiac", and Mark Feld adored it.

Other fledgling rock'n'rollers from the locality remember a distinct lack of chords emanating from Mark's guitar, but plenty of gumption. "I've got this very strong memory of Mark as this chubby little kid in a brown suedette jacket with the collar turned up, whose great claim to fame was that when he combed his hair forward his quiff covered his whole face," remembers Helen Shapiro. Within four years, this eleven-year-old from neighbouring Clapton, had become Britain's biggest-selling singing star. But back in 1957, Mark Feld was the one most likely to. "He was very into the look and the whole rock'n'roll image even then," she says.

The two starlets met via a mutual friend, Stephen Gould, who lived round the corner from the Felds in nearby Fountayne Road. Shapiro, a year Mark's senior, was already attending Clapton Park School and, with her cousin Susan Singer, was already a compulsive singer. "We were friendly with two boys in our year at school, Stephen Gould and Melvyn Fields, and after Stephen was given a guitar for his birthday, he suggested we get together and form a group," says Shapiro.

It was the 1957 summer holiday and the quartet, with Mark Feld and Susan's brother Glenn tagging along, congregated in Stephen Gould's front room to practise their rock'n'roll repertoire. "Stephen and Mark couldn't really play," Helen recalls. "The guitars were twice as big as them anyway. But they looked good. In those days, to have a guitar was the height of sophistication and wonderfulness, because Elvis played – well, held – a guitar. Just to walk along the street carrying one was a thrill."

The six-piece Susie & The Hula Hoops (a name mentioned by Mark years later but which neither Shapiro nor Susan Singer can recall with any certainty) took it in turns to hold the guitars as they wandered the streets of Stoke Newington in search of an audience. They weren't alone: the embers of the skiffle era, when every street had its own DIY group, were still smouldering. "We obviously grew out of the skiffle movement," Shapiro says. "I vaguely recall us having a tea-chest bass for a time, though we never had a washboard. Melvyn kept the beat on the snare drum and brushes while Susan and I sang. There were two distinct camps at the time, skiffle and rock'n'roll. I was in both because I played with my brother's skiffle group from time to time, but Mark was definitely keener on the rock'n'roll thing."

The group's repertoire, which tended to be sung (harmonies and individual vocal leads) rather than played, bears this out. There was plenty of Presley: 'Teddy Bear', 'Got A Lot O' Livin' To Do', 'Hound Dog' and 'Don't Be Cruel' plus 'Heartbreak Hotel', his breakthrough 45. The Everly Brothers' 'Bye Bye Love' and Buddy Holly & The Crickets' 'That'll Be The Day', both hits that summer, were also rehearsal regulars; Susan Singer recalls endless versions of the Holly song at the group's impromptu début in a Stoke Newington cafe (now demolished). "We didn't get paid," Shapiro says, "we just got endless free cups of tea."

Susie & The Hula Hoops also performed at a local school, to children whose parents were unable to look after them during the holidays, before the new autumn term curbed their activities. The group drifted apart, but not before Mark shared his enthusiasm for the latest prince charming in his life, one who was closer to him – both physically and geographically – than Elvis could ever be.

Cliff Richard had been plucked from obscurity to become Britain's answer to Elvis Presley. Difficult as it is to imagine now, in 1958 Cliff was a serious – and potentially panic-inducing – rock'n'roll idol when he charted with the mean and moody 'Move It' that September. Mark's well rehearsed shoulder jerk and lip twisting routine was better suited to mimicking the soft-faced, fast rising British star. Taking off Elvis' surly demeanour and maniacal stare with a face full of puppy fat was never that convincing.

"Mark discovered Cliff Richard before anybody and he wanted to be like him," says Helen Shapiro, who maintains, "He used to do a very good Cliff impression." Harry Feld insists this infatuation represented a genuine watershed in his brother's life. "In his mind, he never ever deviated from the time he started following Cliff Richard. I think he told himself, 'This is what I want,' and he single-mindedly pursued that line until he finally made it."

One of Mark's favourite yarns was the one about meeting Cliff in Soho's legendary 2I's coffee bar when the singer was simply the front man in a combo called The Drifters and in desperate need of a break. "They threw him out!" he remembered gleefully. He even claimed to have auditioned (there was a battered piano downstairs) at the beat hangout in 59 Old Compton Street when he was ten years old. "He was too young," his mother recalled. "I think they only let him do it to keep him happy."

While these stories are clearly nonsense, both were spun out from the basic truth that Mark had been an occasional visitor to the coffee bar, which opened in April 1956 and set Tommy Steele, Cliff Richard and Adam Faith on the road to stardom. By the time Mark Feld walked through its doors, this hothouse of British rock'n'roll was proclaiming itself 'World Famous' and 'Home Of The Stars' and had already become a magnet to tourists and celebrity-junkies. Mark, who spent most Saturday mornings helping his mother on her nearby market stall, found the invitation irresistible. Phyllis would slip him some coppers and he'd run round the corner, dip inside to escape the cold, and help Nora serve the coffees.

Although he occasionally spotted a real star there (Johnny Kidd glowering in a corner, for example), it was the 2I's American-style jukebox that had a more immediate impact, introducing Mark to little heard musical exotica such as The Drifters, The Coasters, Ray Charles and 2I's favourite Bill Doggett's 'Honky Tonk'. "The first record I heard on their jukebox was

'There Goes My Baby' by The Drifters," Mark remembered. "I was knocked out by it." However, the effect of his proximity to stardom at such a tender age cannot be underestimated according to Harry Feld. "Although he was the little'un on the outside, in his mind he was already one of them."

The popularity of rock'n'roll and the rise of a new wave of homegrown talent prompted the launch of Britain's first indispensable television pop show, Jack Good's *Oh Boy*. The shows were filmed on Saturday mornings at the Hackney Empire in Mare Street. Conveniently, the 106 from Stoke Newington stopped right outside, and Harry remembers Mark making the journey on several occasions. The show's most frequent guest was Cliff Richard, but Billy Fury, Adam Faith and Marty Wilde also put in regular appearances. Helen Shapiro managed to obtain Wilde's autograph back-stage, though Mark claimed to have gone one better – carrying Eddie Cochran's guitar when the American appeared on the show in spring 1960, just weeks before Cochran was killed in a car accident. Once again, it's the close encounters with stardom and the star-making process that really matter. Mark was able to peel away the mythology and see his idols as flesh and blood like himself and, reversing the situation, imagine himself as an idol like them.

There's little chance that Stoke Newington's keenest filmgoer would have missed Eddie Cochran make his 1957 film début in *Untamed Youth*. As rock'n'roll made its way onto the big screen, he also saw the all-star *Disc Jockey Jamboree*, featuring Fats Domino, Jerry Lee Lewis and Carl Perkins. By 1959 he had two Cliff movies under his belt: *Expresso Bongo*, which highlighted the dubious role of the manager/agent in the pop process, and *Serious Charge*, which introduced Mark to the illicit thrills of an X-rated film whose subject was homosexuality.

By this time, starstruck Mark Feld was attending the mixed sex William Wordsworth Secondary Modern School, based in Hackney's Shacklewell district. The Palatine Road site was a short walk away (at 14, he moved to the seniors' building in nearby Albion Road), but from his first day in September 1958, Mark resented every second he spent there. "He was in the lower grade, he was lazy and just didn't bother to try," says Harry.

"School was a waste of time, dead," Bolan remembered at the height of his fame. "It wasn't a bad place to be when I was five and we spent our time building bricks. But when the teachers tried to get me to do figurework and writing, I just freaked out." Far more important to him was daydreaming about the world outside and inventing little narrative scenarios to keep himself amused. But one book did leave a profound impression on Mark — though he found it at the local public library. It was, Harry remembers, a biography of Beau Brummell, the 19th century dandy who had been immortalised on screen in a biopic starring Stewart Grainger.

Meticulous about every detail of his personal appearance, this elegant, arrogant aristocrat who'd risen from the margins and was destined to return there, further encouraged Mark to take flight from the habits and conventions of his environment. "He was just like us really," he told *Town* magazine in 1962. "You know, came up from nothing."

"He got the idea of adding a slit in the trouser leg to go over the boot from Beau Brummell," says Harry. But the impact was more overwhelming than that. Reborn as a dandy amid the east London underworld, Mark's every waking moment was now spent endlessly refining his appearance with a precision that was virtually pathological.

2

You Can't Catch Me

"I've got 10 suits, eight sports jackets, 15 pairs of slacks, 30 to 35 good shirts, about 20 jumpers, three leather jackets, two suede jackets, five or six pairs of shoes and 30 exceptionally good ties."

– Mark Feld, *Town* magazine (1962)

"The Mod way of life consisted of total devotion to looking and being 'cool'. Spending practically all your money on clothes and all your after work hours in clubs and dance halls. To be part-time was to miss the point."

– Richard Barnes, *Mods!* (1979)

"I was completely knocked out by my own image, by the idea of Mark Feld."

– Marc Bolan (1967)

In a memorable interview, conducted at the height of his career, Marc Bolan recounted a tale that freeze-framed British subculture in transition. Seated on the porch at number 25, dressed in his black drainpipes, chukka boots and blue, Everly Brothers-style striped shirt, the teenage Mark gazed out across Stoke Newington Common. Engrossed by nothing in particular, he was snapped out of his torpor by a passing Teddy Boy. From the indecent crease in his duck's arse hairstyle to the needle-like sharpness of his winkle-picker boots, this Hackney rebel was a picture of punctilious perfection. Torn between envy and the smug satisfaction that he too could turn heads, Mark returned to his idling.

A little afterwards, a second figure caught his attention. It was, he discovered later, a local Face named Martin Kauffman. "He had on ginger Harris-tweed trousers. Very, very baggy. And a pair of green handmade shoes with side-buckles, very long points. A dark green blazer with drop shoulders, one-button cutaway, very short. (And) his hair was parted straight down the middle, like Hitler, over both eyes." The Beau Brummell of Stoke Newington was delirious. "The impact of having just seen what one thought was really a trendy-looking Teddy Boy and then seeing this cat . . . just the image of him! To this day I still can't trace how he got like that. But I knew something was going on."

It was. The Teddy Boys who'd been casting long and sinister shadows in the streets of Elephant & Castle, Clapham, Stamford Hill and Stoke Newington since the mid-Fifties were losing their lustre. The drape jacket, brothel creeper shoes and bootlace ties that once thrilled and threatened had, by the end of the decade, become frayed and familiar. In its appropriation of the Edwardian look of 1947, a style originally targeted at well-heeled Dandies, Teddy Boy fashion had been an imaginative – and subversive – refusal of mainstream culture. When paraded to the flash, brash soundtrack of American rock'n'roll, the potency of the Ted image soared, investing a power and visibility in youth it had hitherto barely known. But to a new breed of late Fifties peacock such as Martin Kauffman, Teddy Boy apparel was as archaic as the ration book.

Kauffman was undoubtedly an early Modernist, a new generation of obsessive stylists that flourished in London's modern jazz clubs, and whose notion of personal liberation was predicated on matters such as tie width, shoe-stitching or the way a particular pair of trousers hung. The Modernists' microscopic attention to the details of dress was the essence of what later became known as Mod culture. It was consumption, and shameless consumption at that, but in pampering an essentially ungratified self it provided a perfect boost to troubled egos.

The role of a frontline fashion guerilla slaughtering his gracelessly attired rivals (or 'Haddocks') with style was tailor-made for Mark Feld. Within days of witnessing the bloodless battle of mean street elegance, he too had begun to dedicate himself wholeheartedly to the art of sartorial warfare. The self-obsessed, almost exclusively male world to which Martin Kauffman and his contemporaries belonged offered infinite possibilities, enabling Mark to turn his role-playing back on himself, to indulge his manifest narcissism and satisfy the unquenchable desire for constant reinvention in ever more spectacular guises.

The passing of the Teds and the emergence of the Modernists represented far more than a mere change of tailor. While both subcultures flourished in the same working-class districts, and similarly screamed out for recognition, the Teddy Boy rite of passage involved little more than dressing up in the uniform and giving it some 'Wild One' attitude – flick knife optional. The early Modernists were quite different, shunning uniformity for originality, strength for sophistication.

Rejecting the idea of the sartorial readymade, these bricoleurs continually adapted and evolved their style. Any combination was possible for the early Modernist: functional garments for the country gentleman juxtaposed with sportswear, ladies' fashions complementing city slickers' suits. Better still, they'd have their 'clobber' customised by one of the capital's many back-street tailors. This preoccupation with stylish one-upmanship reflected the new mood of competitive individualism that was fast replacing the era of austerity, and in this respect, Modernist culture marked a sharp break with the parochial, herd-like outlook of the Teds. They were the 'in crowd' before it became a crowd.

Frances Perrone noticed the change in Mark. "He used to leave the house dressed up to the nines. He became a real little flash boy who never went anywhere without his rolled-up umbrella." The room at the top of number 25 would still reverberate to the sound of Mark's rock'n'roll 78s – only now visitors would be forced to negotiate the clothes line he'd hung across the room. 'Flash boy' also found another use for his neighbour downstairs. "I used to have a shoe repair shop in Stoke Newington Church Street," Frances recalls, "and Mark was always asking me to make him shoes. I'd got him some made in either lizard or snakeskin, but then it got a bit too much. He wanted shoes every other day."

Mark Feld was too young to have posed a serious threat to the first wave of Modernists. The 'Italian Look' – square-shouldered 'bumfreezer' jackets with thin lapels and two or three covered buttons, narrow trousers without the turn-ups – had already peaked in 1958 when Mark was just eleven years old. Regarded as the height of sophistication and modernity, the style had been introduced to Britain three years earlier by crooner Frankie Laine, who was savaged by the critics for daring to sport such radical attire at the London Palladium. Nevertheless, pre-pubescent Mark, who still lacked the stature to carry classy cloth convincingly, continued to pester his mother for an Italian-style outfit. When Phyllis relented and took him to a local tailor, her son's precise instructions for the cut of the suit exasperated the outfitter. "He didn't even know what it was that Mark was after," Phyllis recalled proudly.

"Knock my talent if you must but not my tailor," retorted a bruised Frankie Laine. As he approached his teens, Mark Feld too understood that he could no longer rely on the goodwill of neighbours or inflexible local tradesmen if he wanted to put on the style convincingly. The need to find cheap, efficient tailors capable of meeting his exacting standards took him beyond his usual environs, away from Stoke Newington, Stamford Hill and Clapton to Bishopsgate, where he'd alight from the train at nearby Liverpool Street Station and head straight to Alfred Bilgorri. Or, a little closer to home, to Kingsland Road in Dalston and Connick's, one of the few places to sell Levi jeans in his size. Sometimes, he'd return to the Feld family's old stamping ground in Whitechapel, where he'd frequent a tailor in Leman Street, or to Borowick's of Bow at the intersection of Mile End Road and Grove Road.

Future Procol Harum lyricist Keith Reid was another young east London Face desperately seeking tailors. "I was about 12 years old, and I couldn't believe that Mark was even younger than me," he says. "All the guys used to meet at a coffee bar in Petticoat Lane on Sundays and then go off looking for clothes. It was a very small scene, so we all knew each other. I'd also bump into him in the Wimpy bar outside Whitechapel Station on a Saturday afternoon."

The search for fine footwear soon led Mark further afield. Harry remembers a Greek shoemaker in Robert Street, Euston, that they both used for a while. "We'd go down on a Saturday morning with a bit of leather or snakeskin and you'd sit on the end of his bed – his wife was often still in it! – and he'd measure your feet. A week later, your shoes would be ready." Never mind the fast turnaround, Mark soon found reason to look elsewhere, to Stan Bartholomew's in Battersea, to the children's department in Ravel's in Wardour Street and to Anello & Davide, the Covent Garden shop renowned for its ballet footwear. That's where Mark purchased his first pair of *après-ski* boots, then a reasonably priced and simply made commodity with distinctive elasticated sides. Within a couple of years, they'd taken off as the world famous 'Beatle Boot'.

The self-styled "star of three streets in Hackney" was beginning to twinkle. According to Harry, this best dressed chicken in town "couldn't pass a mirror". His reflection was Mark's best friend – the one that could be relied upon to tell him when his trousers and jacket, his tie and his button-down shirt, his umbrella, his shoes and his dry-look hair neatly lacquered into position were ready for public exhibition. When he was finally satisfied, Mark would hit the Stamford Hill catwalk, passing the Fairsports amusement arcade (known colloquially as the 'schtip house', literally "to take your money"), the cinema, the salt beef bar and the new bowling alley, one of the first in the country. It was, he remembered in 1971, a "very Jewish, very average, but very funky sort of place".

Mark and his local shmatte-fixated friends – Eric 'Monster' Hall, Mickey 'Modern' Turner, Gerry Goldstein and the considerably older

Peter Sugar and Michael Simmonds – provided a remarkable contrast to the community of Hassidic Jews living in the area. Unmistakable in their beaver hats, alpaca cloaks, untrimmed beards and long, ringleted hair, this closed community remained largely untouched by the modern world. Locked in an attempt to cling on to the 18th century lifestyle of their east European ancestors, they wandered through the streets like extras on the set of a Cecil B. De Mille epic.

Within a decade, Mark too would hold a torch for ancient ways, and with hair that curled like a corkscrew. But for now, as the Sixties began, religion played no role in his life at all, save for the network of youth clubs provided by many synagogues in the Hackney area. Helen Shapiro recalls an unexpected encounter at her local Clapton Jewish Youth Club. "Mark came in with his crowd from a rival club in Stamford Hill and I hadn't seen him for a while. The change in him was unbelievable. He was very slim, taller and dressed from head to toe in his Modernist clothes – bum-freezer jacket, button-down shirt, all the gear. He was obviously the leader of this gang, very aware of himself, and he came in and took the place over. It didn't go down too well. We all thought, 'Who does he think he is?' " Her cousin Susan Singer was less surprised by the transformation. "Most of us were afraid to go too far," she says, "but not Mark. I must say he wasn't aggressive with it. In fact he was always very friendly and everyone at the dances liked him. I thought he was lovely."

Jeff Dexter was a singing, dancing 14-year-old prodigy with the Cyril Stapleton Orchestra, who had a residency at the Lyceum Ballroom. He became Mark's new West End partner-in-style during 1960, and he has a rather different memory of his friend's reputation. "He was hated," Dexter insists, "precisely because he looked so good. Everyone hated anyone who they felt had one up on them. People always tried to pick a fight with you if they thought you were competition. We were surrounded by a lot of very rough firms then. A lot of the Mods would dress up in their posh clothes and then go out and punch shit out of each other. Even Mark often pretended he was out for a fight."

Like Mark, Jeff Dexter was enthralled by a scene that revolved around older and bigger teenagers than himself. Commanding respect in places like the Lyceum, where you had to pass 6'4" bouncers before you could even get in, wasn't easy if you were young and, worse still, small for your age. "You had to be 16 to get in," Dexter recalls. "We were 13 or 14 and probably looked no older than 11, but we both had as much front as Woolworths did. Mark stood out because he was little and he looked immaculate. But when you're small, you had to pretend that you were tougher than you were to stave off the aggro, because you'd often get picked on."

Mark always "acted like he could fight a giant", says Jeff. "I remember one incident at the Lyceum where he got into a bit of aggravation and he did get beaten. The other guy got thrown out but Mark ran off, climbed out of the loo window, smartened himself up then strolled back in as if he'd beaten the guy to a pulp. Of course he hadn't." About a year later, Mark felt confident enough to let the truth slip.

Mark and Jeff were also penalised for their size when shopping for clothes, which made trips to tailors like Bilgorri's of Bishopsgate all the more essential. But bespoke suits hardly came cheaply. "I know that Mark always had fashion at his fingertips," laughs Harry Feld. "Whether they were light fingers, I don't know . . ." Mark knew very well. "I was quite a villain," he confessed to Spencer Leigh in 1976, "although I never hurt anybody. It came about because I was really into clothes, I mean, obsessionally into clothes. I was about 12 and I'd steal or hustle motorbikes to pay for them. Clothes were all that mattered to me."

Hijacked scooters helped fund Mark's passion for fashion, though he once recalled a mass raid on a store in Whitechapel where, he claimed, 40 Levi-loving youngsters liberated an entire stock of the highly desired American jeans. While the other looters raced off without him, Mark was forced, heart pounding, to clamber aboard a moving bus, the spoils safely hidden up his jumper.

The other solution to a young Modernist's cash problems was to purchase items cheaply off the shelf, then customise them at home. Jeff and Mark often checked out the children's department at unfashionable stores such as C&A and Woolworths in the hope of finding something that might then be customised at home – with a little help from a Phyllis or a Frances Perrone.

It was thrift, coupled with the unquenchable urge to flout convention that caused the Modernist scene to flourish and diversify. Soon, the relative ubiquity of the Italian Look had given way to a riot of sartorial juxtapositions. Looking sharp wasn't the half of it; staying sharp was the only true goal, even if it meant travelling across London to supervise a minuscule alteration to a waistcoat, changing outfits several times a day or scouring markets for exactly the right cufflink or pocket-watch. There was simply no other alternative.

According to Nik Cohn, writing in *The Observer* in the mid-Sixties,

"Marc The Mod . . . used to change his clothes maybe four times each day. He was very image then, arrogant and cold and he couldn't even nod to anyone who wasn't hip. By any standards, he had style and he had cool." But, by his own admission, very few friends. "I was a weird kid, very fucked up," he stated grandly in 1972. "I never really got too involved with anyone. I didn't really want friends. I was very into gangs. Not fighting gangs. I was always, like, the leader of all the things I ever did, but very solitary." It was a theme he returned to on many occasions. "I had 40 suits when I was a kid," he boasted another time, "but I never had any friends."

When the Lyceum's all-day Sunday sessions became oversubscribed, Mark, who only deigned to make the occasional visit anyway, would turn disdainfully towards Jeff Dexter and remark, "Too many Mods here." He wanted to be recognised by his peers, but didn't want to be perceived as part of a group – a contradiction that has always undermined the perceived singularity of subcultural expression.

During 1961 and 1962, the term 'Individualist' was adopted by the Modernist vanguard in a vainglorious, though obviously doomed, bid to defy categorisation. These key 'Faces', as they were also known, were sought out early in 1962 by the influential *Town* magazine, then Britain's leading lifestyle publication for upwardly mobile gentlemen. The Features Editor, a youthful Michael Parkinson, packed reporter Peter Barnsley and noted war photographer Donald McCullin (who'd also documented the Teds scene) off to Stamford Hill to document the phenomenon.

Their six-page report was published in the September 1962 issue, a Zeitgeist-seizing 'The Young Take The Wheel' special. 'What are they like? What do they do? What do they want?' asked the magazine. In a piece titled 'Faces Without Shadows', presumably because the pace of a Face's lifestyle was too hurried to cast one, two 20-year-olds, Michael Simmonds and Peter Sugar, together with 14-year-old Mark Feld supplied some provocative answers.

Somewhat at odds with a Face's professed desire to inhabit a perpetual present, Mark, 'the most remarkable of the three', reveals an early preference for self-mythology. "Remember three years ago?" he asked rhetorically. "We used to go round on scooters in Levi's and leather jackets. It was a lot easier then." The very idea of this short, sharp self-assured juvenile ripping up the streets of Hackney thrilled Barnsley, who made Feld the focus of the article.

"You got to be different from the other kids," Mark continued. "I mean you got to be two steps ahead. The stuff that half the haddocks you see around are wearing I was wearing years ago. A kid in my class came up to me in his new suit, an Italian box it was. He says, 'Just look at the length of your jacket,' he says. 'You're not with it,' he says. 'I was wearing that style two years ago,' I said. Of course they don't like that."

Mark's conceit, in accordance with the Individualist's code of conduct, was probably justified, but occasionally his enthusiasm for a good story bore no resemblance to reality at all. During a discussion about the paucity of good tailors in London, for example, Mark's imagination takes flight: "They aren't good on shoulders either," he chided. "They can't make good shoulders like those French shoulders. I brought a jacket back from Paris — I was in Paris with my parents but I didn't like it much — and this jacket was just rubbish over there but it's great here. Great shoulders." The nearest the Felds ever got to Paris was slapping a few onions on their boiled beef and carrots.

But there were some encouraging signs, insisted the Stamford Hill Three. John Stephen, a salesman at Vince's in Newburgh Street who had opened his own shop in Carnaby Street and watched business expand exponentially, inspired both admiration and envy. "All those shops and still only 26 or something," Mark sighed. Success was the key — anyway, anyhow, anywhere. Even though his discovery of American R&B had taken some of the shine off domestic stars such as Cliff Richard and Adam Faith, Mark still respected their fame and endeavour. "I suppose they're had-its in a way but they've done something," he shrugged. "They've made their way at something."

When conversation touched on matters beyond the hated "baggy seats" or the virtues of women's hatpins, the proud young peacocks showed a remarkable nonchalance. The "Ban The Bomb lot" were dead right, believed Michael Simmonds, but he'd never march with them. Mark agreed — seeing demonstrations more in terms of public than principles. "It's all exhibitionist, isn't it?" he announced. "I'm all for that."

The intransigent trio from N16 had hardly given politics a thought, but instinctively they knew which side they were on. "I'm a Conservative," said Peter Sugar. "Conservatives are for the rich, aren't they, and everybody wants to be rich, don't they?" "They've been in a long time and they done all right," added Simmonds. Feld saw no reason to disagree. "Like he says, they're for the rich so I'm for them." Sugar wrapped up the conversation by admitting that he didn't know much about politics anyway.

It wasn't hard to see why working-class Individualists and Faces felt comfortable with the Conservative Party. Staying sharp was, on one level, a symbolic refusal of their class position, the drive to become an Ace Face simply old-fashioned upward mobility in (literally) new clothing. After the evening parade, Mark still went home to a cold bedroom, where his Elvis posters peeled away from the walls and his wet clothes took days to dry. The realities of relative deprivation remained virtually invisible to him. There were, after all, more important things to think about; that crease in his shirt collar, for example. It was politics by association that mattered, and Faces inevitably nailed their bespoke banner to glamour and wealth. "Even though you were an oik at heart, you wanted to be classy," admits Jeff Dexter. "It was the original wannabe culture. Wannabe Boys that wannabe rich, wannabe famous, wannabe loved, wannabe known."

Peter Barnsley's article provides a fascinating insight into the minds of these new young gourmets of elegance though, he concluded, there was something ultimately sad and unfulfilling about these shadowless Faces. "Where is the goal towards which he is obviously running as fast as his impeccably shod feet can carry him?" he asked. "It is nowhere. He is running to stay in the same place, and he knows that by the time he has reached his mid-20s, the exhausting race will be over and he will have lost."

For the moment, though, as Don McCullin snapped away, in a Soho back street and beside the Grand Union Canal, Mark jutted out his jaw in defiance. Defeat and exhaustion couldn't have been further from his mind. The trio were portrayed in a variety of outfits, the details of which were tellingly glossed over in the captions. However, the mix of idiosyncrasy and tradition was self-evident, with one particular image, of the dark-suited Simmonds and Sugar leaning against a wall and a belligerent Mark Feld to the fore, capturing this well.

Mark sports an immaculate hacking jacket, complete with slanting pockets – a garment more usually associated with the hare and hound set from the Home Counties. Close inspection reveals that the lapel has been slightly elongated, a modification that would have been lost on all but the most eagle-eyed observer. Neither the trousers, formal but with razor-sharp creases, nor the collar and tie are exceptional in themselves. But add in a leather waistcoat (this particular Face's *pièce de résistance*) and the look is transformed. Not only was leather virtually impossible to find in Mark's size, it was also prohibitively expensive. In this instance, he'd managed to persuade Mrs. Perrone downstairs to make him the waistcoat.

Years later, Mark described his first spin on the media roundabout as "a bummer article". "(It) came out about seven months after they'd actually come down to see me," he moaned. By which time, of course, a Face's wardrobe would have changed completely – several times over.

In the eyes of Jeff Dexter, Mark's crowning glory was always his thick, buoyant head of hair, sculpted into a particularly brutal style around the time of the *Town* photoshoot. "There was an awful lot of 'horizon line' around at that time," Jeff recalls, "which was a parted, college boy haircut raised at the top of the head. Mark's hair naturally raised in the middle so he always looked absolutely immaculate during that period. I envied that little lift in the middle a lot and spent many hours with a hair dryer in front of a mirror trying to get mine to do the same. It inevitably fell down flat after I'd been dancing." Mark never had that trouble; besides, he rarely danced.

By the time the article was published, in September 1962, the Felds were no longer living in Hackney. They'd spent 17 years on the council's housing list, and had virtually given up hope of ever moving. But when Mrs. Perrone's brother – who'd purchased 25 Stoke Newington Common in the late Fifties – put the house up for sale in June 1960, the situation changed. With the Felds still paying 27*s.* per week as sitting tenants, a private sale proved unlikely. At the end of 1961, Hackney Council stepped in and purchased the property for £2,450. Negotiations to get the Felds rehoused began soon afterwards.

Their destination was Summerstown, an anonymous corner of suburban south London wedged between Wimbledon and Tooting, notable only for its local dog track. Home was now a 'Sun Cottage' on a tiny estate just off Summerstown, a small back road adjacent to the dog track that linked Plough Lane to the busy Garratt Lane thoroughfare. The dozen or so 'Cottages', erected by Wandsworth Council as temporary housing (they were demolished many years later), were actually Scandinavian-designed prefabs that came in two halves and were secured on stilts. With its aluminium skirting and steps that led up to the front door, the Felds' new 'Sun Cottage' was rather like an oversized caravan with a pointed roof.

Although there was no garden, each dwelling was surrounded by a paved area with a wooden fence. Inside, though, there was barely more space than the Felds' were used to in Stoke Newington. They did at last have a family living room, soon furnished with mod cons including a television, but Mark and Harry's shared bedroom was little more than a box room. To Sid, Phyllis and Harry, their Sun Cottage – cheaply made but clean, comfortable and warm – represented a first real stake in the 'Affluent

Society' they'd heard so much about; leaving their old furniture behind in Stoke Newington was both practical and symbolic. Mark saw things rather differently. "Wimbledon seemed very odd to me," he said in 1971. "I didn't relate to it . . . I was totally alone. And a lot of sad things happened."

Nothing hurt Mark Feld more than the day he returned to his Stamford Hill patch and found himself snubbed by a new élite who'd taken over in his absence. The humiliation haunted him: "No one spoke to me and I burst out crying because I couldn't believe it," he remembered.

'Over The Flats', a 1971 demo recording, recounts the misery. "I was dragged here/From my own place/Turned from my old gang/Given a new face," Marc sings excitedly. While "My old man loved it/He had his garden", the uprooted and unhappy Feld Jr. missed his "friend called Pete" who "always looked so neat" and lamented that "the chicks I used to know . . . will never see me grow." Wounded, and with his "reputation gone", he spits out a few words about life in Summerstown: "Here no one knows my name/People all look the same/I walk unnoticed steps/They don't know my rep".

Years later, fellow suburban sufferer David Bowie, a long-time friend and adversary, was moved to write 'The King Of Stamford Hill', which appears to be based on the incident. The track turned up on guitarist Reeves Gabrels' *The Sacred Squall Of Now* album, and hung on the line: "Ain't it fucking curious some other cunts/Are trying to ditch the King Of Stamford Hill".

Stripped of the familiarity of his childhood surroundings, and the adoring eyes of his fellow peacocks and pupils, Mark found himself adrift in a cultural wilderness where the real action took place only behind net curtains. There was a vain attempt to rehabilitate him at school but, enrolling just months before leaving-age, his registration at the nearby Hill Croft Secondary School was little more than a formality. "I spent two weeks at a school there and I just never went back," he recalled. Instead, he continued his education in and around London's West End.

By 1962 Soho, with its labyrinth of clubs and rapidly growing network of boutiques, had become a Mod Mecca. Months after relocating to Summerstown, Phyllis Feld vacated her patch on Berwick Street market; Mark moved and stalked the district's seductive streets with increasing regularity. Often, it was simply to check out the latest trends in Domino Male, Vince's in Newburgh Street or John Stephen's flagship boutique, His Clothes, the place for those hard-to-find narrow-waisted men's trousers. Invariably, these would be too long in the leg for Mark, but with

Carnaby Street still a pop explosion away from tourist trappery, alterations could usually be made on the spot.

The West End's legendary club scene was also experiencing some interesting changes. Faces and hipsters alike could be found watching live R&B at the Marquee and the 100 Club; faking boozy literary conversation at the Establishment, musing over folk in Scot's Hoose, Bunjies and Les Cousins or social climbing at the Saddle Room. Increasingly, Mark and his crowd would go where the latest American R&B/soul sides were being spun – at Le Discothèque, the Scene, the Flamingo (which transformed, Cinderella-like, into the All Nighter Club at midnight), the Roaring Twenties and the Whiskey A Go-Go.

Refused entry to the Saddle Rooms on more than one occasion, Mark, Peter Sugar and Michael Simmonds tended to skulk around the edges of the Mod club dance-floors. While dancing was an avowedly exhibitionist pursuit, many Faces shunned it because too much public exertion didn't sit easily with their *Rebel Without A Cause* cool. "Mark didn't dance," remembers Jeff Dexter. "He didn't want to get his jacket creased. At the Lyceum he used to stand immediately stage left below the balcony, the only spot with light, reflecting from the DJ booth and the exit sign."

Ever since those occasional Sunday sojourns to the Lyceum in 1960, Mark had rarely been more than a bit-player on the club scene. Large groups of people insisting they shared things in common made him feel uneasy, shockingly ordinary. Despite his discomfort, Mark rarely broke the Ace Face code and succumbed to the nerve-steadying bottle. He remained remarkably self-controlled, remembers Jeff Dexter. "It was part of the culture not to drink; Mark certainly would not drink. You wouldn't be seen dead standing in a pub with a pint in your hand. That was oiky." There was an element of pragmatism too, because many of the clubs, including the hugely popular Scene, didn't have a licence.

If the pint tankard was deemed parochial and passé, the scooter was its symbolic opposite. Cosmopolitan, clean and positively gleaming with confidence, the scooter epitomised style, independence and modernity. Ideal for big city mobility, the scooter – to its detractors a portable lavatory on wheels – was perfectly suited to the Mod way of life because its design ensured that its riders' meticulously coordinated outfits remained grease-free.

Unfortunately, Mark was afraid of scooters. In fact, according to Harry Feld, he "was scared of most mechanical things because he wasn't able to understand or control them". Mark Feld never owned a scooter, but in addition to hawking one or two on the black market in moments of poverty, he occasionally rode pillion when the need arose. One day, he bit his lip and set off on the ultimate Mod awayday, the London-to-Brighton scooter run.

The modish Londoners' penchant for visiting seaside resorts like Brighton and Southend *en masse* started around 1959, and had become widespread by the early Sixties. The ritual usually began at 6am in a cafe in London's newspaper capital Fleet Street – one of the few meeting-places open at that early hour – where the Soho all-nighters would replenish their energies with a few black coffees and perhaps a purple heart or a black bomber at 6*d.* a throw. The bravest would head for the coast on their immaculately maintained machines; the rest walked to Waterloo and took the milk train. Seaside punch-ups with greasy rockers weren't on the agenda in those days. "It was a good way of freshening up after sweating the night away on the dance-floor," says Jeff Dexter. "And hopefully you'd find romance as well."

Harry Feld had a scooter. Mark's friend Colin had one too. It was a Vespa GS 150, "a lovely machine", Harry maintains. "It was immaculately painted, and it sounded like a bomber because the exhaust pipe had been cut." Early one Sunday morning, Colin and Mark decided to take it for a run down to Brighton. They never made it. "I'm not sure if they hit a verge or what, but they both went over the top and ended up in hospital," Harry recalls.

Mark Feld's love affair with the seaside – prompted by family visits to Clacton-on-Sea, Lowestoft, Great Yarmouth (where they'd drop in on Sid's brother Arthur), Mablethorpe and Looe in Cornwall – was over. "When he got older," says Harry, "Mark wouldn't go anywhere near the water in case it spoilt his hair . . ."

★　★　★

Since the late Fifties, Mark Feld had been driven by a desire to look good. He was, even if he said it himself, wholly successful in his pursuit of personal perfection. "I was simply knocked out by my own image," he later bragged to *The Observer*.

Music remained a constant backdrop to Mark's perpetual preening. He still followed the careers of Elvis and Cliff closely, but by the early Sixties, both had lost much of their natural lustre, sounding little different from all-American bobbysoxer singers such as Fabian and Frankie Avalon. Mark remained surprisingly loyal to his own idols, eagerly tuning in to Cliff's series of half-hour shows on Radio Luxembourg. It was there that he heard

Roy Orbison, Duane Eddy and Ricky Nelson for the first time – and a new singer dubbed 'The Golden Girl Of 1961', one Helen Shapiro from Clapton E5.

Just four years on from her Susie & The Hula Hoops début, 15-year-old Helen Shapiro – whose unusually mature singing voice became the talk of the nation – was selling 40,000 records a day, travelled in a chauffeur-driven limousine and had just taken Paris by storm. She was also on first-name terms with fellow EMI star Cliff Richard.

The pizzicato cordiality of 'You Don't Know', 'Walkin' Back To Happiness' and 'Tell Me What He Said' was not a sound Mark aspired to, but the transformation of Helen Shapiro from Hackney ne'er-do-well to national heroine had a magical quality about it. Harry maintains that her dramatic change in fortunes left little impression on Mark ("He was already convinced he was going to be famous anyway"), but it is inconceivable that 'The Shapiro Effect' didn't affect him – especially because he seemed to treat life as a competitive sport.*

While Helen Shapiro was becoming every parent's favourite teenager, Mark Feld struggled to find new idols to ape on the early Mod music scene. Many of the groups and singers were black and received little exposure in the media (incredibly, their faces were often excluded from their own record sleeves). Besides, with so many local heroes – spinning the discs, surveying the scene or out on the floor – the emerging Mod movement prioritised the beat over any visual identification with the musicians that made it. At the Marquee or the 100 Club, where hardcore R&B buffs congregated, visiting black Americans such as Memphis Slim and Jimmy Witherspoon would play to hushed, reverential audiences – among them fledgling Rolling Stones and Yardbirds whose admiration bordered on the fetishistic. But in Mod hangouts like the Scene, audiences danced to Wilbert Harrison's 'Kansas City', Ernie K-Doe's 'A Certain Girl' and Hank Ballard & The Midnighters' 'The Twist' without feeling any compulsion to imitate them. There were no self-styled Elmo Lewises (an alter ego favoured by Rolling Stones founder Brian Jones) down at the Scene Club.

* All but one of Susie & The Hula Hoops went on to make records. Stephen Gould became Stephen Jameson and enjoyed a couple of minor hits with 'Walk Away Renee' and a version of Lennon/McCartney's 'Girl' as one half of Truth, before recording several solo singles and an album for Dawn; Susan Singer followed her cousin to Columbia Records, where she released a handful of singles before changing her name to Susan Holliday; her brother Glenn also recorded.

The vision of Mark Feld desperately seeking out the latest in contemporary black music, amassing a stash of 45s on the Sue, London and Stateside labels, is seductive, but it would be incorrect. He loved the full-bodied sound, the heartfelt voices and the street corner jive, but his inability to identify with the performers inhibited his predilection for hero worship.

Jeff Dexter believes that music came a poor second in Mark's priorities during this period. "I don't think we ever really discussed music," he says. "Going to the Lyceum and the Soho clubs was just part of the scene, and you accepted the music for what it was. We did go to record shops together, but I'm not sure if Mark was totally into the music at that time. Our main interests were what we wore and whether we could find things in our size. That provided the basis for our friendship. I think he spent every penny he could on clothes."

There was one thing Mark desired more than music, more even than clothes, and it revealed itself one afternoon in 1963 when the two micro-Mods went to see Cliff Richard's latest cinematic vehicle, *Summer Holiday*. Jeff was mildly miffed because he'd been asked to play one of the film's sun-seeking adolescents and had turned it down. But he went anyway "to see the supposedly good dancing in it that was actually pretty naff". More shocking, though, was Mark's reaction to such bantamweight entertainment. "As we left, he said, 'That's it! I'm gonna sing just like Cliff Richard. I'm gonna be as big as Cliff Richard. Will you manage me?' "

Dexter was horrified. "Cliff was already part of the old school. Mark had this absolute integrity about the way he looked and dressed yet the fact that he wanted to be like Cliff Richard made me cringe. I turned to him and said, 'But you can't even bloody well sing. What's the point?' " Mark dug his heels in. "I'll learn," he snarled. "I'm gonna do it. I'm gonna learn to sing, and learn to play. That's what I really want to do." Jeff heard the spiel many times. "Mark never talked about being a musician. He wanted to be a star. He wanted to be bigger than Cliff."

There was plenty of room for another star on the domestic music scene. The release of 'Dynamite' towards the end of 1959 partially atoned for the heresy of 'Living Doll' earlier that summer, but by the end of the decade, no one believed in Cliff as an authentic British response to American rock'n'roll anymore. Johnny Kidd & The Pirates and the arch-vaudevillian Screaming Lord Sutch brought a modicum of credibility to the British scene; maverick producer Joe 'The Telstar Man' Meek put together a roster of unlikely, hit-or-miss talents; but it was only when The Beatles merged American

R&B, soul and vintage rock'n'roll, adding a few idiosyncratic touches of their own, that people began to care about indigenous pop.

The hysteria that greeted The Beatles' makeover from Hamburg workhorses into a worldwide phenomenon was as surprising as it was shocking. Sociologists, psychologists, sexual analysts, even philosophers struggled to explain how a jaunty beat tune like 'She Loves You' caused an entire generation to howl uncontrollably for John, Paul, George and Ringo. The 20th century had witnessed fan worship before: Valentino, Garbo, Sinatra, even Johnnie Ray had all induced fits, tears and fainting to varying degrees. But the scale of Beatlemania was akin to the adulation afforded political demagogues like Adolf Hitler and Josef Stalin. The true power of pop was revealed.

The Beatles also fomented another change, less heralded at the time, but one that would dramatically widen the parameters of popular music. When, in 1958, John Lennon added a middle eight to 'Love Me Do', one of the first songs written by 16-year-old Paul McCartney, the days when pop singers were mere performing puppets were forever numbered. By the mid-Sixties, The Beatles had become performing artists with the emphasis on art. This licence to create liberated many among their generation in the years ahead, including Mark Feld, who grasped this 'portrait of a young man as an artist' idea with both hands.

3

Little Queenie

"The one thing that sustained me throughout those years of practically doing nothing was that I decided I was going to be a gas. I decided I was going to grow as fast as I could."

– Marc Bolan (1971)

"The Romantic is the one who discovers himself as centre."
– G. Poulet, in *The Romantic Movement* (1966)

"I was very much into my own little world in those days. I'm not a very social person. I was basically a Romantic."

– Marc Bolan (1972)

Some time during the early months of 1963, Mark Feld was invited to attend an interview at the local Labour Exchange. With his school days prematurely behind him, it was time to think about his future. "What, Mr Feld, is your chosen profession?" enquired his interrogator. "Poet," he replied.

Mark's geographically inspired fall from grace, when the "self-styled cult king" turned out to be "a nobody", prompted what he later described as "a time of great spiritual crisis". Spurned by his old inner city muckers, and left behind in the great beat group rush, all the certainties of his life crumbled fast. For a few months at least, life in the Sun Cottage was hardly rose-tinted. Now when he passed a mirror he saw only emptiness. 1963 was Mark Feld's big breakdown year, and neither Cliff, the camouflage of the cloth nor even Mark himself could prevent a showdown with the questions that would lay him bare: Who? Why? And what the hell for?

There were no easy answers, but Mark found a way of confronting them that eased the pain of introspection and self-analysis. That was to seek out others who too had peered beneath the world's polished exteriors and found pain, alienation and, just maybe, a modicum of comfort in

33

being sad. "I had nothing," Marc recalled. "That's why I got into art and culture and books."

It was a necessary and vital discovery, providing both a sanctuary and new sources of nourishment for his crushed soul. Very slowly he began to rebuild, gaining strength from his self-imposed isolation, and new perspectives as he began to view the world with brain as well as eyes.

In *Days In The Life*, Jonathon Green's oral history of the Sixties underground, top Face Steve Sparks claimed that Mark "was an early example of what was the downfall of Mod. He . . . was only interested in the clothes, he was not involved in thinking." It was a harsh assessment, but one that wasn't without some truth. Reborn as a mid-teen Romantic, Mark Feld caught up fast, devouring literature and ancient history in the manner he once feasted on fashion.

In time, he would discover the beat poets, writers like Ginsberg and Ferlinghetti who dressed up metaphysics and social criticism in hipsterspeak. But Mark's first inclination was to eschew the contemporary and plunge himself into the world of the 19th century English Romantic poets, writers like Wordsworth, Keats, Shelley and Byron. His natural inquisitiveness took him further afield, to books on ancient civilisations and to the musical, suggestive verse of French poet Arthur Rimbaud. "When I first read him, I felt like my feet were on fire," he recalled.

For the first time in his life, Mark experienced solitude. He had the Sun Cottage to himself during the day while his father was out driving vans for Airfix and Whiteways Cider, and Phyllis was working as a clerk at the National Savings Bank in nearby Parsons Green. For the moment, Harry was the Felds' glamour boy; he worked in Wardour Street, the heart of London's film industry, in the advertising department at Anglo-Amalgamated.

Words like Etruscan, Dvorak and Abyssinia now formed part of Mark's vocabulary, but his parents weren't averse to using unfamiliar language either: layabout, for example. Phyllis, who spent much of the next five years helping to keep Mark afloat, was supportive but concerned. True to his innate sense of drama, Mark assuaged his guilt by taking two jobs at once. By day, he worked at Edgars menswear shop in Tooting Broadway; by night, he plunged his delicate hands into a washing-up bowl at the local Wimpy bar. The martyrdom lasted all of two weeks. "Nearly dying of exhaustion" and on the verge of a potential breakdown, Mark packed it in. Thus ended his only real acquaintance with the conventional workplace.

When he chanced upon a newspaper advert offering a training course at a top West End modelling school (probably Lucie Clayton's), Mark envisaged an acceptable compromise between work and narcissism. There was one stumbling block: the fee, somewhere around the £100 mark, was astronomical at a time when the average man's weekly pay packet was closer to £15. Phyllis again raided the family savings.

Even though Mark's later claims to have earned £500 or even £1,000 for individual assignments were characteristically overblown, Phyllis' investment was not in vain. Mark obtained at least two significant commissions, for Littlewoods' mail-order catalogue (autumn/winter 1964–65) and for the John Temple high street menswear chain as a male model.

Washable Acrilan viscose trousers were definitely not part of Mark's wardrobe at home, and that 'Littlewoods smile' was no match for the insolence of the *Town* magazine shoot, but at least the work offered anonymity in addition to a decent fee. The commission for John Temple – for whom Mark was, he later claimed, the cardboard cut-out in every store – was reasonably credible. He certainly appeared in the company's Styles To Suit You, Suits To Style You brochure, modelling a high buttoned continental pin-stripe, a rich golden bronzed worsted cloth overchecked in brown and a navy serge outfit complete with velvet collar.

When quizzed about this brief modelling career, Bolan insisted it had fizzled out because he'd been "overexposed". A John Temple spokesman was more prosaic. Mark Feld, he said, had been "just another model selected from an agency in our usual twice-yearly search for new faces. If the figure suited and the face fitted, that was good enough. But he wasn't an exceptional model. And we never used him again."

Modelling shoots aside, the only extant photograph of Mark from 1963 and 1964 was taken at Harry's wedding. Immaculately turned out in a white button-down shirt and a dark suit, his carefully lacquered 'horizon line' hairstyle remained untroubled by the craze for Beatle cuts. But he still followed the music scene as attentively as ever. Tooting Granada hosted many top package tours, and that's where he saw Brian Hyland and Brenda Lee, Little Richard and, on January 12, 1964, The Ronettes, Marty Wilde, The Swinging Blue Jeans, Dave Berry and a fast-emerging R&B combo from London called The Rolling Stones. The white noise of the screaming, beat era audiences damaged eardrums for days. But the memory of those crowds, stoked on anticipation, desire and release, remained with Mark long after everyone else had forgotten.

When Mark Feld used some of his modelling fees to buy a new guitar, he shunned the beat combo-inspired electric in favour of an acoustic model. Financial considerations might have had something to do with it, but the overrriding reason was Bob Dylan. This young American singer, who had yet to enjoy any real commercial success in Britain, was different. He had nothing in common with the beat boom, with the newly imported R&B and Tamla Motown sounds, or with the irrepressible Tin Pan Alley love song. His songs of social commentary had grown out of the American folk-protest tradition; he was more Woody Guthrie than Elvis Presley. In contrast to beat group convention, he operated alone. He was, in the true sense of the word, an Individualist. Intelligent, independent and the name to drop in elitist circles during 1964, he provided a perfect replacement for Cliff Richard as Mark Feld's unknowing mentor.

While Lennon and McCartney were still mimicking their Tin Pan Alley forebears, Bob Dylan was ripping up the rulebook. Both he and his songs were 'real'; this man and his guitar had little truck with showbusiness. The key word was authenticity. His personal autonomy always took precedence over public demands. Dylan was the little man who'd grown too big for his environment; he couldn't be silenced, nor did he want to be. He was cool, calm and remarkably self-assured. He shrouded himself in mystery, and called himself a poet. He answered to nothing but his imagination. His proficiency on guitar and harmonica was negligible, yet that only made him more convincing. Above all, this embodiment of the Romantic values to which Mark Feld now aspired, was on the threshold of stardom.

News of Dylan's emergence energised the British folk circuit, and a new generation of singers – Roy Harper, Ralph McTell, Al Stewart, John Martyn and, most significantly, Donovan – all drew from Dylan as well as Woody Guthrie, Joan Baez, Pete Seeger and Ramblin' Jack Elliott. Many of these singers possessed a strong social conscience. Mark, blessed only with a strong sense of himself, was too awestruck by the singer's linguistic audacity and the air of mystery that enveloped him to notice Dylan's utilitarian observations.

In the days before blanket multimedia pop coverage, audiences gleaned information on recording artists from the back of the record sleeves. On the singer's 1962 début LP, we learn that "Mr Dylan is vague about his antecedents and birthplace, but it matters less where he has been than where he is going," that he "has been soaking up influences like a sponge", that he "didn't agree with school", that he reads a lot, and that he admires rockin' Elvis Presley and Carl Perkins as much as yodellin' Woody Guthrie and Jimmie Rodgers. By 1964, his *The Times They Are A-Changin'* and *Another*

Side Of Bob Dylan albums let Dylan speak for himself through his own prose. The sparkling lines of social commentary were still there, but above all Dylan was now revelling in a linguistic abandon that read more beautifully than ever, but increasingly inhabited a world of its own.

Mark, too, inhabited a private world that he wanted to share with everyone. With his new guitar and a harmonica which hung, Dylan-like in a holder around his neck, he strummed and blew in obvious imitation of the cult hero. Mastering an instrument didn't come easily to him. Beatles songs, which had famously begun to toss in the occasional Aeolian cadence, baffled him, so he searched through the local second-hand shops for rock'n'roll 45s which, once he'd learnt the 'three-chord trick', were far easier to play along to.

Bert Weedon's *Play In A Day* guide was the first port of call for any budding, beat era guitarist. John Lennon, Paul McCartney and Eric Clapton all learnt the basics there; so did Mark. He even met the great man, a regular alongside Wally Whyton, Muriel Young and characters like Ollie Beak and Joe Crow on *The Five O'Clock Club*, which began broadcasting in 1963. He may even have been an extra on the show. What's certain is that one of the show's regular turns, a teenage prodigy named Allan Warren, offered him a lifeline away from Summerstown and towards the heart of showbusiness.

"Mark, like David Bowie, was one of several pop hopefuls who'd hang around the set doing bits of extra work," Warren recalls. "We struck up a friendship and, bringing only his guitar and a carrier bag, he moved in with me." Home was Warren's flat at 81 Lexham Gardens, in a well-placed part of town between Gloucester Road and Earl's Court. Mark moved in some time around autumn 1964 and stayed there for around six months. During that time, he consolidated his musical ambitions, explored his awakening sexuality and cast himself more convincingly in the role of a Pop Romantic.

Mark had a huge room, though Warren remembers him always rooted to his favourite spot in front of the fireplace surrounded by books and strumming his guitar. "He'd sit for hours cross-legged and flimsily dressed playing his guitar," Warren recalls, and would break off only to deliver one of his "When I'm a star . . ." raps. "He'd be absolutely serious and want to talk about it for hours but his dialogue was laughable. He'd talk and you'd be thinking, 'He's never going anywhere with that fucking dreadful music, those cutie bow lips and that broad face.' I just couldn't see it. We used to laugh at him, but he wouldn't give up.

He was tenacious; couldn't give a toot. It was a full-time obsession."

So, too, was daylight, says Warren. "In the daytime, Mark would sit in the drawing room with the curtains closed and the light on. For him, the night never ended and the day never started." It had nothing to do with the black arts, he maintains. "I think it was because he had this pale porcelain skin which he was very proud of. Mark didn't like sunbathing. He just wasn't interested in the day."

No longer the peacock that demanded attention whatever the time of day, Mark Feld now resembled some weird hybrid of idols past and present. Warren, who thought Bob Dylan "tame-sounding when compared to The Beatles and all the groups", remembers Mark's endless attempts to perfect the folk-singer's 'Blowin' In The Wind'. He also insists that Mark found his Cliff habit very hard to kick. "Mark looked like Cliff Richard and he knew it, but he wasn't as handsome. You have to remember that Cliff was still the big thing outside all the heavy groups like The Beatles. He maintained a nice, clean-cut image that Mark still had at that stage. Even his voice was like Cliff's, very toothy, very light."

Allan Warren had heard Mark Feld's singing voice, but virtually no one else had. Late one night, the pair hatched a plot to change all that. "We were talking about Mark," he grins. "Mark was one of those people that would say, 'I've had enough of talking about me. Now, what do you think of me?' I'd think, God, another three hours talking about him!

"Mark suggested I should manage him," Warren recalls, "which appealed to me because I thought I might be able to do something with him through my contacts. The following day, I rang Regent Sound and asked if we could book a studio in a week's time. I turned to Mark and said, 'Right, rehearse two songs.'"

While the budding troubadour prepared for his first proper recording session, Allan tried to get him a spot on *The Five O'Clock Club*. He was unsuccessful. However, a third person in the flat was Gregory Phillips, a regular in *Orlando*, the popular children's adventure series that starred veteran actor Sam Kydd. Mark made a couple of walk-ons dressed as a Teddy Boy. "Whenever they wanted a delinquent, they put me in a leather jacket," he claimed.

There is some discrepancy regarding Mark's recording début, which either took place towards the end of 1964 or during the first weeks of 1965. According to Warren, two songs were recorded during a two-hour session at Regent Sound Studios, in Denmark Street; one a version of Bob Dylan's 'Blowin' In The Wind'. However, a tape exists proving that the session – if it is the same one – actually took place at Vic Keary's Maximum Sound Studios, at 47 Dean Street, Soho. More baffling still, Keary does not remember Mark having a manager in tow. The discovery of the original tape, in the early Nineties, also contradicts Keary's belief that another song, 'The Perfumed Garden Of Gulliver Smith', was recorded that day. The tape reveals that Mark Feld took six tries at 'Blowin' In The Wind' and four (including one false start) of Dion DiMucci's 'The Road I'm On (Gloria)'.

The studio at 47 Dean Street had previously been home to Radio Atlanta, one of the first pirate stations, but when the operation was hastily moved offshore some of the recording equipment got left behind. Keary moved in, late in 1964, and with a basic PA mixer and a couple of ancient tape machines started recording jingles for the pirates using musicians who'd congregate at the nearby La Giaconda coffee bar in Denmark Street. Soon afterwards, he received a call from a young singer eager to record some songs. "I thought he was in the Dylan/Donovan mould, but he didn't really make that much impression on me," he says.

While the 22-minute Maximum Sound Session tape is a remarkable and poignant historic document, it confirms Vic Keary's assessment. Mark Feld's performance had all the assurance of a ship's mate being forced to walk the plank. The voice wandered off-key, chords were fluffed every few bars and the harmonica playing made Dylan sound like Larry Adler. To suck, blow and strum simultaneously proved too much for this musical novice, but at least he had something tangible to offer small independent labels like Oriole and Ember. They turned him down, and even Mark later dismissed the results as "terrible".

'Blowin' In The Wind', the first track on Dylan's 1963 LP, *The Free-wheelin' Bob Dylan*, was already more than a mere staple of the folk clubs; in October that year, the popular American folk trio Peter, Paul & Mary had a huge international hit with the song. An indictment of public apathy to war and wrongdoing in general that had been taken up by the Civil Rights movement in America, 'Blowin' In The Wind' became, in Mark's hands, a tuneful pop melody rather than a slice of biting social comment. Crucially, the verse containing the line "How many deaths will it take till he knows/That too many people have died" was omitted altogether. Mark had mastered the chords, and substituted some blue notes on the harmonica in place of Dylan's erratic flurries, but there was little to suggest that he was anything other than a Cliff Richard soundalike with good taste but sorely lacking in the proficiency department.

If the memory of 'Blowin' In The Wind' still haunts Mark's first manager – "He drove me mad with that fucking song!" – a second song performed that day completely slipped Allan Warren's mind. Another non-original, 'The Road I'm On (Gloria)', was discovered by Mark on the back of an unsuccessful Dion single, 'I'm Your Hoochie Coochie Man'. Best known for pre-Beatles hits such as 'A Teenager In Love', 'Runaround Sue' and 'The Wanderer', the rockin' American pop idol underwent a dramatic change during 1963; 'The Road I'm On (Gloria)', issued in March 1964, featured only acoustic guitar and harmonica accompaniment.

Technically, the performance was grim. The harmonica fills were fumbled, and Mark couldn't get his fingers round the picked introduction – in fact he can still be heard struggling over those same notes as the song fades. Taking the song at a brisker pace, he elected to strum rather than pick his way through the verses, minimising any further mistakes by omitting the last two. Unquestionably the work of an amateur, the most notable element was the voice, rich in melancholy which – thanks to some studio reverb – strives for a maturity beyond its years without ever matching the sense of grief in Dion's original.

There is grief in his performance, but Mark, whose belief in destiny was confirmed with each incremental ration of fame, wasn't to know it. From its title in, 'The Road I'm On (Gloria)' hangs heavy with prophecy, the second verse in particular: "Summer ends and leaves start dyin'/You won't see a robin cryin'/He knows where the sun is hidin'/To another nest he's flyin'." The cruel sense of foreboding in the pay-off ("You gave me reason/Now I've gotta roam/'Cause the road I'm on gal won't run me home") would have stretched even Marc Bolan's imagination.

Selecting the best two takes for the acetates couldn't have been easy, but several pairs were pressed and sent to potentially interested parties, together with a photograph of Mark Feld – the pop hopeful. The photographer was Mike McGrath, a friend of Allan Warren who wrote showbiz stories for girls' magazine *Boyfriend*. The 24 guinea session took place on the balcony of his Earl's Court flat. "I find it hard to believe all that stuff about him being a Face," he says. "He was just a pleasant Jewish boy who looked wide-eyed with wonder and said nothing. He left no impression on me at all." McGrath, already a showbusiness veteran, also remembers two other mid-Sixties subjects, David 'Bowie' Jones and Reg 'Elton John' Dwight, as "silent and colourless".

Allan Warren blames his client's apparent muteness on James Dean.

"Mark would often walk around with a moody expression. Then he'd start talking transatlantic – 'Let's get it on', 'OK, cool man', all that pseudo-American jargon. It used to make me laugh." James Dean, whom Bolan name-dropped many times during his career, was killed in a car accident on September 30, 1957 – Mark Feld's 10th birthday.

There was little of Dean's charisma in the photographs, though. "Mark was like a big fat Tweetie Pie," says Warren, "so we had to disguise the fat face. That's why the cap was there, as a distraction and to give him a bit of height." But the image was more contrived than that. With his jauntily perched peaked cap, thick rollneck jumper, tight fitting suede jacket and white jeans tucked into a pair of suede pixie boots, Mark Feld looked every inch the budding protest singer as he held the six-string acoustic high against his chest. His manner was casual and bohemian, his gaze, directed away from the camera in the press shot, artfully elusive. The Face that had once cast no shadow had forsaken its quixotic façade for the richly toned hues of a Romantic.

For the moment, Mark's hopeful expression was consumed by a void marked 'rejection'. Record companies didn't want to know; neither did Ollie Beak or his puppetmasters at *The Five O'Clock Club*. Even Allan Warren's innate enthusiasm began to wane after weeks of unsuccessful hustling. Mark was less inclined to give up so easily. It's likely that he'd faced rejection before, after turning up on producer Joe Meek's doorstep at 304 Holloway Road, only to be met by a "Sure, kid, record you next week" response.

Rumours abound that the occasion was rewarded with a recording test. It's been suggested that a late 1962/early 1963 song in the Meek archive, 'Mrs Jones' – more poignance – features the voice of Mark Feld, but the quality of the surviving acetate is so poor that it may just as well be Tweetie Pie singing. However, it does seem that Mark was invited into Meek's home-cum-studio, because he remembered the budgerigar that the producer kept in his bedroom. Besides, Meek, who often let his sexual fantasies be the best judge of musical talent, would have been flattered by the attentions of a willing young pop hopeful and former male model.

Eventually, Mark and Allan secured a meeting with EMI A&R man Barry Green. According to Warren, Green listened to the songs, pampered them with endless cups of coffee and kind words – and then rejected them. Yet records confirm that Mark was granted an audition for EMI subsidiary Columbia at Abbey Road on February 16, 1965. Under the auspices of A&R man John Burgess, he was given just 15 minutes, between 3.45 and 4.00pm in Studio Three, to impress. A pianist Sid Hadden had been booked to assist in that afternoon's 'tests', though if this is where Mark recorded Betty Everett's uptempo ballad, 'You're No Good' (that had recently been covered by The Swinging Blue Jeans for the home market), there is no evidence to confirm it. What is certain is that, once again, this star-in-waiting failed to shine convincingly.

Knocked back by the business, Mark Feld sought solace in his awakening sexuality. Harry suspects Mark's first sexual encounter took place back in Stoke Newington with a dark-haired girl with a Mary Quant bob. Both Helen Shapiro and Susan Singer confirm Mark's popularity with Hackney's heartseekers, but there was only room for one in Mark's early love life – and that was himself. "He was definitely more into clothes than girls," says Jeff Dexter. "While he was incredibly flash, he still had a certain shyness about him." Mark once claimed in the soft porn magazine *Oui* that he lost his virginity at nine, but the first evidence of an active sex life only really emerges when he was a 17-year-old living at Lexham Gardens.

"Mark loved the girls, but I think he was very shy with them," Allan Warren remembers. "He was much more at ease with the boys. That was because boys generally took the lead; if Mark fancied a girl, he'd have to chase her." Warren believes that the teenage Mark saw sex as a way to bolster his ego rather than fulfil any notions of romance. "He loved himself and he loved to be worshipped. If someone is going to go to bed with him and do funny things to him, he simply regarded that as another sign of being worshipped."

The rhetoric of the androgynous image underpinned Mark's life, from his early Mod days to the high camp of his final television shows. His idols were invariably male, and extravagance and flamboyance – widely seen as benchmarks of camp – came naturally to him. Invariably, he experimented with bisexuality. "When I was 15, I wasn't very sure of myself," he admitted. "I wanted to find out so I went with a bloke." Mark claimed the experience was short-lived, perhaps even a one-time affair. "It was so I'd never have to look back and wonder what I'd missed out on," he said. "I felt I should try anything once."

Allan Warren remembers otherwise. "He went to bed with anyone because everyone did in those days. It was nothing new. Rather than go to bed alone, if someone was pretty, irrespective of whether they were a girl or a boy, you'd go to bed with them. You really didn't care either way. This wasn't like the dull Seventies or the mundane Eighties when people had different ideas about it."

Jeff Dexter, who didn't see much of Mark during this period of 1963, knew nothing of his friend's bisexuality, but was aware of his involvement in the Hipster scene. "It revolved around several small French clubs like La Poubelle and St. Germaine, where the earliest ('out') gays, dressed in John Michael and John Stephen clothes would go. They had this incredible look. They'd wear low cut hipster trousers with either very tight, sailor-type T-shirts, or very tight Shetland wool jumpers."

The distinction between the Hipster and the early Modernist was blurred. Albert Goldman defined the Hipster as a "typically lower-class dandy, dressed up like a pimp affecting a very cool, cerebral tone – to distinguish him from the gross, impulsive types that surrounded him in the ghetto – and aspiring to the finer things in life". His Hipster was young, American and black. In London, they were almost exclusively white, though similarly disposed to matters both cerebral and sartorial.

The world of the urban Modernist, Individualist and Hipster had much in common with elements within the gay community. Defying convention through the wardrobe; the willingness to use cosmetics to enhance the sense of disguise; the emphasis on consumption; and the abnormal amount of attention devoted to self-image. All, in the eyes of the mainstream, were regarded as 'feminine' pursuits – but the gap between the heavy and the peacock was closer than many assumed.

Mark's nightlife extended beyond the usual Hipster hangouts. He worked briefly in the cloakroom at Le Discothèque in Wardour Street, where he earned most of his money from tips. According to Allan Warren, who says Mark would "go to the opening of a letter if it gave him a free sandwich", he soon found better ways to survive. "People were into beauty in those days, and Mark was young and he was pretty. Many people enjoy taking young men out to dinner; there doesn't have to be anything sexual in it. Mark had all that going for him when he was young. He'd bore someone sick going on about his career, but they'd think, 'Oh, he's pretty,' and order another bottle of champagne.

"You didn't need money if you were a pretty boy in the right part of London in the Sixties. If you had a modicum of talent, and you were persistent, you could get the break very easily. And Mark had youth, looks, talent and ambition on his side. It worked." But it was going to take a little longer than Allan and Mark had planned.

Mark's suspicion that it would only be a matter of time before a 'British Dylan' broke through were confirmed in spring 1965 when an unknown folksinger known simply as Donovan secured a mini-residency on the top pop TV show *Ready, Steady, Go!* Babyface pretty, with a peaked cap, a harmonica around his neck and even something Feld-like about the teeth, Donovan was snapped up by Pye Records. His first 45, 'Catch The Wind', shot into the Top five and he was granted an audience with Bob Dylan when the American arrived in London for his British tour. Despondent, Mark returned home to Summerstown.

"I think he went back to mother," says Allan Warren. "Though we were good friends we had nothing in common. Mark was interested in the pop world; I enjoyed the theatre and playing Jack Buchanan records." Warren also concedes that politics got in the way, too – at least on a playful level. "I was right wing, Mark was left wing, so we often used to argue. I was very into the British Empire and was rather upset that we were losing these colonies. That really used to wind him up. Mark was very liberal and he'd be furious with some of my attitudes, but in the end he just looked at me and laughed."

Such was the union of pop and politics that by 1965 even ex-Tory Mark Feld was moved to nail his colours to those 'Ban The Bomb' "exhibitionists". A photograph taken during a major anti-nuclear (CND) rally in May 1965 shows Mark at the head of the march alongside Donovan, Joan Baez and Tom Paxton. It was an important day for him, as he positioned himself, Zelig-like, alongside some of pop's most progressive-minded folk stars. But it left no impression on Donovan whatsoever. "The first I knew about Mark being there was when someone told me about it years later," he says.

No one, it seemed, wanted anything to do with Mark Feld. There was always another option – be someone else.

*   *   *

'Mark Feld' had been ditched once before, early in 1965 at the Maximum Sound Studios. "He'd come back to pick up the acetates from his 'Blowin' In The Wind' session," recalls engineer Vic Keary, "and it's only because there was so much confusion about his name that I really remember him at all." Initially Keary typed Mark's real name on the label, although he recalls mis-spelling the surname as Felds. "Within the hour, he'd crossed that off and put Riggs. Then he changed his mind again and wrote Toby Tyler."

Allan Warren always knew his flatmate as Mark Felds, and it's quite possible that this was a first, half-hearted attempt to give Mark a stage name. Toby Tyler was taken from the title of a 1960 Disney support feature about an orphan who joins a travelling circus and finds fame – with a little help from a chimpanzee. There was more than a hint of desperation about the choice, as if, by some bizarre act of wish-fulfilment Walt Disney's magic might do the same for struggling Mark Feld. Marginally less improbable, it did have that two syllable ring in its favour, which made uttering the names of Ha-ley, Pres-ley, Ber-ry, Coch-ran, Hol-ly, Fu-ry, Rich-ard, Dy-lan such a pleasure.

But in 1965, the name Mark admired most of all was that of Riggs O'Hara, a young actor friend of Allan Warren and an intimate of theatre director John Dexter. Riggs, whom Mark subsequently dubbed 'The Wizard', became a key character in Bolan's life. Even when recounting his meeting with Riggs in his private 'Big Top' exercise book later that year, Mark – who for a short time experimented with the name Marc Riggs – was coy, almost secretive about him:

". . . Up walks a cool looking hipster all togged up in a dirty grey vest. He told me he was a folksinger, I said I was one too. Soon we had a long cool chat, and eventually became as thick as glue . . . We sang lots of crazy folk songs, blazing in the pale warm afternoon sun. My friends name I cannot tell you, I promised him I would not say, but eventually he became an actor, and acted in a play, hope I'm a dustbin singer someday.

"P.S. I can't keep a secret, his name was Riggs O'Hara – he was a yank.

– Marc Feld Written 12 o'clock pm (Midnight in bed)."

When O'Hara was finally tracked down in 1997, he remembered the meeting in rather less fanciful terms. "We first met at a friend's flat. He was visiting this guy whose name I have absolutely forgotten. I turned up and started to talk about the theatre, and we went out for a cup of tea." It was 1964, probably late that year, and Riggs' new friend was still calling himself Mark Feld.

O'Hara, a serious stage actor affiliated to the Royal Court, widened Mark's horizons socially and culturally. "He wasn't a loner, but he didn't know a lot of people," he says. "Anyone that he met he met through me. It was a period of education for him, of opening his eyes. I took him everywhere I went. I had my own car – with a record player in it! – my own flat and we ate in restaurants and went to first nights."

The pair rubbed shoulders with the glamorous at the Ad Lib, and at the legendary parties of Sandra Caron, sister of Alma Cogan. But, Riggs insists, "Mark never made a beeline for anybody that he thought could help him in his career," He was not in awe of stars or stardom. "We were watching *Top Of The Pops* and there was some guy wiggling around with his guitar and Mark said, 'Anybody can do that.' And he did. He was self-educated in almost every respect. He decided one day to teach himself to speak properly, and he did that too."

There is some overlap between Mark's months with Riggs O'Hara and the time he spent with Allan Warren. To confuse matters further, Riggs also claims to have paid for Mark's first demo disc. "It was in a small studio on the ground floor, I don't think there was a producer and it cost something like £20," he says. "Mark had quite a thin voice, although he stood right in front of the microphone, and I don't think it was him playing the guitar." O'Hara cannot remember the title of the song Mark performed that day, but confirms that it was neither 'Blowin' In The Wind' or a Feld original. Betty Everett's 'You're No Good', perhaps? "It might have been. Betty Everett was fabulous – he got that from me."

During the early months of 1965, Riggs O'Hara shared his flat in Lonsdale Road, Barnes, with Mark and actor James Bolam, star of a new television series *The Likely Lads* (launched on December 16, 1964). Riggs was the first in a long line of Mark's 'name' companions, friendships struck on the basis of the sound of a person's name. If Mark could find enchanting things in a name, then a trip with worldly Riggs O'Hara to Paris – at the time still the ultimate destination for romance, sophistication and culture – was likely to set his mind ablaze.

Mark gave his most detailed account of the vacation to Dick Tatham in *Diana* magazine. "We went by boat and train," he said. "A couple of mornings later I went on my own to see all the art treasures at the Louvre. I was standing there looking at a statue when I heard a voice behind me comment on it. I turned and saw a man of about 40. He looked very distinguished and intellectual and I was particularly struck by his eyes. They were very bright and penetrating."

This gentleman, apparently an American living in Paris with a young girlfriend, invited Mark back to his castle-like residence for a meal. And that's where he stayed for an unspecified length of time, digesting the vast collection of books on magic and watching in amazement as his host read people's minds, levitated, conjured up spirits and performed many other acts of white magic. "I don't think anyone has influenced me as much as he did," said Mark.

Several variations on this story appeared in print over the years, although the sinister embellishments from his early telling of the story were later dropped. "They crucified live cats," Mark claimed in October 1965. "Sometimes they used to eat human flesh just like chicken bones. From a cauldron. I don't care whether you believe it or not. It's a bit scary however false it sounds. But what can I do? You tell me. It sounds ego, yet it's true." As late as 1976, he was spinning his own spin. "They made out I lived in Paris for four years and all this shit, and I was only there for three months," he deadpanned.

No one close to Mark ever believed in the finer details of the trip to Paris. "The story I heard," says his brother Harry, "was that they checked into a hotel when they got there. But Mark found a slug in the bath, said, 'That's it!' and they came straight back home. They were only there for a matter of days, a week maybe, but certainly not six months. And there was certainly no wizard."

Jeff Dexter agrees. "I always thought the Paris trip was total bullshit. Once he was over the initial shyness of a situation, Mark could turn on the crap till the cows came home. He was obsessive about building up his own self-importance, but he was a lot of fun as well. We all had our own little fantasies that we were a bit more special than we really were."

There was no wizard, no cannibalism and no sacrificial felines, but the Paris trip was not a figment of Mark's imagination. "It was a long weekend and we did it proud," remembers Riggs. "Mark had never been to a foreign country, and we did everything – late night crazy clubs with extraordinary elaborate revues, a boat trip on the Seine, the theatre, the Louvre. It was his first eye-opening experience and I'm sure for someone like him it seemed like six months. We stayed on the Left Bank on the Rue St. Benoit at the Hotel Montana."

Mark had the time of his life. So much so that he built an entire mythology around what was, after all, little more than a citybreak. "The Wizard? Well, there was only me," says Riggs. "The stories that Mark would invent about the Wizard being somebody else was his way of protecting me. All of the myth that has grown up was his invention. He never knew anybody but me."

And Mark had grown extremely close to Riggs O'Hara. "I remember when I had to go to New York for two weeks," says the actor, "and when I came back he was practically waiting at the door. I realised that he cared about me because he wasn't the kind of person who usually showed how he felt."

Despite their closeness, Riggs saw little of the avaricious sexual being that Allan Warren remembers. "Mark didn't pick guys up, he just didn't. If I had to say anything about Mark's sexuality, I think that all of his sexual drive was invested in what he wanted to be and do. There was no way he was gay, or even bisexual." But, he adds, "If he went to bed with a man it was because he had some kind of affinity with that person, some understanding, liking, caring. If he happened to feel that way for you, then that was fine."

Eventually the pair drifted apart, and Mark once again went back to mother. "There was no fight or argument, it was just the right time for both of us," says Riggs. "That day when he decided that he should leave, we went down to Camden and in this shop right on the corner of the market there was this little green statue of Pan. He liked it, and I bought it for him. That was the last time I spoke to him." Mark treasured the statue, which reappeared several times in his later career, most visibly on the back sleeve of the second Tyrannosaurus Rex album.

The Paris episode marks a critical point in the young singer's life, career and, above all, mythology. It was the moment Mark Feld ditched his dreams of becoming Cliff or Dylan or even Toby 'troubadour' Tyler and instead switched to the fantasies that grew inside his head; the ones that filtered out, untouched by cynicism, to coat ordinary events and people and things in what might reasonably be called Bolanic fairydust. It was daft, indulgent and often rather charming, but to Mark it was the culmination of where he'd been heading all his life. It was also a solution of sorts, affording him protection from life's hard knocks, though privately at least, there were sometimes moments when the gloss of enchantment failed to illuminate his darkest fears.

"Observing life through Mark Feld's looking-glass was irresistible and seductive." says Simon Napier-Bell, who became Mark's manager the following year. He'd been spun the wizard story, too, that Mark had met a magician in a forest in France and remained with him for three months. "It turned out that he'd been to some gay club and this conjuror had picked him up and taken him back for the night!" he claims, colourfully if incorrectly. "Mark didn't want to face up to a situation that was as mundane as trying to find somewhere to stay for the night in Paris. It was magical, absolutely wonderful. And that's what he managed to do all the time, to take a mundane situation and see it as some wonderful poetic fantasy. He really was a poet."

Napier-Bell had also heard much about Riggs O'Hara. "He kept on about him, and in my mind, he was this six-foot two Texan oil guy or a great-looking Hollywood actor type. That's how Mark genuinely saw him. He even put him into a couple of his songs. Then one day, we were out to dinner somewhere and this little fat chap called out, 'Hey, Mark!' And it turned out to be Riggs O'Hara. Mark didn't see things; he imagined things."

The culmination of Mark's Francophile fantasies came in late summer 1965 when both 'Toby Tyler' and 'Mark Feld' were dumped for something more exotic – and permanent. There are at least four credible and sometimes overlapping theories about how Mark Feld from Stoke Newington became Marc Bolan. The most likely comes from his brother Harry. "Around this time, Mark was friendly with the actor James Bolam. They fell out shortly afterwards, and I have a feeling this was because Mark used his name as inspiration."

"When Mark changed his name, Jimmy got very offended as he thought it outrageous that Mark would take his name," adds Riggs O'Hara. "Mark just changed the 'm' to an 'n', as simple as that. Mark liked the sound of it. He couldn't understand why Jimmy was upset. He thought it was absolutely ridiculous that Jimmy thought he was going to be as big as Mark was. Mark always knew that he was going to be more famous."

Typically, Mark's own explanation contains little more than a half-truth. "The only thing Decca (Records) did for me was to change my name," he complained in 1972. "From Mark Feld they changed it to Bolan, which was originally spelled B-o-w-l-a-n-d." With characteristic nonchalance, he added, "I didn't really care, to be honest."

No more convincing is the theory that finds Mark, who liked to pass himself off as "French Cockney", marrying a touch of Euro glamour with his latest guitar-swinging object of desire. Mark becomes Marc; and with a bit of juggling, Bob Dylan becomes Bo(bdy)lan. It looked good, and it had that two-syllable sound. However, at least one letter survives that bears the signature 'Marc Feld', which suggests that the route to Marc Bolan came in two stages.

Another possible explanation comes from Mike Pruskin, the latest in Mark's string of publicists-managers-flatmates. "He wasn't calling himself Toby Tyler at the time we met," Pruskin recalls. "He was just plain Mark Feld, but he was desperate to find a name." When asked how the pair arrived at Marc Bolan, Pruskin suggests the name was simply "plucked out of the air". Later on he added that it may have been inspired by the French fashion designer Marc Bohan. Considering Bohan's profile at the time – he'd replaced Yves Saint Laurent as couturier for Dior in 1961 – and Mark's penchant for all things French and fashionable, it seems a likely alternative source for the Marc Bolan name.

"Originally," says Pruskin, "there was an umlaut over the 'o' (Bölan), which was even more chic." This is confirmed in a contemporary magazine caption that read: "Helen Shapiro chatting about schooldays with folk singer Marc Bölan".

When Pruskin met Mark Feld, he was an 18-year-old freelance publicist who worked out of Phil Solomon's New Oxford Street office. He had Van Morrison's Them and The Nashville Teens on his books, but striking an instant rapport with Mark, he dropped both in order to promote his new friend. The pair drew up a contract, and moved into an £8-a-week flat at 22 Manchester Street, round the back of Baker Street and comfortingly close to EMI's headquarters. The bill was picked up by an older man called Geoffrey; "Landlord's a queen", quipped Mark in his diary.

The flat consisted of a kitchen, a living room, two bedrooms and a green telephone, which was typically pinned to Pruskin's ear. On the walls hung an acoustic guitar and Mike's self-portrait that he himself described as "very hermaphroditic". A small black kitten named Loog – after the Rolling Stones' ace publicist/manager Andrew 'Loog' Oldham – also shared the basement lair, quietly oblivious to all the dreaming and scheming. There wasn't much clutter: a fur hat that had seen better days sat on the windowsill; Mike's engagement book lay on the floor, always open.

One day early in October 1965, Mike convinced *Evening Standard* pop writer Maureen Cleave to pay them a visit. Her report, published in the October 17 edition of the paper, was titled 'Knit Yourself A Pop Singer: Marc And Mike Will Tell You How'. Its purpose was to identify a new breed of pop singer who strove single-mindedly to attain the inevitable glory that was rightly his. Cleave had come to the right place.

"Big is the way every pop singer now thinks," she wrote. And Marc Bolan, a folk singer who admired Bob Dylan because he was "artistic and aggressive", gave her what she wanted. "The prospect of being immortal doesn't excite me," he deadpanned, "but the prospect of being a materialistic idol for four years does appeal." He also reminded her just how irresistible he was: "If I go into a room and there are ten girls, nine of them will fancy me. I've never failed yet."

Cleave wasn't to know that, with only a handful of male suitors behind him, Marc had yet to enjoy a serious relationship with a woman. That changed during the Pruskin months when Torquay-bred Theresa 'Terry' Whipman, who had a flat in Maida Vale, began sharing nights with Marc at Manchester Street. In their thin, his'n'hers corduroy trousers, suede mosquito boots and navy blue reefer jackets, the pair looked blissfully androgynous, an impression accentuated by Terry's boyish bob and Marc's coiffeured waves that framed his soft, feminine face. Marc spouted poetry, she put it down on paper for him. "She was devoted to him," Pruskin recalls.

Initially at least, Marc was rather less private with his favours. Pruskin, who couldn't make up his mind whether Bolan was gay or straight, believed the singer "used his sexuality to get what he wanted." If it suited the greater cause then "that is the sort of game you played in order to get on." And, since meeting Pruskin that summer, Marc at least appeared to be getting on.

Inspired by Manchester Street and the optimism he felt there, Marc stayed in the flat as often as he could, filling notebooks with florid, fantastical prose, and writing at least three original songs. Two of these, 'The Wizard (In The Woods)' and 'The Third Degree', were played to Leslie Conn, a Denmark Street agent, who was impressed enough to buy into a deal with Pruskin on a 50/50 basis.

Conn's role in Bolan's career is small, but he did make two significant introductions. One day, he took Bolan and another of his keenly dressed charges, David Jones, to see Beatles' publisher Dick James. Kenneth Pitt, who went on to manage David 'Bowie' Jones in 1966, remembered an unimpressed James sending all three packing with the words: "Get those long-haired gits out of here!" Thus began Marc and David's complex friendship, which, during the mid-Sixties, usually consisted of little more than exchanging the latest career knockback over cappuccinos in La Giaconda, the music industry hangout just doors down from Conn's office.

A second meeting yielded almost instant results. Jim Economides, an American known for his work with pre-Beach Boys harmony group The Lettermen, was an independent producer working out of an office in Albert Gate Court adjacent to the barracks in Knightsbridge. With the right Bacharach and David or Sonny Bono song, he envisaged a fine future for Marc as a soloist, and promptly introduced him to Dick Rowe, the hapless Decca A&R man who had infamously turned down The Beatles. He daren't make the same mistake again; Marc Bolan was offered a one-single record deal.

With a roster that included The Rolling Stones, Them, The Zombies, The Nashville Teens and The Moody Blues, Decca Records was fast challenging the supremacy of EMI. When the label signed Marc in August 1965, the Stones were hot on The Beatles' tails, and Rowe's continued belief in solo artists was vindicated by the label's recent successes with

Tom Jones, Billie Davis, Marianne Faithfull, Twinkle, Dave Berry, Lulu and P.J. Proby.

Years later, Marc said the idea was that he'd become "Decca's Donovan", though that idea was probably his. Dick Rowe was less convinced and packed him off to Decca's in-house Musical Director Mike Leander. "He turned up at my central London flat in a lovely denim suit and denim hat looking every inch the clean-rinsed Bob Dylan," recalls Leander. "What appealed to me most at that stage was his voice, rather than the material. 'The Wizard' was quite good, but the other songs were so-so."

The Dylan effect was clearly in evidence. "It was very early days for singer-songwriters and Marc was very folky. But he definitely had new things to say lyrically. He was different, and though he seemed confident in himself, I think he was unsure about the subject matter of his songs because they were a bit off-the-wall."

Leander's flat was barely a stone's throw away from Manchester Street, and Marc visited the arranger several times prior to recording the single, strumming the basics on his acoustic while Leander fleshed out the simple chord changes on his piano. Despite the material's original flavours, when Leander and producer Jim Economides discussed the forthcoming session, they played safe and opted for a tried-and-tested formula.

"We always recorded solo singers with an orchestra behind them back in the mid-Sixties," says Leander. "Because I was a bit stumped as to know what to do with Marc, I put him in the same light folk category as Marianne Faithfull, who I was working with at the time. On reflection that was quite the wrong thing, but at that stage, nobody quite knew what he could do. We just thought, here's a little hot guy who's going to make a lot of noise one day."

On the morning of September 14, 1965, Mike Leander, Jim Economides, Mike Pruskin and Marc Bolan congregated at Decca's Broadhurst Gardens studios in West Hampstead. A small backing orchestra, comprising string section and pop instruments, and The Ladybirds vocal group were briefed and awaited further instructions from Leander. It was ten in the morning and everyone knew that the session would be over by lunchtime.

It was. Marc, in a thick black sweater and, says Pruskin, "very nervous", stepped into a booth and sang guide vocals to ensure that the key was correct and give the musicians a feel for the tempo. Once a satisfactory backing track was in the can, he stepped forward a second time, pulled the headphones over his ears and – just as Elvis and Cliff had done so many times before him – cut his vocal master. By the time Leander and

Economides had finished, the hideous memory of Marc's 'Blowin' In The Wind' session was banished forever. Leander's tightly arranged beat backing, embellished with howls of oboe, flute and bells, was complimentary to Marc's musical mystery plays.

Three songs were recorded that morning: two originals, 'The Wizard' and 'Beyond The Risin' Sun'; and a Chicago blues song, 'That's The Bag I'm In'. The first two were coupled for Marc Bolan's début 45; the latter, a recent inclusion on a Phil Ochs album, stayed in the vaults. No matter: it was 'The Wizard', with its beguiling content, insistent beat and Dylan-like vocal intonation that would make Marc Bolan a star.

'The Wizard' was released on November 19, 1965, the latest product of a newly Dylanised pop world. Marc knew it: "I sounded like Bob Dylan," he admitted in 1972. It was hardly surprising. According to Mike Pruskin, "He'd listen to Dylan all the time, pulling out phrases and expanding them for his own purposes."

By winter 1965, Bob Dylan didn't just write and sing about freedom; he epitomised it. The ragged trousered troubadour, who eulogised Woody Guthrie and knew which way the wind blew, had turned his back on the cosy certainties of protest and instead became the new Christ of chaos. What Charlie Parker had done for jazz, and Jackson Pollock for art, Dylan – by tapping into a highly crafted but seemingly spontaneous creative vein – was now doing for popular music. No one was more responsible for the impending uprising, the one that left a lasting chasm between pop that was fun, fleeting and neatly dispensed in three-minute chunks, and rock, which signified something more meaningful and lasting. Marc was an eager witness to pop's entry into adulthood, though like Dylan, he too would later flout its boundaries.

For now, Bob Dylan's most immediate gift to Marc Bolan was poetic emancipation. *Bringing It All Back Home*, issued in spring 1965, had confirmed Dylan's headlong dive into symbolist, even surrealist imagery. There's no doubt that songs like 'Gates Of Eden' – rich in couplets like "The motorcycle black Madonna/Two-wheeled gypsy queen/And her silver-studded phantom cause/The gray flannel dwarf to scream" – left an immediate and indelible impression on the newly literate Londoner. Had Mark Feld been invited to volunteer his desired profession in 1965, he would no doubt have answered 'Pop Poet'.

Dylan was also the archetypal Romantic rock artist – contrary, inspired, cloaked in mystery, outrageously opinionated and disarmingly prone to self-promotion. The cover of *Bringing It All Back Home*, which provides a telescopic leap into Dylan's carefully constructed private world, illustrates this perfectly. Freed from the gestures of social solidarity, the newly domiciled singer is 'back home' with his artefacts and commodities, a beautiful woman by his side and a Persian cat for company. This paragon of authenticity, now draped in conspicuous consumption and decadent pleasures, had become a pariah to purists, an inspiration to the modernisers.

Poet, moderniser and so hung up on self-importance he could swing, Marc Bolan was perfectly prepared to become pop's latest boy wonder. Hot on the heels of the *Evening Standard* piece came an enthusiastic profile by George Melly (who was "attracted to Marc", says Pruskin) in *The Observer* that compared Marc with Walter De La Mare. Meanwhile, the Decca publicity machine got to work with the preposterous Wizard story. A lavish, illustrated press release read:

"Marc Bölan was born in September 1947. After 15 years had passed he travelled to Paris and met a black magician called The Wizard. He lived for 18 months in The Wizard's chateau with Achimedes (sic), an owl, and the biggest, whitest Siamese cat you ever saw.

"He then felt the need to spend some time alone so made his way to woods near Rome. For two weeks he strove to find himself and then returned to London, where he began to write.

"His writings mirror his experiences with mentionings of the magician's pact with the great god Pan. In London walking down King's Road, Chelsea in the dead of night he chanced to meet a girl named Lo-og who gave him a magic cat. This cat, named after the girl, is now his constant companion and is a source of inspiration to him.

"Now the Wizard's tale is set down for all to hear on Marc's first recording for Decca."

Quite a few people heard 'The Wizard'. Many more had read his intriguing story. But not one of them bought the record. "It was a great disappointment when those first tracks made no impression whatsoever," remembers Mike Leander. The reviewer in *Disc* was suspicious of the Dylan-like phrasing, though Derek Johnson at *New Musical Express* gushed: "Try and catch Marc Bolan's self-penned 'The Wizard'. It has a most intriguing lyric, and his Sonny Bono-like voice is offset by a solid thumping beat, strings and ethereal voices." Perhaps it was all a bit too ethereal, a hippie fable on 45 before there were any hippies around to appreciate it.

'The Wizard' was the first of many personality songs Bolan would write over the next decade or so, many glorifying male characters, imagined or real. It was a characteristic he shared with fellow Londoners, The Kinks'

Ray Davies (creator of the gender-bending 'Lola') and The Who's Pete Townshend (whose Tommy was a wizard at pinball) – though neither mangled reality so thoroughly as Marc did.

The intonation may have owed much to Dylan – the way Bolan let his voice drop wearily at the end of each line, for example – but the lyric was more obviously whimsical than anything in the American's repertoire. Both 'The Wizard', who "turned and melted in the sky" in a visionary 1'45", and the sharper and even shorter flip, 'Beyond The Risin' Sun', were sonic fairytales more akin to C.S. Lewis' Narnia chronicles or *The Wizard Of Oz*, where strange things happened behind magic doors.

Donovan, the original British Dylan, was another likely source for Marc's mythological tales. "I'd begun to take a great interest in the myths and legends of the distant past," he remembers. There was an American connection, too: "The folk songs that came from Britain, especially Ireland, Scotland and Wales, regions with a strong Celtic tradition, were taken up by singers like Joan Baez. She sang the Child ballads, songs that had been passed down through the centuries, carrying with them a view of the world that was made up of the remnants of myths and legends." Donovan's late 1965 album *Fairytale* was rich in mythology.

The pair crossed paths again on November 19, at the second Glad Rag Ball, a huge charity event organised by students from the London School of Economics. A last-minute replacement for John Lee Hooker, Marc walked out onto the vast Empire Pool, Wembley stage to face 8,000 boisterous students, zanily attired and more interested in slapping shaving foam over each other than in the nervous unknown who stood quaking before them. Worse, still, Marc was given a semi-acoustic guitar so that he could make himself heard, distracting film cameras wheeled around the stage recording the event for an ITV television broadcast on December 8, and his short set was blighted by equipment failure. His later insistence that Donovan, by then an accomplished performer with two Top five singles under his belt, "died a death" at the show sounds suspiciously like projection – although the billtopping Glaswegian was booed by a rowdy audience who expected a no-show Kinks.

Although Marc claimed to Maureen Cleave that he'd sung in a few folk clubs "ages ago", he certainly wasn't accomplished enough to regard himself as a natural performer. Concerts were virtually non-existent. Mike Pruskin remembers one performance at the Pontiac Club, at 100 Upper Richmond Road, Putney in west London. The Pontiac, famed for its R&B sounds bouncing around the op art decorated walls, catered for a hip

Mod clientele. Recent visitors included The Byrds, who played one of the least successful shows of their British tour there.

"Marc's performance was a total disaster," says Pruskin. "It was like a cartoon, with fights everywhere and people diving all over the place. He really wasn't much good on the guitar at that time." Janie Jones, whose 'Witches Brew' was rather more successful than 'The Wizard', also remembers playing a couple of shows with him. "It was somewhere in the wilds," she says, "but I do remember that he was very nervous."

Things weren't much better in the television studio. A critical appearance on Rediffusion's *Ready, Steady, Go!*, broadcast on November 12, was marred by the backing band playing out of sync; although subsequent visits to *The Five O'Clock Fun Fair* and *Thank Your Lucky Stars* seem to have passed without adverse comment. And at least one person, a teenage girl from Teddington, took notice: she started the very first Marc Bolan fan club. It didn't last very long.

After working with Marc on a morning shoot in Holborn on October 23, Decca's in-house photographer David Wedgbury treated his subject to lunch. "He really opened up while he was eating, telling me how much money he was going to make. He had it all sussed – he was really going to be big and make a lot of money." But by the end of the year, 'The Wizard' had done his disappearing act, and the mists of apathy had lifted to reveal Marc Bolan as small and impoverished as he ever was. Wedgbury's assessment – "I dismissed him as a young kid" – was looking more apt than any of Marc's arrogant declarations of imminent stardom.

Helen Shapiro had also heard the spiel. "I hadn't seen him for several years until I ran into him at Fleetway House, where I was attending a party for *Fabulous* magazine. I said, 'What are you doing here?' and he told me how he'd been trying to break into showbusiness. He had his Donovan cap on and we discussed old times for a while. Then he told me he'd been living in Paris with this wizard. He was very enthusiastic about it, but I didn't really know what he was going on about. Marc always did have a very strong imagination."

Marc Bolan couldn't believe that everything hadn't immediately fallen into place. Recording for one of the country's leading record labels, a pop TV regular who'd been invited to join all-star concert bills and attend music-business parties, and the subject of several magazine profiles – everything, it seemed, had been carefully planned. Photographers scrambled to immortalise his handsome image – in the studio, beside classy oil paintings or in a doorway clutching his black cat. He'd even been asked for his autograph. The decade-long dress rehearsal ought to have ended here.

Dressed in his smart suede boots, mid-length reefer jacket with brass buttons, his crown of thick, wavy hair now liberated from its lacquered inflexibility, Marc looked every inch the fashionable Bohemian. If it wasn't quite the poverty chic of the middle-class American beatnik, it was a lot more relaxed than the aspirational one-upmanship of his Mod days. Yet this casual exterior, a cool, art school indifference that again can be traced directly to Bob Dylan, was a façade – at least according to Jeff Dexter.

"Once someone like Marc or I had reached the end of our schooling, we just wanted to be out there. We wanted to be grown up and bigger than we were, and the thought of being a student again was abhorrent to us. Art school kids were all spoilt brats who had too much of everything." Marc had certainly embraced the art school worldview, but coming from the streets and not the salon, his priorities would always be different. "I think he really just wanted to make money," Dexter maintains. "Ultimately, he always wanted to make it rather than create it."

There were a few people at Decca who still shared his belief. Jonathan King, a recent Decca success and a scout for the label, was a convert. "I knew Marc four years ago and I always knew he would be a monster hit," he said at the beginning of the Seventies. "At that time there were only three people I would allow to sing me their songs. They were Marc Bolan, Scott Walker and Cat Stevens." Stevens was another Decca hopeful, and his manager Mike Hurst shared an office with Jim Economides. The pair often commiserated with each other, though a little more than a year later, when Stevens started having hit singles, their fortunes diverged dramatically.

Mike Leander, too, was happy to give Marc another shot and on December 30, 1965, the pair returned to the studios to record four new Bolan originals. This time, there were no Ladybirds or string and woodwind sections, simply Marc accompanying himself with some rudimentary guitar chords. Again, none of the songs broke the two-minute barrier, with 'Reality' and 'Song For A Soldier' barely lasting a minute apiece. The willingness to defy verse-chorus-verse convention, evident on both sides of the début 45, was keenly, maybe even necessarily maintained. So was Marc's preference for sword-and-sorcery lyrics with added Dylanish touches, and a voice that still vacillated somewhere between Sonny Bono and Bob Dylan.

Both 'Rings Of Fortune', which had been written during the summer around the time of 'The Wizard', and 'Highways' (later retitled 'Misty Mist') were re-recorded by Bolan several months later. But there was no second chance for the crude sermonising of the Donovan pastiche, 'Song

For A Soldier', or the ephemeral 'Reality', which languished in the late Mike Leander's archive until acetates of all four songs came up for auction in spring 2002. Neither Decca nor Leander was sufficiently impressed by the material to offer Bolan a second single. When Jim Economides nagged his protégé for more songs, Marc – to whom songwriting was becoming easier by the day – duly delivered.

Economides booked an independent studio and a batch of session musicians, including future Led Zeppelin bassist John Paul Jones. Two songs were recorded one day in spring 1966, both in stark contrast to the Leander-arranged single taped in West Hampstead. 'The Third Degree' was a twin-guitar, two-chord R&B assault closer to Dylan's 'From A Buick Six' (from his latest album *Highway 61 Revisited*) than the folkish flamboyance of 'The Wizard'. The acoustic troubadour was more clearly evident on 'San Francisco Poet', though the uncharacteristic 3/4 rhythm was carelessly handled. (Marc's later claim that the song was never intended as anything other than a demo is probably true.)

'The Wizard' had been a spectacular disaster. The fate of 'The Third Degree', licensed to Decca for a single in June, was a dismal dull affair – no press, no promotion, not even a humiliating public performance to rue later. There was one brief moment of titillation, though only Marc appreciated it. Through the cluttered sound a few blearily delivered words shone back at him: "Philosophising mad psychiatrist closing off my mind in darkness". What he heard was the power of alliteration, and its innate musicality; the more exotic the words used, the more thrilling the effect. Marc Bolan rarely agonised over the art of lyric-writing again.

There was agony in failure, though, and despite his comic identification with the Outsider on 'The Third Degree' ("Everywhere I go people laugh at me"), the mask of Marc Bolan so immovable in public was increasingly slipping in private. At the time of the Decca 45, *New Musical Express* writer Keith Altham remembers Marc as a familiar figure, hustling in and around pop places like the Brewmaster in Leicester Square. "We used to regard him as a bit of an upstart. Marc was small, pretty and very full of himself. He'd always have a new demo tape or a tale like the one about living with the wizard in France, which we all thought was a bit dubious. Then he'd start coming out with these outrageous statements, that he was going to be bigger than Elvis Presley, and we'd all say, 'Sure Marc, sit down and have a Coca-Cola.' Then he suddenly disappeared."

★　★　★

Marc Bolan had packed up his guitar, his box full of diaries and notebooks, his meticulously maintained file of press cuttings, his beatnik trousers and a head full of shattered dreams and gone home, his diary sarcastically noted, to his "penthouse suite in Upper Tooting". From his box room in the Felds' Sun Cottage in Summerstown, Marc began to replenish his creative cupboard without interruption. We know this from the scrap pages, the journals and diaries, the poems and short stories, the songs, the love letters and the typed manuscripts for the modern mystery plays that constitute a vast legacy from these months of literary hyperactivity.

The self-improving bibliophile of 1963 and 1964 had now become a fully fledged creator, gripped by a desire to discover, expose and eventually to succeed through the thrilling dexterity of his own awareness. Inspired by Dylan and the subterranean worlds, the vibrant language and the glorious defeatism of the Beat writers, Bolan's self-importance had strayed headlong into 'Artist' territory. The old Mod clotheshorse was now flirting with a kind of cerebral striptease, one that sought to peel away falsity and wallow edifyingly in miserablism.

Most of all, though, Marc indulged his passion for creating otherworlds. Sometimes, these would simply be idle reflections on his daily routine, which he'd transform into micro-sagas written enthusiastically in beat-lit vernacular. One, 'A Bitova Diary' includes many of beatnik Bolan's pre-occupations: the chaos of sexual orientation, the allure of drugs, identification with black culture, class, cars, hustling, dreams, encounters with strangers, shopping for records, even lavatory humour. And, of course, the man in the mirror: "Wonder if I'm as beautiful today as I was yesterday," he concludes.

The piece begins at home in "Upper Tooting", his streetwise euphemism for Summerstown. Marc gets up, takes some aspirins, eats "crapo cornflakes", eggs and "some ploppy coffee" and says to himself: "I'm a born loser." Pulling on his Levi's and a denim jerkin, the penniless wretch hitches a lift to central London and is beset by more bad luck: "Only I can get picked up by the only 97-year-old granny-type nymph in Tooting, man I tell you they were down to her knees." After punting round Piccadilly for an hour, where "nobody tries to pull me – oh no, not another off day", he earns 7s. 6d. busking, grabs a Coke at a Wimpy bar and asks himself, as every good rent boy (real or imaginary) would: "Where did all the queens go?"

Using his last shilling to go to Knightsbridge via the underground ("the only place where the negro is top dog"), he remarks on the abundance of

E-type Jags ("kinda posh") and bumps into a girl he knows. "She's awful pretty, got long straw-like hair and high flying cheek-bones, full red lips and big huge breasts, and lovely legs." Unfortunately, she mistakes him for Donovan, leaving Marc "feeling real squishy"; he goes home.

As the piece continues, Bolan plays a gig in Chelsea, buys a Jesse Fuller LP, *San Francisco Bay Blues*, meets "a guy who looked just like Jesus" and winks at him "knowingly". He gets stoned and imagines he's Prime Minister "Harold Wilson in his caveman aspect and I'm catching dinosaurs and beating my chest in leopard-skin briefs from John Stevens." Rather less imaginatively, he uses "the loo only to see that the last person to do numbers didn't pull the chain, and it was floating about like a little ship". That little trauma over, he goes to sleep and dreams of death: ". . . a real spook dream, as if things ain't bad enough down here, without Jesus and his Dad pissing off and leaving us alone". Things improve next morning when Bolan gazes into his mirror and sees "a young river God – his hair a-dripping and his body wet and fish-like".

"He was very picaresque," remembers Mike Pruskin. That was certainly true. Marc regarded the thrill of the unfolding narrative, where new secrets would be revealed at the turn of each page, as literature's deepest pleasure. In his earliest writings, he'd often put himself at the centre of his narratives, but by May 1966, and with his literary wings flapping, he devised a plot that owed more to the fantasy writings of Tolkien and C.S. Lewis than to a day in the life of Marc Bolan.

Pictures Of Purple People was the first of Marc's many attempts to create a world where good invariably triumphed over evil. As creator of this world, Marc was omnipotent, acting out his hopes and fears through a huge cast of humans and supermen, tyrants and trolls. "I am Napoleon. I am Joan of Arc. So don't cry now baby I've the keys to the darc," he wrote on May 8. And it was darkness, rather than drugs, that tended to ignite his imagination.

The script, handwritten by Marc over 27 pages of an exercise book and subsequently amended for a 14-page typewritten version, had originally been sketched out on a piece of paper marked 'Play'. "A drug is discovered by a small boy (17) and he and a group of hippys (are) all transformed by the drug from dull old ordinary Milliannes to groovy do-gooders diggin' victars and their god. Only the drug (is) manufactured by Scenescoff to be the all power, and their constantly fightin' off evil trolls and dragons. And no matter what they (are) always as high as the sky. Most scene only in their minds, but one goes on a Quest to kill."

Theresa Whipman, who faithfully put Marc's thoughts down on paper, was little more grammatically assured than her lover, but the central thrust of Bolan's archetypal tale is discernible. In the two completed versions, this hallucinatory scenario – where Scenescoff's acid-induced bid to dominate the minds of the younger generation is thwarted by his inevitable destruction – is fleshed out with Magical Persons, Scenescoff purples, winged horses and dragons, wart-infested Trolls, two-headed Angels, Black Unicorns, horned baboons and suchlike. Everything is transformed: "All telegraph poles become huge white crosses and the Baker Street Gnomes become white saints with silver white beards, some even riding white horses."

Incidentally, as well as The Baker Street Gnomes, there are references to Manchester Street ("where I once lived"), Tooting Broadway, Garrett Lane in Wimbledon, "Smoky Old Leicester Square" and Terry's patch Maida Vale. In one scene, Jerry (the suspiciously familiar small, cool-looking boy-hero) sees three heroic images staring down from a wall. And up there with Marlon Brando and Bob Dylan is . . . Marc Bolan.

In a diary entry dated April 27, 1966, Marc complained: "If you're on my scene (music), you'd wanna get some songs sung and dig studios n things. All down to the mind if you can ever get at it after all the shit humans put on it. O those broken shoe depression blues. Alas, will I ever be a millionaire." In his way were those music industry 'Scenescoffs' – his term for downer people – who, if they weren't neglectfully failing to recognise his talents, were busy lining their pockets at his expense.

The confidence Marc had in his own abilities wasn't replicated when it came to dealing with the pop powermongers, hence his preference for agent/friends like Mike Pruskin and Allan Warren. But even something as simple as the deal struck with Warren, sealed with a primitive contract and yielding just a handful of acetates, had caused problems.

When Warren's champagne lifestyle eventually took its toll, and he found himself owing three months rent at 35 guineas a month, he approached landlord David Kirsch with a proposition. "I went with Marc's record and photograph under my arm, and I said to him, 'Don't you think this is marvellous? This guy could be a star.' I said, 'Instead of paying you rent, you write off my debt and I'll give you his contract. And you, with all your money, can make him a star.' " Kirsch was convinced. "What a good idea," he told his precocious young tenant.

"Long after Mark and I had parted our ways, David came to me one day and said, 'I've had the most terrible thing happen with that silly contract you sold me. An angry woman called Mrs. Feld came into my office while I was in the middle of some business and complained that I was doing nothing for her son. I told her she was right; I had done nothing." Phyllis Feld took the contract and tore it up right there in front of him.

There were other problems. According to Mike Pruskin, Marc's first publishing deal was worth a paltry 15s. for 'The Wizard' and 6d. each for his other songs. On January 8, 1966, in a bid to get shot of Les Conn, Pruskin offered him to Kenneth Pitt. Pitt declined, and in April signed another Superstar-in-waiting, David Bowie. Mike Pruskin also remembers meeting Simon Napier-Bell, a young songwriter about to take his first steps into management, but nothing came of it at the time.

Meanwhile, Jim Economides had been trying to convince his young pop poet that perhaps his greatest asset was, after all, his looks. Despite Marc's careful cultivation of the Beatnik-inspired poverty chic, he couldn't help but dress down with panache. Towards the end of their relationship, Pruskin still recalls the continuing obsession with image, the talk of Marc being reinvented in the James Dean mould and his own feeling that he'd struggled enough trying to make Marc Bolan happen. "We weren't making any money and so we parted," he recalls. "The crunch came when we got so broke that we had to do a bunk from the flat." Pruskin assumed that events had precipitated another crossroads for mutable Marc. "I really thought he was going to pursue a career in acting," Pruskin maintains.

Marc may have been tempted by the idea during his Riggs O'Hara days, but by 1966, there was only one role for him and he was still busy working on it. Acting offered fame in exchange for the ability to experience the world from a variety of perspectives. It was a bargain he'd find virtually impossible to fulfil. "I never felt that close to acting," he said later. "I didn't see it as something that would really turn me on. It seemed so slow." Marc Bolan didn't need scripts. He needed a Svengali.

"I'd never heard of Marc Bolan before," says Simon Napier-Bell, indicating that the earlier discussion with Mike Pruskin had been on a distinctly casual basis. In either September or October 1966, Marc telephoned Napier-Bell out of the blue, and fixed up an instant meeting at the manager's flat. A short time later, he was on the doorstep clutching his beaten-up six-string acoustic, but without the promised demo tape of his original songs.

Napier-Bell liked what he saw. "I thought he was a Charles Dickens urchin," he recalls. "It's now become very fashionable to wear old clothes, two jackets on top of one another, that sort of thing. Back then it was unique. I certainly hadn't seen fashion like that before." He invited Marc in. "He sat down quite unabashed and played me all these songs. His guitar playing was appalling, but I just loved the voice."

Between recording 'The Third Degree' in late spring and meeting Simon Napier-Bell in the autumn, something had happened to Marc Bolan's voice. The impressionable, self-conscious attempts to mimic Cliff Richard or Bob Dylan or even Sonny Bono had given way to a style of singing that was virtually unheard of in the pop world. It was a remarkable transition with no obvious precedent, though Bolan later claimed it was derived from spinning Billy Eckstine records at 78rpm. Comparisons have often been made with Bessie Smith's agonised blueswailing, though a more likely contemporary influence was Buffy Sainte-Marie, the Amerindian folksinger whose dramatic and lachrymose vocal flutters would have reached Marc's ears during the mid-Sixties.

The voice that reverberated around Simon Napier-Bell's living room marked an extraordinary break with convention. It broke every professional code. Where once there was diction, intelligibility and 'holding the note', there was now an unrefined haemorrhage of sound, a quivering vibrato that mangled words into an unrelenting warble, punctuated at frequent intervals with bursts of shrill bleating. Marc Bolan sang as if his larynx had become diseased. Just what the doctor ordered, enthused thrill-seeking Simon Napier-Bell.

Two years later, Marc was asked about his distinctive singing style. "I suppose we're trying to imitate the instruments," he said almost instinctively. It was his standard response to his underground press inquisitors. On this occasion, though, he elaborated. "It's just a development of my mind," he admitted. "I never used to like singing but now it is a great fulfilment, like flying. I think it mirrors what I feel inside." Bolan could have written poetry and prose for the next 50 years and not impressed a soul. But the moment his exotic sounding verbiage came gushing out via his new, sense-shredding bleat, it marked the triumphant birth of a unique and truly distinctive texture in popular music.

Inspired by Marc's self-confidence, his attractive image and that voice, Napier-Bell could barely control himself. He telephoned several recording studios in the hope of finding one available that same evening. The only one with free time – and it may well have been days rather than hours later – was De Lane Lea Studios in Kingsway, central London. During a quickfire session, that took anything from 50 minutes to two hours (Napier-Bell's memory has stretched over the years), a staggering 14 demos were recorded. Given that the Summer of Love was still months away, Bolan's song titles were almost as unique as the vocal styling – 'Hippy Gumbo', 'The Perfumed Garden Of Gulliver Smith', 'Pictures Of Purple People', 'Charlie', 'I'm Weird', 'Mustang Ford', 'Horrible Breath', 'Hot Rod Mama', 'Jasmine 49', 'Eastern Spell', 'Black And White Incident', 'You Got The Power', 'Observations' and 'Cat Black'.

None of the arrangements were particularly intricate. In fact, most were endearingly under-developed, with just one, 'Hot Rod Mama', lasting longer than two-and-a-half-minutes. But Napier-Bell was convinced of their greatness. "I think they were the best songs Marc ever wrote," he insists. "They had great poetry and imagery, which was lost later when he got commercial." Bolan, too, was more than satisfied with the session. "He said, 'Well, there's the album,'" Napier-Bell recalls. "I had to tell him that the idea was to listen to those demos, and then make one into a record."

At the time of the session, Simon Napier-Bell was still managing and producing The Yardbirds, steering the R&B firebrands through a turbulent period in their career. After the departure in June of Napier-Bell's confidant Paul Samwell-Smith, ace session man Jimmy Page joined on rhythm guitar, teaming up with the gifted but cantankerous lead guitarist Jeff Beck. Years later, when Marc contested the public release of these tapes, he claimed that "the only interesting thing that came out of that period was watching The Yardbirds work. Jimmy Page and Jeff Beck were with them then, and I used to go to their sessions and watch them". On another occasion, he claimed to have been present at the session for 'Happenings Ten Years Time Ago', The Yardbirds' glorious three-minute blast of Eastern-tinged chaos issued that autumn.

The Yardbirds were already well established virtuosos who could outplay The Rolling Stones and thrill America, but they were "a dreary lot," says Napier-Bell who had become bored by their internecine conflicts. By contrast, Marc Bolan was "a lot more interesting", a nobody with a great face, a distinctive voice, a handful of good songs and bags of enthusiasm. Napier-Bell was transfixed by the 19-year-old who sat dwarf-like in his armchair, though he was less convinced by Marc's 'I'm weird' patter.

"There was never an element of mysticism about him," he insists. "Marc was a wonderful, charming fraud. That was his own fantasy he had about himself. There was nothing mystical in the fact that he was prepared to sit down, quite unabashed, and play all these songs to me – and his guitar playing was appalling. He was absolutely unaware of his own shortcomings. I just loved the voice. He also happened to be an extremely interesting person who had a great approach and musical attack."

Inevitably, there was a 'Scenescoff' element to Napier-Bell's adoration. "I thought Marc would be the biggest star in the world," he admits. "Even some of his fantasy about making it rubbed off on me. His voice really sounded magical and I thought people would want to hear it. And the lyrics, in terms of the words and feeling, were tremendous. At his best, he wrote some of the best poetic lyrics I've ever heard in pop. He often talked about being a poet."

Among the most startling of the De Lane Lea demo session recordings was 'Observations', a walking, talking blues and Marc's most wordy song to date. Echoing many of the elements that had already appeared in the *Pictures Of Purple People* play, the song anticipated Bolan's later distinctive lyric style. A masterclass in conspicuous association, it namedrops locations (Brighton, West 1, Maida Vale and Chelsea), characters (crazy Sally), stars (Barbra Streisand), rock'n'roll songs ('See You Later Alligator') and street hardware, and still finds time for strange encounters with "guys with paintings in their eyes" and "rockin' preachers".

Marc at last had found the wildly enthusiastic patron and Svengali figure he'd always wanted. Napier-Bell, although committed to his new discovery, had other matters to attend to. "I remember him complaining once that he couldn't come round and sit in my flat all day when he wanted," he recalls. "Marc saw a manager as a substitute parent – someone who would help him, guide him, be his partner, talk with him, provide a home, provide him with some pocket money and be a manager. Someone who'd do everything for him so that he could go ahead and become a star. There was an element of laziness in Marc."

The relationship soon assumed a closeness that rivalled Marc's romance with Terry Whipman. "I would imagine that his relationship with Terry was rather inventive, like a brother and sister learning together," Napier-Bell speculates. "I thought Marc was more gay than straight. All the figures he admired were men, and I think he admired them to the point of finding them sexually attractive. If his sexuality was more or less evenly balanced, I think he found gay life and gay chat infinitely more amusing. You only have to hear his off-the-cuff interviews and chat between takes. He was always fun."

An entry in Bolan's 1966 journal, dated April 23, suggests that Marc's sexual interests were confused and possibly more prurient than pleasure-seeking. "There's this huge fat man clutchin a new shinin kettle, man he was Fat & ugly to, well not so much ugly as repulsive like he looked very dykey (lesiaban) – no mostly no sex, & bein Fat he had boobs (tits) n Id imagine no dicky to speak of (I read somewhere it grows inwards or something) – (I even imagined havin him lay on me all sweatin & maybe 1 or 2 greasy black pubic hairs) . . ."

Napier-Bell insists that Marc "had no great hang-ups about sex" by the time they met. "Obviously, I was aware of his sexual relationship with me; I was aware that he had Terry; and I was aware that he'd had affairs with various people. He used to come round on the early morning bus from his parents' prefab in Wimbledon and get in bed with me in the morning. How can you manage anybody and not have a relationship with them? The sexual borders had completely collapsed by that time. Straight people thought they shouldn't be straight. In fact, in the Sixties, it was pretty difficult to have any sort of relationship with someone without it being sexual. There was a feeling that you were not entering into the spirit of what that decade was about. There was not necessarily any closeness or commitment involved, though. It was of no more consequence than smoking a joint together. I think Marc had a whole series of people with whom he went around having very intimate but very nice, easy relationships."

Marc's early morning bedroom discussions with his manager were, more often than not, plotting sessions for ways of hatching the all-new Marc Bolan on an increasingly sophisticated record-buying public. By the end of 1966, American folk-rock – Dylan, The Byrds, Sonny & Cher, The Lovin' Spoonful, The Mamas & The Papas – had just peaked. Having soaked up its influence, The Beatles and The Rolling Stones had begun to look further afield for musical inspiration. Dylan had turned his back on politics, Lennon and McCartney had virtually killed off Tin Pan Alley. The Beach Boys' *Pet Sounds* and 'Good Vibrations' and Bob Dylan's *Blonde On Blonde* were among the records that got everyone talking that year. The pop world was taking giant strides. Marc and his paternalistic manager knew that it was only a matter of time before its quest for innovation would catch up with Marc Bolan.

The song the pair chose to relaunch Marc's career was 'Hippy Gumbo'. One of the original De Lane Lea demos, it was re-recorded at a slower pace and with added vocal tremors, and fleshed out by a seductive, menacing string section and three double basses. A brooding, almost indecent arrangement, it provided a perfect backdrop for Bolan's new vocal technique. The effect was menacing and claustrophobic, and not dissimilar to the early work of Dr. John. The lyrics were uncharacteristically compact, and disturbingly evocative of a Grimm Brothers fairy tale ("Hippy Gumbo he's no good/Chop him up for firewood"). 'Misfit' on the flipside was oddly out of place, with Marc's best asset – his voice – struggling to be heard against a conventional beat backing with added brass.

'Hippy Gumbo' was fashionably freaky but it hardly sounded like a hit record. Napier-Bell's enthusiasm was infectious, but even he couldn't charm a record deal for it. Eventually, he used his contacts at EMI (The Yardbirds were on its Columbia subsidiary) and secured a low-key release on Parlophone. Marc Bolan was now only a few catalogue numbers away from The Beatles, but in terms of mass appeal, he remained a frustrating failure.

Marc performed the song on *Ready, Steady, Go!* on December 13, 1966, the same edition that featured the British television début of the Jimi Hendrix Experience. The two hirsute hopefuls exchanged a few words backstage. "He said he dug the way I sung," Marc recalled with pride. "And he said, 'One day, you're gonna be very big.' I thought bullshit, you know."

Meanwhile, Simon Napier-Bell was already plotting his next pop sensation, one that would soon play a small but significant role in the future destiny of Marc Bolan and finally land his face on a magazine cover, his song in the charts and his life in the hands of a rioting audience. These new pop playthings were a ramshackle bunch from Leatherhead called John's Children.

4

Let It Rock

"John's Children – First Of The Anti-Lust Groups."
  – Headline in *New Musical Express* (March 18, 1967)

"All I've done is recreate John's Children, or at least what I wanted John's Children to be like when I was with them. I'm writing exactly the same stuff as I was five years ago. It's no different really except that hopefully it's a bit better and has a bit more insight. And I can play it now; I couldn't then."
  – Marc Bolan, *Zigzag* (1971)

"It was like ducking Marc in the deep end and then pulling him out again and saying, 'See, you can do that. That's what you can get away with without being any good. Imagine what you could do with a good band and some good songs.'"
  – Chris Townson, drummer, John's Children (1992)

The first time Marc stepped outside Britain he enjoyed a civilised weekend in Paris in the company of a cultured friend. For his second continental trip, in April 1967, he was an active part of a travelling rock'n'roll freak circus that wreaked such mayhem across Germany that the group was forcibly packed off home. "It was total smash-up media," Marc claimed in 1972 and this time it was no exaggeration.

John's Children provoked howls of disgust – from the German police obliged to pick up the pieces after their shows, from the media who mistrusted their sensation seeking antics, and from an outraged British serviceman stationed in Germany who caught the group's short, incendiary performance in Düsseldorf on April 11, 1967. Describing the group as "the most atrocious excuse for 'entertainment' I have ever seen", he singled out "the lead guitarist (who) kicked his equipment, beat the stage with a silver chain, and sat in a trance between his speakers producing deafening sounds on his guitar." That was Marc Bolan. "It was sickening," insisted the military man. "Britain was shamed on that stage."

Until they were eclipsed by their little-known support act, The Who were Britain's premier Pop Art destruction unit, whose shows invariably culminated in a mess of mangled microphones, smashed guitars, bashed-in drums and screeching howls of feedback. These frenzied climaxes were often celebrated as wanton destruction and nothing more, though guitarist and spokesman Pete Townshend claimed a direct link with the auto-destructive art theories of Gustav Metzger. Metzger was interested in the relationship between violence and creativity. Pete Townshend was interested in testing those theories out on rowdy beat club audiences.

On Wednesday April 12, 1967, several thousand young West German pop fans crowded into the large Eberthalle in Ludwigshafen to witness The Who sacrificing their equipment in the name of auto-destruction. John's Children, the Who's label-mates on Kit Lambert and Chris Stamp's newly formed Track imprint, were theoretically the least significant of the four bands on the bill that night, another of whom was The Rattles, the German group who later scored a hit in Britain with 'The Witch'. Much of the audience had been dispersed by the time The Who came on, but they'd already had more than their fair share of destruction that night.

The memory of that evening's events have stayed with the ex-band members ever since. "Most of our gigs ended in some form of disarray," says singer Andy Ellison with a culpable grin, "but that one was way over the top. We'd only played about three or four longish numbers, and then the customary feedback, the thunderous drumming and the vocal chants took over. Marc began to whip his guitar and amplifier with a heavy chain. Meanwhile, I'd jumped into the audience and started stirring the crowd up by throwing feathers everywhere. Before long, the whole place was covered with them.

"People tried to pick fights with me, but I scrambled back on to the stage and had the usual preconceived battle with John the bassist, complete with fake blood capsules. I think that's what sent the audiences mad on that German tour. At Ludwigshafen, the crowd started picking up chairs and throwing them through windows. Everyone was fighting and there was a hideous noise from the audience. I remember thinking it had all gone berserk. While this was going on, the feedback continued and Chris carried on banging away on his drums."

Not for long, though. John's Children's shows usually ended with Chris Townson alone on the instrument-spattered stage pounding hell out of his kit. But at Ludwigshafen, with the stage under siege and mayhem all around, he beat a hastier retreat than usual. "It was very dangerous," he remembers, "almost like mass hysteria. I remember John laughing like a maniac – out of fear, I think, not because he was enjoying it."

The turning point was the Viking. "The audience surged onto the stage, and there was this huge guy who looked like a Viking. He was wearing an RAF roundel T-shirt like the one Keith Moon always used to wear. As I decided to make a run for it, this guy bore down on me. I thought my time was up, but instead of beating me up, he gave me this huge wet sloppy kiss. Eventually, I got away from him, kicked my kit towards the crowd and ran."

While Chris grappled with the latter-day sea wolf, Andy Ellison, John Hewlett and Marc Bolan cowered backstage having already beaten a hasty retreat from the unwanted attentions of the security guards and officials who – forewarned of the band's stage antics – had turned out in force. "All the bouncers in those days were leftovers from the old Nazi regime," claims the group's manager Simon Napier-Bell. "They only went to rock concerts so they could bang people's heads together. These were the most vicious people you could ever meet, so when we tackled the gig in what was more or less our customary way, they felt justified in responding like that. The whole place just went mad."

There was no time to listen to The Who's angry protestations, or those of their manager Kit Lambert, who had suggested taking John's Children on tour in the first place. What followed next was pure Mack Sennett. With a small cavalry of enraged concert stewards snapping at their heels, Napier-Bell and his young charges hot-footed their way through a maze of backstage corridors leaving their equipment and personal belongings behind. As they raced towards their manager's limousine, a fleet of water cannons arrived outside the hall, their hoses dangled through every window in a last bid to subdue the crowd.

While the audience sluiced around in a lagoon of chair legs and feathers, John's Children swerved out of the car park, headed for the nearest auto-bahn and sped off towards the calmer environs of Munich. Under the freeway lights, they compared bruises. Chris bore the brunt of it, his chest tattooed by a massive jackboot mark. Andy, already nursing a damaged neck after falling from the stage the previous night in Düsseldorf, sat in the tattered remnants of his stage outfit. Marc and John picked feathers from their white uniforms in virtual silence. The next day, Napier-Bell received a call from Kit Lambert. John's Children were going home.

★　★　★

John's Children were an unlikely vehicle for the poetic ambitions of Marc Bolan who, according to Mike Pruskin, "always wanted to do it on his own". Marc had spent the past year or so piling on the integrity, but in spring 1967, he found himself part of a group that relied on shock tactics on stage and session musicians on record. "All that John's Children were at that period were what I am now," he claimed in 1972. "I'm only doing the same thing I wanted to do then." It wasn't quite that simple. Like T. Rex, John's Children were a four-piece rock band with electric guitars and some Marc Bolan songs. But any similarities ended there.

Early in 1967, Simon Napier-Bell returned to the studio with Marc to record a new song he'd just written. Titled 'Jasper C. Debussy' it was punctuated by a 3/4 fairground-style motif between each verse, and paid more respect to pre-psych Brit-pop quirkiness than it did Bolan's fast-developing *oeuvre*. It was another of Marc's character songs, this time portraying a mischievous individual whose "kinda fun" was tying people to railroad tracks. An upbeat boogie-woogie tempo and Nicky Hopkins' trademark bar-room piano-playing underscored the darkly hued comic-book humour.*

Initially conceived as the follow-up to 'Hippy Gumbo', 'Jasper C. Debussy' was soon shelved in favour of the latest Napier-Bell brainwave. The two acts he most wanted to succeed were both lacking in some essential way. There was the gifted songwriter with a voice so abrasive that few dared listen. And the band with boundless energy that couldn't write a decent song. Why not introduce the songwriter to the band? It could hardly fail . . .

John's Children had been playing in one form or other for at least as long as Marc Bolan had. The group started out in 1964 as The Clockwork Onions, and after shedding Louie Grooner and Martin Sheller, the nucleus of the band – bassist Chris Dawset, Geoff McClelland on guitar, drummer Chris Townson and vocalist Andy Ellison – continued as The Few before becoming the more artfully named The Silence.

By spring 1965, they'd begun gigging with a noisy mix of Who and Kinks covers, interspersed by R&B standards such as 'Smokestack Lightning' and a version of Booker T & The MGs' 'Green Onions' that seemed to go on forever. The decidedly unmusical John Hewlett stepped in to fill Chris Dawset's shoes. The rest weren't much better, so to compensate for

---

* John Paul Jones and guitarist 'Big' Jim Sullivan on guitar were among the other backing musicians.

their technical inadequacies, The Silence began to dress in moody stage gear and crank the volume up. Andy Ellison found the innate showman that lurked inside him and developed a stage act that began with a furious shaking of his maracas and ended with a headlong dive into the audience. That hurt when there were only a handful of heads watching.

At the time Ellison lived in Finchley, North London, while the group's base was in Leatherhead, Surrey, a good ten miles beyond the city limits. That was where The Silence became regulars at the Chuck Wagon, a club based at 22a Bridge Street which, in early 1966, became the Bluesette Club. For a while, things looked good for the group. Pop impresario Don Arden, then handling the fast-rising Small Faces, offered them work and The Silence played several major shows with the diminutive Mod combo.

Being part of a group was, says Andy Ellison, "a load of fun and a good way of picking up birds", and in August 1966, Townson, Hewlett and Bluesette co-owner Gordon Bennett ventured down to San Tropez looking for more of the same. It all went horribly wrong: cheques bounced, Bennett mysteriously disappeared and the two band members went their separate ways in a bid to escape the attentions of the French gendarmes. Also sunning himself at the resort was Simon Napier-Bell. One lunchtime, the aspiring pop impresario bumped into John Hewlett in a club.

Napier-Bell gave Hewlett the fare home; in turn the bassist suggested that he check out The Silence on his return to England. True to his promise, Napier-Bell drove down to Surrey to catch The Silence performing at an outdoor party held at the Burford Bridge Hotel, just off the A31, where the group had set up dangerously close to a swimming pool. By now, they'd become a semi-competent, Who-influenced R&B band, retaining an element of performance that sometimes threatened to overshadow the music.

"We couldn't afford to smash up our amplifiers every night like The Who," Ellison remembers, "so we used to destroy ridiculous things like the maracas – in fact anything that just happened to be on stage that wasn't ours. The night of the open-air barbecue we excelled ourselves. Some of the amplifiers ended up in the pool, and I can clearly remember being up on the diving-board singing, then diving into the water with the microphone. I think Simon was quite taken aback, but he must have seen something in the band. Complete madness probably."

"It was primarily sexual," Napier-Bell confesses. "Like most people in the Sixties, I was very hedonistic, and here were three provocatively attractive boys. Brian Epstein only signed The Beatles because he fancied them. Andrew Oldham only got involved with The Rolling Stones because he liked Mick Jagger. What did I have? The boring old Yardbirds who were the straightest, dullest bunch ever. I thought, it's all very well learning about this business and making money, but I'm not getting any fun out of it."

Napier-Bell has a theory that explains why there were so many gay men in management during the Sixties. "In those days, pop music was selling primarily to teenage girls, and only a gay man has the ability to see the artist from the perspective of a teenage girl and that of a businessman. That was a very valuable thing to have." He, too, was seduced by the idea of pop management. "It seemed the ideal way to mix business with pleasure," he recalls. "It was the modern equivalent of being the choirmaster. But in the Sixties, instead of being arrested for the nasty little things you did round the back of the church, they gave you a million pounds and made you a hero."

Napier-Bell put a lot of money into John's Children and got very little back. But he enjoyed every minute of it. "They were one of the most intelligent and fun groups I ever met," he says, "but they weren't very good. Andy couldn't sing but he looked great on stage. Chris could only just play the drums, though he was probably the best musician of the lot. When I saw them, I thought they were probably the worst group I'd ever seen, but it was just too tempting. I jumped in quickly, ignoring the fact that they weren't good musicians. I then realised that I had to do something with them." He quickly spotted that the group had little rapport with guitarist Geoff McClelland. "I decided to put Marc in the band instead."

Napier-Bell's first move after taking the band under his wing in autumn 1966 was to rename them in honour of the tone-deaf bassist who had first introduced the band to him. John's Children, as they were now known, were kitted out in Persil-white outfits, gold medallions swayed around their necks and their hair was trimmed into a smart, boyish late-Mod style.

John Hewlett, who was a willing puppet at the time, now regrets the band's willingness to be manipulated. "I seriously think we were on the way to Hell," he deadpans. "It was the frustration of youth. We wanted to express ourselves, but the truth was that we were not in touch with what we really wanted to achieve." He respects Napier-Bell's talent-spotting instinct, but rues the fact that "he responded to the fun element and the sexual aspect, and tried to manufacture something out of that".

Worse still, he claims that "I can never recall him addressing our talents or encouraging us to work at it. All I can recall is negativity, the feeling that we could con the world, which later became part of the punk ethos. The difference was that during the punk era, bands were far more aware than they were in the Sixties. The punks clearly understood what they were saying and doing. We didn't have a clue."

At a time when pop musicians were starting to take themselves very seriously, spending weeks on songs, and sometimes months on albums, the idea of a manufactured, blatantly hyped group that didn't always play on their records was repugnant. John's Children weren't even Britain's failed response to The Monkees. Their recorded legacy is threadbare, often badly played, blighted by strange edits and a production sound that gambled and lost. Yet amid this mess is a handful of extraordinary gems which, when coupled with the kudos afforded the group on the basis of Bolan's brief involvement, has secured them an unexpected place in rock history. What was an inconsequential aberration back in 1967 is now held in high regard by connoisseurs of British freakbeat. And it's the band's slim output recorded with Marc Bolan on which that reputation is based.

Before Marc joined, towards the end of February 1967, John's Children were already veterans of two singles and had an album lined up for release in America. Through Napier-Bell's contacts at EMI, the group were installed on Columbia in the UK, with separate deals made in Canada, America and Germany. The début 45 was 'Smashed Blocked' (re-titled 'The Love I Thought I'd Found' for the drug-fearing home market), a colossal freakbeat classic that announced itself with 30 seconds of pulsating weirdness and a deranged plea: "I'm losing my mind . . . help me!"

The remainder of the song, which had been recorded in Los Angeles using session musicians, was reminiscent of The Turtles, but much of its oddness was down to Simon Napier-Bell's passion for meddling with the tapes. "After we recorded something, Simon would always take the tapes away and cut them about," Ellison says. "There are edits all over the John's Children's recordings." He claims that the habit was a likely legacy from Napier-Bell's background in film editing. "It made life very difficult for us. We'd rehearse a number in a certain way, and then find that Simon had chopped the last chorus and put it somewhere else, or he'd dropped in a middle section from another track completely." Ellison remembers the group having to re-rehearse songs from the records so they could replicate them live.

'Smashed Blocked' enjoyed enough local success in parts of America to creep into *Billboard*'s Top 100 singles chart. This in turn encouraged the independent White Whale label to commission an entire album from the group. John's Children had yet to perform in front of a screaming audience, but that didn't prevent Napier-Bell from pressing on with the idea of a faked 'concert' LP. He had the band play their set at Advision Studios in Gosfield Street, central London, then he obscured their rudimentary musical skills by running a tape loop of screams lifted straight from The Beatles' *A Hard Day's Night* film. He titled the record *Orgasm*.

The album wasn't even offered to Columbia. White Whale intended to release it, but after the reactionary pressure group the Daughters Of The American Revolution heard about the title, it slipped quietly from the schedules. (By 1971, the 'O' word was deemed rather less controversial and the album finally got a release – and failed dismally.)

While Marc Bolan was still awaiting the release of 'Jasper C. Debussy' on 45, a second John's Children single, 'Just What You Want, Just What You'll Get', appeared, again with characteristically odd production. But this time it was written without the guiding hand of their manager. However, the flip, 'But She's Mine', a blatant recycling of The Who's 'I Can't Explain' riff, illustrated the paucity of original ideas. The songwriting situation was never as bad as Napier-Bell later made out for, unknown to the public, the group wrote and played almost everything on the shelved *Orgasm* album.

By the time of the much-hyped single's release, in February 1967, it had become obvious that Geoff McClelland was not comfortable in the group. The guitarist, whose job it was to faint when the band ran out of songs to play, thus giving them an excuse to cut their concerts short, just wasn't suited to outrage. Simon Napier-Bell wanted to heighten the contrast between the four angelic looking pretty boys who stepped onto the stage in ultra-brite white outfits, and their sudden transformation into wild men who'd drag their equipment across the stage and thrash it – and each other – with belts and chains. "At first I wanted to be a good drummer," maintains Chris Townson, "but there was a transition after Simon took over. In the end, playing well didn't matter. The performance was much more important than what we sounded like."

Napier-Bell stoked up the mayhem. "The more outrageous the better," says Townson. "And we were happy to go along with it. It was like saying to a child, 'Go and smash that kitchen up.' He'd do it with glee. We were like that, but Geoff couldn't carry it off. When Pete Townshend smashed up a guitar, you knew he meant it. When Geoff did it, it made you want to laugh, which was not what we wanted."

Increasingly uncomfortable on stage, Geoff McClelland made the mistake of agonising over his lead break during the recording of 'But She's Mine'. Napier Bell called up Jeff Beck, who delivered the break in one take. Geoff McClelland was on a one way trip back to Leatherhead.

★ ★ ★

It's been said that Simon Napier-Bell served Marc Bolan with an ultimatum: join The Yardbirds or John's Children. The very idea of Bolan's bungling guitar exertions finding a home in the virtuoso R&B band is preposterous. In John's Children, though, his inexperience would matter little.

From childhood, Marc Bolan had never been a team player. When he imagined himself in the role of a pop idol, it was always as a soloist in the manner of Elvis or Cliff or Bob Dylan. As he stayed awake through the night filling his exercise books with passages so purple they reeked of violet, Marc fully believed that true creativity could only be attained through solitary endeavour. To be part of a group was an admission of defeat, but in accepting Napier-Bell's invitation, Marc had chosen to defer the undiluted path of the Romantic artist in favour of naked opportunism. Besides, the buzz around John's Children suggested a more likely route to stardom than 'Jasper C. Debussy' could.

Simon Napier-Bell insists that Marc was a willing conscript. "He was obsessed with being in a band. Marc wanted to be a rock'n'roll star, and so when I put the idea to him, he was immediately taken with it." The manager maintains it was all part of a long-term plan. "It was rather manipulative of me. I knew that John's Children were about to succeed and I knew I couldn't sell Marc's voice to the public. If Marc was a backing singer behind Andy, and the band had some hits, I figured that the public would get used to his voice. Then I'd take him out of the group and he'd re-emerge as a solo artist with a ready-made audience. That's what I really had in mind when I put Marc in John's Children. We made 'Desdemona' with exactly that in mind."

Unwittingly, John's Children were subjected to a mild form of brainwashing. They'd find photographs of Marc Bolan scattered around the recording studio and in Napier-Bell's office; conversations would be punctuated by the sound of yet another Bolan demo wafting in from an adjoining room; and, increasingly, they'd be lectured to by their manager on the subject of his unwavering belief in Marc's songwriting talents. Sometimes, Marc would sit in, almost unnoticed, on the group's evening sessions at Advision. Only Geoff McClelland – for obvious reasons – seemed to be aware of his presence in the studio. "There was this little guy there," he remembered. "Actually, I wasn't too sure if it was a guy. He was sitting, playing an acoustic guitar, very influenced by Dylan and Donovan. At around 10.30pm, he suddenly leapt up and said, 'Look, I've got to go now otherwise my parents will be really mad at me.' And he ran out. That was Marc Bolan."

One day in February 1967, Napier-Bell decided to force the issue and drove Andy Ellison down to Summerstown. Marc wasn't in the habit of receiving many visitors there – only his girlfriend Terry and an old Mod adversary who was now living in nearby Stockwell. "He used to sit and write songs with Keith Reid," remembered Sid Feld many years later. "They'd just sit together and write music from morning till night. That's all they'd talk about – music. That and what they'd do when they were well known." Reid says, "I'd lost touch with Marc. Then I read about him in the *Evening Standard* and called him up. It was strange that we were both trying to pursue a career in music. We didn't write songs together, though. Those daytime sessions were more about showing each other what we were up to musically. He was very motivated and extremely into his career."

As soon as Andy Ellison arrived, Marc raved to him about a book he'd just been reading, Günter Grass' *The Tin Drum*, a remarkable tale about a child's refusal to acknowledge the horrors of the adult world. They listened to Bob Dylan records – Bolan had been playing *Blonde On Blonde* for months – and ate mushrooms on toast, cooked by the host. Marc ran through several songs on his acoustic, including 'Desdemona' and 'Cat Black', before the pair started work on Bolan's latest idea, 'Midsummer Night's Scene'. The enforced encounter between the easy-going singer and the keen, slightly confused songwriter went well. "I was really impressed with his songs," recalls Ellison. "They were great and simple – exactly what John's Children needed."

Simon Napier-Bell now had all his delicious young things together. John's Children had the gifted songwriter they needed, and Marc Bolan had a fresh outlet for his songs. The vibe, visually at least, was good: John's Children looked stunning. "We were all about the same size," says Ellison. "Simon must have known that he could market us as four pretty boys." In retrospect, though, John Hewlett feels that Bolan's recruitment was a wasted opportunity. "He was probably the one person who could have made John's Children more than just a band of drinkers and womanisers. He'd been around longer than us, was more streetwise and had his heart set on success, whereas we were more loony. He was definitely the right person for the band and I think the combination, short-lived and poorly guided as it was, showed signs of working really well."

John's Children's refusal to take anything seriously wasn't the only problem. Marc found the group's devil-may-care camaraderie difficult to penetrate – not that he was ever in the habit of bending to the needs of others. Caught between a desire to refashion the group in his own image, and an innate reluctance to 'join the gang', Marc was first among equals but found himself virtually powerless.

Track boss Kit Lambert had agreed to sign John's Children on condition that Marc was incorporated as a Pete Townshend figure – writing songs, providing musical direction and taking the entire project forward. John's Children benefited from his songwriting, but with Marc unable to establish himself as the group's guide and guru, his stay was destined to be brief. "He entered into this really wild, over-the-top band and he was flabbergasted," Ellison explains. "That Townshend-type relationship was never given a chance to develop, because we worked on the material democratically. I never once heard Marc say, 'This is how you play the song.' We used to work at it together."

On an interpersonal level, Marc's impact was negligible. In the recording studio, however, his arrival instantly transformed the band. Between mid-March and mid-June 1967, John's Children recorded around a dozen Marc Bolan songs: 'The Perfumed Garden Of Gulliver Smith', 'Hot Rod Mama', 'The Third Degree', 'Sara Crazy Child', 'Lunacy's Back', 'Jasper C. Debussy' (as 'Casbah Candy'), 'Mustang Ford' (re-done with non-Bolan lyrics as 'Go Go Girl'), 'Hippy Gumbo' and 'Sally Was An Angel' (both with Marc on lead or shared vocals), plus the two A-sides, 'Desdemona' and 'Midsummer Night's Scene'. Both structurally and melodically, most stuck remarkably close to his original demos.

It's possible that other Bolan songs were taped during his spring fling with John's Children. Simon Napier-Bell's cavalier attitude towards master-tapes meant that he was just as likely to erase original parts, even voices, as he was chucking in screams or wildcard edits. Marc's tenure was brief, his official output restricted to just three sides of two 45s, but the legacy of his spell with John's Children is more significant than has been previously suggested.

A good case in point is 'Cornflake Zoo'. Ostensibly it was an Andy Ellison B-side from April 1968, tucked away on the flip of 'You Can't Do That'. However, it began life as a simple guitar and vocal demo recorded by Bolan early in 1967. The tape was later resurrected by Napier-Bell who simply erased Marc's vocal and replaced it with an Andy Ellison melody that bore no resemblance to the original. As further evidence of John's Children's appropriation of Bolan's swelling repertoire, the group continued to perform his 'Cat Black', and possibly even 'The Third Degree' in concert long after he'd left.

Bolan's arrival was deemed significant enough for Simon Napier-Bell to cancel the planned John's Children single, 'Not The Sort Of Girl (You'd Take To Bed)'. The title alone had been enough to arouse disquiet among the executives at EMI, and Napier-Bell had no qualms in accepting Kit Lambert's offer of a new home at Track Records. Now with a tried-and-tested songwriter in the ranks (albeit one with a failure rate of three out of three), the projected third 45 – which sounded like Dave Dee, Dozy, Beaky, Mick & Tich taking on Captain Beefheart – was shelved and the newly constituted combo began work on the latest Marc Bolan song. Titled 'Desdemona' after the character in Shakespeare's *Othello*, it would become John's Children's sole claim to pop greatness.

By all accounts, drummer Chris Townson was the only half decent musician in the band. As soon as Marc Bolan plugged in for his first rehearsal, at the Bluesette Club in Leatherhead, the rest began to feel a whole lot better about their own abilities. Wielding a Gibson SG he'd recently purchased from The A-Jaes' Trevor White, Bolan was the idiot savant of the solid-bodied guitar. His style, though technically crude, was more percussive than melodic – a trait he shared with The Pink Floyd's Syd Barrett, Marc's latest pop godhead.

It wasn't easy to hear what he was playing because the group's new "folkie" (as *New Musical Express* inaccurately described him in March) always turned his amp up to ten. A ruse to disguise his shortcomings, it also allowed him to bask in the fantasy of the guitar hero, as the new Eric Clapton or Pete Townshend or even Track's fast-rising hippie hero, Jimi Hendrix. Only the aforementioned would have had the sense to tune their instrument before plugging it in. Marc Bolan didn't seem to think it mattered. Chris Townson did, and one day, he decided to tune it himself. Narked, Marc found it "insulting and unnecessary", Chris remembers.

Rejoicing in energy and volume, and finding at least some comfort in the company of the Surrey-based strangers, Marc Bolan's ego was in recovery. The songs kept coming but, to his regret, so did the day he'd have to perform live on stage with the band. Early in March, John's Children arrived at a hall in Watford, Hertfordshire; Marc was completely drunk. When the band were told to stop playing after two songs, the guitarist – uncharacteristically reckless and legless – broke down and cried. For the group's next show, at the Bluesette on March 10, Marc again hit the red wine, but it wasn't long before the rest of the group demanded that he brave an audience without alcohol. However, on-stage sophistication was never going to be the group's forte. "With Marc in the band, we'd swapped a little clunky noise for a huge indistinguishable blurge," says Chris Townson. "There was no way that John's Children could ever get a feel or tick. It was just a manic thrash."

None of this helped Marc's slow integration into the John's Children way of life. The on-stage hyperactivity was more than an act for Andy, Chris and John, who pursued a vigorous social life once recording at Spot (alias Ryemuse) Studios in South Molton Street was over. Heading off to the Soho club scene, or sometimes a wild night at the Lotus House restaurant in Edgware Road, Marc would usually go the other way and make his way back home.

"Marc sometimes joined in," says Andy Ellison, "although even when we were on the road, I remember him staying in the car and writing in one of those notebooks he used to carry round with him." The private Marc Bolan was, the singer says, "quiet, very shy and rather nervous". To begin with, being on stage only magnified these tensions. John's Children changed all that, Ellison insists. "We had to force Marc to be a nutter on stage. Eventually he got into it, going over the top with his chains and playing the guitar above his head."

The idea of Marc Bolan as some kind of reluctant showman is a difficult one to grasp but that's because, like many intrinsically shy individuals, he flaunted his protective façade as if it was a virtual colossus. Ever the schemer, there was another reason for his haughty manner and self-imposed segregation. Refusing to concertina the complete Marc Bolan into one quarter of John's Children kept the vista of a glory-bound future of his own making within his sights. His long-term desire was hardly a secret. In the 'First Of The Anti-Lust Groups' piece published in the March 18 edition of *New Musical Express*, Marc confessed that "I still hope to record independently as a solo artist," adding that "as far as this group is concerned" Andy Ellison is the lead singer.

Costume was still a vital tool for Marc in terms of maintaining his sense of apartness. He was obliged to fall into line with the group's striking snow-white image, though inevitably he customised this limited wardrobe by wearing T-shirts with embroidered motifs and draping scarves and cravats round his neck. His hair, thinned out and fringed in line with the rest of the group, was cut in a style suggested by Simon Napier-Bell. The John's Children image was ripe with juxtaposition – mischievous purity, innocence corrupted – and no one in the band seemed to embody this as convincingly as Marc Bolan.

After a couple of shows at the end of March and early April, at Tiles in Oxford Street and back at the Bluesette Club in Leatherhead, John's Children took off for Germany. There were five shows, including the fateful Ludwigshafen concert, each tingling with tension as The Who sought to preserve their reputation as rock's premier demolition kings by any means possible. Already under pressure back home from The Move, whose latest on-stage wheeze was to demolish television sets with an axe, The Who – and Pete Townshend in particular – were irritated by John's Children's almost immature appetite for destruction. Reviewing the first night of the tour, on Saturday April 8, a Nuremburg newspaper reported that John's Children "rolled over the floor, writhing convulsively, beat themselves up, smashing lamps and chairs". It was performance art, but not as Gustav Metzger understood it.

"We don't just do a musical performance," Marc explained at the end of the tour. "It's a 45-minute happening. Sometimes we're barely conscious of what we're doing. It's like a big turn-on seance between us and the audience. I've seen Andy go quite mad like a witch doctor in a tribal dance. He leaps off the stage and runs round the audience or sometimes he attacks one of us. In Düsseldorf he got in a fight with John, and they both fell 15 feet off the stage onto Andy's head."

Abroad for only the second time in his life, Marc Bolan flourished as his latest continental caper unfolded, dragging amps around the stage and flagellating his guitar with whatever came to hand. He even took John's Children's theatrics into a different dimension, devising his own stage prop – a pair of folding vanity screens covered in silver foil – that stood in front of his amplifier. The idea was to reflect the sound back in order to produce ear-splitting feedback. It seemed to work but, inevitably, Bolan's sound reflector screens were ripped to bits during one of the early shows.

The battle of the bands got more intense with each show. Loving every minute of it, Simon Napier-Bell goaded his boys to push the act to its limits, and the NASA-patented Jordan equipment – the loudest on the market – he'd specifically imported for the dates further aggravated the headliners. One night, The Who borrowed the John's Children backline and drum-kit and proceeded to demolish it. Keith Moon did untold damage to Chris' drums, but the Jordan gear proved invincible – even to Townshend's infamous amp assaulting tactics. Marc, who singled out the guitarist as the most antagonistic Who member, confided to Terry by letter: "The tour's going OK. The Who are a drag but we're going down quite good . . . we're outplaying The Who in most shows . . ."*

Naturally, relations between the groups deteriorated rapidly. On the night of the Ludwigshafen concert, Kit Lambert – who'd suggested the group change its name to The Electric Bunnies to better reflect their stage performances – requested that John's Children tone down their act, which created such an atmosphere among the crowd that The Who found it difficult to play. Simon Napier-Bell encouraged the band to turn the heat up another notch – with near-catastrophic results. "Kit told me, 'If they do that again, they're off the tour'. I thought, if we don't do it, there's no point being on the tour. So let's do it."

That moment of bloodymindedness cost Napier-Bell dearly – supposedly around £25,000, mainly due to lost equipment. He also claims it marked the beginning of the end for John's Children. The group arrived home a full three weeks before the release of 'Desdemona', their first 45 with Marc, but everyone concerned cites Ludwigshafen as the turning point in the band's fortunes. "They came back from the tour and Marc never played anything else with John's Children," insists the band's ex-manager. "The relationship with Kit and Track had soured, we'd lost the equipment and I'd wrecked my car. I don't think they recorded again."

Such was the trauma of the German tour that most of those involved now suffer from a collective amnesia about the events that followed it. Contrary to Napier-Bell's assertion, Bolan didn't bow out on the band's return to Britain. Far from it; he remained with the band for at least another two months, during which time John's Children recorded several more of his songs at various studio sessions; released two further singles, one to a publicity fanfare that put the group on the cover of *New Musical Express* and in record shops for signing sessions; played a handful of gigs, including the legendary 14-Hour Technicolor Dream all-nighter concert

---

* Another letter suggests that the set list during the tour was likely to have been 'The Third Degree', 'Jagged Time Lapse', 'Smashed Blocked', 'Desdemona', 'Mustang Ford', 'Hot Rod Mama' and 'Remember Thomas A'Beckett' followed by a "freak out".

at Alexandra Palace on April 29; and recorded a session for BBC Radio.

However, all are agreed that Marc's attitude changed once the group were back in England. The 'Ally Pally' show was, says Chris Townson, "a bit of an anti-climax. There was definitely something odd going on. Marc didn't play at all that night. He was there, but he didn't play. He plugged in, let his guitar feed back, and wandered around the stage with it on his head. I pounded out a beat on the bass drum, occasionally throwing bits of the kit around. I don't think we even pretended to play any numbers; it was minimal even by our low standards. That performance was the equivalent of throwing buckets of paint around. We did that using noise." The audience response was in complete contrast to the sieg-heiling violence they encountered in Germany. It was the night that London's hippie community came out. In their tripped out reverie, few noticed that the group had been on stage.

Marc wasn't the only guitarist behaving badly – or madly – that night. The Pink Floyd, the London underground's house band for the past 12 months, quit the stage prematurely when it became obvious that frontman Syd Barrett wasn't going to touch his instrument. Perhaps Marc had seen his new hero's performance and opted to follow his example? June Child, lover of Syd and Bolan's future wife, maintained that Marc was strongly influenced by Barrett – which showed in his choppy guitar style, as well as the obvious visual and lyric similarities.*

It was unfortunate that John's Children's enthusiasm dropped off after Ludwigshafen. May 5 saw the release of 'Desdemona', the much-anticipated Bolan-penned single that offered the group their best chance of success. Reviews were generally good, and press coverage impressive, but despite healthy sales the single narrowly missed a chart placing. That was due in part to the "Lift up your skirt and fly" refrain at the end of each chorus. Marc claimed the phrase simply described how a witch mounts her broomstick, but it proved too risqué for the BBC, who promptly stuck a ban on it.

Interviewed at the time, John Hewlett raved over Marc's songs. "They're super-dimensive," he claimed, "not just double meanings but millions of meanings. Take 'Desdemona'. A lot of people say that 'Lift up your skirt and speak' is dirty, but it's not. Marc wrote those words because

---

* Andy Ellison's final memory of John's Children with Bolan still in the ranks was of the group huddled round a jukebox repeatedly listening to 'The Scarecrow', the B-side of the Floyd's 'See Emily Play' single which charted on June 22, 1967.

they gave him a buzz . . . they weren't meant to mean anything."

Nevertheless, the song marked an important development in Bolan's songwriting. Unlike the three-chord tricks he'd previously employed, or the tentative finger-picking that characterised his early sessions for Simon Napier Bell, 'Desdemona' was a wonderful study in extravagant minimalism, hinging on a single chord that merely moved up a key at the start of every verse. Tightly structured and with more hooks than before, it was also the first in a long pedigree of Bolan songs to pay homage to the music of the Fifties – in this instance, Gene Vincent's 'Rollin' Danny'. It was also the most professional sounding record of John's Children's career.

Leaving aside its lack of commercial success, 'Desdemona' was precisely what Simon Napier-Bell had in mind when he introduced Marc Bolan to the group. Andy Ellison lent a common touch to Marc's lyrics (which evoked Paris, rhymed "rude" with "nude" and namechecked Toulouse-Lautrec), which made Marc's bleated "De-de-de-Desdemonaaah" response during the chorus sound all the more kinky. There were Bolanic touches everywhere, including the guitar break, a barely restrained burst of Clapton-like drones.

Had 'Desdemona' succeeded, John's Children could have gone on to become a very British response to The Velvet Underground. Boasting a lyricist with literary aspirations, musicians who couldn't help but defy the rule-book, a producer who paid scant attention to the conventions of pop production and a stage show that was as striking visually as it was musically, John's Children were no less iconoclastic. The difference was a matter of intent: The Velvets flirted knowingly with form and cared for little else; John's Children simply wanted fun and fame.

As if to make amends for refusing to broadcast 'Desdemona', BBC Radio invited John's Children to record a four-song session for *Saturday Club*, broadcast on June 17. If 'Desdemona', with its clean production and tight performance, suggested a new improved John's Children working at the intersection where beat meets psychedelia, this, virtually Marc's last gasp with the group, was rock'n'roll at its most ramshackle. The session featured two Bolan originals, 'The Perfumed Garden Of Gulliver Smith' and 'Hot Rod Mama', one pre-Marc song, 'Jagged Time Lapse', and a version of the incendiary R&B number 'Daddy Rolling Stone' (previously covered by The Who).

Bolan's guitar remained blissfully out of tune throughout, as he battered his way through the songs, letting Townshend-like power chords resonate over Townson's impressive drumming. Occasionally, a guitar overdub squealed out of the mêlée, atonally but rarely artfully. It was ragged, to put it mildly, but sometimes gloriously so. 'Hot Rod Mama', on which Bolan and Ellison alternated verses, confirms that on their day John's Children were Britain's premier garageland rockers.

If Marc recorded anything else with John's Children, it would only have been to add overdubs to a song that he later claimed precipitated his departure. That was 'Midsummer Night's Scene', a title that – in the wake of 'Desdemona' – confirmed Bolan's rock'n'roll Shakespearean intentions. This extraordinary recording was first taped on May 5 and went through many changes over the course of several sessions until June 12 when a final mix was readied for release. By the time early copies were distributed, on July 7, 1967, Marc Bolan had walked out, ostensibly in protest at the way his latest masterpiece had been butchered.

"All of us were in tears because we knew we had a Number 1 record," he later explained. "We were so happy. Next day, we went back into the studio and listened to it, and the guy who was producing had totally destroyed the song, so much so that I walked out and never came back." On another occasion, he claimed, "It was incredible . . . it really made it. But it got rearranged by producers and things, and when I heard the way it had been produced and mixed, I left the group because it really brought me down."

He gave his most detailed explanation to Danny Holloway in 1972. " 'Midsummer Night's Scene' was an interesting song as I had it. When I rehearsed it, it didn't really work out. We did one take and it sounded good, really tight but very raw. I felt like it was going to be huge. It was much better than we were. I went home and I heard it the next day, and it was a totally different thing. Simon had overdubbed all these oo-bee-doos. He had to edit everything. And I heard it and I quit the next day."

Bolan was right about the production. In its final form, 'Midsummer Night's Scene' marked a return to the muffled cacophonies created by Simon Napier-Bell in the days of 'Smashed Blocked' and *Orgasm*; none of the group were happy with the finished record. But neither can anyone recall any big bust-up precipitating Marc's departure. Wounded by the ruination of his work, he simply shrunk away unwilling to stand his ground or create, uncannily given the approximate date of his departure, yet another midsummer night's scene.

'Midsummer Night's Scene' was extraordinary, but not in the way that, say, The Beatles' just-released *Sgt. Pepper* album was. In many ways, it was the antithesis of the new classically inspired rock music. With no instrument prepared to anchor the song, its rhythm was awkward and tentative, while the individual parts were as shockingly interlocked as on any rock record made before or since. The cash-in "petals and flowers" vocal overdub lost time with each successive verse; Chris Townson's percussive thuds played a cat-and-mouse game with Hewlett's cranked up bass; while Marc jettisoned rock'n'roll guitar completely for some freaky, Syd Barrett-inspired fretboard fun with a bottleneck.

The confused claustrophobia of the A-side may not have been what Bolan or the band intended, but it was no accident; there was more of the same on the flip. 'Sara Crazy Child', another Bolan original, also lacked the production rigour and commercial appeal of 'Desdemona'. Again, Marc used his guitar ornamentally rather than as a rhythmic centrepiece; his strange, piercing single notes paying little respect to the key of the song.

For, or perhaps because of, its eccentricities, 'Midsummer Night's Scene' remains one of the most enduring records from the Summer of Love. Unfortunately, few ever got to hear it, because the single was cancelled just prior to its official release date.* It was hastily substituted with the Bolan-free 'Remember Thomas A'Beckett' (previously coupled with 'Desdemona') now retitled 'Come And Play With Me In The Garden'. John's three remaining Children were photographed naked behind some strategically placed flowers, but true to form, the caper once again failed to translate into record sales.

After it became clear that Marc Bolan was not coming back, John's Children reshuffled, bringing in an old friend Chris Coville on drums with Chris Townson switching to guitar. The group made a return trip to Germany, where they played the Star Club in Hamburg and appeared on television. But trouble was rarely far away and new tensions between John and Chris eventually exploded in a particularly angry confrontation at the Flamingo Club in Redruth, Cornwall. Chris Townson walked, and John's Children were finished.

Simon Napier-Bell continued to look after Andy Ellison for a while, and the spectre of Marc Bolan – already apparent on John's Children's reworking of 'Mustang Ford' for an October 1967 single – continued to

---

* It's now one of the rarest, most coveted 45s in the world, its estimated price of £2,000 in the 2002 edition of *Record Collector Price Guide* having been exceeded in deals among private collectors on the very rare occasions it comes up for sale. Of the small amount pressed, it is believed that over half were used as frisbees by John's Children.

shadow the singer's work. However, neither master nor apprentice could get a grip on the musical changes that occurred during the late Sixties, and both dropped out of the music industry for the best part of a decade.

★ ★ ★

"One day," recalls Chris Townson, "Simon, Marc and I played a game in the back of the Bentley after we'd broken down in a German town. I was Marc's manager and Simon was the big record company magnate, and I had to convince Simon that this new protégé of mine was going to be a big star. It was a funny idea for a game. I remember us all doing it in Jewish accents. But Marc really took off.

"I 'introduced' him to Simon, and then we both just sat back and listened as Marc outlined everything he was going to do. And it was the truth! He had the confidence to come out with it because it was in the context of a game, but it was obvious that to him it was serious. It struck me then that he knew exactly what he wanted and where he was going. I remember thinking that it all sounded completely feasible."

Chris Townson was right. Bolan knew what he wanted, but popular music was developing at such a pace that he was uncertain of the best means to achieve it. John's Children had outlived their usefulness, that much he knew. As a member of a bona fide pop group, Marc had learned much about the industry, and he'd also grown in confidence as a song-writer and as a performer. So much so that on June 11, 1967 the following advert appeared in *Melody Maker*. "Freaky lead guitarist, bass guitarist and drummer wanted for Marc Bolan's new group. Also any other astral flyers like with cars, amplification and that which never grows in window boxes. Phone WIMBLEDON 0697. 9am–3pm."

As he began to piece together his own underground rock group, Marc Bolan kept his hand in with Simon Napier-Bell, recording 'The Lilac Hand Of Menthol Dan' at Advision with John's Children as the backing band. The group had occasionally performed the song live as 'Dan The Sniff' complete with requisite sniffing. Marc's version, his first 'solo' recording since 'Jasper C. Debussy', is important because it's the first song where he finally lets out his full 'Larry the Lamb' voice, a cry-baby bleat that howled most spectacularly during the "Dan, Dan Dan, you don't understand" chorus.

It was yet another portrait of a young man, and one that again contained several self-referential moments, not least the cautious soul "with the face of an angel and the mind of a man", who breaks out from his monastic cell, falls into "the art of truth" and suddenly understands everything. Musically, 'The Lilac Hand Of Menthol Dan' was eclectic: its rock'n'roll opening was a direct lift from Eddie Cochran's 'Something Else', while the guitar break was closer to the untrained genius of Janis Joplin's band, Big Brother & The Holding Company.

'Menthol Dan' was deemed unfit for public consumption, and so was Marc's new band – but unfortunately the verdict came far too late. "He got this gig at the Electric Garden in Covent Garden," says Napier-Bell, "and I think it was on the evening of the day that his advert in *Melody Maker* appeared. I asked him where he was going to rehearse, and he said, 'Who needs a rehearsal when you know you've got the right musicians?' At three o'clock he was auditioning; by five o'clock he had the musicians, including full-kit drummer Steve Peregrine Took and pipe-smoking guitarist Ben Cartland, and by eight o'clock they left to make their début." Napier-Bell refused to attend.

"The gig was exactly how you'd imagine it – five people who'd never played together before on stage with no songs. It was a disaster. The experience wrecked his ego forever. He came straight back from that gig and said he would never use an electric instrument again. He was booed off and thrown out. Marc always had this fantasy that things just happened, and if you got it right, things would come together without any effort. But he hadn't even picked good musicians. He only chose those who looked good or who had interesting names."

This notorious concert, which may or may not have taken place on June 11, 1967, is still shrouded in mystery, not least because the only person who remembers it is Simon Napier-Bell and he wasn't even there. Intriguingly, a poster from another Electric Garden show, on Saturday July 22, shows 'Marc Bollam & Tyrannosaurus Rex' bottom of a bill that also includes Pandemonium, Apostolic Intervention and 117.

Another poster advertising gigs at UFO suggests that Marc's new band may have débuted at the legendary Tottenham Court Road hippie hangout the previous night, but this may well have been cancelled. Steve Took seemed to think that his first show with Marc took place at the Covent Garden venue (which later became Middle Earth). "We smoked a bit, went back to my place, had a few drinks, had the rehearsal and did a gig. It was dire," he admitted. He remembered the pipe-smoker and another guy "nearly dead from stomach ulcers" trying in vain to pull off a set made up of John's Children songs and some "12-bar rock numbers". Took also recalls a violinist briefly being on the scene.

"I'd originally wanted a five man rock'n'roll band," Marc recalled in 1970. "It was going to be like John's Children because I wanted to keep the sound I got on 'Desdemona', which I really dug. But I couldn't find others that I could work with." Then, to cap it all, Track Records requested the return of his electric guitar.

A few months earlier, in mid-March, Marc had witnessed an extraordinary concert given by a musician who looked good, had an unusual name and made music that, even by the standards of 1967, oozed mystery and charm. On the way home from Germany, John's Children had taken a scenic diversion through Luxembourg and ended up at a concert in the capital city's town hall. "It was a Ravi Shankar performance of Indian music," remembers Simon Napier-Bell.

"It was an incredible contrast to what we'd just experienced on the John's Children tour. This man played to a hushed, reverential audience in the simplest way imaginable – seated on a carpet and surrounded by joss sticks which filled the air with a pungent smell. That really tripped Marc's mind. I think that was the moment he realised what he should be doing. After giving it one more try with that electric gig, he went the whole Ravi Shankar way."

5

Beautiful Delilah

"Civilisation now is very plastic, people have the wrong sets of values. So I write about different lands – places where the good things are good, and not just because we've been brought up to accept them that way."

– Marc Bolan (1968)

"Nowadays, people consistently ignore the hippie thing about the group in the early days. Tyrannosaurus Rex was a completely different concept to what T. Rex is now. I guess for a while Marc was a good hippie."

– Steve Peregrine Took (1972)

"Marc wasn't a hippie. Most hippies practised free love and took a lot of drugs like acid. He abhorred drugs in those days, and he certainly wasn't into free love. He was a Mod dressed up as a hippie."

– Tony Visconti (1992)

One morning in July 1967, Radio London's underground disc jockey John Peel received an innocuous looking envelope. Marked for his attention c/o "The Perfumed Garden", the show he broadcast from the station's off-shore home on board the Galaxy, it was, he assumed, one of those regular messages of gratitude thanking him for playing the latest Blues Project or Liverpool Scene record. But this one, embellished with what looked like a child's illustration of a castle, was different. It was from Marc Bolan, the singer whose extraordinary voice had recently become a fixture of Peel's late night broadcasts, and its arrival ignited a friendship that would last for the next four years, a period in which the fortunes of both men were to change dramatically.

Marc wrote: "John. <u>Thanks</u> for playing Hippy Gumbo, it gave me a real high knowing you turned on to it. I did a session on Monday night and we (tyrannosaurus rex = steve porter on tablas and assorted auxilliary) are diping our hearts in the sounds and trying to xtend our musical hi over the

"I ain't no square with my corkscrew hair."
(*Music Sales Archives*)

Simeon and Phyllis Feld at their wedding, on January 31, 1945, at Fulham Registry Office, London. (*Feld Family Archives*)

Private Mark Feld, Marc Bolan's uncle after whom he was named. Mark Feld died as a result of injuries sustained in an attack at an Army barracks in 1946, a year before his nephew was born. (*Feld Family Archives*)

The infant Mark Feld, aka Marc Bolan, born Hackney, East London, September 30, 1947. (*Feld Family Archives*)

Five-year-old Mark Feld (second row up, third from the right) and his brother Harry (top row, second from left) with classmates at Northwold Road Primary School, Stoke Newington, pictured during celebrations for the Coronation of Queen Elizabeth II, in June 1953. (*Feld Family Archives*)

Harry (left) and Mark Feld, circa 1954. "Mark took after his mum. He was much more jolly and sociable," says neighbour Frances Perrone. (*Feld Family Archives*)

Mark, circa 1956, sporting a quiff inspired by Elvis Presley, his first rock'n'roll idol. (*Feld Family Archives*)

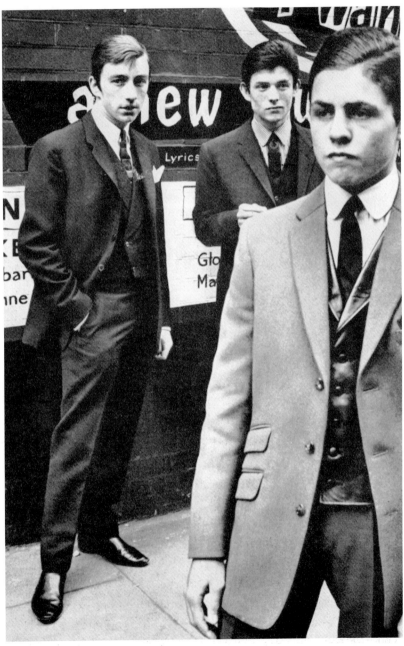

Fourteen-year-old Mark Feld featured in a *Town* magazine special, published in September 1962. With him are two older Stoke Newington Mod faces, Michael Simmonds and Peter Sugar. (*Town Magazine*)

Mark pictured during his brief period as a teenage model, circa 1963.
(*Feld Family Archives*)

Mark Feld as Toby Tyler, photographed during the winter of 1964/65 in Earls Court, London. "He was just a pleasant Jewish boy who looked wide-eyed with wonder," says photographer Mike McGrath.
(*Mike McGrath*)

Mark – now Marc – pictured by David Wedgbury on October 23, 1965. "He really opened up while he was eating, telling me how much money he was going to make," says Wedgbury. "He had it all sussed - he was really going to be big and make a lot of money."
(*Popperfoto/PPP*)

Marc with his cat Loog at the Manchester Street flat in London's West End, October 1965, just prior to the release of 'The Wizard'. (*Popperfoto/PPP*)

Marc with John's Children in 1967; left to right: John Hewlett, Chris Townson, Andy Ellison and Marc. (*Rex Features*)

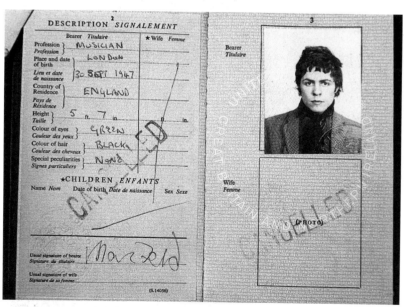

Marc's passport obtained for the aborted John's Children German tour with The Who in April 1967. "We had to force him to be a nutter on stage, and eventually he got into it, going over the top with his chains and playing the guitar above his head," says singer Andy Ellison. (*Rex Features*)

Marc and Steve Peregrine Took as Tyrannosaurus Rex, in a previously unpublished shot taken in 1968. Unusually, Marc is seen playing a mandolin.
(*Photographer unknown*)

twitchy hangups of the <u>hard</u> world and get the communication of a BE IN into everything we do. The twelve things we did are for White Whale in the States and are being put out in late September — its a real heart hang up about *The Garden* vanishing but it really is a bopping concern. Thanks again for coming thru' for hippy and I'd truly like to talk or turn on or something. I'm on the phone at WIM 0697 so maybe we'll talk.

So long keep hi

Truly Mark bolan"

There were no concrete plans to release the Tyrannosaurus Rex demos on White Whale. The invitation to 'turn on' was fraudulent, because most of Marc's late Sixties friends and associates remember him as one of the few longhairs that didn't meddle with drugs. Mention of 'Be-Ins', those psychedelicised-sexualised-spiritualised affairs that only really happened in San Francisco, was a particularly ham-fisted show of Marc's counter-cultural hand. But 1967 was the year of the great divide: you were either turned on or off, way in or way out, chasing white rabbits or dancing the last waltz forever. Marc knew which side he was on, and which side John Peel was on too – his side.

Throughout his life Marc Bolan craved everything: sounds, stories, philosophies, fashions, friends, faces, names, numbers – it hardly mattered what so long as it amused or inspired him. He was, as his ex-wife June fondly recalled, "a wonderful, wonderful sponge". Sometimes, this compulsive need to know, discover and digest left enduring legacies, such as his devotion to Elvis and Dylan. Often the little details and the big words would be eagerly refashioned into one of Marc's fantasy scenarios. Once in a while, he'd become bored and move on.

The emergence of the hippies during 1967's Summer of Love prompted a mass outbreak of wonderment. Minds were blown and blow was smoked and blokes looked like girls and Marc Bolan's fast-sprouting curls were fashionably 'in'. In many ways, the hippie was an extension of the Romantic rebel that, in pop terms at least, had its archetype in Bob Dylan. That same Dylan who had already proved that popular music could also function as a vehicle for social criticism and give vent to the kind of personal expression usually restricted to literary figures.

By 1967, the limits of the form – even the medium itself – was being stretched further as a new generation of musicians weaned on The Beatles, the Rolling Stones and Bob Dylan looked beyond the three-minute song and outside the industry's infrastructure. This insurrectionary mood was also reflected in new voices that emerged to head the hippie underground

– flag-wavers for racial and sexual liberation such as Jimi Hendrix and Janis Joplin, outsiders and misfits like Frank Zappa and Captain Beefheart and committed anti-stars The Grateful Dead and Pink Floyd. The hierarchical, good-guy star system to which Marc Bolan had always been in thrall had now begun to look decidedly uncool.

Since he began writing his own material in 1965, Marc had regarded his songs as personal expression rather than pop cant. His position as part of the malleable, manager-led John's Children was always ambiguous; by late spring 1967 it had become untenable. The group was not, after all, the perfect launching pad to stardom as Napier-Bell had suggested. Besides Marc had turned on, metaphorically at least, and turned his back on 'The Man' and all those greedy, grasping souls seduced by his meaningless rewards. For a while, at least. "You'll laugh at this," Marc said in 1976, "but I left John's Children because I thought they were getting too commercial." There was some truth in that.

Bolan's growing distaste for mainstream pop was confirmed at the end of June when his girlfriend Terry won a pair of tickets to see The Monkees at the Empire Pool, Wembley. The experience prompted a tirade in his notebook where, noting that "the show was an impossible drag," he reflects upon the relationship between audience, star and manager:

"Hung up young babes Full of Monnkee faces worship/hitch up there magazine hearts + turn over too long stocking tops into sweet sally black scented turn on suspenders. They bop & dream there lily white bodys to unknown to them stoned, wanked out bored w/ the people + truly-true to there wives cardboard pop stars – a weird triangle – sorta like some christians & some christs. a manager with a marked face & goopy eyes always is around, at first cool – your his babe – later a first class leather arsed drag of the first order who every time you do-the-true calls you moody & makes up sudden expenses – yes indeed a triangle."

Marc Bolan wasn't ready to make his peace with mass popularity just yet.

Tyrannosaurus Rex, Marc's makeshift group that had débuted so disastrously at the Electric Garden, embodied the era's 'Just do it' ethic. By the end of July, the violinist, the pipe-smoker and the ulcer-ridden mercenaries had gone, though there was nothing professional about the set-up they'd left behind. "Steve (Porter) had been a kit drummer in a lot of groups," Marc recalled in 1972. "But he had to sell his drum kit for us to live. We nicked somebody's bongos" – "a cat named John," said Steve in 1968" – "and for the first year the guitar I used had a broken neck that was taped together. It cost me six quid. I used that for a long time. We never had a p.a. for two years."

Born in the south east London suburb of Eltham on July 28, 1949, Stephen Ross Porter was almost two years younger than Bolan. Unlike his colleague, Porter was neither gregarious nor self-assured; he was a nervous child blighted by eczema and asthma, whose reddened skin prompted the occasional 'leper' taunt from his classmates. Withdrawing into his own world, he shared with Marc a passion for animal books and inventing stories, with which he would amuse the younger children in the neighbourhood. His self-esteem received another blow when his father left home, leaving his wife to fend for her two sons alone.

After leaving school, Steve gravitated towards the nascent hippie scene, a refuge for the genuinely disassociated as well as fashion tourists. A wiry, striking figure, he grew his hair long, dressed in silks and velvets and – probably at Bolan's command – adopted the name Steve Peregrine Took after one of the central characters in Tolkien's *The Lord Of The Rings*, the Bible of the weird beards. 'Peregrin Took' was a Hobbit of the Shire and a loyal companion to Frodo Baggins in Tolkien's epic.

Marc had also let his hair grow, and had exchanged his bleached-out John's Children wardrobe for a second-hand girl's blazer and a pair of crumpled, loose fitting trousers. The Modernists had dressed to impress, their apparel a portmanteau of poshness that mocked their social status as have-nots. Hippies tended to be middle class rebels who delighted in poverty chic, a symbolic 'V'-sign to the 'natural' social order. The doctrine of the longhairs was a complete reversal of the Mod *Weltanschauung*: anti-materialist, anti-urban and anti-straight society, it celebrated the countryside and sites of mystic importance, open-air festivals, sexual libertarianism, natural foods, unnatural drugs, supernatural myths and legends. It was a subculture ripe for fantasists and flamboyant dressers and Marc, who quickly embraced what he called the "flower-power summertime", soon blossomed into one of its most cherished creations. It was the most significant transformation of his life, for Marc Bolan as we know him – through his modest yet richly embellished music, his florid poetry, his iconic image, in short the very T. Rexness of him – was the product of that happy, hippie summer of loveliness.

A highly skilled changeling, Marc played his new role to perfection. His hair sprouted a crown of corkscrew ringlets like a modern-day Medusa, the Gorgon sister of Greek classical mythology who, infamously, had a head of snakes. With dark curls cascading around his face, the emphasis subtly shifted from the determined jaw-line to his sensuous, Theda Bara lips, his wide, honest eyes and broad smile. Bolan's 5'7" stature emphasised the veneer of waif-like vulnerability; his wide-eyed innocence and androgynous beauty epitomised the hippie ideal.

Marc's songwriting, steeped from the start in mysticism, couldn't have been more suited to a culture determined to extricate itself from old 'common sense' ways. Much of his mental agility had been Dylan-inspired, at least initially, though the true Pied Piper of pop mythology and Utopian vibes was Donovan. During '66, the British Dylan released two songs that became foundation stones for a peculiarly English take on the psychedelic sounds lately emanating from San Francisco. 'Sunshine Superman' and 'Mellow Yellow' were hippie hymns that luxuriated in love, peace and blissfulness.

"It was natural for romantic bohemian musicians to think pop would become an art form," Donovan remembers. "Many of us saw ourselves as painters and artists, and we dressed ourselves in our dreams. The interest in the ballad tradition seemed natural because it was in direct contrast to the materialistic world that we grew up in. I think we were searching for our own indigenous religion, which is Celtic, but which had disappeared in the face of the Christian teachings. We looked to the East, because we felt that we could enter the secret world only through meditation which wasn't taught in the West." Marc Bolan was far too hyperactive to dedicate himself to meditation, but he did have a head full of secret worlds ripe for public scrutiny.

The hippie underground had incited an epidemic of benevolence and beatitude, but that didn't mean that self-obsessed fame seekers weren't allowed to join in. When he quit John's Children, Marc hadn't given up on ambition; he had merely renounced a capricious pop world that continued to reject him. Opportunism as much as cultural instinct prompted the decision to reposition himself as part of the new underground – though the hippies' 'anything goes' disposition was certainly helpful when it came to the matter of Marc's music, which was distinctive though hardly accomplished.

Novelty has always been a quintessential pop ingredient, but such was the pace of change during 1967 and 1968 that the more 'strange', 'weird' or 'far-out' anything was, the greater its chance of an audience. Hippies not only courted the bizarre, they positively revelled in it; and Marc, already the owner of one of pop's more peculiar voices, quickly put the failed rock band idea behind him and opted instead for what he called an off-beat "acoustical" set-up. Both folkish and faux-Eastern, the new-look Tyrannosaurus Rex became a thrift-shop duo that enabled Marc and Steve to rebuild from the bottom up without having to answer to 'uncool' managers or musicians and, crucially, gave Marc greater control over his destiny.

Simon Napier-Bell loathed the underground's 'showbiz-ain't-where-it's-at' pose. "Initially, I was surprised by Marc's reinvention," he says, "because I knew what he really wanted. Everything he did as a hippie was not what he wanted, but he didn't want to make a fool of himself again, like he did at the Electric Garden. He sensed that the prevalent hippie attitude would not accept a glossy rock star, and that he was going to have to go along with it. It was obvious to him that becoming a hippie was the right thing to do."

It wasn't that cynical. The trappings and the collective interests of the hippies were an extension of the Romantic quest Marc had been pursuing since embarking on that voyage of personal and cultural discovery back in 1963. The hippie underground was an ideal cultural space for an aspiring musician whose teenage years had been distinguished by a zest for flamboyant fashion and a fanciful attitude towards intellectual pursuits. Even the return to an acoustic style, fashionably uncontaminated in accordance with underground ideology, came naturally.

However, Marc was hardly a deferential folkie who'd pass a hat round among a pub crowd feasting heartily on beer and sandwiches. With pin-up looks and a vocal style that forced audiences to jam their fingers in their ears for all the wrong reasons, Bolan was in little danger of being mistaken for Ewan MacColl. Instinctively, though, he sought to deflect any hint of a soft centre with a hard shell; and thus Tyrannosaurus Rex was born.

It was a passage in a Ray Bradbury short story, *A Sound Of Thunder*, in his 1952 collection, *R Is For Rocket,* that was the catalyst for the group's name. A tale of time travel concerning a group of people who venture back to prehistoric times in order to shoot dinosaurs on safari, it included a passage that ignited Bolan's imagination: "A Tyrannosaurus Rex. The Tyrant Lizard, the most incredible monster in history. Sign this release. Anything happens to you, we're not responsible. Those dinosaurs are hungry."

Reading the Ray Bradbury story, Bolan said in 1968, reminded him of his childhood fascination for dinosaurs. "When I was in bed with measles, aged eight, I read about prehistoric monsters and dug the whole scene. They were so like dragons that could have breathed fire and smoke and somehow, because they existed, they justified unicorns and centaurs and the whole Narnia scene." He also claimed to have been "really freaked out" by the sequence in Walt Disney's *Fantasia* where the bestial struggle of the prehistoric predators is battled out to the inflammatory strains of Stravinsky's *Rite Of Spring* "All the eight- and nine-year-olds got really hung up with it," he remembered, adding that "it's nice to make them happy thinking of it."

Marc had been stockpiling songs ever since 1966, and so when he and Steve met to rehearse in the Feld or Porter living rooms, it didn't take long to work up a set. Sometime in August, within a couple of weeks of the catastrophic Electric Garden gig, Tyrannosaurus Rex were ready to record. Simon Napier-Bell, who still looked after Marc at this point, booked the duo into the studio for two sessions, the first with a bass player (probably Ben Cartland) and Marc's girlfriend Terry in attendance. "That was another first night," he remembers. "I took Marc and Steve upstairs to the studios in South Moulton Street, sat them on a rug with their first joss-stick and they played for about an hour."

These first Tyrannosaurus Rex sessions featured slimmed down versions of material John's Children had been using ('Sara Crazy Child', 'Hot Rod Mama', 'Sally Was An Angel', 'Lunacy's Back' and 'Jasper C. Debussy'); 'Rings Of Fortune', 'Highways' (alias 'Misty Mist') and 'Beyond The Risin' Sun' from the Decca era; and three more recent songs, 'One Inch Rock', 'Sleepy Maurice' and 'The Beginning Of Doves'. These sessions, most of which subsequently turned up on *The Beginning Of Doves*, blue-printed the Tyrannosaurus Rex sound that became a regular fixture on the underground over the next couple of years.

Even by the standards of the time, that sound was already decidedly outré and hardly easy on the ear. Taking Marc's warble as a benchmark, Steve Took quickly made his presence felt, and by the second session, was already deploying a range of toy whistles, panpipe blasts, handclaps and vocal falsettos to supplement the manic flurries of bongo beats and the rich serenity of an occasionally struck gong. With Marc's guitar style now flirting with mock-Eastern flourishes, Tyrannosaurus Rex resembled nothing so much as a pair of musical jesters capable of erupting into nonsense sound at a moment's notice.

The spontaneous and discordant noises created by this pocket-sized pop duo provided a perfect backdrop for Bolan's florid fairyland romps sung in the manner of a deranged storyteller. That voice, though settled on a style, was still in transition. Marc still spoke with a strong Cockney tone ("Bi' o'

Jeffus'n Air-o-plyne," he suggested during one of the early sessions), and unlike his earlier recordings, there was little pretence at maintaining perfect diction when he sang. Instead, he peppered his indistinct, poetical lines with James Cagney-inspired Bronx-speak ("at da time") and joyful pre-language utterances ("da-da-da da-da-da-da") that accentuated the aura of childhood abandon.

Excepting the odd inflection on 'One Inch Rock', Marc had moved on from his days as a Dylan obsessive. But there is little doubt that his new, sound-as-message vocal style, which foregrounded its own strangeness more than any lyric 'message', owed much to the mumbling nonconformist. It was this vocal defiance of 'the order of things' that captivated disc jockey John Peel, who was poached from Radio London to join the team at the BBC's new beat-the-pirates station, Radio 1. "I liked Tyrannosaurus Rex initially because I've always been drawn to extreme voices," he says, "and I really liked the noise of Marc's 'Larry the Lamb' stuff. I also liked the lyrics, which read terribly but when they were sung took on another dimension." Even Peel admits he "could only ever pick up the odd isolated word" when Marc sang.

When John Peel first met Marc, either at the end of July or very early in August 1967, they bonded quickly, swapping nuggets of hippie wisdom and sharing an insatiable – and unfashionable – appetite for old Gene Vincent and Eddie Cochran 45s. Marc gave Peel some recent Tyrannosaurus Rex acetates, ensuring that his new champion had a complete collection of his work to date. Peel, suitably impressed, frequently dipped into his Bolan bag during his final days as a Radio London DJ. On his last show, broadcast between 12.00am–5.30am in the early hours of August 14, 1967, Peel played half-a-dozen Marc Bolan songs: two solo singles, 'The Wizard' and 'Hippy Gumbo'; John's Children's 'Sara Crazy Child' and 'Desdemona'; plus two songs from the first Tyrannosaurus Rex session, 'Rings Of Fortune' and 'Highways'. He'd play many more on his new *Top Gear* show on Radio 1, which was able to reach audiences that neither he nor Bolan could have dreamed of months earlier.

Now moving in circles where the boundless energy and business-like manner of Simon Napier-Bell was regarded as old school and uncool, Marc was ready to loosen the ties of management. "There was no place for me in Marc's new world," Napier-Bell recalls. "I told him that if he wanted to get gigs on the hippie circuit, he'd be better off without a manager. At first, he wanted me to call up and get the contract and the money sorted out, but I said, 'I can't do that if you're going to sit on a prayer mat and play surrounded by joss sticks.'" Napier-Bell remains baffled by 1967 and the brief flowering of counterculture values. "It was an incredible feeling that swept through the country for a year or so," he shrugs.

Fast becoming a recognised member of the freak fraternity, Marc gained in confidence as the shock of the new continued to turn perceptions upside down and reduce old homilies to dust-encrusted rubble. Rankled by the music industry's refusal to recognise his special gifts, he welcomed the underground's iconoclasm wholeheartedly, so much so that the musical extremes he'd begun to embrace can also be heard as the rancorous ravings of vengeance. In 1972, he admitted: "The reason our earlier records were so ragged and bare was because I was so paranoid of someone coming along and saying, 'Hey kid, you gotta put strings on that.' For years everyone said that you had to have orchestras, you've got to have bass and drums and make it like a pop record. In my head, there was this little block against anything like that. I thought, 'No man, I don't want it.'"

What Marc Bolan wanted was a home for his music, and in that home a family eager to listen to his latest fireside fantasy. Initially, Marc and Steve carried their instruments on the tube to Hyde Park, where they'd entertain small crowds of stoned hippies and curious passers-by with their strange, pastoral sounds. Then John Peel got a regular DJ spot at Middle Earth (which the Electric Garden had, in homage to Tolkien's fantasy land, become), and Tyrannosaurus Rex made the first of many appearances on the underground venue's all-night weekend bills in September. Adverts inviting the public to 'Trip softly with Denny Laine's Electric String Band, the Piccadilly Line, Tyrannosauras (sic) Rex and John Peel' won the group a considerable following of hippies and students, and Tyrannosaurus Rex remained Middle Earth regulars until July 1968.

This wasn't solely down to John Peel's patronage. Jeff Dexter, Marc's old mate from the Lyceum days, had also exchanged his Mod threads for hippie tat and had become a leading underground scenemaker. "I'd heard that Tyrannosaurus Rex were around and I remember John talking about this incredible guy called Marc Bolan. He said, 'You gotta meet this guy.' I was also MCing at Middle Earth by that time, but I think I met Marc in Hyde Park. We took one look at each other and it was like . . . Aaaaarrghh! There was a slightly nervous reaction from him at first because he knew I was DJing all the underground live shows, but it was great to see him again. He wasn't busking that day, just standing around looking great."

The last time Jeff had seen Marc was in the audience on the set of *Ready, Steady, Go!* in 1965. "A lot had happened since then. We'd been chained up by all that competitive Mod stuff, and now we were freeing ourselves, blowing away the cobwebs. It was a totally different world, particularly after coming into contact with LSD, but I don't know how much Marc truly let himself go. I immediately assumed by his look that he was into the same thing, and I never realised until a few years later that he wasn't really into acid. Marc was very careful.

"I went back to Middle Earth and said to the owners, 'You've got to see this band. They're great looking . . . old mates . . .', and he was on about two days later. I loved it because it was so different, although I found it difficult to come to terms with the idea of Marc singing." That wasn't the only change Dexter noticed. "I was also taken aback by the fact that this east London Face I'd known was now so *wordy*. He must have really worked at it, researching everyone else's lyrics and reading absolutely everything to find out what was going on. And he was into the spiritual path. We all were."

Bolan continued to plough his way through shelves of books, and during the months of hippie ascendency, he joined his fellow rainbow chasers and dived deep into the fantasy worlds of C.S. Lewis (the *Narnia* adventures) and J.R.R. Tolkien *(The Lord Of The Rings)*, and the mystic poetry of Kahlil Gibran, all further nourishing his appetite for escape. "There are so few books like *The Lord Of The Rings* and the *Narnia* books, that once you've read them, you want more, and there just aren't any around. So I just write my own things," he told underground magazine *Gandalf's Garden* (itself a homage to Tolkien). Yet in pursuit of his career, Marc's mind managed to work in wonderfully pragmatic ways, sniffing out deals and contacts like James Cagney in a poncho.

While Marc was still part of John's Children, Simon Napier-Bell had taken him to see David Platz, head of Essex Music, the international music publishing company which had close associations with Kit Lambert's Track label. Marc signed a deal with Platz, left John's Children and formed Tyrannosaurus Rex all in a matter of a couple of months, confusing Lambert who had envisaged him as a new kind of intelligent pop soloist in the Cat Stevens mould. He sent for Joe Boyd, a producer/engineer who operated out of Sound Techniques Studio in Chelsea.

Joe Boyd had already worked with several luminaries of the British underground, including The Incredible String Band and The Pink Floyd. The Floyd were best noted for their interstellar jamming, though it was the short, wistful, nursery rhyme-like material on their summer 1967 début album, *The Piper At The Gates Of Dawn* (a title taken from Kenneth Graham's children's novel, *The Wind In The Willows*), that most impressed Marc. These songs, all written by the group's singer/guitarist Syd Barrett, shared some affinity with Bolan's own: awe-filled, they created hermetically sealed new worlds of wonder that seemed to be written, more often than not, from the vantage point of the playpen. Barrett drew from similar sources, too. Ancient wisdom, in the form of the *I Ching*, found its way onto 'Chapter 24'; 'Matilda Mother' invoked medievalism; 'The Scarecrow' a charming rusticity; and 'The Gnome' infant storytelling.

The parallels were uncanny, and could be stretched beyond shared creative sources and reality defying inclinations. Barrett and Bolan were both dark, curly-haired and incredibly cute Aquarian Age pin-ups with suggestions of androgyny who radiated airs of unblemished innocence. (And in June Child, Syd and Marc would share the same lover, too.) There was one crucial, distressing difference. Within months, Barrett's diet of acid and Mandrax had detached him from his pop star responsibilities, and he was quietly coerced out of the Floyd and into a dark, cultish corner where he remains to this day. Bolan, meanwhile, was in full command of his faculties. He never forgot Syd's towering influence, later describing him as "one of the few people I'd actually call a genius . . . he inspired me beyond belief".

When Joe Boyd first met Marc Bolan and Steve Peregrine Took, the producer recalls the pair as keen Incredible String Band fans. He also admits a feeling of "slight condescension" towards Tyrannosaurus Rex. "Marc seemed like someone who had decided that being a hippie was the 'in' thing, and had switched from taking Black Bombers to smoking good Afghan hash. I felt there was no real conviction in his acousticness. It was just a musical change that went along with the change of drug and the change of dress."

Marc later rejected comparisons with The Incredible String Band, a Scottish duo of multi-instrumentalists who took their passion for indigenous folk and international music extremely seriously. And with good reason: it was unduly crude. Whereas Bolan invariably worked within the standard A/B/A/B pop song format, the String Band weaved intricate melodies around a progressive, linear A/B/C/D structure. The main similarities were in the surface textures – the use of acoustic instruments usually excluded from rock and pop (bongos, bells, toys), and the vague aura of Eastern-tinged exoticism. For the time being, though, it suited Marc to namedrop The Incredible String Band, if only to catch a ride on the tide of popularity created by the duo's 1967 album, *The 5000 Spirits Or The Layers Of The Onion*.

"The Incredible String Band approached it on a much more deeply spiritual and intellectual level," insists Joe Boyd. "They came to the music via a genuine fascination for ethnic sounds, and there was a depth to their approach which I related to. Marc's approach was to take what were essentially pop tunes and play them in an acoustic, folksy way. It didn't have the musical signposts I was looking for, but I have to confess that I saw the appeal and the potential, even if I wasn't struck on the music." The String Band's Mike Heron concurs. "I don't think our styles were ever that close," he says. "Although Tyrannosaurus Rex were acoustic, Marc's songs were always rock orientated."

Despite his initial reservations, Boyd was sufficiently intrigued once Marc and Steve sat themselves down in front of his fire and played their songs. He accepted Lambert's challenge and booked the pair into Sound Techniques for two sessions. The absence of any conventional musical ability troubled him, so for the second session he called upon ace session acoustic bassist Danny Thompson to anchor the sound. "I think Marc seemed pretty unsure of what he wanted at that session," Thompson maintains, "though I was immediately struck by his nature, which was an endearing mix of gentleness and shyness together with an aura of confidence." Perhaps feeling insecure at the prospect of working alongside the technically gifted bassist, Bolan boldly informed Thompson that he'd trained with the Westminster School Choir.

Until recently, just one song was believed to have survived from the liaison. That is 'Chateau In Virginia Waters', a blissfully serene slice of psychedelia enveloped in a whirlpool sound, created by the old George Martin/Beatles trick of running the bass through a Leslie speaker. As John Peel suggests, lines like "Her one rich wish is to write a book about/A Venetian mother's problems on a barge in Little Venice" didn't translate well onto the page, but Bolan's barely decipherable trill sent the DJ raving about the demo in his column for *International Times*, the Bible of the British underground. In the piece, Peel also mentions other songs recently recorded by Tyrannosaurus Rex for Track Records – 'Dwarfish Trumpet Blues', 'Child Star' and 'Highways' – all recorded at the earlier session.

The producer had hoped to establish a working relationship with Track but soon after these sessions, taped on November 6 and December 12, 1967, this fell through and Marc was obliged to hawk the acetate around elsewhere. Cheerleader John Peel floated the idea of forming a record label and informed his *International Times* readership that if he had the cash he'd sign Tyrannosaurus Rex immediately. Marc later claimed that The Beatles' newly formed Apple label had approached him but, he added incredulously, "it didn't feel very good". Instead, Marc's publishers Essex Music stepped in and paid Boyd's studio bill, for they had their own plans for Tyrannosaurus Rex.

Meanwhile, John Peel arranged a photo session for the group late that autumn with Ray Stevenson, who recalls seeing Tyrannosaurus Rex in concert at one of Peel's *Perfumed Garden* evenings at the Marquee. Marc suggested Holland Park as a location because he thought that the fence painted with the figure of Dougal, the shaggy haired dog from the popular children's series *Magic Roundabout,* would make a suitable jokey-dopey backdrop for the shoot.

Dressed in a striped, school-style blazer with the collar turned up, his hair furiously backcombed but not yet a Medusa mass of curls, Marc – with a hint of Clara Bow lipstick on the night shots – gazed determinedly into the camera lens. Steve Took looked towards him, adopting the secondary role he'd later come to resent. However, the Stevenson session was rejected because, the photographer says, "Marc thought he looked too much like Dylan." No longer the John's Children plaything, Bolan had vowed to take a firm control over the presentation of himself and Tyrannosaurus Rex.

Few people had heard or seen Tyrannosaurus Rex, but news of the fun-sized duo with the grand name began to filter out through concert listings and namechecks in magazines, hip hearsay and, most of all, through the insatiable enthusiasm of John Peel. The *Top Gear* DJ convinced producer Bernie Andrews that the group were worthy of a specially commissioned 'Peel session' (the first unsigned band to be granted one), and on October 30, 1967, Tyrannosaurus Rex taped six songs for a trial broadcast, five of which went out on *Top Gear* on November 5. 'Misty Mist' (as 'Highways' was now more groovily known), 'Hot Rod Mama' and 'Pictures Of Purple People' were remakes of material demoed for Track in the summer; the remainder, 'Child Star', 'Dwarfish Trumpet Blues' and 'Scenescof', were new.

'Scenescoff' (the second 'f' was dropped later) had been the villain in Marc's 1966 play, *Pictures Of Purple People*, an evil underworld figure who harboured "illusions of taking over the minds of the younger generation". Literally "to scoff at the scene", the term was usefully applied to any 'spoiler' who dared infect Bolan's late Sixties idyll with 'heavy' vibes. The new song (key line: "I don't need anyone/To dictate all my fun"), which was twee even by Tyrannosaurus Rex's fragrant standards, appeared to be a musical attempt to disarm bad karma. When interviewed by John Peel on *Top Gear* on February 4, 1968, to coincide with a second broadcast of the session, Bolan described the character as "a villain in all the songs", a relative of the "people who are hung up with outward things" on 'Pictures Of Purple People'.

Despite Peel's eagerness to share his enthusiasm for Tyrannosaurus Rex with the rest of the world, the BBC's selection panel was still deliberating whether the duo had a future on national radio at the taxpayers' expense. Almost three months had elapsed since the initial session before, on Valentine's Day 1968, the corporation's decision was posted to him accepting Tyrannosaurus Rex for future sessions. The committee's report showed an awareness of the need to reflect the new underground, describing the group as "very far out" and "very way in", though one dissenter was moved to call the work "crap, and pretentious crap at that". Nevertheless, with the immortal words, "OK for *Top Gear* I suppose", Tyrannosaurus Rex were passed for further sessions – a decision that had a great bearing on Marc Bolan's future career. It wasn't the only stroke of good fortune he enjoyed that winter; by the time he received the news, Tyrannosaurus Rex had signed a record deal and were about to begin work on a début album.

★   ★   ★

Brooklyn-born Tony Visconti began his musical career as one half of the husband-and-wife harmony duo, Tony and Siegrid. By the mid-Sixties, he was writing songs and producing records for the New York-based Richmond Organisation. That's where visiting UK producer Denny Cordell, on a scouting trip to the States to look for an assistant, found him; and he promptly persuaded Visconti to try his luck in England. It was June 1967 and Procol Harum's Cordell-produced 'A Whiter Shade Of Pale' (with lyrics by Keith Reid) had just become one of Britain's most talked about Number 1 hit singles. Having secured his reputation as a producer with The Moody Blues' 1964 hit, 'Go Now', Cordell was now a high-flyer producing hits for both Procol Harum and pop-psych pranksters The Move. He'd also established a unique relationship with Essex Music where, in exchange for the publishing rights and copyright ownership of his New Breed productions, Essex financed his studio time. It was a deal that would make the publishing company inestimably more wealthy than Cordell.

The relationship was further cemented in July 1967, when Cordell joined forces with Essex boss David Platz to form the Straight Ahead/New Breed independent record production company. Within a month, they'd secured a deal with EMI, reviving the stagnant Regal Zonophone label (which had been reduced to issuing the occasional Salvation Army record) as an exclusive outlet for Cordell's productions. Prior to this, Cordell's work had been issued via Decca's Deram subsidiary, though the writing was on the wall when that label's Ken East defected to EMI. Consequently, Procol Harum and The Move ended up on Regal Zonophone, the oddball outlet that also became home to Straight Ahead's future signings.

Straight Ahead operated out of Dumbarton House, Essex Music's Oxford Street offices, the production company occupying a few rooms at the front of the building. That's where Denny Cordell, his enthusiastic new assistant Tony Visconti and secretary Richard Kerr shared a small office, and from where they'd seek out and nurture new talent for the ambitious company.

Visconti's new career got off to a dismal start when his first production, Manfred Mann's 'So Long Dad', resulted in a rare flop Fontana 45 for the group in September 1967. Matters quickly improved, though, when the young American was invited along to The Move's session. The group were recording 'Flowers In The Rain', a song with hit single potential but still lacking a certain something. Visconti suggested embellishing the song with a woodwind quartet, the session continued and 'Flowers In The Rain' went on to become a huge hit and a *Pop Quiz* perennial (it was the first song to be played on Radio 1).

While 'Flowers In The Rain' maintained Straight Ahead's extraordinary chart profile that year, Tony Visconti was about to familiarise himself with the London club scene. One night that winter, he remembers going to UFO (though he is likely to have meant Middle Earth), the legendary underground hangout where anything could happen. "I'd been working with Denny for a while," he recalls, "and he thought it was time I found my own group. It was my very first night of talent scouting, and I walked round the corner from Oxford Street into Tottenham Court Road where the club was, and saw a poster for this group called Tyrannosaurus Rex. When I walked in, there were around

300 people sitting around the stage in silence, watching this strange little person seated on the floor singing in what I thought to be something other than the English language."

Tony Visconti was mesmerised but admits, "I felt awkward approaching Marc. He gave off an air of being very precious, very special and powerfully charismatic. I fell in love with him. Whereas Steve just looked like a hippie, Marc resembled an exotic gypsy with his curly hair, his tiny waistcoat, a tattered silk shirt and a scarf tied to his arm." The producer introduced himself to Steve Took instead.

"Steve mumbled something about Marc being 'the leader', so I finally approached him and said I'd like to work with him. 'Oh man, you're the eighth producer that's come up to me this week,' he told me – in perfect English, of course. 'John Lennon came up to me last night.' That was the first of many lies Marc told me! He had the arrogance of a New Yorker and I loved it. Marc knew exactly what he wanted; he knew he was going to be big. And he had everything to back it up: talent, imagination, great songs, extremely good looking. His melodies were absolutely superb."

After all the well-wishers and amateur impresarios and avaricious Scenescof-types, Marc Bolan had finally met The Great Enabler. Visconti gave Bolan his telephone number; next morning, as he walked through the door at Straight Ahead, the phone was already ringing. It was Marc. Eager to impress Denny Cordell with his new find, the fledgling producer invited the duo to the offices to give an impromptu performance for his boss.

"I told Denny about Marc's great voice and strange songs. I thought everything about them was extraordinary. An hour or two later, Marc and Steve showed up with the Oriental carpet under their arm, the guitar with the missing peg on the G string and the bells, Pixiephone and one-string fiddle. They did the entire set from the previous night uninterrupted. Denny was agape and I just glowed with pride."

Denny Cordell was confused but soon succumbed to Visconti's powers of persuasion. The producer remembers that, "As soon as Marc and Steve were out of the door, Denny said, 'I don't understand them at all, but we'll sign them as our token underground group.'" Cordell then went to discuss the matter with his partner David Platz. "There was no question that it was Tony's enthusiasm that carried the day," recalls the music publisher. "My first impression of what Marc was doing was total uncertainty, but whatever convincing I needed was soon complete when I saw the audience reaction to him."

Platz instinctively recognised that Marc was no ordinary hippie. "I was also struck by his utter determination to succeed. He knew he would, but he put it across in a way that was completely disarming. It was absolutely charming. Most artists at the outset of their careers usually come across as rather shy and diffident, but that was never the case with Marc. I think that confidence had a lot to do with his later success. He was overjoyed at the signing and I remember him saying to me, in front of Tony and several other people, that he guaranteed he would stay with me forever if I could make him successful. Of course, that didn't happen."

Even before Platz and Cordell had hammered out a deal, Tyrannosaurus Rex were rehearsing their songs in the front room of Tony Visconti's flat at 108 Lexham Gardens, Earl's Court – just yards from the rooms Marc shared with Allan Warren in winter 1964. Eager to impress with his first major assignment, he captured the songs on a two-track recorder so that he could familiarise himself with the material. The tape, which he still has, was a blueprint for the first Tyrannosaurus Rex album, a remarkably clear-sounding *vérité* document that also included updated versions of 'Hippy Gumbo' and 'Lunacy's Back' plus the evocatively titled 'Puckish Pan' (alias 'Rock Me').

Buoyed by a string of Move and Procol Harum hit singles, Straight Ahead Productions nevertheless regarded the new project as something of an experiment for both band and producer. A minuscule budget of £400 gave them just four days at Advision, where a brand-new eight-track recorder had recently been installed. No one knew how to handle the equipment, and the time restrictions meant that any lavish production flourishes Visconti may have envisaged had to be scotched. In fact, just one song, 'Strange Orchestras', topped and tailed with Punch and Judy-style nonsense vocals, sounded as if it benefited from being recorded in a studio – and even that cried out for a string backing which Marc later claimed the production company wouldn't pay for. At least three songs – 'Dwarfish Trumpet Blues', 'Child Star' and 'Chateau In Virginia Waters' – were nailed in two takes.

"It was very bad," said Marc remembering the sessions. "It was the first LP (Visconti) had ever produced and it was done at Advision on an eight-track – the first in the country – and they didn't know how to use it. The stereo was awful. When we were doing it, it sounded good, but on record it sounded very thin and nasty. But we did it in two or three sessions – the whole thing only cost £200 to make, and 'Debora' only cost £30. I like the feeling of the first LP but as a production, I can't listen to it."

'Debora' was Marc's latest song, written at Visconti's flat and sung down the telephone to a delighted John Peel immediately afterwards. With its insistent beat and memorable refrain, it was an obvious candidate for a Tyrannosaurus Rex single, and was premiered on *Top Gear* on March 13 together with five songs from the forthcoming album, 'Mustang Ford', 'Strange Orchestras', 'Knight', 'Afghan Woman' and 'Frowning Atahuallpa'.

Spring 1968 inspired a glut of 'girl' songs: The Monkees' 'Valleri', The Hollies' 'Jennifer Eccles', Tom Jones' 'Delilah', Scott Walker's 'Joanna', and the more generic 'Young Girl' by The Union Gap and Bobby Goldsboro's maudlin 'Honey' all charted in April. 'Debora', sung in Bolan's best cry-baby voice and boasting lines such as "Your sunken face is like a galleon/Clawed with mysteries of the Spanish main", was different. *New Musical Express* summed up the general press reaction: "All very clever and intricate — probably too complex to register." He was proved right. But Bolan's apparent shunning of the commercial world had a surprising, and immediate payoff; 'Debora' narrowly missed a Top 30 placing, stalling at number 34 in May. It was quite a feat for a producer who barely knew how to produce, a percussionist on borrowed bongos and a songwriter for whom more than three chords was a luxury.

'Debora' is archetypal Bolan, a song that bustles with such energy that it appears more intricate than it actually is. The secret is in its structure, the oddly positioned verses, chorus and bridge that toy with pop convention, a subversion rendered palatable by making every line a virtual hook. Marc's undulating vocal onslaught, which occasionally broke into pure vocal noise ("nah-nah nah-nah nah-nah naaahhh") was becoming a trademark, too. The souped-up voice and unfamiliar backing aroused the wrath of many, who tended to regard Tyrannosaurus Rex as an irritant that would wilt with the summer flowers, but even John Peel couldn't have predicted the song's relative success.

Obviously more people were tuning in to *Top Gear* than Marc and Peel imagined. The March 13 Tyrannosaurus Rex broadcast was repeated twice (in a modified form) between March and May. Given that the duo had rarely ventured out of London, this must account for the success of the début Tyrannosaurus Rex album, which elevated the group from Hyde Park minstrels to moderately successful artists in just over six months. By the end of July, the record, *My People Were Fair And Had Sky In Their Hair . . . But Now They're Content To Wear Stars On Their Brows*, was outselling the latest Pink Floyd and Jimi Hendrix Experience LPs.

It was well over a year after San Francisco had ceremoniously proclaimed 'The Death Of The Hippie', and several months since the Summer of Love, but Marc Bolan's Tyrannosaurus Rex had clearly kept the faith. From its self-consciously wordy title to the children's story that closed the second side, *My People . . .* struck a chord with the whimsy-stricken elements within the British underground. Chief among them was John Peel, who narrated Marc's 'Woodland Story', a tale about Lionel Lark and his playmate Kingsley Mole who, "not even caring if he dirtied his Rupert trousers", knew in his "moleish mind . . . that playing was special". "Marc probably thought he was doing me a favour by letting me recite that on the LP," says Peel with inevitable bashfulness. The DJ's sleevenote, which recounted the group's brief history in flawless hippie vernacular, confirmed the degree of Peel's entanglement with counter-cultural flights of fancy:

"Tyrannosaurus Rex rose out of the sad and scattered leaves of an older summer. During the hard, grey winter they were tended and strengthened by those who love them. They blossomed with the coming of spring, children rejoiced and the earth sang with them. It will be a long and ecstatic summer."

"The whole hippie thing had very little grasp of reality," Peel offers by way of explanation, "but I think Marc had more of a grasp of it than I did. I can't think of anybody alive who didn't; I was quite astonishingly naïve. We all wanted things to be true so much that people would blind themselves to a lot of what was really going on." So while Saigon braved America's 'napalm diplomacy', indigenous Rhodesians hung lifelessly as Ian Smith clung desperately to minority white rule, while Martin Luther King and Robert Kennedy were cruelly gunned down and students and workers sought to topple the de Gaulle government in Paris, change-seekers in Britain were either flat on their backs, fraying their jeans or frying their minds with a compound of hallucinogens, hash and hedonism. Of course it stopped the war; they hardly knew it was going on. And, anyway, everything looked beautiful through psychedelic peepers – especially with the strange, sumptuous sounds of Tyrannosaurus Rex perfuming the air.

George Underwood's artwork for the album sleeve evoked the music perfectly. A netherworld in lilac, metallic blue and green, it roped in a cast of stock fantasy figures – winged masters, Greek gods, galloping horses, maidens with flowing, blonde hair and full breasts, flashes of bright light, serpents, even glimpses of a subterranean hell. The painting was also the first image to iconise Marc Bolan as a Samson-like character defined by the hair that cascaded in ringlets down his neck.

The painter, a schoolfriend of David 'Bowie' Jones whose fist was responsible for the singer's odd-eyed appearance, had first met Marc at La Giaconda in the mid-Sixties when they were both involved with Les Conn. "Marc thought I was famous because I'd once been on *Thank Your Lucky Stars!*" George recalls. By 1968, Underwood had ditched his musical ambitions to pursue a career in fine art. When Bowie heard Marc was looking for someone to paint an image for the *My People . . .* sleeve, he recommended his old Bromley mucker. "I asked Marc what artists he liked and he said William Blake," the painter recalls. "So I had this William Blake thing in my head, a sort of visionary feel, and I had an acetate of the album and figured it out from there." Underwood's Blake-like spectacle was inspired by two Gustave Doré woodcuts, Inferno and Purgatorio, which he adapted for the work.

Within the album's mythologically rich sleeve were a dozen songs which Marc duly dedicated to the C.S. Lewis characters "Aslan and the Old Narnians". The record opened with several strikes of a Chinese gong, launched into the primitive 12-bar thrash of 'Hot Rod Mama', and over the next 35 minutes or so, convincingly maintained a mood of otherworldly abandon where strangely titled tunes were performed as if through a looking-glass that miniaturised everything. Taking the opposite route to the heavy, improvisation-led explorations of Pink Floyd or acid-rock power trios such as the Jimi Hendrix Experience and Cream, Tyrannosaurus Rex tripped in smaller doses but did so no less convincingly.

Beneath the flamboyant fog created by Bolan's vibrating voice, and Took's percussive accompaniments, the songs were simple to play and, in the case of 'Hot Rod Mama' and 'Mustang Ford', rooted in vintage rock'n'roll. Only 'Weilder (sic) Of Words', where Marc lashed his larynx with barely controlled yelps of childlike abandon, and the pair assailed their instruments as if seeking to invoke the god of goodliness, hinted at musical intoxication, though the valedictory 'Frowning Atahuallpa (My Inca Love)' became gloriously mired in an Eastern-styled mantra, a sonic spell rudely broken by John Peel's deadpan prose reading.

The overall ambience, though, was one of deliriously joyous pastoralism, as if Tyrannosaurus Rex had somehow decamped to a shady glade in the New Forest and set up their bells, bowls and Pixiephone to an adoring audience of elves, animals and kindly witches. One of the album's most blissful songs is 'Child Star', a tricky arrangement which threatens to fall apart until the chorus, when the pair's harmonies lock spectacularly and the rise-and-fall melody divulges its real charm. "They did not see what a precious gem you'd be," Bolan sings in the mournful manner that would become his trademark. The song namechecked several classical prodigies, though like the self-referential 'Strange Orchestras', it was obvious where the real inspiration came from.

Allen Evans in *New Musical Express* picked up on the inherent sadness of Bolan's songs of love and escape. "Do not adjust your record players," he warned in his brief LP review. "This is how Marc Bolan and Steve Peregrine Took sing – as if they are about to break out crying." On the surface, though, Bolan was hardly lamenting the passing of his childhood, not when his records were selling for the first time, and Tyrannosaurus Rex were playing prestigious venues such as the Royal Albert Hall and the Purcell Room on London's South Bank. With the active support of influential figures such as John Peel, Jeff Dexter and a cub reporter and Peel acolyte Bob Harris on his side, his name was spreading throughout the music industry's subterranean chambers. And he had the backing of a powerful music publisher, of a successful production company and, more recently, a hip young management team.

The days of performing at Middle Earth for a stick of incense and a mug of jasmine tea had been banished by late spring when, through a Tony Visconti connection, Tyrannosaurus Rex were picked up by Blackhill Enterprises. Run by Pete Jenner and Andrew King, a pair of London Free School renegades whose hippie sensibilities were trimmed with entrepreneurial acumen, Blackhill managed Pink Floyd and were about to start empire building.

When news reached Andrew King that Tyrannosaurus Rex were playing a lunchtime concert at Ealing College, he instructed secretary June Child to prepare the company Rolls and take him to west London. He was impressed enough to invite Bolan back to Blackhill's Alexander Street office in Westbourne Park, where Marc told Pete Jenner: "What The Pink Floyd do electronically we do acoustically." Jenner agreed; Tyrannosaurus Rex were invited to join the Blackhill revolution.

As late as July 1968, Tyrannosaurus Rex were still putting in the occasional appearance at Middle Earth, though by now they'd become headliners, leaving acts such as The Third Ear Band, Hapshash & The Coloured Coat and a mime-obsessed David Bowie to aspire to their bill-topping greatness. The ramifications of the Blackhill deal were soon apparent, as the group played a prestigious show at the Royal Festival Hall on

June 3, followed by 'Midsummer High', the Blackhill-promoted free concert at Hyde Park (an idea often credited to Marc) supporting Pink Floyd.

One drawback of this greater exposure was that they no longer played solely to audiences blasted by dope and bleary-eyed with tiredness, but clear-sighted reviewers who watched the group struggle to win over seated audiences in rarified settings. Reporting back from the Festival Hall show, an *International Times* reviewer lamented the transition and called the performance too long, too unvaried and "a bringdown". Suggesting that Bolan's decision to get the audience to clap was "a wise move because it covered up some of his off-key notes", the writer speculates that the poor performance may have been the result of "nervousness . . . Every time I have seen them at Middle Earth they have always been of a fairly high standard."

The Blackhill liaison barely lasted the summer, but the introduction to June Child in the company's west London office was to leave a more lasting impact on Marc's life. The long-suffering Theresa Whipman received a credit − as "Euterpian Dancer Terry Mosaic" − on the *My People . . .* sleeve, but she wouldn't be around for the next one.

Marc's relationship with Theresa had consolidated during 1967 as the bisexuality of his late teens subsided, but with Tyrannosaurus Rex increasingly making demands on his time, his apparent love for her was compromised by his increased detachment. Nevertheless, Terry seemed able to deal with Marc's occasional lapses into self-pity (a card sent at the end of the year came "with love from a Christmas elf metamorphosed into a sad little flower"), and after they fought, which was often, he apologised with palpitating poetic flourishes. On January 17, 1968, he wrote:

> "My Dearest Teresa
> Just the thought of your Torqauy smile + your ballerina body brings tears from so deep within me I qauke . . . I'm ever so sorry that we fight but all close people seem to have to endure them, a divine error or a purifacation for a blissful after life. I love you coz your uniqe Teresa of the childhood dancing nights, Truly Mark x"

Terry, of whom Marc also wrote, "She's not beautiful, she's not ugly/ yet her heart shaped face smilin resembles the dawn", received letters that were signed in a number of ways − 'Marc Feld', a schoolboy-like 'Cram', even, romantically, 'Marc Whipman'.

Another letter to Terry, probably dating from early 1968, gives a rare insight into Marc's long-term aspirations: "Here's to the gates of my very own castle happy where I'll live with foxes and ponys and my true love. Here's to my true love who live with me when I'm me." Its Sixties city dweller's vision of country quietude is predictable, especially since Marc's greening during his hippie months. His reference to "when I'm me" is of interest, suggesting a sense of becoming and being only partially complete, a situation that could only be resolved by achieving stardom, and with it the financial means to disappear to his castle retreat. It also suggests that Marc was acutely aware that until such time, he would be caught up in games, adopting masks and strategies, a series of temporary 'me's.

R.D. Laing's fashionable book, *The Divided Self*, published in 1960, posits a similar dichotomy at the centre of his study of schizophrenia, where he states that attempting to sustain the split between the real self and the invented personality is the motor behind what is generally referred to as madness. It is a state that commonly afflicts those people thrust, by whatever means, into the public's gaze.

More recently, the post-Freudian psychologist Jacques Lacan, in his theory of the subject, bypasses Laing's categories of 'invented' and 'real' in favour of the role of social experience in the construction of self. Lacan suggests that a child becomes aware of a difference between 'self' and 'not-self' during what he calls the 'mirror stage', a metaphor for infant ego construction. According to this idea, self-awareness is intrinsically bound up with image, and an idealised one at that, which in turn reduces any abstract division between 'invented' and 'real' to a nonsense. Marc Bolan, who spent much of his life exercising his own formidable ego with a series of playful character hops, seemed to have an instinctive grasp of this apparent delusion.

Whether Bolan's "when I'm me" prognosis meant the removal of false identities or the discovery of a true one is a difficult one to call. Like most of us, he was in the grip of contradictions, and there's evidence to support either perspective. From his teenage years, he'd sought to discover himself both by extending reality through exaggeration and adoption, and by a gradual acquaintance with his inner needs; both were didactic pursuits that brought new knowledge to Mark Feld.

While there is nothing necessarily false about the flexibility of self-image, there is nothing particularly true about a person's essence. More than most, Marc was acutely aware of the reality of the image; during the late Sixties, in particular, he was drawn into the collective search for the 'true' self. Subsequent developments indicate that he was probably more successful in the former quest, but his being a cultural butterfly opened doors to a wide range of perspectives, and his insatiable appetite for all kinds of knowledge put at his disposal skills which, so he might have assumed, would have enabled him to find that elusive "me" more quickly.

A key lesson picked up by this self-starter was that both wisdom and stardom couldn't be achieved in a vacuum. Marc enjoyed his own company but without the help of well-placed friends he was going nowhere. John Peel, who still refers to Marc as his "best mate" during the late Sixties, is honest though hardly damning about the nature of their relationship. "He obviously saw me as a means of promoting Tyrannosaurus Rex and getting his music heard," he says. "I knew he had a hard side to him, as we all do, but in those early years I really didn't see it very often."

Contrary to the chimerical Marc Bolan of the early Tyrannosaurus Rex records, Peel maintains, "He was a more practical person, but I don't think he was being cynical and manipulative. That's not the Marc I remember. He had his eye on something in the distance but he didn't work towards it in any kind of obsessive way as far as I was aware." That was probably because Marc, for the most part, was genuinely immersed in hippie pursuits, which satisfied his natural inquisitiveness and flattered his desire for recognition. Even at his most bitter, in 1972, Steve Took conceded that, "I guess for a while Marc was a good hippie."

That didn't mean Marc Bolan couldn't be cruel or, at least, opportunist when it suited him. And so one day, the bundles of elegant prose dripping with daft thoughts and proclamations of love stopped arriving at Theresa Whipman's door. The girl once destined to share Bolan's stately home in the sticks was displaced overnight after the odes to joy started arriving at the feet of June Child, who ran the Blackhill Enterprises office. The pair clicked almost as soon as they were introduced, and by the time Marc had returned home, his passion burned sufficiently enough for him to call her up and invite her over. It was an uncharacteristic move; despite being a virtual slave to the whims of fashion, Marc preferred the stability of regular, long-term partners.

When June arrived in Summerstown, a picture of calm assurance with her long fair hair and steely blue eyes, Marc welcomed her with a romantic poem from his hieroglyphic hand and they exchanged cosmic thoughts and business secrets over a shared bowl of muesli. The pair's mutual admiration society intensified by the minute. Strong, opinionated, clued-up and five years Marc's senior, June Child was powerful and irresistible, a mother-lover figure and an ideal partner-in-pop, a more astute and authoritative voice of encouragement than Theresa had ever been. Marc had found his greatest ally and protector.

Marc and June immediately dumped their respective partners, June ending a four year relationship with jeweller Mick Milligan, and these instant soulmates headed for Wimbledon Common where they spent four nights in June's Commer Cob van, hastily fitted with a mattress in the back. George Underwood, who met Marc soon afterwards, remembers the pair hopelessly lost in the first flushes of romance. "Marc and June Child were sitting crosslegged on the floor facing each other and not speaking for 20 minutes. That's cosmic! They were like two little pixies just staring into each other's eyes."

June soon found them a place to live, a cold-water attic flat at 57 Blenheim Crescent in Ladbroke Grove, close to the Blackhill offices and in the heart of the capital's hippie community. There wasn't a great deal of money coming in – Bolan's record and publishing deals and his regular concert appearances hardly provided for an opulent lifestyle – but the £2 8s. 6d. per week rent they'd scraped together for the love-nest secured them a room, a two-ring gas cooker and the use of a shared bathroom. It was more than enough for their humble needs.

Pete Sanders, a close friend during the late Sixties who photographed Marc's next four album sleeves, is not alone in stressing the importance of the role June played in laying the foundations for Marc's later success. "She was the person who kept his feet on the ground," he says, "or should I say enabled him to float in his own world while she took care of all the day-to-day business – money, gigs and getting from A to B. She obviously loved Marc a lot, gave him encouragement and was very loyal to him." Jeff Dexter agrees: "June was wonderfully organised. She had a little van, worked at Blackhill and knew everyone, had access to a telephone and could make things happen. She made a lot of difference."

The sexual chemistry between the pair was complemented by the neat compatibility of their chosen roles. After years of solitary endeavour, Marc's creative urges welcomed outside nourishment, while his career aspirations required support from the industry men who mattered. June, who was both literate and a skilful PR operator, could deliver on both counts, introducing Marc to new writers and poets by night and singing his praises to sceptical suits during business hours.

To the adoring crowds at Middle Earth and the bedroom hippies who tuned into *Top Gear*, Marc Bolan was cultish and handsome, a latter-day

Romantic who couldn't help but write songs and poetry or give off vibes of innocence and sensitivity wherever he went. Later, June keenly betrayed the mythology that sprung up around his artistic aspirations, maintaining that Marc was "a businessman who regarded his fellow musicians as wage earners. His motivation for organising cut-price concerts was simply that he'd reach more people, who in turn would go out and buy his records," she said with a mild sneer back in 1992.

That didn't prevent him from indulging in a bit of animism every now and then. Marc's fondness for escape, intrigue and a sense of wonder at the world enabled him to embrace even the most outlandish hippie hogwash with a straight face. While June looked after the cheques, Marc looked towards Poon, a statue that lived on his mantelpiece at Blenheim Crescent, for inspiration in times of need. Eyewitnesses recall seeing written notes to Poon in Bolan's unmistakeably runic hand placed around the statue. Poon, almost certainly the statue of Pan that Riggs O'Hara had given Marc back in 1965, was Marc's muse.

Throughout his life, Marc often made mention of the external forces that governed his life; words such as reincarnation and destiny were part of his everyday vocabulary. Sometime during his first months at Blenheim Crescent, he was persuaded to take this quest further. Tony Visconti, a student of Buddhism and meditation, brought his teacher Chime Rinpoche round to Marc's for tea. "I said to Marc, 'You're into mysticism, this guy's a real mystic. You should meet him.' Eventually he agreed, and the meeting was the only time I ever saw Marc in a humble posture. They were seated cross-legged facing each other, and Chime, dressed in his splendid gold waistcoat, the maroon robes of a monk and with a crewcut, said to Marc, 'Tell me about yourself.. Marc bowed his head, clasped his hands tightly and said, 'Well I'm very young . . .' I thought I shouldn't listen in on such a private conversation and I joined the others at the other side of the room. But I'd have loved to have heard the rest of the story. Marc was very impressed with that meeting."

Among the many tenets of Buddhist philosophy is the one that recommends the gentle eradication of vices such as greed and self-delusion, but Marc's keen interest in personal enlightenment didn't persuade everyone that he'd dumped his old Mod baggage. John Peel preferred to ignore what he dubs the "harder side", but some like Steve Sparks, the Ilford 'Ace Face' who went on to become a rock executive, maintained that Bolan's ego was beyond redemption. "I knew him from when he was a Mod, when he was Mark Feld," he recalled in Jonathon Green's *Days In The*

Life. "He was a shit, a cocky little shit."

Journalist Keith Altham, who knew Marc at most stages of his career, is more measured in his assessment: "Marc had that inner drive, that intuitive and instinctive feeling to do something that was a bit special, a bit magical. He was intrigued by some of the trappings of hippie culture, but I don't think he appreciated the likes of Tolkien in a deep, literary sense. He was a chameleon, a butterfly, taking what he wanted out of something and then moving on."

During 1968, Marc played the role of the hippie anti-hero impeccably, his ambition a by-product of his creative endeavour rather than something that existed for its own sake. "We're not looking for publicity," he told underground magazine *Gandalf's Garden* that summer. "We're not doing interviews at all, ever, as far as I'm concerned." Yet at the same time, Tyrannosaurus Rex were beginning to find considerable success almost despite themselves. A second single, 'One Inch Rock', briefly hit the British Top 30 in September, a feat probably helped by three noteworthy summer festival appearances – at Woburn in July, Kempton Park early in August and the first Isle of Wight Festival at the end of that month.

More palatable to sensitive ears than 'Debora' and not dissimilar to 'Jasper C. Debussy', 'One Inch Rock' was an effective two-minute burst of upbeat rock'n'roll that, with its "oochie-coochie-tie-dye" refrain and homespun sound, anticipated the simplified pop of bands like Mungo Jerry, The Mixtures and indeed T. Rex. The critics thought so too. "Undemanding, good fun and blues-chasing," reckoned Derek Johnson in *New Musical Express*. "We're all pretty unanimous that this will be a big hit for the two lads," predicted Peter Jones in *Record Mirror*. "Very commercial material." A feature in *New Musical Express* that August went further, declaring "Tyrannosaurus Rex: Pop Monster In The Making" in bold type. The group's abrasive, inimitable style continued to polarise opinion, one *Melody Maker* correspondent recommending that "Tyrannosaurus Rex be stamped out, along with their gaseous aider and abetter John Peel."

The song's storyline – a "liquid poetess" invites the narrator back to her "shack", unties her buckskin dress and gives him "the horrors 'cos I'm one inch tall" – raises the spectre of sexual inadequacy. However, the unmistakable sound of Marc squeezing additional mileage from his pocket-sized cuteness can also be distinctly heard, a familiar cry that summer. "I'm very unmusical. I don't know any chords or anything," he told one interviewer, as if to underscore the naïveté at the heart of his being. "When I write, the words and music come together, normally very roughly, but I start getting high on it and just can't stop, until I blow my mind off and it all comes bubbling out."

By July, and with the *My People* . . . album only just in the shops, Marc's fantasy factory had already produced enough material for a second album. Tyrannosaurus Rex returned to Advision, Marc still clutching his £14 Suzuki acoustic guitar, Steve Took now unpacking an African talking drum and kazoo as well as the bongos. Talking to *Beat Instrumental*'s Rick Sanders during a break from the sessions, Marc claimed that the first LP "doesn't really represent us as we are now". Months later, promoting its release in November, he refined his opinion: "With this album, we're more relaxed and we treated it differently. For every two hours we spent recording we spent another three on production, perfecting it technically."

Its title was more succinct, and it was better produced and marginally less manic than the duo's début LP, but there was nothing on *Prophets, Seers & Sages The Angels Of The Ages* to suggest any dramatic change in direction. Although renowned for his sharp ruptures in style, growth for Marc from 1967 onwards was organic and evolutionary, often – particularly after 1972 – to his detriment. *Prophets* was a consolidatory affair, a slightly muted echo of the "two sorts of music – loud and freaky and soft and pastoral" that Marc was insisting characterised the Tyrannosaurus Rex sound.

Much of the freakiness was used up for the opening 'Deboraarobed', a less frenetic re-recording of the single which, as its palindromic title suggested, went into reverse mode midway through the song. 'Juniper Suction', an obvious allusion to the new woman in his life, was a compelling, mantra-like tone poem, that Marc plucked out mid-interview in 1973 to illustrate a moment he felt he was "getting somewhere" as a songwriter. Perhaps it was the subject matter: " 'Juniper Suction' is about making love," he confessed.

The genesis of 'Salamanda Palaganda', one of a trio of furiously paced songs on the record and a favourite of John Peel and his girlfriend Sheila, was more typical. "The title is really nothing to do with the song," Marc admitted around the time of its release. "We were driving along in the car one day, and I was looking for a name. Then suddenly I thought of 'Salamanda Palaganda' and I couldn't stop saying it."

Straining to hear lines such as "Dungaree dome is decked like a pagan temple to Zeus/He drinks acorn juice", tends to distract from perhaps the most overlooked aspect of Marc's songwriting – his melodies. But *Prophets* . . . illustrates the full range of Bolan's style, from the conventional singalong charm of 'Stacey Grove' (from which the above lyric comes) to the extraordinary invention of 'Salamanda Palaganda', which combines giant feats of vocal acrobatics with infinitesimal though highly effective shifts in pitch – all in just over two minutes.

If anything, the record represented a further retreat from the vagaries of the corrupt and fast-changing modern world, towards a purer way of living that instead celebrated mysticism and innocence. An aphorism printed on the rear sleeve read: "In the head of a man is a woman/In the head of a woman is a man/But what wonders roam/In the head of a child." Animals, too, provided another key to Bolan's disillusionment with the real world. Describing 'Trelawny Lawn', another track on the LP, he says it "tells the story of a different earth. It's the man versus animal theme and the man is bad and the animals are good."

In a revealing interview with Derek Blackwood in *New Musical Express* in November 1968, he defended his anti-materialist tendencies. "I dislike cities and the realities of modern life; I find plastic things repellent. My innermost thoughts are classical, and away from everyday life." Cars, telephones and television aren't inherently bad, he suggests, but they have been misused: "We can't seem to be able to control the things that we invent. The television's continually on . . . telephones often intrude especially when some crank starts breathing heavily down the other end of the line." Lorries, a daily talking point in the Feld household, were "noisy and release exhaust fumes everywhere".

Aside from standing apart from the crowd (and the further apart the better), Bolan's greatest ambition, which troubled him from the mid-Sixties to the end of his life, was to construct an epic world along the lines of Tolkien's scrupulously constructed *Lord Of The Rings*. The scale of Tolkien's undertaking, which involved mapping out Middle-earth and the Undying Lands, and the creation of a huge cast comprising hobbits and elves, dwarves and dragons, gods and monsters, wraiths and demons, orcs and ents, took the literary Grand Vizard years. It was an impossible task for Bolan, whose creative urges came in flashes and never stayed long enough to broach the boredom threshold. However, that didn't stop him trying.

Prophets, Seers & Sages . . . concluded with 'The Scenescof Dynasty', a Marc monologue accompanied only by a simple, playground-style hand-clap. The plot of the original 1966 tale had been ditched, leaving an impressionistic word assault that only loosely mirrored the good-over-evil scenario. Of course, it made no sense whatsoever ("The cello stairs reduced in size/The sunken landscape eclipsing into/A pair of blue

Tasmanian eyes"), but it was 1968 so it didn't need to.

Inevitably, Marc was asked to explain the piece – which he attempted to do at length. "Scenescof is a very bad man, very evil," he told Derek Blackwood. "And he sucks two people into him through his eyes . . . the story is about their travels through his body, starting off at his head. At first they don't realise that he's evil, but they gradually discover it. Then Scenescof sends a Gorgon after them, but the Gorgon changes sides and helps the two people. And because they're inside the body they realise that it's easy to kill him – a thing Scenescof hadn't thought about. So the couple go back up the body to the head and kill him."

The basis of the song had been 'The Scenescoff Dynesty' (sic), a 33-verse poem that had been lovingly transcribed over 13 pages by Terry Whipman the previous year. However, in the spring of 1968, Marc had filled at least three notebooks with a spontaneously written epic fantasy set in the imaginary land of Beltane. Titled *The Krakenmist* after John Wyndham's 1953 horror tale, *The Kraken Wakes* (in turn inspired by Alfred Lord Tennyson's 1842 poem *The Kraken*), it remains the only surviving piece of Bolan's extended writing and confirms that he was thoroughly in the grip of Tolkien during the earliest Tyrannosaurus Rex days.

The Krakenmist is hardly an easy – or enjoyable – read and belongs to its time even more than the music of Tyrannosaurus Rex does. But as Delf the Unicorn and Agadinmar do battle with the mighty Kraken Mist, and the Elf Lord Quador confronts Rark Stang the monster Stoad maker, Marc's open, compassion-filled face and soft poet's voice melt to reveal, once again, a worldview based on tumult and competition. It was a contradiction that Marc Bolan was continually grappling with, no more so than in the late Sixties.

While attempting to disarm and perhaps punish 'scenescofs' and assorted wrongdoers through his work, Marc found solace in the work of Kahlil Gibran, in whose memory *Prophets, Seers & Sages . . .* was dedicated (pity his name was spelt wrong on the sleeve). A founding father of the hippies' poetic revolution, Gibran was an early 20th century Lebanese mystic whose best known work, a book of aphorisms titled *The Prophet* (1923), was invariably sandwiched between the obligatory Tolkien and I Ching on every longhair's bookshelf.

Sharing the writer's fondness for Biblical and Blakean references, Marc was captivated by Gibran's gentle message of love and peace couched in imagery that was already familiar to him. In Gibran's world, which mighty and lofty wise men with swords shared with eagles and minstrels, the

119

moon shone spectacularly and trees swayed majestically, and Beauty, Love, Life and Death all warranted capital letters. Unknown to Marc, Gibran had little formal education, couldn't spell, and even had his own 'wizard', Selim Dahir, who had encouraged him in his search to attain higher knowledge.

John Peel has reservations about the depth of Marc's interest in the works of Gibran and similarly vogueish writers. "The idea of him sitting down and studying anything would have been anathema to him," says the DJ. "Most people used to get their ideas from reading the backs of paperbacks in W.H. Smith. You'd leave books by Gibran and Hesse and *The Tibetan Book Of The Dead* lying around because they were part of the uniform. You could lie on the floor, smoke dope, listen to the new Donovan album, talk a load of shite and it was all rather pleasant."

He is not alone in his scepticism. Tony Visconti, who knew Marc well from late 1967 until the end of 1973, cannot ever recall seeing him reading a book, though he insists that Bolan was acutely aware of the sources of his influences. During the early weeks of their friendship, Marc gave him copies of *The Lord Of The Rings* trilogy and *The Hobbit* with a few gentle words of advice: "If you're gonna record me, you gotta read these."

While Marc was recommending Tolkien and Gibran as panaceas for the "plasticity of civilisation", others spent 1968 in cabalistic corners fingering the world's oppressors and plotting their hideous downfall. Western democracy's tolerance for dissent was exposed as batons rained down upon the heads of protesters in Chicago, in Paris, and even in London as protesters marching on the American Embassy in Grosvenor Square left nursing bloody wounds and vowing revenge. Even pop musicians, who post-Dylan had felt obliged to form an opinion on matters far and beyond the proverbial 'What's your favourite colour?', began to sense that their Pied Piper moment had arrived. Come the 'Revolution', bolshie Beatle John Lennon was undecided whether to count himself in or out; The Rolling Stones idly celebrated the 'Street Fighting Man'; and Columbia Records capitalised on the mood with their 'Revolutionaries Of Rock' promotional campaign.

The children of Marx and Coca-Cola seemed momentarily to unite, and the rock world was poised to envelop and inspire both. The union was short-lived, especially so in Britain, where the radicals' cause was only rarely espoused. This reluctance was common among mid-Sixties' pop Romantics, who tended to regard conventional left/right wing political affiliations as obsolete obstacles to self-knowledge and discovery. Drugs only served to deepen the chasm: "Politics is pigshit" declared *International Times*, whose editorial content betrayed a deep mistrust of politicians of all persuasions and instead reflected a rabid libertarianism. *Challenge*, the broadsheet of the Young Communists, was deeply sceptical of this bourgeois search for personal enlightenment, rechristening its key text "Sgt. Pep-Ups Phoney Thoughts Club Band". Rock culture's prevailing mood, though, was encapsulated by Elektra Records' boss Jac Holzman, who proclaimed: "We think that the revolution will be won by poetry not politics, that poets will change the structure of the world."

Marc Bolan, the emerging hippie folksinger who sat cross-legged as he played, who interrupted his concerts with brief poetry readings and who was in the habit of telling interviewers that his "Guardian Angel does all the writing; I'm sure it's not me," was firmly entrenched on the out-to-lunch wing of the British underground. Now dedicating his mind and body to creative acts, he was the epitome of the 'poetry not politics' Little Englander who passed up Mao and the Maharishi for Dylan. Asked about the rock underground in December 1968, he explained: "Really, it all belongs to Bob Dylan. We are all producing a monster – a 55-group image of Dylan. We are all now forming a big statue of Dylan in different aspects."

By now, Tyrannosaurus Rex concerts had become reverential gatherings of the flower children who'd refused to wilt. The underground had exchanged its rainbow aspect for bluesier hues, as evidenced by the success of Fleetwood Mac and Chicken Shack, and *Prophets, Seers & Sages . . .* failed to chart. Convinced of the sanctity of their mission, and with John Peel making it a condition of his university and college gigs that Tyrannosaurus Rex be allowed to perform on the same bill, the duo travelled the country. Even by the standards of the time, Peel remembers they were regarded as "elfin to a degree beyond human understanding".

Keith Altham was baffled by the transformation of the ex-Mod, ex-Beatnik, ex-John's Children dynamo. "I saw Tyrannosaurus Rex at the Albert Hall and they bored me to death," he says. "I remember thinking that Marc's guitar playing had improved dramatically, but that the whole affair was terribly insular." It was, but Marc's audience continued to grow. So did Marc's understanding of the pop process. "I think he learned a lot during that period, especially about the business," Altham maintains.

He did, but for now Marc Bolan was the child out of time, guaranteed to bring last year's hippies out of the woodwork whenever Tyrannosaurus Rex hit town. Such was the debate surrounding the group's love it or shove it sound and anachronistic whimsy that few noticed when Marc's pretty pixie looks starting winning him the beginnings of a female fan following. A Tyrannosaurus Rex Fan Club was set up in February 1969, and within a month, the organisers were forced to plead: "Because so many of you have requested locks of Marc and Steve's hair, they are now beginning to go a bit thin on top, so please all you adorable fans, no more requests for locks of hair." However, Marc maintained an open-door policy backstage, and would sometimes surprise his keenest fans with handwritten letters signed "with deepest love".

Bolan's private life mirrored his public image during these early months of minor pop stardom. There were day trips to Glastonbury Tor and Stonehenge with June, John Peel and the DJ's girlfriend Sheila. Bolan and Peel would also feed their voracious appetites for new sounds with regular treks round the record stores. Visiting obscure junk shops in Wimbledon and the modish Musicland in Berwick Street, Soho, they'd indulge their shared enthusiasm for the latest Donovan import or James Burton guitar solo tucked away on an obscure Ricky Nelson B-side. And when Marc wasn't performing at places like Mothers in Birmingham or the Arts Theatre in Cambridge, nights were usually spent indoors at Blenheim Crescent (where the doorbell was marked 'Bolanchild'), where poems and songs would flow as liberally as the jasmine tea and vegetarian food.

The climax of this period of unbridled Romanticism came with the publication, in March 1969, of *The Warlock Of Love*, a 12s. 6d. collection of Bolan's richly descriptive blank verse in a slim hardback volume. Published rock poets were still a rarity, although Dylan's example had encouraged writers such as Leonard Cohen to embrace rock culture and songwriters to think poetically. Marc's knack of stringing attractive sounding words together was instinctive, if untroubled by academic rigour, but his florid style, so perfect for its time, soon fell foul of fashion.

Lacking in any obvious emotional content, and devoid of any symbolic worth apart from its simple, escapist instinct, his work has little relevance outside the culture from which it sprang. Yet Bolan's poetry encapsulates both his vainglorious attitude towards himself, and his oddly individual take on accepted wisdom. Cloaked in the richly patterned language of the Romantic, *The Warlock Of Love* boasts a stream of seemingly unrelated images and characters that leap from the page – a mirror of Marc's visual style – and virtually scream out for attention. And while all around him songwriters – Dylan included – were seeking out a new economical style,

Bolan refused to recognise any limits to his literary ambition.

"The writings are very rich in romantic imagery," says Donovan. "You can link it back to the Victorian's embracing of medievalism. There are many references to myths and legends, and it's full of the images of the pre-Raphaelite painters. Marc had a very colourful view of the world."

There is little more maligned in rock'n'roll than the self-styled poet. Bob Dylan was acceptable, because he was the first, the most original and his work was rich with philosophical, socio-political and symbolic meaning. There were few qualms, too, when award-winning Canadian poet Leonard Cohen transposed his rhymes to music, or when Pete Brown, a mainstay of the British poetry scene since the early Sixties, began writing rock lyrics for Cream. Bolan's literary voice, controversial even during those few heady months in 1967 and 1968, was rarely taken so seriously.

Even comparisons with Syd Barrett failed to stand up in the eyes of his peers. "Syd was much more convincing," Pete Brown maintains, "because he was much less self-conscious about his poetic content. The thing that Syd did was to address British subjects and he made it work. He had been through that whole art school background which gave him a greater sophistication." Brown acknowledges Bolan's Dylan-like aspirations but insists that his efforts were doomed. "When Dylan used mysticism, it more often manifested itself in Biblical imagery and was much harder-edged than anything Bolan did," he says.

"Cloak me in ermine Merlin . . ." "O nosediving eaglet stormed on a mountain . . . " "The chariots diminish high on the chartered hills of science . . ." "Yon ravelling Mage . . ." Marc pulled no punches with his opening lines and *The Warlock Of Love*, dedicated to "the woods of knowledge", finds Bolan at his most fanciful, adrift somewhere between King Arthur's enchanted forests and the epic landscapes beloved of the 19th century Romantics.

Pete Brown found the escapism unbearable. "There was a lot of phoneyness about the hippie thing, and its twee side always annoyed me. All that Tolkien stuff which was co-opted by the hippies was bullshit. They felt they recognised something in it – fantasy, Utopias, good and evil. To me it was an abomination and it fucked people's heads up. The combination of that stuff and acid was lethal. It sent people off to a kind of numbskull cloud cuckooland."

Bolan's lyric fleet-footedness was better confined to song lyrics, where any pretensions were largely rendered redundant by the obscurantist magnificence of his vocal delivery. John Peel – himself credited as 'Poet' on the sleeve of the début Idle Race album – regards Marc's literary aspirations as very much a product of the time. "He did regard himself as a poet, or at least, he was encouraged to do so," he remembers. "As much a part of the corrupting process are the fans and people like me who tell musicians how wonderful they are. So few have a steadying hand on them to say, 'Frankly, that is shite.' A lot of people would benefit enormously from such a figure in their lives, though I don't think Marc would have taken kindly to such criticism."

Peel has little doubt that Bolan's love of words was genuine, and suggests that he approached them in the manner of an idiot savant. "Marc liked words, and sometimes he'd ask me what a particular word meant. When I told him and its meaning seemed inappropriate, he'd say, 'Well, it doesn't fit but I like the sound of it,' and so in it would go." It is this playfulness, this flouting of rules he didn't always care to understand, that lend Bolan's lyrics an inventive abandon that eluded many of his more angsty contemporaries. Throughout his career, Marc never once doubted his poet status, and though even he would have later retracted *The Warlock Of Love* as primary evidence for this, there is a fine case to be made for the flamboyant idiosyncrasy of his song lyrics. As he moved closer to the mainstream of popular music, the ornate language, the mischievous lyric juxtapositions, and the immediacy of his memorable word couplings made him the most talked-about lyricist in pop. In that respect, the meaning of Bolan's lyrics was at least as important as anything discussed in the lecture theatre.

In September 1968, Marc recorded an interview and recited 'Juniper Suction' for *The Voice Of Pop*, a Radio 1 documentary about the importance of lyrics in popular music. That same month, plans were unveiled for a full-length album dedicated to the new rock poets recited by John Peel. Among those asked to contribute were Marc, Arthur Brown, Tim Rose, Syd Barrett, Roger Waters, Traffic's Chris Wood, Keith West, Captain Beefheart and, oddly enough, The Move's Carl Wayne. "What an awful idea that was," recalls a horrified Peel. "I'm glad we had the wisdom to pack that in before it got too serious. I think I got as far as taping Syd Barrett's 'Effervescing Elephant' and 'Baby Lemonade'."

By late 1968, it was clear that the dream – mind-altering for some, a fashion accessory for many – was well and truly over. Weekend hippies, the acid-frying of some of the best minds of the generation, and the desire to translate musical disorder into new heights of sonic sophistication marked the end of the party. As the hippie subculture began to fragment, the diffusion was reflected in the music. Hard rock began to replace the soft, Eastern influences that had floated mysteriously into Western pop; musical gurus like Dylan, The Beatles and The Rolling Stones embraced a new rock simplicity; and a fresh wave of ambitious, album orientated groups prised open the divisions between elite and mass musical tastes still further.

Bolan was acutely aware of the changes but, not for the last time, he moved much more slowly for fear of losing his audience. Despite his deep-seated ambition and his abhorrence of drugs and slothfulness, many of the facets of hippie culture – the sartorial flamboyance, its fraternal elitism, the flight from normality – had coincided with his own passions, and the movement had given him the opportunity to taste genuine commercial success. John Peel saw little to suggest that Marc Bolan would one day happily exchange cult cosiness for a way of life he once condemned as commercial and plastic. "Marc was just an amiable lad who was quite ambitious and enjoyed the fashion aspects of life," Peel insists, while refuting any suggestion of a Bolan masterplan. But while there was no plan other than a continual desire to succeed on his own terms, Marc's 'quiet ambition' slowly gained pace over the next two years as he sought to expand his creative horizons without jeopardising his benevolent hippie mien.

6

No Particular Place To Go

"I feel Marc is as genuine as it is possible to be within the rather narrow corridors of pop. He has never been in the big hype scene and the music has gone through logical, unforced progressions."
　　　　　　　　　　　　　　　　　　　　– Tony Norman, *Music Now!* (March 1970)

"I think our time for singles may come again."
　　　　　　　　　　　　　　　　　　　　– Marc Bolan (spring 1970)

*"And now where once stood solid water
stood the reptile king,
Tyrannosaurus Rex, reborn and bopping."*
　　　　　　　　　　　– Marc Bolan, *The Warlock Of Love* (1969)

In early 1969, Marc and Steve were no longer alone. The indomitable John Peel and June Child were still cheering loudly from the wings, providing valuable airplay and business acumen respectively. But, uncharacteristically for an underground group, Tyrannosaurus Rex now had a fan club. Established during 1968 after a keen fan called Suzy placed an advert in the music press requesting members, the club acquired a degree of professionalism early in 1969 after Annabel Butler and a colleague called Maxine, who both worked for the Bryan Morrison Agency, brought it in-house.

By March 1969, there were over 100 members, including four from Germany, three from France and two from Norway. Each received a monthly newsletter, and a document titled 'Life Lines', one of those at-a-glance personality profiles that proffered indispensible information such as height, colour of eyes, favourite clothes, pets and drinks. Typically, it tells us rather more about Marc than Steve Peregrine Took; that he was born in the "ancient city of London", and now lives in a "Chateau in the west", that his favourite clothes are "medieval and elfen", that he eats vegetables but dislikes "meat, uninspiring persons monsters (human kind)", that he enjoys "the writing of C.S. Lewis, the musical work of Devorak (sic) and the dawn", that his favourite group is The Beach Boys, that he has a cat called Flute and sips on wine and grape juice.

It was an idyllic portrait of the artist as a gentle aesthete and when, in February 1969, Maxine assured club members that, "I have never heard either of them raise their voices above their normal talking voices," there was little cause to doubt her. But there were distinct rumblings within the Tyrannosaurus Rex camp that spring which threatened the group's existence. In March, midway through the sessions for the duo's third album, Marc bought himself a new electric guitar. It signalled his determination to develop the group's sound. But the loudest commotion came from the fast deteriorating relationship between Marc and Steve Took.

From the beginning the partnership had been one-sided, but with Took now a charismatic figure in his own right on the Ladbroke Grove drug scene, the percussionist was no longer content to remain in Bolan's shadow. Fraternising with various Pink Fairies, Pretty Things and pre-Hawkwind members, Took had landed himself at the opposite end of the hippie spectrum, where hard drugs were preferable to softback editions of fantasy fiction, and where hardwearing biker leathers and dirty denims were favoured over kaftans and girlish shoes. If Marc was the stay-at-home poet, Took was the anti-social deviant whose favourite band was The Pretty Things, who adored the horror films of Vincent Price and Christopher Lee, and who (unlike Marc) voiced public support for the rapidly fading Syd Barrett. There was trouble ahead . . .

Because Tyrannosaurus Rex had so perfectly personified the exuberant mood of 1967, the group's appeal was bound to be limited when the real world invited itself back into youth consciousness. *Prophets, Seers & Sages* had failed to capitalise on the success of the début album, and those not immediately smitten by the duo's work found the music one-dimensional, boring and passé. Lacking the profound, psychedelic appeal of Pink Floyd or the eclectic musicality of The Incredible String Band, Marc and Steve's Tyrannosaurus Rex, far from being a powerful beast of sound, was in danger of being typecast as lightweight and anachronistic.

Kenneth Pitt, who'd toyed with the idea of managing both Bolan and David Bowie in 1966 before plumping for the latter, secured a support slot for his artist on Tyrannosaurus Rex's seven-date *For The Lion And The Unicorn In The Oak Forests Of Faun* tour during February and March 1969. Despite Bolan's success and Bowie's miserable string of failures, despite the imminence of the third Tyrannosaurus Rex album and Bowie's decision to shun songs on the tour in favour of a mime piece, Pitt insisted he'd made the right decision. "There was something shallow and crude in Marc's performance," he wrote later, "and it gave me no reason to believe that it would ever be otherwise, but David invested his work with a couth intelligence that held great promise for the future."

Bowie had followed Marc's fortunes closely, via Tony Visconti who worked with both, and through an infrequent social relationship. This was put under some strain late in 1968 when Marc and June had driven out to Edenbridge in Kent, to the family home of David's girlfriend Hermione Farthingale – with Steve Took and photographer Ray Stevenson in tow. In Bowie's mind, Marc had hijacked the day in the country for a photo shoot, which nevertheless went ahead in 'Marnie's garden. But he had the last laugh. Marc later gave him the Stylophone on which he wrote 'Space Oddity', the song with which he would briefly leapfrog Marc in terms of popularity late in 1969.

There seemed no middle way for Marc Bolan. For every manager or industry executive who'd fallen for his voice, his songs and his personal charm, there were dozens that had laughed him out of their offices. It was a similar story with audiences. During 1969, while David Bowie's eclecticism appeared to pay off, Marc maintained his purity: letting his heart rule his head, and brushing aside criticism, he pursued his magnificent obsessions ever more doggedly.

When Marc did defer to the advice of others, for instance when he was encouraged to release 'Pewter Suitor' as a single in January 1969, the outcome – downright failure – only served to strengthen his self-belief. Reviewing the record, singer Barry Ryan cautioned: "I should imagine if you were in a stoned state at a party, you'd think this record was fantastic." There was some truth in his comment. Finicky even by Tyrannosaurus Rex's standards, 'Pewter Suitor' possessed little of the duo's characteristic charm, its high-pitch two-chord hook more inclined to irritate than enchant. Only in its final moments did the song ignite, disintegrating into a glorious mess of percussion and some near-hysterical wailing from Bolan, as *Melody Maker*'s Chris Welch amusingly noted. "Their rattling pots and tiny voices get quite heated at the end, rather like a couple of rough gnomes bashing each other with toadstools." "It was an album track," Marc suggested two years later.

If 'Pewter Suitor' had damaged the group's reputation as a bankable singles act, 'Warlord Of The Royal Crocodiles' on the flip ("which I really dug," he added) marked a new departure, with Bolan's voice multitracked to good effect and Took's percussion enhanced by studio trickery. Despite a string of encouraging – though hardly overwhelming – concert appearances at reasonably sized venues, Bolan was seriously questioning the direction being taken by Tyrannosaurus Rex. In a postcard sent to John Peel apologising for not seeing much of him lately, Marc admitted: "I've had strange wrestles with the gaolers of my destiny causing much upset in my usauley sweet calm life."

That wrestling, which invariably involved the Steve Took problem and the creative turbulence that had produced such a flustered 45, was partially resolved on *Unicorn*, released in mid-May 1969. This, the third Tyrannosaurus Rex album, was a notable departure in a number of ways. The lo-fi, guitar-and-bongos-in-the-park ambience of their earlier work was now camouflaged in a production sheen that paid homage to Phil Spector's wall of sound. The meandering and bountiful lyrics had been clipped in favour of neatly crafted four-line verses sung – occasionally at least – with a new-found clarity. The greater emphasis on production also meant more time was made for overdubs, most notably the double-tracking of Marc's voice, which significantly strengthened the melody lines. Once in a while, Marc would lighten the mood further with an uncharacteristic lead guitar phrase.

Even the structure – alternating an upbeat, highly produced song with a sparse-sounding recording – suggested that the record had been carefully planned. "The album is in two parts," Marc explained to *Circus* magazine. "Six tracks have just guitars and bongos, but the others have many instruments on them. I bought an organ, learned to play it, and became interested in many different sounds. There are 20 kinds of percussion on the album as well as bass and drums."

That barely disguised Spector touch was immediately apparent, the opening 'Chariots Of Silk' trampolining wildly on a heavily echoed drum pattern, double tracked voices and a giant-sounding tambourine. Even more impressive was 'Catblack (The Wizard's Hat)'. Using the standard rock'n'roll ballad C-Am-F-G chord progression as its template, the song's mock-Spector sound was filled out with some rudimentary Tony Visconti piano ("Thankfully it was in the key of C," the producer recalls) and concluded with some knowing "Da-doo-ron-rons". "That song was really inspired by those 'Runaround Sue' songs – the chords and so on – and I wanted to do that sort of melody with nice words," Marc said in 1970. "I brought the piano in so that people who are into rock'n'roll piano could relate to it a bit."

Not everything was recognisably rock'n'roll. 'She Was Born To Be My Unicorn', which again reverberates around a cavernous, Spector-like production, echoes Marc's mantra form that tore into rock'n'roll's verse-chorus-verse rulebook. Despite its 22 overdubs, 'Romany Soup' was even more minimal, a nine-word mantra to a dish Marc and June sampled during a brief holiday in Cornwall in December 1968.

If there was the faint trace of fashionable progressive rock about *Unicorn*, it wasn't merely in fleshing out the basic guitar/bongo/percussion/vocal front line with piano, a full drum kit, harmonium, bass and fonofiddle. Nor was the authoritative tone of Marc's brand new Suzuki acoustic, which rang with exceptional clarity throughout, a major factor. Away from songs like 'Catblack' and 'Chariots Of Silk', Marc's melodies were getting ever more intricate, as evidenced on 'The Pilgrim's Tale' and the magnificently mournful 'Iscariot', which found him mangling the meaning of his words with a showy display of vocal incomprehensibility.

There was something altogether less manic about *Unicorn*. Despite the obvious Spector affiliations, a song like 'Nijinsky Hind' (which took nine takes to perfect) was more typical of the 16-track set – its melodies more subdued, its hooks less insidious, its subject matter more obviously earthly. "Nijinsky was a dancer in the Twenties," Marc told *Zigzag* in 1970. "He was huge for three years, and then he freaked. He was very similar to Syd Barrett in that he was so into what he was doing. Then he freaked partially and everybody kicked him in the face. Everyone said he was mad, and he died about four years later. I just liked the idea of a creature, an animal as agile as Nijinsky . . . and the song just explains what a gas the creature was. *Unicorn* was very much into that."

As if his material wasn't fanciful enough already, Marc proudly stepped outside the pop discourse to reveal some of the sources for his inspiration on the album sleeve. "Marc had very strong ideas about what he wanted," recalls Pete Sanders who shot the session in the kitchen of the flat he shared with John Peel, at 2 Park Square Mews, off Upper Harley Street in central London. "He brought some objects over for the session – I think the Gibran books were his, as were *The Children's Shakespeare* and Blake's *Complete Writings*, but the Singer sewing machine and the photo book of the Cottingley fairies (which has since been proved a fake) were mine." During the session, Marc and Steve held sparklers to create what Sanders calls "a more wizardy effect", but these shots were passed over at the picture edit stage.

"Marc was very generous," Sanders insists, "because I wasn't a very good photographer then. But we did work well together. He was always meticulous about the sessions and was incredibly aware of the power of image."

Shortly after the session, Pete Sanders quit the flat. "Marc and June had moved out of the attic at 57 Blenheim Crescent and down to the more spacious floor below, so I moved in above them." John Peel, who had recited a second 'Woodland Story' on *Unicorn*, kept the flat, from where he hatched great plans for his own Dandelion record label, which he'd got off the ground at the start of 1969.*

Nevertheless, the DJ, who had witnessed many Tyrannosaurus Rex performances over the past year, continued to MC for the duo, and was still firmly committed to the shared Utopian philosophy as his 'John Peel proving the existence of fairies' billing at the Queen Elizabeth Hall on January 13, 1969 attests. Lower down on the bill that night was a new American singer named Melanie who, like Marc, polarised audiences with an anguished vibrato that oscillated wildly. Once again, Chris Welch was left harbouring some reservations: "A pretty evening of wafer-thin material presented in such a civilised way it became charming and satisfying."

Tyrannosaurus Rex continued to rotate heavily on John Peel's *Top Gear* radio show; the May 11, 1969 broadcast was the pair's sixth session in just 18 months. During that time, Bolan had also joined his DJ pal on air to discuss his work, recite his poetry and comment on the current state of pop. Predictably, there was a backlash. As Clive Selwood, Peel's manager and the architect of Dandelion Records, remembers: "John got a letter from the Controller of Radio 1 which ordered him to stop playing Tyrannosaurus Rex on the basis that listeners were complaining that John had a financial interest in Marc's affairs – which of course was not true. John ignored it, and rightly told them it was madness."

"I used to get a lot of critical mail," Peel says, "and of all the artists I used to play regularly, Tyrannosaurus Rex was always the name that used to be mentioned. 'C'mon, you can't *really* like all that stuff, all that bleating!' And of course, the more people react like that, the more I'm drawn to it." The rumours didn't stop at nepotism either. "Another thing that people used to say was that I liked the band because I fancied Marc. They also thought that was why I moved in with Pete Sanders, because he was immensely beautiful as well. Actually, I didn't fancy either of them."

---

* The label and its publishing arm were named after his two hamsters, Dandelion and Biscuit, gifts from Marc and June.

Resisting the charms of beautiful Bolan and pretty boy Pete, the decidedly heterosexual John Peel instead found his life-mate in Sheila, whom he'd met in 1968 on the set of Tony Palmer's *How It Is*, BBC-TV's alternative pop show. In spring 1969, he was in front of the cameras in his own right, fronting a pilot show for Granada TV provisionally titled *John Peel's In Concert*. Inevitably he brought Tyrannosaurus Rex along with him, though to little avail. Apart from a faint memory of a dog wandering onto a makeshift stage to join the duo, Peel remembers little else about the show – which was junked after one trial episode.

Marc, too, was enjoying the heterosexual life. His relationship with June had grown from instant attraction into a formidable business team – he the product, she the salesperson. An active campaigner on Bolan's behalf, June defended her corner even when pitted against an imposing music industry figure such as publisher David Platz, who recalls her giving him some testy times.

June Child's role in Marc's career took on even greater importance after the pair's shared love affair with Blackhill Enterprises came to an abrupt halt. It had begun so well, too. According to photographer Ray Stevenson, prior to the release of the first Tyrannosaurus Rex album, Marc had suggested that Blackhill stage a free concert in London's Hyde Park. A couple of months later, on June 29, 1968, an audience of 7,000 spent a midsummer's day chasing bubbles and boating down the Serpentine to the sounds of Roy Harper, Jethro Tull, Pink Floyd and Tyrannosaurus Rex.*

It was the pair's insatiable appetite for each other that provoked the departure of both June Child and Tyrannosaurus Rex from Blackhill. That's because Andrew King returned home from honeymoon to find the pair romping in his bed. June took care of Marc, and Marc took Tyrannosaurus Rex off to the Bryan Morrison Agency which, by the end of 1968, also handled Pink Floyd, Captain Beefheart & His Magic Band, The Pretty Things and Aynsley Dunbar's Retaliation. Morrison's impact was swift, booking the duo on a series of continental shows, including appearances on German and French television. For a few months during 1968 and 1969, his office at 16 Bruton Place in central London provided a second home for Bolan: Morrison's Lupus Publishing Company, which published *The Warlock Of Love* in March 1969, was based there, as was the Tyrannosaurus Rex Fan Club.

---

* The event was a dry run for Blackhill's legendary Rolling Stones Hyde Park show in July 1969 which attracted a 250,000-strong crowd.

The Club's March 1969 newsletter gives an indication of Bolan's desire to maintain a degree of independence, even though the size of the concerts the group now played meant that Marc and Steve could no longer simply turn up and plug in. With John Peel and June both capable of transporting the group to Bromley Technical College or Bath Pavilion, Tyrannosaurus Rex now took their own WEM 200-watt PA with Shure microphones, purchased with the proceeds of their record sales, which meant decent sound and sound business sense.

Members were also told that all four members of Pink Floyd – conveniently also on the agency's books – were big fans of the group. "Steve and Marc are a gas," Dave Gilmour was quoted as saying. "They play such beautiful music and make terrific records." Nevertheless, the gentle sounds and good karma that Tyrannosaurus Rex once epitomised were fading fast.

The process seemed to accelerate after Marc bought an electric guitar – his famous Fender Stratocaster embellished with a teardrop symbol – in March, towards the end of the *Unicorn* sessions. For months, he'd been playing around with Tony Visconti's electric while at the producer's flat, dissecting the latest Beatles or Beach Boys record or guardedly exchanging tips with Visconti's other protégé David Bowie. Having embellished the Tyrannosaurus Rex sound on the latest album, Marc's third flirtation with electricity was prompted less by imagining himself as an Eric Clapton, a Jimi Hendrix or a Pete Townshend, and more as a response to one simple fact: rock music was now sounding increasingly robust.

Rising groups such as Led Zeppelin, Jethro Tull, Humble Pie and, from America, Creedence Clearwater Revival, based their acts on high energy blues rock. For the moment, Marc Bolan's model for a new electric Rex eschewed foot-stomping 12-bar boogie for something throbbing and sinister sounding. That was 'King Of The Rumbling Spires', the fourth Tyrannosaurus Rex single, on which Marc's usually strong melodic sense was obliterated by pounding, punk rock drums and a dark, descending guitar motif that soon became something of a Bolan trademark. A descent into a Scenescof-like abyss, the song's disquieting fusion of hard rock and progressive intent, enriched by Mellotron 'strings' midway through, was reminiscent of the new breed of classically inspired British groups such as King Crimson and The Nice.

Issuing 'King' on 45 in July 1969 was an unusual move because, as Derek Johnson of *New Musical Express* rightly pointed out, "whether it will have mass appeal is a moot point". Chris Welch, on a secret mission to help Tyrannosaurus Rex succeed, saw it differently under a prophetic "Electrified Teenybop!" headline in *Melody Maker*. "This is Bolan's most commercial production to date," he claimed wildly, "and with Steve Took rocking feverishly on regular drums . . . they could easily crack their chart problem." They didn't. Sales were up on 'Pewter Suitor' but 'King Of The Rumbling Spires' disappointed those expecting the group to capitalise on the upbeat, commercially successful *Unicorn* album.

There was cold comfort on the flip, too. Its opening line, "Her face was like a cult to me," was open to interpretation, but there was little doubt that 'Do You Remember' had similar intentions to the top-side. Dense, austere and with an attacking ambition that anticipated the proto-punk sounds of Pere Ubu, both sides revealed Bolan's willingness to adapt and survive but the move was short lived. That's because the greatest threat to the group's existence came from within.

A close listen to 'Do You Remember' reveals that Took and Bolan share the lead vocal, with Took alone introducing that easily misheard first line. Previously undocumented outtakes show that the first four takes of the song were recorded with Took alone handling the vocals, though by the fifth and final take, Marc had changed his mind prompting the compromise that can be heard on the released record.

According to David Platz, Steve Took was someone who "floated more than walked". Certainly the percussionist's love of excess was in marked contrast to Bolan's restraint, but it was the lack of professionalism that resulted from Took's recklessness which most bothered Marc. After all, in spite of the cool hippie demeanour, Bolan had been encouraging fans to clap along at concerts ever since a performance at the Royal Albert Hall in June 1968. (He could be partially excused – it was to help him keep time during an a cappella performance of 'Scenescof Dynasty'.)

Took's grievances were of the usual power struggle variety common to those who feel their contributions have been unduly restricted or, worse still, ignored. His harmonies were strange, compelling and technically accomplished, his percussion flurries inventive and teetering on the manic, and lately he'd been expanding his role as a multi-instrumentalist. Now, Took wanted a larger slice of the action, demanding that Tyrannosaurus Rex record his songs and allow him the occasional vocal. This did not sit easily with Bolan's understanding of the group's internal politics.

Tyrannosaurus Rex material was conceived in Toadstool Studios, the fittingly named patch of floor-space Marc had cordoned off in his flat to enable him to write and play undisturbed. The songs, which, Marc claimed, sometimes came courtesy of his Guardian Angel, were his prerogative; it was Took's job to garnish Bolan's basic melodies and tempos with suitable percussion and harmony parts – preferably with a minimum of fuss. During the early stages of the group, this subordinate role hadn't been a problem for Took, who was younger and had little experience of the pop world. To Simon Napier-Bell, Took was "a bit of a yes-man; he got the hash, lit the joss sticks, carried the carpet", but once he realised that his own songwriting ambitions would find no outlet within the group, frustration set in. A close friend in whom Took confided maintains that, "Marc seemed to be some kind of power maniac who only wanted his own songs recorded. I think Tony Visconti tried to encourage Steve to contribute more but Marc wouldn't have it."

The friend, who prefers to remain unnamed, maintains that at one time there was a strong bond between the pair. "Marc and Steve were incredibly close, and despite the bitterness, you could still sense that years later. When Steve talked about Tyrannosaurus Rex, it was always with a mixture of real love and a feeling of hurt and anger at being rejected, but it was largely his own fault." The key to the problem, she insists, was drugs. "Basically, he took too many, though he functioned better on acid than most people did. Because he took so much of it, he became slightly immune to its effects."

His immunity to Marc's delusions of grandeur was somewhat less effective. "Steve was often cited as the quiet one of the group, but he was very charismatic," says his not so public defender. "People either loved him or hated him. He'd get right up people's noses so they'd end up wanting to kill him. Marc and Steve could both be difficult people, so it's no wonder they clashed."

With Marc remaining close to June, and Steve pursuing an itinerant existence, the two unequal halves of Tyrannosaurus Rex rarely met socially. While their early companionship may have waned, until that cataclysmic spring of '69 the relationship hadn't soured completely. When, for example, Steve was busted for possession of drugs, Marc and June were incredibly supportive, hiring a top lawyer and hiding their friend's hippie demeanour for the court appearance, kitting him out in a blue pin-stripe suit and stuffing his long hair down the neck of his shirt. On this occasion, the moral support and image management was in vain and Steve was briefly packed off to a remand home, an institution not generally suited to sensitive, vegetarian types. Recalling the episode, Visconti insists that, "Marc treated Steve with great love."

135

The producer was also aware of Steve Took's musical aspirations but maintains he was more "supporter than creator. He worked out his own backing vocals and they were chromatic, really quite ingenious. His voice was probably more sophisticated than Marc's. But his songwriting left a little to be desired," says the producer. "He slept over my place on occasion and we'd do some of his songs but they were awful. He wanted equal say on the albums, and I think Marc was quite justified in sacking him."

It seems that Took was on his way by the middle of the year, though the pair agreed to undertake a long planned tour of America before making the break official. "He wanted to burn down the city and put acid in the waterways," Marc recalled in September 1971. "We agreed to break up, but we were legally tied to do our first American tour. We did do it, but it was a shambles." It was also an essential stepping stone. The US visit had been announced back in March 1969, and Marc was keen to fulfil the dates. After all, an earlier attempt to take Tyrannosaurus Rex to the States had been mooted the previous August, but the planned September tour of US colleges with Pink Floyd fell through and the duo were packed off for a short trip to Germany instead.

The projected May tour was set in motion by Steve O'Rourke from the Bryan Morrison Agency, supposedly in conjunction with Blue Thumb, the group's new American outlet and home to fellow Peel favourites Captain Beefheart & His Magic Band and Love. The original intention was an exchange visit that would take Tyrannosaurus Rex, Pink Floyd and Aynsley Dunbar's Retaliation to the States, and bring Love, Captain Beefheart and The Byrds to Britain. After first being postponed to June 15, Marc and Steve eventually set off with road manager Mick O'Halloran on August 6 on an exchange that brought Bob Dylan over to Britain for the Isle of Wight Festival at the end of that month.

Marc outlined his aspirations for the tour in an interview with John Peel circulated on a promotional 45 in advance of the visit. "I want to play to people there with a quieter thing," he said in a delicate tone that belied his East End upbringing. At the same time, this English man of peace spoke of performing "with an excitement which equals rock'n'roll but doesn't have any of the violent feelings. If people dance or move about or scratch at the air, it's because they want to and because they're enjoying the music as music, not as a theme to violence."

While Tyrannosaurus Rex were being packed off to the hippie heartlands, Marc was well aware that America – the land of Mighty Joe Young, Elvis, Davy Crockett, James Dean and numerous other childhood fantasies – was by 1969 in the midst of a violent upheaval. A significant minority of the nation's youth seized the moral initiative, exposing the racism, imperial ambition, consumer madness and spiritual bankruptcy at the core of the nation. Assassinations, riots and combative demonstrations were ripping the country asunder. Marc, who had quietly banished social concerns from his mind after his momentary flirtation with CND and protest songs in the mid–Sixties, imagined he'd bring a green and pleasant vibe to a distressed nation, hoping at the same time to emulate the success Donovan had enjoyed there.

The six-week tour, which took in around 25 club and support dates plus a couple of mid-table pop festivals, confirmed the breakdown of Marc's relationship with Steve Took. However, any hopes of breaking Bolan in the States were dashed by indifference and that summer's major talking points – the moon landing, Woodstock and the Tate-LaBianca murders.

Things didn't go to plan from the start; Steve Took failing to rise from his bed on the morning of the departure was an early omen. According to the August Tyrannosaurus Rex newsletter: "Even on the day they had to catch their plane, we could not get Steve to answer the phone. Eventually, after persistent telephone calls, we sent Ron (the roadie) around to his pad with instructions that, if necessary, he was to throw a brick through the window to arouse Steve from his slumbers, which bear some resemblance to a coma. However, bricks were not necessary as the window was open and Ron squeezed in, and with the application of some force, was able to shake Steve back to consciousness and reality."

Took began as he meant to go on. "During that disastrous tour of the States, he was constantly supplied with acid and was really out of it," says a friend.

After touching down in Los Angeles on August 6, the pair motored up the coast to Hippie Central San Francisco for three shows as third on the bill to Berkeley luminaries Country Joe & The Fish. "Lovely" was Marc's back of a postcard verdict, though he was even more enamoured of Los Angeles when the duo returned there for three nights at Thee Experience. "We're going to buy a house in Los Angeles with Aynsley Dunbar and Pink Floyd," Marc told one local interviewer, adding that he would like to divide 🌸 time between London and California. "Things are so different here. In Los Angeles, there is an open invitation from the underground stations to go into the studios and talk and play when you want. Can you imagine that ever happening in England?" Or Arkansas?

By the time Tyrannosaurus Rex were tucked away in the Drake Hotel[*] in New York by the third week of August, Bolan had changed his tune. "John, we're terribly homesick," he complained in a postcard to his DJ pal. "It's such a strange alien country . . . We hate New York." However, the earnest receptions and string of well-meaning interviewers gave Marc some cause for optimism. "The gigs are going well and in time I think it will be very big," he added.

Reviewing the last of a three-night residency at the Café Au Go Go on Bleecker Street in Greenwich Village, *Billboard*'s Fred Kirby was clear about the group's cultish appeal. "Tyrannosaurus Rex, one of today's most unusual acts . . . might not appeal to all tastes with their distinctive vocalising, but their effect is telling on those who dig them . . . The effect can be spellbinding." He was one of only a handful to file a review from the tour, though Marc did give several interviews, most notably to Dave Marsh, then contributing to the independent, influential *Creem* magazine based in Detroit.

Marsh was treated to an impeccable display of 'Bolanchild' at his dreamy, dove-like best. "I draw much of the things I use from the dawn of time," he insisted. "I believe that man, when he was first, was truly first, had a golden age . . . when he had complete control, mentally and physically, of his body and of nature." A Rousseau-like champion of unfettered man in harmony with the natural world, Marc attempted to sell the hippie dream back to the States. "I only ever do things that are true completely," he claimed. "Guiltless things. This is a callous world, an unbelieving world, a very harsh world. Most anything that is tender and real is suspect." Even the falling out with Steve was transformed into a wondrous thing: "We're breaking up in two weeks' time. Not breaking up . . . Steve's gonna leave and do other things. I have someone else I'm gonna work with. But it's cool. It's nice, really."

In another Stateside interview, given to *Circus* magazine, Bolan declared, "I don't want to know about society as it is – it brings me down," then provided a thumbnail sketch of the Utopia he yearned for. "I wish I could get away to another place where mountains rise unspoilt to the sky and you could ride horses as far as the eye can see," he mused.

Effortlessly switching from spiritual to material matters, Marc raved about the musical changes he'd recently undergone, declaring somewhat

[*] Marc and June were offended by the grubbiness of the infamous Chelsea Hotel, Took remembered sarcastically.

prematurely that "we are completely electric now – soft electronics that is . . . somewhere between The Kinks and The Incredible String Band." Despite his impeccable hippie charm and lofty ideals, he also boldly claimed he was "a pop writer" but that nobody recognised him as one. "I can't see it when people say they can't understand our music – there is nothing to stop them," he complained. "The songs are agreeable melodies with nice words." Of the future, he was decidedly upbeat. "I want to learn more about music. I can hear things in my head which I can't express yet," he said. Bolan was abroad; Took was going overboard; and creatively Tyrannosaurus Rex were all at sea. "I don't know what direction we're going in," Marc admitted, "just that we are completely free."

After a couple of dates in Chicago, where the small entourage visited a temple and stayed at the Tides Motel, Tyrannosaurus Rex moved on to New Orleans and Houston, Texas at the end of August, where they appeared alongside many of the top West Coast bands at two open-air festivals (a provisional booking for the earlier Woodstock Festival had fallen through). Marc expressed his disappointment at some of the established acts such as Jefferson Airplane, Grateful Dead, The Byrds and Janis Joplin, but left raving about the lesser known It's A Beautiful Day and Santana.

It's A Beautiful Day, the floaty 'Frisco outfit that shared a vague musical affinity with Tyrannosaurus Rex, headlined the final shows of the duo's summer '69 US tour in Seattle on September 19 and 20. But the only friends Marc picked up during this first Stateside visit were Howard Kaylan and Mark Volman. The pair were singers with The Turtles, who'd started out as Byrds-inspired folk-rockers before making a successful cross-over into cheery harmony pop during 1967 and 1968 with a succession of hits including 'Happy Together', 'She'd Rather Be With Me' and 'Elenore'. Musically, The Turtles were way off Bolan's track, although the Americans had belatedly embraced psychedelia with the Ray Davies-produced *Turtle Soup* album.

Bolan met Kaylan and Volman at an aftershow party in Detroit where Tyrannosaurus Rex had supported The Turtles. It was the Englishman's wit – not something that Marc was particularly renowned for – that endeared him to the Americans, who promised to pay Marc and June a visit when they were next in London. Contrary to Marc's benevolent hippie image, Howard Kaylan explained that the friendship was based on a competitive kind of conceit. "Marc isn't one of the most humble guys we've ever met," he said a couple of years later, "but neither are we, so that gives us a really good rapport." According to Tony Visconti, the mere presence of Kaylan and Volman would inspire an abundance of Jewish humour that Marc revelled in. Out of this humour came the pair's assertion that Bolan was nothing more than a "cosmic punk", a name that Marc would identify with increasingly in years to come.

In September 1969, though, Steve Took could probably rightly lay claim to such an epithet. Cosmic thanks to the hallucinogenic holiday he'd enjoyed abroad, punkish because he wrecked some of the concerts by removing his clothes on stage and performing bloody-minded acts of musical sabotage; Took had simply gone too far. If Marc Bolan was to fulfil the ambitions that filled his head, it was clear that he could do without his incapacitated, self-destructive companion.

Three years after the split, by which time he'd become more cosmic and punk-like than ever, Took gave his side of the story. "I was a flower child," he said, "and there are things that a flower child can't do. Being a natural born rebel, I wanted to do all the things I was meant not to do. That caused a lot of raps with the management and a lot of raps with Marc." Although an air of innocence and independence enveloped the group, Took had sensed little of it, finding himself cowed by Marc's ego and barricaded by management diktats. "I was getting really shat on by them," he said. "A typical thing was when I used to go out and jam occasionally with The Deviants and The Pretty Things, the management would come and say, 'Boy, don't go and jam with this group, it's bad for the image.' And I'd go, 'What image? I'm Steve Took, well-known drug addict.'"

A Blue Thumb press release suggested that Took left to form The Pink Fairies All-Star Motorcycle Club and Rock and Roll Band. Took later insisted that he'd stuck to his hippie roots: "Basically, all I want to do is sit under an orange tree, play my guitar in the sun, get stoned and dig the smells and colours," he said with a hint of wistfulness. Marc rarely mentioned his ex-partner again, though in February 1972 he claimed that he "was never excited that much about Steve's drumming. The one thing he did really well was sing. He was a very good singer; he really had harmony."

Steve Peregrine Took may not have handled a full kit with too much subtlety, but there was no doubt that he was the most inventive percussionist Marc Bolan ever had.

* * *

Bolan wasted little time in looking for a new partner. On October 4, 1969, a boxed advert simply headed 'Tyrannosaurus Rex' appeared in

Melody Maker: "Wanted to work with T. Rex a gentle young guy who can play percussion, i.e. Bongos and Drum Kit, some Bass Guitar and Vocal Harmony. Photos please. Box 8679."

The 300 or so replies piled up undisturbed, because through Pete Sanders in the upstairs flat, Marc had been introduced to a good-looking young painter/would-be musician with an appealing, unlikely name — Mickey Finn.

Most among Marc's immediate circle of friends were known by various *noms de plume* – John Peel, Steve Peregrine Took, Jeff Dexter, even Howard Kaylan and Mark Volman ('Flo and Eddie') were every bit as fictional as Marc Bolan. June Child had been an unlikely exception; so too was Mickey Finn. His name may have been a euphemism for a spiked alcoholic drink, but it was his own.

Michael Norman Finn was born in Thornton Heath, Surrey on June 3, 1947, and attended All Saints Primary and Rockmount Secondary Schools, neither of which had dampened his passion for rock'n'roll or for painting. Like Marc, he'd grown up idolising far off Fifties figures such as Elvis Presley and Gene Vincent before switching his allegiance to group sounds with the arrival of The Beatles and The Rolling Stones. After leaving school, he attended Croydon College of Art, and spent most weekends at the Orchid Ballroom, Purley, where he first met fellow scenemakers Pete Sanders and Jeff Dexter. After a year at college, he quit so that he could earn money to purchase his first motorbike.

In an echo of Marc Feld's teenage cravings, the finely chiselled Finn enrolled with Mark Palmer's English Boy Model Agency, which enabled him to flirt on the fringes of London's fashionable set. But by 1967 formal modelling was unhip. The streets – King's Road and Portobello Road in particular – were the new hippie catwalks, and Finn instead found irregular employment with Michael English and Nigel Waymouth (who traded as Hapshash & The Coloured Coat), helping them to paint an Art Nouveau-inspired mural at their Granny Takes a Trip boutique in the King's Road.

"I used to do painting, scenic painting and shop fronts," Finn remembers. "I had a good name. I had The Beatles under my belt because I did their clothes shop, the Apple boutique in Baker Street. I was making a reasonable living doing murals and things. I had a couple of guys working for me at the time I met Marc, so it wasn't like I was on the breadline."

Mickey Finn's entry into Tyrannosaurus Rex was fittingly gentle. "I think Mickey was coming round to visit me," says Pete Sanders, "and somehow he got introduced to Marc, told him he liked getting quietly stoned and banging away on the bongos. The next thing I knew he was part of the band and they were practising away together downstairs." Marc once claimed that Nigel Waymouth recommended Mickey Finn to him, though Jeff Dexter corroborates Sanders' version, and pinpoints exactly why Mickey was drafted into the band. "He looked great and he said yes to everything Marc wanted. He could hardly sing or play, but he had a wonderful character and a great feel for what Marc was doing at the time."

At some point, Marc and Mickey arranged to meet in the Seed restaurant in Bishop's Bridge Road a short distance from Blenheim Crescent, where they discussed the vacancy over a macrobiotic meal. "I was amazed at how much energy he had," Mickey remembers. "We got on like a house on fire." Bolan turned up wearing a multicoloured patch waistcoat fringed with long tassles, green girls' shoes and a cascading crown of Pre-Raphaelite hair. Mickey Finn, five-foot eight with long straight hair and the incipient stubble of a beard, made a fine partner – visually, at least.

From the cheap seats, it looked like nothing had changed, just as Marc had intended. Tyrannosaurus Rex remained a two-piece, consisting of a singing, guitar-playing frontman and a subordinate bongo player. Musically, however, there were obvious differences. Finn's grasp of the laws of vocal harmony was poor, and his proficiency as a percussionist questionable, as he readily admits. "I just used to play for my own satisfaction. I had no intention of picking up percussion instruments. I used to knock the shit out of somebody's chests at the bottom of a bed. They just bought me a pair of clay bongos and I just carried on."

But there were distinct advantages. There was no suggestion that the affable, easy-going Mickey Finn would ever question Marc's authority. And besides, as Tony Visconti maintains, "Mickey Finn was instantly likeable, had a great sense of humour and was a breath of fresh air after Steve who was very heavy. But I immediately assessed that he wasn't anywhere near as good as Steve." That was of little concern to Bolan. By late 1969, he was busy tinkering with the basics of Tyrannosaurus Rex; the technical deficiency of his new, good-looking, easygoing sidekick was of little consequence.

Took's departure gave Marc the opportunity to rethink the entire Tyrannosaurus Rex project and its place in the fast-changing rock market. After years of stylistic shifts and musical fads, he'd found stability and established some roots of his own in the tolerant climes of late Sixties hippie culture. His poetic and musical reveries were given room to flourish, and there was a ready-made audience eager to listen. But now, with the end of the decade weeks away, minds were concentrated on old eras closing and new dawns beginning. It was obvious that the 'anything goes' tolerance of the underground was in retreat, that the musical ambition unlocked by *Sgt. Pepper*, the development of studio technology and those uncritical, stoned audiences were coalescing around new, niche market formulas.

Rock music seemed to lose some of its flamboyance as it withdrew into an increasingly isolated, self-satisfied world of studios and stadia. The collectivist anthems of peace (The Beatles' 'All You Need Is Love', The Youngbloods' 'Get Together') and revolutionary activism (Jefferson Airplane's 'We Can Be Together') were ousted as a new catchphrase took hold: 'The Personal Is Political'. Hippie idealism had been discredited as bogus and ineffective. "Everyone dressed up but nothing changed," spat John Lennon bitterly. Instead, sincerity seekers turned to a new generation of singer-songwriters, tortured troubadours such as Cat Stevens, Leonard Cohen, Joni Mitchell, James Taylor and Neil Young, most of whom followed Dylan's lead. Marc's suggestion that rock musicians were merely components of a towering edifice known as Bob Dylan, which he'd made 12 months earlier, had been satisfyingly prescient. Not that he was about to join them. He couldn't anyway. Disrobing his soul in public just wasn't his style.

The quest for 'authenticity' also manifested itself in the search for roots, another Dylan-prompted pursuit inspired by two 1968 albums – Dylan's own *John Wesley Harding*, and *Music From Big Pink*, the first record by his backing group The Band. While the music of black America had engineered the slow transformation from 'Rock Around The Clock' into the Woodstock Nation's reinterpretation of 'The Star-Spangled Banner' (courtesy of Jimi Hendrix), country music remained the forgotten element of those early Presley, Carl Perkins and Jerry Lee Lewis sides. Dylan's duet with Johnny Cash in 1969 on *Nashville Skyline* symbolised his return from art rock extravagance into a recognised tradition, and a new-fangled country rock was patented by The Band, and taken up by numerous American groups in need of a soft landing after overdosing on stoned improvisations.

Neither properly took root in Britain, where its own indigenous tradition – Celtic and folkish – was eclipsed by a distinctly European classical approach that privileged technique over history. Gifted musicians formed 'supergroups', every blues and hard rock band had its own guitar hero (and, often, a bass and drum darling too), and a most extraordinary contest was set in motion to become 'progressive', a word that suggested superhuman ability and classically inclined aspiration.

Marc Bolan reflected the mood of these times but he managed to remain detached from it. He was earnest: "Most rock musicians really care and are desperately trying to say something," he said early in 1970. He even respected tradition of a kind: "The music of T. Rex (his abbreviation) is about what's around us, which has been there for thousands of years but which for the past hundred or so has been neglected. My way of expressing it is through pop music." But above all, Marc was idiosyncratic; his small cult of personality and his unique, Lilliputian music that was neither folk nor rock, adrift on a magic carpet ride all of its own.

There was still a place for Marc Bolan amid these changes – he was, after all, a changeling of the first order – but he was unwilling to gamble with sales of around 20,000 per album to make any monumental shifts. On his return from America, though prior to Mickey Finn's arrival, Marc recoiled from the threshold of freedom he'd been telling US writers about and admitted to Chris Welch that, "There won't be a new direction . . . Tyrannosaurus Rex is still a very young thing and although it has gone electric, it will still be much softer and more harmonious than most groups."

Even in the face of increasing public apathy for hippiefied 45s, Tyrannosaurus Rex had always issued singles. But now, Bolan clearly found that corner of the market frustrating. "Forget England for singles," he complained. "People keep telling me to make singles and we always get good reviews. But John Peel is the only DJ who will play us here – and Alan Freeman." As for the emerging hard rock sound, Marc contrasted his own destiny with that of Steve Took, whom he said was "wanting to get into this heavier group thing with Twink from The Pink Fairies". Meanwhile, Marc and Mickey Finn headed for the countryside.

Plas Tan Y Bwlch, a mansion house set in huge grounds in the heart of the Snowdonia National Park, north Wales, provided a perfect autumn refuge. Installed in a nearby cottage, Marc unwound from the traumas of America, Mickey was shown how to tap meaningfully and in time, June ensured the bonding process went smoothly and Tyrannosaurus Rex emerged with enough material for a new album. They'd also reworked the live set so they could hit the British concert circuit and replenish the fast depleting Bolan coffers.

It wasn't Marc's first visit to wildest Wales, a land so rich in legend and mystery that a red dragon motif appears on its national flag. Marc and June favoured this north-west corner of Wales, with Portmeirion, the fairytale village used for the filming of the 1967 television series *The Prisoner*, and Harlech (home to Lord Harlech, father of June's friend Alice Ormsby-Gore), both within easy reach. There was no electricity so Marc chopped wood for the open fire. There was little sound bar the babbling of brooks and the bleating of sheep, so the London-born Larry the Lamb sang his songs on the foothills of the mountains. Hackney seemed miles – centuries – away and a part of Marc was temporarily seduced by the lifestyle. On a postcard from an earlier visit, he had written: "People wear peace, deep green peace as a halo here."

Back in London, his thoughts swung pendulum-like away from the calming influence of landscape, folklore and wildlife as his ego – replenished and perhaps a little more rabid – sought to rescue Tyrannosaurus Rex from the brink of oblivion. With Steve Took flat on his back somewhere in Ladbroke Grove, Marc now lacked a demon figure, someone onto whom he could project his frustrations. Conveniently, on January 8, 1970, Tony Visconti invited him along to a session he was producing. It was for the next David Bowie single.

For five years, Bowie had tried his hand at virtually everything – fronting R&B groups, folksinging, film acting, cabaret-style songs, scriptwriting, Buddhism, mime, UFO spotting, even advertising ice-lollies. To his manager/mentor Kenneth Pitt he was a genius in waiting, and no matter how many times his charge was dropped by a record company Pitt was unwavering in that belief. So too was Bowie, whose never-say-die attitude finally paid off in October 1969 when 'Space Oddity' gave him the hit he'd long coveted.

The recent death of his father and his spell as an Arts Lab activist had tempered Bowie's attitude towards pop stardom. Late in 1969, he cited Marc as "a great influence on me, not so much with his music, but with his attitude to the pop scene. He shuts himself off from the destructive elements and prefers to get on with his work. That's how I intend to be."

This graft and endeavour attitude towards his career meant that, even on his 23rd birthday, Bowie preferred to labour through the night if it meant bagging the appropriate follow-up to 'Space Oddity'. Two songs were up for consideration – 'London Bye Ta Ta' and 'The Prettiest Star'. "Initially, we recorded them with an all-black band called Gass," says the producer, who remembers backing vocalists Sue & Sunny and Lesley Duncan also being at the session. "When they left, I replaced the bass part, then I asked Marc – who was just starting to play electric – to record a guitar part.

"He came in and it was daggers. Everyone's having a good time, and Marc comes in and the atmosphere just chilled up. I gave him a tape to rehearse with and he came up with this beautiful solo guitar line. By the end he was having a good time. But then, as Marc is packing up, June viciously turns on David and says, 'This song is crap. The best thing about it is Marc's guitar,' and the two of them walk out. June went through this period of viciousness." It was an unhappy conclusion to Bolan and Bowie's only fruitful studio collaboration, a melancholy-tinged hymn to celebrity featuring London's premier curly-topped stargazers. Worse still, the single flopped.*

In a short piece in an American magazine, published towards the end of 1969, David claimed that, "Marc Bolan . . . is the only friend I have in the business." However, recalling the night twenty years later, he admitted, "There was quite a lot of rivalry between Marc and myself. We had a sparring relationship. We both knew we were going to do something in the future, but he was a few rungs up – he was really starting to happen . . . I don't think we were talking to each other that day. I can't remember why, but I remember a very strange attitude in the studio. We were never in the same room at the same time. You could have cut the atmosphere with a knife."

"That rivalry – as well as a mutual admiration – was there from the beginning," says Tony Visconti, who has worked extensively with both. The pair met infrequently during the mid-Sixties while hustling in and around Denmark Street, though it was the producer who brought them together socially. "I started inviting them round to my flat," Visconti remembers, "because I had a gramophone and they didn't. They were both living at their mums' at the time." Marc and David would occasionally jam together, but the trio's main preoccupation was "to get high and listen to Beach Boys and Phil Spector albums.

"We weren't big *Pet Sounds* fans. *Smiley Smile* and *Wild Honey* were the ones we used to sing along with. We used to play 'Vegetables' over and over. We also noted that on 'Heroes And Villains', every time the word 'villains' was sung, it would be obliterated by a loud whistle. We speculated that there was some spiritual significance in that. Hey, come on, it

---

* It's worth noting that Marc's solo was copied note-for-note by Mick Ronson when the song was re-recorded for Bowie's 1973 *Aladdin Sane* album.

was the Sixties!" The producer also remembers the photo shoot at Hermione Farthingale's family home. "I set it up, but they never even spoke to David or thanked Hermione for the use of her parents' garden. The rivalry was always there."

That antagonism was intensified by the many parallels in their lives since the pair loitered in obscurity, Mark Feld in Stamford Hill and Wimbledon, and David Jones in the south-east London suburb of Bromley. Like Marc, David had played skiffle as a schoolboy, became a teenage dandy and declared on leaving school that he was going to become a singer. He also started his professional career at Decca in the mid-Sixties, and underwent an exotic name change, his surname deriving from a knife that graced many Hollywood westerns including, of course, those early Davy Crockett movies.

Neither singer allowed rejection and failure to get the better of their determination and self-belief, and by 1966, both had fallen into the arms of managers eager to share their aspirations. Simon Napier-Bell listened attentively while Marc dreamed aloud; Bowie had Kenneth Pitt campaigning on his behalf. While Bolan struggled with some poor early publishing deals, Bowie beat him to a deal with Essex Music, signed in December 1966. It wasn't particularly lucrative — he received an advance of £500 for the first year, rising to £1,500 in 1968 — but the association with Essex put Bowie in contact with Tony Visconti, who befriended the young songwriter after Denny Cordell had turned him down for New Breed.

Visconti produced 'Let Me Sleep Beside You' and 'Karma Man' for Bowie at Advision on September 1, 1967, but this projected single was shelved and there were no more David Bowie records until 1969. Like Marc, though, he found an outlet on Radio 1 and Tony Visconti was brought in as Musical Director on some of these BBC session recordings. While one of his few champions, John Peel remembers the late Sixties Bowie as, "not a joke exactly but a chap who was full of extraordinary ideas and notions, none of which seemed very likely to ever come to fruition".

George Underwood has confirmed that, during this period, he and his odd-eyed pal from Bromley were, like Bolan, "never into drugs and booze – we were stoned on imagination". Inevitably, then, Bowie – who fully embraced the Romantic notion of the all-creative artist by taking up mime, dance and acting – though more wary of the counterculture than Marc ever was, was sufficiently inspired by its anti-materialism to look

Eastwards, taking a keen interest in Tibetan culture and philosophy.

For all these shared referents, until the night when Visconti brought them together for 'The Prettiest Star', there had been no notable collaborations. However, Steve Took did contribute some impromptu backing vocals to Bowie's May 26, 1968 *Top Gear* session. "He slept on my floor the night before and came along to the session the next day for the fun of it," Visconti recalls. "I have a clear vision of David, Steve and myself standing around a microphone and adding various 'oohs', 'aahs' and hand-claps on those tracks." Took is particularly prominent on the falsetto "slow down" harmony on 'Karma Man' and can be heard droning at the beginning of 'Silly Boy Blue'.

When 'Space Oddity' made its slow ascent up the singles chart on the back of the NASA moon landing in July 1969, Marc felt a mixture of vindication and discomfort. For when Bowie first played him the song in demo form, Bolan's response was an ecstatic "It's going to be a hit, Davie!" His judgement was better than his producer's – Tony Visconti disliked the song so much he declined to work on it and fellow New Breed producer Gus Dudgeon duly stepped in to claim the glory.

Marc's enthusiasm for 'Space Oddity' dampened once he started to read the kind of press Bowie was attracting towards the end of the year. "If he reminds you of anyone," wrote Penny Valentine in October, "it is a gentle mixture of Bob Dylan and Donovan with 90% pure (himself). He says he sings like Dylan would have done if he'd been born in England — and he's an absolute charmer. His charm is so overpowering that it has given him more freedom to achieve his ideals than you would have thought in this day and age." This flattering portrait of David Bowie could easily have been written about Marc – but it wasn't.

The success of 'Space Oddity' was probably responsible for Marc and June's uncharacteristically bad behaviour at the session for 'The Prettiest Star'. According to Visconti, "Marc was in rivalry with everybody. He simply couldn't stand attention going in anyone else's direction. He was a total megalomaniac, God bless him. David, on the other hand, is a very gregarious, open-minded person, and apart from a normal, healthy type of rivalry, he was never obsessed with Bolan. David always loved Marc. He loved to be with him. He would come home after a social session with Marc feeling quite hurt after Bolan had taken too many digs at him."

On the night of January 8, 1970, the birthday boy must have wanted to swallow the words he'd just sung, ostensibly directed at his new girl-friend Angie but which could just as easily have applied to his irascible guest: "One day, tho' it might as well be someday/You and I will rise up all the way/All because of what you are/The Prettiest Star." Tony Visconti suggests that the balance of power was never quite what it seemed. "Yes, Bowie was openly in awe, always very respectful and affectionately called him a cosmic punk. He made all the effort to become Marc's friend, but it was Marc who was covertly in awe of Bowie. He secretly admired him." It was an admiration that rankled all the more once the stakes were raised.

Another friend of Marc's also enjoyed a flicker of fame during 1969. That was Marsha Hunt, whose extraordinary take on Dr. John's 'Walk On Gilded Splinters' had given her a minor chart hit in May. Tony Visconti was slated to work with her and, he remembers, "She showed up one night while we were recording *Unicorn*. By chance, it was the one night June wasn't there." Marc stood transfixed. "The two of them just looked at each other and it was like magic. You could see the shafts of light pouring out of their eyes into each other. They were eating each other up alive. We finished the session unusually early, and Marc and Marsha walked out into the night hand in hand. He said, 'See you tomorrow, Tony,' and gave me a wink. He'd never behaved like that before. It was a total shock to me."

Although their affair was short-lived, Marsha Hunt was sufficiently impressed by Marc's songs to record four of them that spring.* "Marsha loved 'Hot Rod Mama'," Visconti recalls, and the song duly appeared – as 'Hot Rod Pappa' – on the flip of 'Gilded Splinters' – itself eerily reminiscent of Marc's 'Hippy Gumbo'. 'Desdemona' and 'Hippy Gumbo' were coupled for her next single, and with 'Stacey Grove' (featuring woodwind mimicking Marc's voice), turned up on her *Woman Child* album, issued on Track (with Visconti sharing production credits with Gus Dudgeon and Kit Lambert) in 1971. Marc later put in an early guest appearance on Marsha's version of The Supremes' 'My World Is Empty Without You', bleating a brief line ("Hickory Dickory Dock, the mouse ran up the clock") from a children's nursery rhyme.

Like Marc, Marsha was young and gifted. Unlike him, she was a black American with a good academic record and a tendency to court controversy, first as a cast member of the so-called hippie musical *Hair*, then when one of her breasts popped out on *Top Of The Pops* and later as the mother of Mick Jagger's daughter Karis. In her fringed jacket, leather

---

* She wasn't the first to cover his work, though. That honour goes to French singer Sylvie Vartan, who had recorded 'Beyond The Risin' Sun' in the mid-Sixties.

pants, thigh-length boots, hula-hoop earrings and wild afro hair, she turned more heads than he did, too.

Marsha claims in her autobiography, *Real Life*, that there was more to the relationship than physical attraction. "I personified things which Marc rejected," she writes. "He was reclusive, macrobiotic, and professed aversion to success. He had no money and acted as though he was opposed to it on social grounds. Maybe his choosing to be with me was an indication that he was changing." While Marc was still looking towards Poon on his mantelpiece for inspiration, he teased Marsha about her success. "I almost believed he spurned it, except he brought it up too much . . ." He was, she insists, a self-professed cultist. "To Marc, my visibility was commercial, and this wasn't appropriate to the serious art of music which he implied was validated by obscurity. (But) his undercover enthusiasm for The Ronettes and Melangian girl group vocals made his protestations about pop and rock success seem hypocritical."

Marc seemed to have a strange effect on young black actress/singers with a track record in *Hair*. During the 1969 Tyrannosaurus Rex tour of America, Marc and Steve attended a party in Los Angeles thrown by Miss Mercy of the infamous, Frank Zappa-sponsored all-girl groupie rock band The GTO's (Girls Together Outrageously). Also there was Cincinatti-born singer Gloria Jones, cast member of the Los Angeles production of *Hair*.

"Jobriath was the one who introduced me to Marc," she says. "He was in *Hair*, too, and he came to the dressing-room and said you've gotta go to this party; Tyrannosaurus Rex are over from England. I didn't know who they were. I was in theatre. I'd been in Jack Good's *Catch My Soul* and in *Revolutions*. I was sitting at the piano singing and playing when Marc came in. He went to the back of the house, where Jobriath's timid Afghan dog was. Marc and the dog didn't get along. Apparently, he said the dog was trying to smell his balls! He kicked the shit out of this dog, you know. I went out back and I said, 'Do you always do that?' That was the first encounter."

Dog-kicking, professional jealousy, a clandestine affair – Marc's near religious adherence to hippie cool was showing signs of weakening. Breaking that precious, unspoken bond with June hurt remorse-filled Marc. His partner's forgive-and-forget attitude only served to remind him that she was the one with reserves of inner strength. When June found out, she turned up on Marsha's doorstep and cleared the air. Marc flagellated himself emotionally to such a degree that in an act of unbridled passion, he turned his back on à la mode sexual mores forever and asked for her hand in marriage.

It was a spur-of-the-moment decision and, having notified the local Kensington Registry Office a couple of days earlier, Marc and June took their matrimonial vows on Friday January 30, 1970. Just five close friends were invited along – Mickey Finn and his girlfriend Sue Worth, Jeff Dexter (in a three-quarter length fur coat), and witnesses Alice Ormsby-Gore and Pete Sanders. After posing outside for a few photographs, Marc impishly delighted and with his hair flecked with confetti, June, vaguely art deco in her crocheted cloche hat, and the revellers celebrated with a meal and too many drinks. Sid and Phyllis Feld found out about Marc's marriage some time later, but they'd long known that their second son had a habit of doing things very much his own way.

7

Almost Grown

" 'Be like you could' all my friends say."
— Marc Bolan, 'Summer Deep' (December 1970)

"The ego pop things are a drag. You can't believe all that stuff – no one's that important. Marc Bolan as a plastic cut-out has got to be a drag."
— Marc Bolan, *Zigzag* magazine (March 1970)

"The credibility of the band was lessened by the fact that people associated us with Flower Power, and that was a long gone era. I wanted people to look at the thing in a new light, and the only way to do that was to have a label change, and change the music, and change the name, but not lose any identity either way."
— Marc Bolan, *Creem* magazine (1972)

With the tortured howl of a fuzzed-up electric guitar still ringing in his ears, John Peel got up from his perch beside the small stage and made his way towards the microphone. Tyrannosaurus Rex had just finished performing 'Elemental Child', one of a batch of new songs destined for the duo's imminent fourth album, and the DJ was thunderstruck by the six-minute electric storm he'd just witnessed. "Scotty Moore would be proud of you," he said, knowing Marc would be thrilled by the comparison with the guitar legend who had energised the early Presley sides.

It was New Year's Day, traditionally the most relaxed day in the annual calendar, and Marc Bolan, erstwhile sprinkler of sonic fairydust, was on his feet and performing guitar god heroics on his Fender Stratocaster. The concert, at BBC's Paris Studios in Lower Regent Street, central London, was being recorded for a new Radio 1 programme called *John Peel's Sunday Show* (forerunner of the long-running *In Concert* series). Tyrannosaurus Rex, who had played no more than half a dozen shows with Mickey Finn in the line-up, were a last-minute addition to the programme because flu-stricken Family vocalist Roger Chapman could only be expected to grind out a

30-minute performance. John Peel knew exactly who to call on to fill out the rest of the show.

"Once or twice a week, Marc comes round to Peel Acres to listen to Ricky Nelson, Gene Vincent, Elvis and James Burton's guitar work," Peel explained. But these were rock'n'rollers; the new aggression in Marc's guitar playing owed more to contemporaries such as Jimi Hendrix, Alvin Lee and Eric Clapton. It was no coincidence that in recent weeks, via June's friendship with Alice Ormsby-Gore, Marc had spent "some time" with Clapton in the Surrey retreat he shared with his fiancée. Photographs of Marc and June in Clapton's garden show Bolan with his Les Paul, which lends weight to his claim that he'd been taking lessons from the guitarist known as 'God'. Any instruction is likely to have been informal; "I sat at the feet of the Master," Marc later told Visconti.

By comparison, Marc was an entry level student, his electric soloing limited to repetitive runs through a fuzz-box which, to untrained ears, tends to make any novice sound like Hendrix. Marc's electric guitar work lacked finesse but there was something of the old Hackney audacity about his playing. 'Elemental Child', built around almost all of Bolan's favourite electric chords – E, D, A minor, C and G – consisted of two short verses. Its second part (recorded separately for the studio version) was a loud, lengthy, guitar coda in the open (and simplest) key of E that chugged and howled like a boogiefied version of the Pink Floyd's 'Interstellar Overdrive' for a cacophonous four minutes.

Far from inciting squeals of "Judas!" and other such profanities, 'Elemental Child' was greeted with keen applause during the half-hour set that had begun gently with 'Hot Rod Mama' and ended with an acoustic reworking of 'The Wizard' that, at over eight minutes, slightly outstayed its welcome. The absence of Steve Took's manic bongo-playing and maniacal vocal interjections had reduced 'Debora' and 'Hot Rod Mama' to shadows of their former glory. However, a trio of new songs – the acoustic 'Pavilions Of Sun' and 'Dove', and the electric 'By The Light Of A Magical Moon', again with a flamboyant electric coda – suggested that Bolan was now writing almost exclusively with voice and guitar in mind.

Work on the fourth Tyrannosaurus Rex album had begun on October 31, 1969, shortly before the duo completed a short British tour towards the end of November. Despite the lengthy spell in America and Took's departure, Tyrannosaurus Rex had been booked into medium-sized venues in major cities such as Newcastle, Birmingham and Manchester. However, around this time Marc also thought it prescient to turn up at the offices of *Melody Maker,* acoustic in hand, to remind journalists that he was still around. Mickey Finn's rudimentary percussion skills went unnoticed because he'd left his bongos behind, preferring to keep time by tapping his hands on a table.

A five-song session taped for *Top Gear* in November anticipated changes that were soon apparent on *A Beard Of Stars,* issued in March 1970. Marc's songs were becoming less complicated, with simplified structures, more hooks and increasingly audible lyrics. The voice and guitar were foregrounded more than before, four of the five songs featured electric guitar and one, 'Fist Heart Mighty Dawn Dart', even had a rumbling rock'n'roll bassline on the chorus.

By far the most commercial new song from the sessions was 'By The Light Of A Magical Moon', though Bolan's agnostic attitude towards the singles market allayed his disappointment when the 45 stalled in January. 'Magical Moon' was enchanting, frivolous even ("I'm a-gonna dance," the now upright Marc begins optimistically), but with little radio support and no killer hook its instant obscurity was virtually assured. The subtle, talismanic audience screams that Visconti had woven into the mix failed to work their magic.

A Beard Of Stars is probably the closest Marc Bolan ever got to making a solo album. The negligible role of Mickey Finn had something to do with it, though most telling were the arrangements, simple in essence though with neat ornamentation, the obvious result of Bolan crafting the songs on tour in America and back at 'Toadstool Studios' alone with a tape recorder. Gone was the Spectoresque production; absent too was the range of instrumentation used on *Unicorn.* Now there was even more Marc Bolan than before – multiple guitar tracks, both acoustic and electric and, critically, crisp double-tracked vocals that accentuated what was undoubtedly his greatest asset.

This gave the album an intimate, bedroom bard feel, a direct line to Bolan that was enhanced by crystal clear production and a more streamlined lyric style. Verses were shorter and often repeated, lines were more succinct and, more unusual still, words could be understood. This confidence was also reflected musically, both in the assured performances now liberated from instrumental clutter and in Marc's fast improving technique. The musical parameters had been widened, too, from the monstrous virtuosity of 'Elemental Child' to 'Dove', a sparse, plaintive love ballad that was probably as conventional as Tyrannosaurus Marc ever got.

Another sign of Bolan's musical growth was that two titles – 'Prelude' and 'A Beard Of Stars' — contained no lyrics at all.

According to the Blue Thumb publicity machine in the States, *A Beard Of Stars* was virtually an act of revolution. "Yes, the switch is on to electricity and so is Tyrannosaurus Rex. Can you imagine Marc 'The Bopping Imp' Bolan on electric guitar?" it asked. Notwithstanding the noise he'd already made with John's Children and, more recently, on the 'King Of The Rumbling Spires' single, the impression of a full conversion to electricity was misleading. While several songs on the album featured lead guitar embellishments, most of the material was still acoustic based, with only 'Pavilions Of Sun', 'The Woodland Bop' and the title track (a speeded-up instrumental that sounded like The Shadows on acid) dominated by high voltage.

Grandly dedicated to "The Priests of Peace, all Shepherds and Horse Lords and my Imperial Lore Liege — the King of the Rumbling Spires", the subject matter was much the same as before, albeit more simply wrapped. Lyrically at least, 'The Woodland Bop', 'Dove', 'Lofty Skies' and 'Dragon's Ear' (a labyrinthine piece peopled with Druids, Dworns and a witch with "a dagger on her lip") could have come from any of the previous albums. On 'Great Horse', Marc's excessive vocal gymnastics sailed remarkably close to self-parody.

'Great Horse' was one of a handful of tracks initially recorded with Steve Took, though his parts were replaced by Finn or Visconti or else mixed out completely. "Marc was terrified of paying Steve any royalties," says the producer. Took was disappointed. "I didn't like the whole scene over *A Beard Of Stars*," he complained years later. "That was a bummer." Mickey Finn certainly remembers many rehearsals during his early months in the group. "I used to spend all my time up at Marc's place just off Ladbroke Grove. He had a broom cupboard that was his recording studio at the time, and in it was a snare on a stand, percussion equipment and an acoustic guitar. We were in and out of it all day long."

Across the other side of London, in Beckenham, north Kent, David Bowie was laying the foundations for a new rock movement and ideology. On the way out were worthiness and endeavour in favour of a lighter more mischievous attitude, and the name of Bowie's new band – The Hype – said it all. Hype: the word was a stentorian profanity amid the vibey lingo of rockspeak. Hype was a curse on the scene, cheaply purchased praise that masked a woeful lack of authenticity. "I suppose you could say that I chose Hype deliberately with tongue in cheek," Bowie suggested later. Tony Visconti, now living as part of David's enlarged family in the singer's Haddon Hall flat, insists that the short-lived and little known Hype were a harbinger for Glam Rock – and he's probably right.

The group, featuring Bowie, drummer John Cambridge, new guitarist Mick Ronson and Tony Visconti on bass, followed Tyrannosaurus Rex onto Radio 1's new live concert show later that spring. A shambolic performance, the broadcast was noteworthy for a lengthy new hard rock piece, 'Width Of A Circle', a vehicle for Ronno's Jeff Beck-style guitar workouts that effectively reduced Bowie to a sideman for lengthy passages. It was an indication that the singer, for so long the centre of attraction in his single-minded quest for recognition, was content to bask in a new, more effortless form of extravagance.

The Hype's real claim to pre-Glam infamy was a show they played on February 22 at London's premier underground Mecca the Roundhouse. "We decided to dress up," Visconti recalls. "David was dressed as Rainbowman in lurex, pirate boots and with all these diaphonous scarves pinned to his clothes. I was Hypeman in a mock Superman costume with a white leotard, crocheted silver knickers and a big red cape with a collar. Ronson wore a gold lamé double-breasted suit and fedora, so he was Gangsterman. And John Cambridge was Pirateman wearing a kind of buccaneer's outfit." Someone else was also there that night.

"David showed me some photos from that gig a few years ago," Visconti continues. "He told me to look closely, and there was Marc Bolan in blue jeans and a floppy hat resting his arms on the edge of the stage watching us. We never knew he was there on the night. He wasn't into his Glam thing yet. We were!" According to Bowie, "Marc Bolan was the only person that clapped . . . He was open-mouthed that we had the balls to camp it up so much."

Although The Hype name was quietly dropped, Bowie hung on to his hard rocking combo as he continued to toy with the career he'd spent so long building up. "He was so frustrating to work with at this time," says Visconti recalling the sessions for *The Man Who Sold The World*, recorded during April and May 1970. "I couldn't handle his poor attitude and complete disregard for his music." Shortly afterwards, Visconti and Bowie went their separate ways. It was three years before they worked together again – by which time the producer was saying the same things about Marc.

Bowie was the one-hit wonder who aspired to be a latter-day Renaissance man. Marc Bolan already had a substantial cult audience but he was becoming increasingly restless. Neither could achieve what they wanted – stardom on their own terms – or determine in which direction the new cultural wind would blow. Their uncertainties were also reflected elsewhere, though it was the new apocalyptic rock of Bowie's spring 1970 sessions that best caught the mood. Unluckily for Bowie, again beset by record company problems, *The Man Who Sold The World* wasn't released in Britain until April 1971 when it was surprisingly overlooked. But an enforced change of record company had the opposite effect on Marc Bolan. Streamlining his best assets, and abandoning extraneous baggage from his past, he used the occasion to transform himself quietly into a marketable pop idol. Only the market didn't yet know what kind of idol it wanted.

Stars were in short supply during 1970, not least because the concept of stardom had been devalued since 1967 at least in its glitzy, *Sunday Night At The London Palladium* kind of way. But there was always the fashionable misnomer of the countercultural anti-hero – Bob Dylan, Jimi Hendrix, Janis Joplin, even Frank Zappa, all with distinctive, colourful personalities and instantly recognisable faces that looked good on wall posters. Dylan's arrogance, Hendrix's crotch, Janis' Southern Comfort bottle and Zappa's lavatory humour were inextricably bound up with their work — like the poets and painters of antiquity, their art was inscribed in the act of being alive and enjoying a particular lifestyle.*

By 1970, record companies had begun to realise that this credible kind of star – self-aware and capable of sustaining a career in the lucrative album sector – was a better long-term investment than a cheap 'n' chirpy bubble-gum tune sung by one-hit wonders who didn't even play on their own records. Like the Dylans and Joplins out there, Marc was a recognised album artist in command of his work, and the image that sustained it. Unlike them, his appeal was distinctively English. There was another crucial difference, too. Bolan possessed the potential to break out of that long-haired, long-playing market, to take on the three-minute charlatans and reinvent himself as the pop idol he always knew he was.

The cover photograph for *A Beard Of Stars*, shot by Pete Sanders, had been the most blatant selling of Marc Bolan – The Icon yet. "Image was very important to him," Sanders remembers. "He had very strong ideas about what he wanted." What Marc wanted in spring 1970 was a

---

* The import of Jimi and Janis' art was further enhanced by their premature deaths later in the year.

Tyrannosaurus Rex cover to reflect that *he* was the band. No winged horses or busty maidens, no Steve Took, not even the hapless Mickey Finn, whose face was relegated to the LP's back cover. Disarmingly, this first Bolan cover typifies his pretty, poetic hippie look.

"Marc was a very gentle character and the cover really personifies that for me," says the photographer. "What you see – Marc dressed in a velvet coat and ruffled shirt – is just a small part of a negative. He went through the contact sheets with June and suggested I enlarge that small portion of the photo." This gave the image a soft, grainy effect, "a Pre-Raphaelite feel with all those wispy curls", Sanders says. Inevitably, some lysergically minded fans saw more in the photo than Sanders or Marc ever did. "I got letters that said, 'I've looked at the photo through a blue filter and discovered the heads of Dylan and The Beatles in Marc's hair,' " Sanders recalls.

So it *was* true: Marc Bolan did wear stars in his hair. Soon enough, and with far greater consequence, he'd be wearing them on his brow.

★　★　★

Simon Napier-Bell had been laughed out of every record company office in London when he spun Marc Bolan's 'Hippy Gumbo' demo to bemused A&R men. The beat was pedestrian, but worse still was that voice. Four years later, thanks to the hippies' willingness to fete the weird and wonderful, audiences had warmed to it – especially now that Marc had softened its abrasive edges. Then, in June 1970, just three months after *A Beard Of Stars* had stalled at number 21 in the LP chart, all of Europe seemed to be singing in vibrato voices. The reason for this mass outbreak of musical madness was not Marc Bolan, though; it was Mungo Jerry's 'In The Summertime', a sunny, seasonal hit as maddeningly infectious as a dose of holiday STD.

"What really made Marc a star was Mungo Jerry not Marc Bolan," Napier-Bell claims. "He could not make any headway with his voice other than as a hippie act playing to 300 people at universities for £20 a night. His albums were selling in reasonable quantities but he wasn't really going anywhere. When Ray Dorset pinched his voice and put it into a super-commercial hit song, suddenly that voice was acceptable. I don't know what Marc must have thought when he heard that voice; it must have been terrible for him. But it was a turning point." Recalling the episode a year later, Marc played it cool: "It was a bit of a rip-off, I suppose, but he could have been copying an old blues singer for all anyone knew."

It wasn't the first hijacking of Bolan's braying. At the end of 'Cold

Turkey' on the *Live Peace In Toronto* album, released in December 1969, John Lennon says, "I couldn't get that voice," before emitting a hasty bleat to illustrate his point. Then again, he might have been trying to emulate his new wife Yoko. There was no mistaking Ray Davies' appropriation of the Bolan vibro-voice on 'King Kong', which had appeared on the flip of The Kinks' 'Plastic Man' back in April 1969. "Everybody wants to be King Kong," he predicted, oblivious both to the Tyrannosaurus man's ambition and earlier Mighty Joe Young fixation.

And then there was David Bowie. His June 1970 single, 'Memory Of A Free Festival', included a harmonium-led coda that was a direct lift from 'Iscariot' on the 1969 *Unicorn* album. But the most obvious acknowledgement, a few warbled lines followed by a full-throated bleat on 'Black Country Rock' recorded in the spring, had yet to appear on *The Man Who Sold The World*. "It was spontaneous," remembers Tony Visconti. "David did it as a joke, but we all thought it was cool so it stayed. We actually re-recorded it to get it 'right'; I thinned out David's voice with equalisation to get it to sound more like Bolan's. The fascination these two men had with each other's careers is obvious." Even the verses on 'Holy Holy', Bowie's last recording with Visconti and issued on 45 the following January, undulated like a Bolan melody.

In an extensive interview in *Zigzag* magazine, published in March 1970, Bolan revealed another dimension to his sparring with Bowie. "Sexually, I believe that one should love what one loves, and I quite enjoy the Greek idea of two warriors going to war and mentally being very close – they didn't actually screw each other on the battlefield, but mentally they were really into each other." Then his thoughts turned to Bowie. "I really dig David – I like his songs and we have a very good head thing . . . but we don't make love. To make love wouldn't be repulsive to me. It would just be a bit of a bore with bums, and it'd hurt."

And Marc Bolan was easily hurt. He was sore at Ray Dorset, whose chart-topping parody boomed out from transistor radios wherever he went that summer. And he was so angered by the critics' reaction to Bob Dylan's new album, *Self Portrait*, issued in July, that he dashed off a heart-felt riposte to *Melody Maker*. His letter was published in the paper's July 11, 1970 edition:

> I've just listened to Dylan's new album, and in particular 'Belle Isle', and I feel deeply moved that such a man is making music in my time.

Dylan's songs are now mainly love ballads, the writing of which is one of the most poetic art forms since the dawn of man.

'Belle Isle' brought to my memory all the moments of tenderness I've ever felt for another human being, and that, within the superficial landscape of pop music, is a great thing indeed.

Please, all the people who write bitterly of a lost star, remember that with maturity comes change, as surely as death follows life."

Coming from someone about to embrace change on a star-making scale, it is a remarkable document, and probably says as much about Bolan himself as it does his mentor. Marc, who was fiercely competitive when it came to his close contemporaries, stayed loyal to Dylan, though like his arbitrary namedropping of John Lennon on the January 1, 1970 Tyrannosaurus Rex radio performance, its publication also worked as a neat piece of self-elevation by association.

Even zealous Bobphiles regarded the amorphous 24-track double set as the singer's idea of a joke (and time – the oldest healer – has failed to re-habilitate the record). Among the baggage were three instrumentals, a cover of an old standard ('Blue Moon') and a few lukewarm live recordings of material from Dylan's catalogue. Worse still, the rich, inspired imagery that made each Dylan album such an eagerly awaited event was missing. Bob was coasting but Marc, who remained remarkably faithful to his idols, still found reason to keep the faith.

After visiting Bolan in his two-room Blenheim Crescent flat, *Music Now!*'s Tony Norman emerged with a portrait entirely in keeping with the soft-focus image on the sleeve of *A Beard Of Stars*. "I feel Marc is as genuine as it is possible to be within the rather narrow corridors of pop," he gushed. "He has never been in the big hype scene and the music has gone through logical, unforced progressions." Norman also described Tyrannosaurus Rex as "the smallest rock'n'roll band in the land"; at precisely the same moment, Marc was seriously reconsidering the group's format.

Speaking to *Zigzag* that same month, Marc Bolan floated the idea of expanding the line-up for concert performances. "This album (*Beard*) is fuller than any other Rex album and I have been thinking about this problem a lot recently. Perhaps when people have really got into the new songs, we may get another guy to come on and play bass for a couple of songs." But he was clearly uncomfortable with the idea of dealing with a third musician. "Another idea I had was to pre-record a bass line and then play that over the speakers while we do other things live. But whatever happens, we won't get another full-time member. I don't want to lose the tight sound we have now," he insisted, adding that The Incredible String Band's work had suffered when they expanded the line-up.

For the time being, Marc recreated the rockier sound of some of the more recent material by strapping on his white Fender Stratocaster towards the end of Tyrannosaurus Rex concerts. Initially, audiences thought it was a joke and greeted the sight of Marc's guitar and amp with laughter. Things had improved since April 1969, when Steve Took joined Marc on bass for a couple of songs at the Lyceum, an experiment that Bolan later described as "disastrous". "Concerts are very exciting for us now," he said in spring 1970. "We had 200 people up on the stage when we did a gig at the Fairfield Hall in Croydon recently. That's the way it should be. They don't have to sit quiet and listen." Once again, he repeated the mantra that Dave Marsh had heard in America the previous summer: "We have always been a little rock'n'roll band," Marc insisted.

The revival of interest in vintage rock'n'roll that began in 1968 continued to grow. A 'Rock Revival Show' held at the Roundhouse in March featured Marty Wilde, Joe Brown, Tommy Bruce and the original king of the fumbling wires Bert Weedon. Doorstopped at the show, Marc raved about Frankie Lymon's voice, the guitar playing of Lonnie Mack and Link Wray, and insisted that, "It's nice to get back to the originals." In reliving his past, he was able to glimpse the straitjacketing of the present. "We were thinking of going on at the Festival Hall with 400 watts each and freak 'em out!" he gently threatened. "All the kids will come to see freaky Bolan quietly doing his thing and then . . . Nearh!"

As it was, the Tyrannosaurus Rex set had changed considerably as the duo maintained a hectic concert schedule booked by the ambitious new management company EG, founded by David Enthoven and John Gaydon. April and May saw brief visits to Austria and West Germany in between prestigious shows such as the Pop Proms at the Roundhouse and Extravaganza '70 at Olympia, Kensington, and a short tour of Scotland supporting Ten Years After. They also trawled the summer festival circuit for the third year in succession, and a performance of 'By The Light Of A Magical Moon' at the Kralingen Festival in Rotterdam, Holland, subsequently turned up in the film of the festival, *Stamping Ground*. A typical set from mid-1970 kicked off with acoustic versions of 'Debora', 'Hot Rod Mama', 'One Inch Rock' and 'Wind Quartets' from the Took era, 'Organ Blues' (featuring Marc on his £6 Woolworths keyboard), followed by a second half of electric material, including 'Pavilions Of Sun', 'By The Light Of A Magical Moon' and 'Elemental Child' all from *A Beard Of Stars*, before climaxing with a lengthy reworking of his début 45, 'The Wizard'. Now, it seemed, Marc was reclaiming his own past in order to construct a new future.

Most dramatic of all, though, was the inclusion, from June onwards, of a new song, 'Jewel'. Aired nationally on Radio 1's *Stuart Henry Show* on June 25, alongside 'Elemental Child' and an electric reworking of 'One Inch Rock', the song marked Marc's psychedelicised take on blues-based rock'n'roll, a hypnotic, sexualised, fuzzed-up explosion of sound that found him stumbling, glorious and incoherent, into guitar hero territory. It was acid rock of a kind, though Marc had rarely touched the stuff – until recently.

"None of the (Tyrannosaurus Rex) albums were written under drugs," Marc maintained in 1976, adding that he came to drugs late and never wrote under the influence of any kind of stimulant. But he admitted taking acid "about four times in 1970" and that he "didn't like it. I was spiked with STP and was under sedation for two weeks. I came out and wrote 'Ride A White Swan'," he said, stretching the truth a little. Marc looked down on acid as a short cut to a way of viewing the world he'd been experiencing since childhood. Jeff Dexter suggests that the truth was rather less romantic. "I think he was slightly afraid of dropping acid. He read all the books, knew all the words, but I don't know if he actually learned the song."

Dexter was with Marc the night he was spiked. The pair had been at a party for the launch of the British version of *Rolling Stone* magazine in Hanover Square, off Regent Street in central London. When June, who'd been working late, arrived to pick Marc up, she found him dazed, confused and mumbling something about wanting to eat himself. According to her account in Jonathon Green's *Days In The Life*, she intended to drop Jeff off at his place in Haverstock Hill, but with Marc screaming, salivating and hopelessly out of control, she drove the three of them direct to Blenheim Crescent. A doctor friend, Bernie Greenwood, eventually managed to get him out of the car and into the flat, administering a healthy dose of Largactyl that sent Bolan to sleep. This process was repeated for the next couple of days until Marc finally came down. "He was absolutely petrified and he made me promise that nobody would ever give him acid again," said June.

The bad trip confirmed to Marc that his flight from the complexities –

and insecurities – of the psychedelic experience was right. That summer, as Mungo Jerry were spreading a little seasonal happiness, as the country marvelled at the exemplary football beamed back by satellite from the World Cup Finals in Mexico, and as Fleetwood Mac were being dubbed 'the new Beatles', Marc and Tony Visconti released some silly season entertainment of their own.

"David Platz got me some free time at a studio (LTW's Studio 5 in Wembley, London)," Visconti recalls, "and I went in and recorded a song as Yankee Dayglo, which was a play on my Italian-American background. Steve Took was on that too, as Skinny Rose, and Bowie loved it. It was a funny version of Tyrannosaurus Rex. Then Marc said he had this song, 'Baby Baby', which he wanted me to sing. So we got in John Cambridge and Rick Wakeman to help out." "It was a one-off, a bit of a laugh, and we had a lot of fun," is how Wakeman remembers the March 24, 1970 session.

For musicians more used to singing songs about madmen and mythological creatures fun meant having a crack at the ballooning bubblegum market, a place fit for Edison Lighthouse, White Plains, Pickettywitch and The Pipkins but, it seemed, no one with any hint of durability. The quartet spent six hours in the studio, apparently watched by Mick Ronson, and emerged with two songs so dizzy and featherlite they floated away onto record collectors' wants lists the moment they were released.

"David Platz wanted nothing to do with it," Visconti admits, but the producer, who sang and arranged a sprightly string section that wouldn't have been out of place on a late Sixties Motown production, found an outlet in the independent Bell label. The two songs, 'Oh Baby' and 'Universal Love' and credited to Dib Cochran and The Earwigs, were issued in August – and promptly forgotten about. In truth, the "Oh Baby" hook was hardly 'Yellow River' or even 'Groovin' With Mr Bloe', but the session was significant because it enabled Marc and Visconti to tap into their deep atavistic yearning for pure pop without compromising their reputations. Despite its inglorious failure – not least because it received minimal promotion and no airplay – the 'Oh Baby' session gave the pair a tantalising glimpse into the possibilities of pop. "It was definitely the precursor of T. Rex," says Visconti.

A new pop aesthetic also gave a healthy glow to sessions for the putative fifth Tyrannosaurus Rex album that summer. Marc's voice was doubletracked and more prominent than ever, the percussion, including drums, had a new no-frills directness and several simple bass lines added muscle. The rock'n'roll influence, for so long quietly understated in Bolan's music, now ran riot through at least half a dozen of the songs taped at the sessions. Even Marc's lyrics had a freshness and brio about them, with many allusions to the joys of instantaneous pop pleasure that virtually amounted to a clarion-call for his new-found bubblegum boogie: "I want to give every child the chance to dance", "Boy, wouldn't you like to rock", "Light up the world with poems from within you" and, presciently, "One day we change from children into people".

The new songs spoke loudly of transition and wish-fulfilment; one in particular managed to encapsulate everything Marc Bolan had been looking for. At one session, on July 1, 1970, he asked Tony Visconti to start rolling the tape. He wanted to put down a new song, 'Ride A White Swan'; "Let's call it 'Swan'," Visconti called back from the Trident Studios control booth, unaware that the next few seconds would reveal the key to Marc Bolan's glorious future. With his cherished Gibson Les Paul around his neck (stained orange in homage to Eddie Cochran's six-string), Marc formed an open E shape chord above the capo he'd strapped over the fourth fret, and kicked out a clipped rock'n'roll chord just like James Burton on those old Ricky Nelson B-sides. Almost the instant Visconti flicked a switch, adding a small amount of tape echo on the guitar track, Marc shouted back emphatically: "I want that sound!"

'Ride A White Swan' not only sounded simple; it was simple. The ingredients were few – that clipped, three-chord-trick guitar, Marc's cautious vocal (sung from a page hastily typed by June), handclaps on the offbeat and a rudimentary Bolan bassline (played on Visconti's Fender Precision bass), offset by a modest, Visconti-arranged string section and that trademark Tyrannosaurus Rex falsetto backing drone. The lyrics – just twelve short, sweet lines – were similarly economical even by Marc's recent standards. And the crucial parts that Dib Cochran and The Earwigs lacked – a genuine voice, and a rock'n'roll backing – were here in abundance.

"When we heard what we had got," recalls David Platz, "it was simply so exciting that we knew we had a potential Superstar on our hands. It had such a different sound, and was exactly right for that particular time." Releasing 'Ride A White Swan' as the band's next single seems in retrospect to have been an expertly judged calculation, but at the time its success took almost everyone by surprise – even Marc whose memory was already saturated with misplaced hopes. In fact, the route to number two in the British charts in November 1970 was tortuous and complicated, with several factors contributing to the success of 'Ride A White Swan'.

Although Marc could will the musical changes, and instil a new sense of ambition in those around him, even he doesn't take credit for the series of coincidences that enabled his 'Swan' to take flight. "People associated us with Flower Power, and that was a long gone era," he said after the stardust had settled. "I wanted people to look at the thing in a new light, and the only way to do that was to have a label change, change the music and change the name but not lose any identity. I make it sound very controlled, but it wasn't at all. It all happened in three days, and I got put on Fly Records. I didn't choose to be there. That happened because the company I was with signed with those people who formed Fly Records."

The crucial month was September. With the launch of Fly Records imminent, Marc chose to drop the cumbersome Tyrannosaurus Rex name in favour of T. Rex, an abbreviation many had been using for convenience's sake. Tony Visconti remembers Marc's initial reaction: "He came to my little office at Essex Music one afternoon, looked at my recording calendar on the wall and took great offence at all those references to 'T. Rex'. I told him it was for my eyes only and that it was too tedious writing Tyrannosaurus Rex 15 times on the same page." In fact, Marc had used the same abridgment when he advertised for a replacement for Steve Took 12 months earlier. After the incremental advances of the previous three years, the name change marked a brutal, crucial break with the past – though the motivation was as much practical, giving DJs like Tony Blackburn and Dave Lee Travis the opportunity of playing the band's records without screwing up their syllables.

Tony Visconti puts the success of 'Ride A White Swan' down to two things: "The image change, and the fact we had a string section in there." He claims that he had to beg David Platz to pay for the four violins used on the single and on a couple of album tracks. "Fly had nothing to do with Marc's success," he declares. "We never had any support from them. T. Rex was a legacy from the old days. We were almost an embarrassment to the company."

That may have been true, but the newly constituted Fly Records could not afford to back too many losers. There was a lot riding on Marc's 'White Swan' when it appeared in the racks on Friday October 9, 1970. For all Visconti's reservations, the company – set up by David Platz in partnership with Track Records' Kit Lambert and Chris Stamp – had splashed out on a mass-produced picture sleeve that utilised a moody Pete Sanders portrait of Marc and Mickey. And the decision had been taken to release it as a value-for-money maxi-single with two songs on the B-side.

"You'd be surprised how many kids can't afford an album," said Marc, hot on the scent of a new audience.

There is no doubt that 'Ride A White Swan' was intended to invigorate Bolan's career and provide a flagship for the new record company. The careers of Procol Harum, Joe Cocker and The Move, all brought over from New Breed's previous Regal Zonophone outlet, were at stake; both the label and its first single were expected to succeed.

The Fly launch was beset by problems and last-minute changes. Label manager Malcolm Jones, who'd been poached from running EMI's progressive Harvest imprint, had initially named the new operation Octopus. A small handful of (now priceless) acetates for the first 45 had been pressed bearing the (now legendary) catalogue number OCTO 1. Extant copies show that the guitar-heavy 'Jewel' was tipped for the flipside alongside a wobbly version of Eddie Cochran's 'Summertime Blues' – though it was later replaced by another, less abrasive cut from the forthcoming LP, 'Is It Love'.*

After a distribution deal with Chris Blackwell's Island fell through, Lambert and Stamp got involved, and it was Kit Lambert who came up with the Fly name. With the Christmas rush imminent, Platz returned to EMI who agreed to distribute the label, a logo was hastily knocked up by Track's in-house design team and by early October 'Ride A White Swan' was ready to go. Everyone involved expected the record to make some impact, though the scale of its success meant that Malcolm Jones quickly ran into difficulties. "I was so busy trying to get records pressed and sleeves printed," he recalled, "that the disc appeared on brown or lilac labels. That was because I purchased Immediate Records' lilac paper after they'd gone out of business – simply to get records pressed quickly at any cost."

"The business was at a very low ebb at that point," Marc admitted several months later. "There was nothing really going down. When we put ('Ride A White Swan') out, I was well prepared for it to bomb. I expected to get a lot of aggravation from people saying, 'It's too electric,' or whatever, and it was a hit in three weeks." Actually, it was only a minor hit at that early stage, but after strong support from the BBC – T. Rex recorded five separate Radio 1 sessions between October and December – and the music press ("their most commercial song yet", raved *New Musical Express*) 'Ride A White Swan' took off.

---

* A full colour picture sleeve for this original pressing also exists, confirming that a little cost-cutting took place prior to the single's eventual release – in a black-and-white cover.

The campaign had been launched on a wing and a prayer, but encouraging a new audience to T. Rex concerts by pegging ticket prices to 10s. (50 pence) during an extensive October/November tour of Britain was a masterstroke. The concerts soon sold out, and after the October 15 show at the City Hall, Sheffield (just six days after the single's release), the gentle applause that usually followed Tyrannosaurus Rex performances ("As usual, they were greeted with a silent but totally involved reverence," wrote Chris Welch of the duo's September 6 Roundhouse gig) had given way to boisterous reactions and mob-like scenes outside the stage doors.

"The low admission at our shows has meant the younger kids can come – the Teenybop Heads," Marc told *Disc*'s Tony Norman in October. "I've been given lots of beads and things like that. We got mobbed when we played in Nottingham. Everyone was freaking and dancing around in front of the stage. When we finished they just leapt up and surrounded us. I think that sort of excitement has a lot to do with the electric music we are playing now. At these recent shows there has been a real frenzy the second we got on stage. Usually you have to build the feeling up, but this time it has been there from the start. We can only relate this change to the price. I think that as the seats are cheaper, the kids are coming with a nicer attitude, they want to enjoy themselves."

Just weeks earlier, Roy Hollingworth had written a think-piece in *Melody Maker* under the title "Is Fan Worship Coming Back?" In it, he described the uncritical hysteria that had greeted virtuoso groups like Taste, Free, The Moody Blues and Ten Years After at the recent Isle of Wight Festival. He didn't for one moment imagine anything like this.

Neither had Marc's faithful fans, some of whom were beginning to resent 'their' cult hero appearing on *Top Of The Pops*, inspiring star-struck teenagers to rush the stage at concerts and recording radio sessions for uncool shows such as Dave Lee Travis' Sunday morning broadcast and the *Radio One Club*. The controversy was fanned by B.P. Fallon, who'd first met Marc on the set of *Ready, Steady, Go!* in December 1966 and had become his publicist after Tyrannosaurus Rex signed to the EG management company the previous winter. His slogan, 'The Last Of The Great Underground Groups', was fed to the music press and inevitably intensified the debate. For the next two years, the letters pages of the music weeklies played out the same old question: Had T. Rex 'sold out'?

Their concerts certainly had. But with Marc and Mickey under pressure to reproduce the group's recorded sound on stage, it was clear that while Tony Visconti could sit in on bass for radio sessions and the occasional

167

show (he joined the duo at Oxford Town Hall on November 12, for example), T. Rex required a permanent bassist. The group took ten days out of their hectic schedule to redress the situation, and after some intense rehearsals, the three-piece T. Rex was unveiled in Guildford's Civic Hall on November 24.

Marc disliked confrontation – at least if it meant someone in the band disagreeing with him. "I have no time for tension in groups," he once said, which suited 22-year-old Steve Currie, who had no burning ambition other than to earn a living from music. After an audition in south London, Currie was offered the job and accepted immediately, even though he wasn't particularly fond of Tyrannosaurus Rex's music. He was delighted when Marc assured him that the old acoustic sound wasn't going to be around for much longer. "We are not a little folky duo anymore," said Marc just days before Currie joined. "We want to spend the next year working very hard and getting everything out of the music we can. I want it to be very exciting."

Born on May 20, 1947 in Grimsby, Currie had been playing in groups since the mid-Sixties. He started out in a jazz band called The Rumble playing the local South Bank Jazz Club on Friday nights. During the day, he worked in a shipping office and by the late Sixties, he'd become a qualified ship broker. But music was his first passion, and when The Rumble relocated to London in the hope of getting a deal, Currie gambled on his professional career and went with them. It ended in tears: the group returned home deep in debt, though Steve, whose girlfriend Hazel had found a steady job in the capital, stayed. He joined a band called The Meteors, but an advert in *Melody Maker* in November 1970 took him to a school hall near the Elephant and Castle where he was invited to join T. Rex. Confident of the group's imminent success, Currie celebrated with a bottle of whisky, ordered a special licence from Willesden Registry Office and married Hazel the next day.

The addition of Steve Currie was announced in the music press on December 12, 1970, and the following week, the first T. Rex album appeared. In contrast to the infamous wordiness of those early Tyrannosaurus Rex titles, it was simply titled *T. Rex*. (This was probably a last-minute decision, because documentation exists that suggests at least two provisional titles: *The Wizard* and *The Children Of Rarn*.) Although the summer sessions had marked an exciting new departure, it all sounded a bit flat by December, when 'Ride A White Swan' was right behind *Dad's Army* actor Clive Dunn's mawkish chart-topper 'Grandad'; when fans were starting to scream "MARC!" at concerts; and when T. Rex had become the country's fastest growing Lilliputian power trio. In interviews conducted around the time of its release, Marc – now writing songs faster than ever – kept his distance from the record, protesting that it had been recorded months ago and apologising for it not sounding heavier. His coolness helps explain why the album narrowly failed to crack the Top 10.

The *T. Rex* album offered a similar balance of electric and acoustic material to *A Beard Of Stars*, and even included its own 'Elemental Child' freak-out moment in the epic reworking of 'The Wizard'. In a way, that was a sop to those purists lamenting the passing of the duo's hippie-era vibe, with Bolan turning in some of his most extreme Punch and Judy vocal yelps. 'Summer Deep', 'Suneye' and the blissfully tranquil 'Root Of Star' could have been Tyrannosaurus Rex songs refined and reborn; 'One Inch Rock' literally was, now rockin' and rollin' where before it had Fred 'n' Barney'd its way along on square wheels. This second reclaiming of a vintage Bolan original was a unique development, too, as if Marc somehow needed to repossess his own past in order to build a new future.

At the core of the album was a quartet of rock'n'roll songs – the afore-mentioned 'Jewel', obviously inspired by June Bolan ("Her thoughts are gold/her eyes 'lectric blue"); the second 'Swan' B-side, 'Is It Love', which neatly retained Marc's mantra style, both in the voice and in the persistent fuzz-box hum buried in the mix; 'One Inch Rock'; and 'Beltane Walk'. The latter was a direct lift from Jimmy McCracklin's 'The Walk', recorded in 1957, which the Chess R&B star later maintained he'd written to illustrate how simple it was to have a rock'n'roll hit. Ironically, McCracklin's ungainly riff (which Marc used as the basis for at least three other songs) itself can be traced to an earlier recording – Chicago slide gui-tarist Hound Dog Taylor played an approximation of it as 'Taylor's Boogie' in the mid-Fifties.

The record was topped and tailed by brief snatches of symphonic rock, both titled 'The Children Of Rarn' which, Marc claimed would soon be developed into a full-length, science fiction concept album. The project, which he was still talking about years later, was initially envisaged as a double-album set with a spin-off book. According to Tony Visconti, Marc had earmarked either John Peel or *Catweazle* actor Geoffrey Bayldon to narrate parts of it. A demo of Marc's multi-part Rarn epic recorded a few months later suggests he was entirely serious about the idea, but by the turn of the year, there were too many distractions for him to give it the attention he felt such a piece deserved.

Once again, Pete Sanders was asked to shoot the photo for the cover, a semi fold-out poster sleeve that depicted Marc and Mickey looking more like weekend hippies than the real thing. If the *A Beard Of Stars* cover masqueraded as art, the T. Rex sleeve was pure pin-up, a sanitised version of the long haired cult that now seemed more acceptable to mainstream tastes in the face of the emerging Skinhead culture. In light of this new brutalism, T. Rex went for a more androgynous, angelic image than ever. "We went down to my mother's house in Sussex and did the session in the garden," Sanders remembers. "Marc and Mickey wore white make-up which gave their faces a porcelain-like effect. It was all part of the new electric image Marc was trying to create. And that's why he wanted to be pictured with his electric guitar."

The 'Bopping Imp', a phrase coined by *Melody Maker*'s Chris Welch back in 1968, had truly come to life. In November 1970, while 'Ride A White Swan' was still making its way up the singles chart, Marc claimed in *Disc & Music Echo* that, "I've suddenly tuned into that mental channel which makes a record a hit, and I feel at present as though I could write number ones forever. Let's face it, the majority of pop hits are a permutation on the 12-bar blues and I've found one that works." This time, it was no idle boast. "There are no barriers," he added. The changeling was ready to move on.

8

Let It Rock

"You can sell all the albums you like, but until you get a hit single, you don't feel successful. I always wanted to be a rock'n'roll star."

– Marc Bolan (August 1971)

"People said he sold out when he made the transition from Tyrannosaurus Rex into T. Rex, but he wanted to be the Marc Bolan of T. Rex from the time he was 14. He wasn't really interested in being the esoteric, underground cult figure that had emerged from Middle Earth. He played that role and did it well, but he always wanted to be the Star."

– Keith Altham (1992)

"The one quality they all shared was their remoteness, a mental and physical inaccessibility which manifested itself in the purchasing of white Rolls-Royces and lightweight Lambourghinis. They gave the audience something to look up to again."
– *Melody Maker* on the rise of the new pop idols (January 1972)

In the spring of 1970, when Tyrannosaurus Rex comprised a novice percussionist and a guitarist who concealed his technical shortcomings behind a fuzz-box and a wah-wah pedal, Marc Bolan predicted a modest future for rock'n'roll: "People are abandoning the idea of the group," he claimed. "Musicians have realised that if the music is not right then the success and money don't mean a thing." But not for himself: "In the past bands have stayed the same and got very bored," he continued. "We only do three of the old songs now. All the rest are new and fresh."

Less than 12 months later, Tyrannosaurus Rex had taken so many giant steps they had rendered themselves extinct. As 1971 began, the new and fresh T. Rex were still rising up the charts with the slow burning 'Ride A White Swan' and Marc Bolan was thrilling both the media and the audiences they served with an endearing display of braggadocio long missing from the self-serving rock community. He had genuinely good reason to be pleased with himself.

"Marc Bolan became a star and T. Rex a supergroup on Monday," claimed Chris Welch reviewing the group's concert at the Lyceum, London, on January 25. "It was heart-warming for those who have followed the career of the unlikely duo down the years." More ominously, he added: "Several doubts arose during the almost unbelievable response . . . something a little disturbing about the readiness to cheer what was frequently unmusical . . . The elements that make up the web of fantasy, fun and pop of Tyrannosaurus Rex are being uncomfortably stretched to the limits of credibility."

Marc's ears were attuned only to the cheers of the crowds and the call – which he felt in the pit of his stomach – for another hit single. There was no hint now of abandoning the idea of a group. Bolan had refined his sound and, galvanised by the vast new audience within his sights, he was writing songs more quickly than ever. "Reaching a wider public is what we want," he told *Beat Instrumental*'s Steve Turner. "If 'underground' means being on a show screened at midnight and watched by 15 people – then we're out of it. If we're asked to do *Top Of The Pops* we do it, and if we're asked to do John Peel we do it."

"I realised after 'White Swan' I had to have a drum kit on the records," Bolan recalled in 1972. Mickey Finn switched briefly to a full kit, but Marc missed "the funky feel" of the hand drums. "So I said I must have a drummer now or I'm never gonna play again. I got very dramatic. And then suddenly it was all there and I thought, 'Man, I got a band.' The second we played, it was just so right."

That drummer was Bill Fifield from the group Legend, whose self-titled album Tony Visconti had produced several months earlier. "Tony came up to me in the pub one night and asked me if I wanted to sit in for T. Rex," he recalls. "I didn't really know much about the group, but he told me they were working in the studio and wanted to try out drums for the first time. I went straight up to Advision Studios off Oxford Street, met Marc – who I remember was being fairly flamboyant in a green suit – Mickey and Steve, and we recorded 'Hot Love' and 'Woodland Rock' straight away."

Marc and Tony were making it up as they went along. The last-minute decision to bring in a proper drummer for the January 21, 1971 'Hot Love' session yielded what everyone believed would become an even bigger hit than 'Ride A White Swan', but Bill didn't instantly become part of the furniture. Only when 'Hot Love' entered the charts in mid-February – and with an American tour on the horizon – was the decision taken to audition for a full-time drummer. Many candidates were called; Marc got bored and often left Mickey and Steve to entertain the queues of hopefuls. None seemed right for the job.

Born in Barking on May 8, 1944, Bill Fifield had grown up in east London, and took up drums while still at Mayfield School in Ilford. He'd begun by tapping out rhythms on his school desk to rock'n'roll songs strummed and sung by a mate, Stewart Tanner, and by the late Fifties, he'd progressed to playing drum and brushes in the Boys' Brigade. After leaving school, Bill and Stewart formed The Teenbeats, who became The Zodiacs, then, at the height of Beatlemania, The Epics. When the band were booked for a season in Scandinavia, Bill put his job first, and was replaced by Mike Blakely, brother of The Tremeloes' Alan Blakely.

Caution was Bill Fifield's middle name. Despite enjoying limited success drumming for Legend, he'd hung on to his day job as a design artist at Bryant & May in east London's Bow district. He'd virtually forgotten about his session for Bolan when 'Hot Love', issued on February 12, 1971, started receiving regular airplay. Then, a couple of weeks later, he took a surprise call at work. It was June Bolan. Would he like to audition for T. Rex, she asked. The drummer begged, bought and borrowed as many old Bolan albums he could find to prepare for his date with glory. "I needn't have bothered because it was all rockin' and rollin'," he remembers. "Marc was already on another kick by then. The chart success had really whetted his appetite."

The audition took place at Gooseberry Studios, a small demo studio in Soho. As the four-piece ran through standards such as Eddie Cochran's 'Summertime Blues' and 'C'mon Everybody', and Bolan's own 'Ride A White Swan', 'Hot Love' and 'One Inch Rock', the drummer, who'd recently backed British rock'n'roll idol Billy Fury, played it simple and instinctively. It was exactly what Marc wanted. Not that he was able to tell Bill in quite that manner. "My status wasn't clearly established at all," says the drummer. "Tony Visconti asked me how it went, and I told him that Marc had mumbled something about getting the gig in a low-key way. I didn't realise that was his way of saying I was in. There was no big introduction. We rarely ever got any feedback from Marc," he shrugs. The four-piece T. Rex spent the next few days rehearsing in a cheap and dingy cellar below an estate agent's on the corner of Tachbrook Street, Pimlico. On April 9, the new quartet made its concert début far from the maniacal crowds in Detroit, Michigan, USA.

As T. Rex flew out of London on April 6, 'Hot Love' was midway through its extraordinary six-week stay at number one in the British singles chart. "The very simplicity of the number is the key to its assured popularity," predicted Derek Johnson in *New Musical Express*. Unlike the speculative 'Ride A White Swan', 'Hot Love' had been written with success in mind. There was no way that Bolan was going to blow the opportunity with a bloodyminded reversion to Tyrannosaurus type. That luxury was reserved for one of the flipsides, 'The King Of The Mountain Cometh', a heady, 'King Of The Rumbling Spires'-like slice of psychedelia and an obvious sop to the old loyalists.

Marc, whose wonderfully idiosyncratic hyperbole was brightening up the pages of the pop press, had a name for 'Hot Love' and the new T. Rex sound. Uttered during the song's lengthy coda, it was, he said, "Cosmic Rock". The phrase, more commonly applied to Hawkwind and Pink Floyd, was meaningless on purely musical terms, but it worked both as a metaphor for Bolan's sky's-the-limit stargazing and at the level of suggestion. To a pop audience otherwise exposed to Ray Stevens' 'Bridget The Midget', Jackie Lee's 'Rupert' and serene ex-Beatles singing odes to 'My Sweet Lord' and, mundanely, 'Another Day', there was something weird and utterly wonderful about Marc Bolan. It was as if the Plastic Ono Band's white sack that contained a wobbling, warbling Yoko Ono had been tapped with a witch's wand and up popped this strange boy-mystic with corkscrew curls, an impish smile and a poet's demeanour.

That such a delightful apparition was responsible for the most infectious pop anthem since the Beatles' 'Hey Jude' over two years earlier made Marc Bolan all the more intriguing. "I know it's exactly like a million other songs," he explained, "but I hope it's got a little touch of me in it too. It was done as a happy record, and I wanted to make a 12-bar record a hit, which hasn't been done since 'Hi-Heel Sneakers' really."

He was right about it being a happy record if little else. 'Hot Love' was built on a rock'n'roll template that had been used, with varying levels of success and originality, since the mid-Fifties. As for reviving an ancient form, well, Dave Edmunds ('I Hear You Knocking') and Mungo Jerry ('Baby Jump') had already topped the British charts in the first two months of 1971 with similar digressions on the 12-bar formula. What made 'Hot Love' different was its classic simplicity – a distillation of everything Marc and Visconti had learned together – and its star-spangled salesman.

Structurally, the song differed little from 'Hot Rod Mama', the opening cut on the first Tyrannosaurus Rex LP. But the details had been significantly refined. Instead of the tense, acoustic clutter there was now a rolling, clippety-clop pulse, electric and pronounced. With Larry The Lamb trussed up and on a one-way trip to the death factory, Marc's voice now sounded confident and clear. The production, utilising a 16-track machine, was skilled and seemingly effortless. And the trimmings – graceful backing vocals, swooning strings, on-the-beat handclaps – were exemplary.

At the heart of the record, and of Marc's routing of the pop world that year, and of the entire Glam Rock/Glitter Rock shibboleth that piled up in his wake, was vintage rock'n'roll. Its sound was ingrained in Marc's psyche, its attitude responsible for Elvis, The Beatles, Hendrix and most everything else associated with vibrant youth culture. And, of course, it had been rock'n'roll that had rescued the young Mark Feld. 'Hot Love' drew unashamedly on familiar sources: Marc's "Uh, uh, uh" vocal, bathed in Sun Studio-style reverb, echoed Elvis on 'All Shook Up'; the guitar break was bussed in from 'Heartbreak Hotel'; and Howard Kaylan and Mark Volman's backing vocals, taped at four in the morning over a convivial bottle of Remy, sounded merrily surf-inspired. Even the coda was a homage – to the Beatles' 'Hey Jude'. The inspiration for 'Woodland Rock', the second flipside, was even easier to identify. Take Elvis' 'Jailhouse Rock' and Little Richard's 'Long Tall Sally', add a little Bolanic mischief, mix and serve.

Among the many questions Marc had been asked since the success of 'Ride A White Swan' was how he envisaged himself in 15 years' time. "A science fiction writer who sings," he replied. Although his commitment to pop Superstardom had been unyielding from the moment he'd first sniffed at it, he couldn't help but see himself at more than one remove from 'ordinary' stars. Throughout 1971, this innate competitiveness was preoccupied by a battle between Marc Bolan past and present, and was neatly channelled into the rapid-fire development of the T. Rex metier. He was too busy watching himself to bother about the activities of his rivals.

"I am just pleased that a lot of people are listening to ('Hot Love')," Marc told *New Musical Express*' Nick Logan in March. "That is what excites me. I love putting singles out. Lennon's into that, and 'Hot Love' is so right because it's so new. It's the last song I had written at that time." This contrasted favourably with the old ways of Tyrannosaurus Rex. "I used to say that albums were behind what we are doing but singles like 'Hot Love' are well ahead."

Marc's relatively rapid transformation from cross-legged hippie troubadour into a swaggering pop idol was now forcing him to abandon many of the certainties of his previous life. "I don't know what I want to do yet and I am forcing myself to grow," he admitted. "In the past I wouldn't have taken any risks but everything I am doing now is a risk." Even the peace-loving, home-loving, animal-loving, wife-loving, friend-cherishing, body-respecting Marc Bolan, whose tender tongue could delight in an instant with its lexicon of exquisiteness? "I am very self-destructive," he added. More Marc fantasy, everyone assumed.

Success at home breathed a much-desired air of urgency into Marc Bolan's life. In America, where the band spent the whole of April on tour, interspersed by hurried recording sessions in Los Angeles and New York, it was a different story. Now signed to Reprise, the band were second and sometimes third on the bill to a variety of acts, none particularly well-matched to T. Rex's emerging 'Cosmic Rock' sound. Mountain, Johnny Winter and Humble Pie were all hard or blues rock bands renowned for volume and virtuosity; T. Rex, though, barely had time to gel as a unit – the tour's opening night, on April 9 in Detroit, marked the live début of Bill Legend (as Marc had renamed him). And, apart from some primitive soloing from Marc on 'Elemental Child' and an extended version of 'Jewel', virtuosity was off the agenda. "Bands that were huge in England like T. Rex couldn't get arrested in America because they couldn't do it live," claims Humble Pie drummer Jerry Shirley.

Disc And Music Echo's US correspondent Lisa Mehlman witnessed the comedown first-hand: "When T. Rex played the Fillmore East the reception was mixed. Some said they were awful, loud and non-musical," though matters weren't helped when Mountain jammed and posed for their attendant film crew for so long that T. Rex were unable to soundcheck. "The New York audience is a bit jaded anyway," she continued. "Everyone has heard so much heavy music." Reactions improved on the second and third nights, but "there wasn't much of the usual Fillmore East hysterical ovations and demands for encores."

Marc reminded the reporter that things were different back in Britain: "We like people to get excited at our gigs, so we've had a lot of riots!" He also played down the 'Sell Out!' debate that raged in the music press. "We could always fill a concert hall," he declared. "All that's happened now is that our records sell half a million as opposed to 40 or 50 thousand! Our fans are very cool. They realise that as a musician one has to grow and I've grown," he continued optimistically. "We didn't sell out or change the music; the music's the same. It's just that it's now timed in the cosmos to be successful." But not, alas, in America.

Prior to the American visit, T. Rex spent a day at Trident Studios on

March 16 putting down basic tracks for two new songs, 'Mambo Sun' and 'Cosmic Dancer'. Other than trying to steal short bursts of studio time in between the multiplying mountain of concerts, interviews and television appearances, there was no great masterplan for the second T. Rex album. In fact, if Marc had planned to record in advance during the American trip, he hadn't conveyed that fact to Tony Visconti, his producer for the past three years. "I wasn't invited," he says. "It was a risky period because he was going to make those recordings in America without me. It was only by chance that we hooked up. 'Hot Love' was already a hit, so I had decided to go back home to New York and see my mum. It was my first holiday since coming to England in 1967."

Recording on the hoof was a necessity at this critical moment in Bolan's career, but a significant by-product of this arrangement was that there was now little time to labour over material. The meandering, progressively inclined demo he'd recorded sketching out his *The Children Of Rarn* epic – momentarily envisaged as a follow-up to the *T. Rex* album – was put aside. "I think we did well to remember the songs," says Bill Legend. "We used to run through a song three or four times and then we'd go for a take. I used to invent my drum breaks as I was playing. It was all done so quickly. Nothing was well prepared but it did give an edge to those records. They were really powerful."

Tony Visconti, who was back in the control booth for a session in New York's Media Sound Studios in mid-April, agrees that in their raw, pre-overdubbed state, the American recordings were primitive – and deliberately so. "We'd set up with Bill in the same room so the drum sound would leak out into other mikes," he explained in his notes for the remastered *Electric Warrior* CD, "and that gave depth to the rest of the sound." According to Marc, "What I did in America when we cut the album was not rehearse the band, just go in and mike everything live and play ... We recorded (it) like the early Sun records." It couldn't have been more simple: the group stood facing each other, relying only on Marc's visual cues and their own intuition as the songs journeyed from solo demo to complete take within the hour. Sun boss Sam Phillips would have been proud.

At least two songs, 'Jeepster' and 'Monolith', had been laid down in New York. With the likelihood of further recording opportunities during the band's stay in Los Angeles – where they played two nights at the Whisky A Go-Go billed as Tyrannosaurus Rex – Marc continued to write at a furious pace. "He called me into his room while we were in New

York," recalls Bill Legend, "and asked me to bring my snare drum along. We sat on the bed and he played this song through, giving me a rare opportunity to work out all the stops. He said, 'I'm thinking about using the song as a follow-up to 'Hot Love'. We're gonna record it when we get to Wally Heider's.' And we did." On April 18, 1971.

That was 'Get It On', one of a handful of tracks taped in Los Angeles, with added Flo and Eddie backing vocals which the group had rehearsed around the swimming pool in Howard Kaylan's Laurel Canyon hideaway. But time had been limited, and when the group returned to Britain on May 3, 1971, the real work was only just beginning. "We didn't even know we were making an album while we were in the States so in that sense, *Electric Warrior* was a relaxed record to make," says Visconti. "It was only when we took all the tapes back to London that the record was really conceived."

The group returned home to find 'Hot Love' still loitering close to the top of the singles chart almost three months after its release. Fly's cash-in Tyrannosaurus Rex compilation, the misleadingly titled *The Best Of T. Rex*, was also in the racks. While it put some much needed pennies in the Bolan purse, Marc (who had first mentioned such a collection the previous autumn) was mildly annoyed by its appearance because his break with the past had been hastened by his success, by events in America and by his new creative impulses.

"There's nothing in my life that I've felt is as important as this one," he told *Sounds* writer Penny Valentine on his return to Britain. "Really, because I'm so exposed on this album. I've never actually ever written about me. I've always disguised it. All those songs were disguises, and this album is a rip-off. Every song is about me – all very erotic songs." He wasn't kidding. There was an animal grace to Marc's new-fangled rock'n'-roll sound, a funky sexuality that seemed inextricably connected to his success. In this heightened state, Marc had a fleeting affair with Barbara Nessim, an artist friend of Tony Visconti's and several years his senior, while in New York. And, as some leaked studio jams confirm, he'd begun to channel some of this into his guitar solos, which were beginning to go on a bit in the tradition of the climax-fixated guitar hero.

Back home, the assiduous, seemingly unflappable June Bolan had helped set up a major British tour with concert promoters John and Tony Smith, the band's first as a four-piece. Initially, Marc found it difficult to acclimatise. "I didn't even know where England was," he said midway through the tour. "It took me two days to relate to June, to remember who she was. Because I didn't know who I was." It was an ominous remark.

Marc had been lost in the stars for years. Fame, which as many observers eagerly pointed out, seemed to come naturally to him. He was a skilled media player with the gift of the gab, and his cheerful, flamboyant presence illuminated hotel rooms and concert stages alike. But like an alcoholic who senses oblivion the moment a glass reaches his lips, the threat of intoxication was rarely far away. The destabilising effect of fame on his music may have infuriated some but in creative terms Marc was, in his own words, reborn and bopping. "I've always been a very consistent person musically up to the single hits," he told Penny Valentine, "and now I'm totally inconsistent. That's not in a bad way; it's really good."

The changes would inevitably have a personal dimension too. " 'Hot Love' caught us by surprise," says Tony Visconti, "because before that the albums were hitting the 20,000 mark. I'm sure Marc and I were going through a similar period of shock, wondering what we were gonna do with all this success. But he recovered very quickly and started to really take control of the image. He knew he was at the forefront of something."

During T. Rex's May tour of Britain, Barry Dillon in *Sounds* reported on a show at the Portsmouth Guildhall. "Marc Bolan gyrated around the stage like the new Elvis Presley," he wrote. "Girls clambered on the stage to kiss him. Others, with a touch of hero worship, reached their arms across the stage to grab him as he hop-scotched around. The few to remain seated jumped up and down like dervishes as T. Rex pounded their exciting message home." The demographic downshifting of the audiences witnessed back in January and February had intensified; now a younger, predominantly female following ousted any remaining stragglers from the Middle Earth days.

"People used to tell him, 'As soon as you're on telly, Marc, it'll be fantastic. You're bound to happen,' " says Jeff Dexter. They were right. That line on 'Ride A White Swan' – "Catch a bright star and place it on your forehead" – turned out to be rather prophetic.

★　★　★

Oblivious to the private psychodramas, sometimes indifferent even to the music, were the star-starved teenage fans who sat adoring at Bolan's feet and gazed longingly into his eyes. At least that's how it felt to those in thrall to the extraordinary magnetism of the musician in whose face they found a curious blend of the sensitive poet and the self-satisfied pop idol. In the words of cultural theorist Iain Chambers, Bolan represented "a sensationalist aesthetic of the strange", a new breed of star who turned the progressive rock rulebook on its head by transforming his own body into an awe-inspiring feat of virtuosity. This new Glam Rock aesthetic shattered the old divide between pop 'falsity' and rock 'naturalness'. Now, the construct of 'The Star' had become an integral part of the musician's creative process.

Whether pegging concert ticket prices at affordable rates, issuing three-track singles, tucking posters inside album sleeves, sending out seasonal messages on record and making himself available for autographs at the stage door, Marc played his 'man of the people' card well. His acute understanding of – and empathy with – the role of private fantasy in the fan/star equation won him an audience renowned for its loyalty, a devoted congregation that put its faith in Marc Bolan first and foremost; the work existed to confirm his omnipotence.

There was also a whiff of hippie humility about this personal touch, which could veer alarmingly close to mawkishness. A programme produced for the May 1971 tour included a short poem of gratitude to his new friends:

> "Many's the time on a windy day
> I've wanted to hold the hand of all the people that ever
>   thought my name
> But hands are many and the days grow fewer
> Now I know you, and like it."

There was little sense of humility, though, when on Wednesday March 24, 1971, T. Rex performed 'Hot Love' at BBC's Lime Grove Studios for the *Top Of The Pops* cameras. The single had just reached number one and Chelita Secunda, a hot, swanky publicist pal of June Bolan's, spontaneously suggested Marc celebrate his first chart-topping 45 with a bit of panache. "Chelita was the first person to really make up Marc," Tony Visconti told *Glam!* author Barney Hoskyns. "She didn't just put some eye make-up on him; she threw glitter on his cheeks."

As well as daubs of glitter under his eyes (that looked a little like tears), Marc also pulled on a silver lamé top for the performance. The effect on the High Street was instantaneous; for manufacturers of glitter and anything else that sparkled, Christmas had indeed come early that year. In the months ahead, Chelita, who had extravagant tastes and great style, accompanied Marc to King's Road boutiques Alkasura and Granny Takes A Trip, purveyors of crushed velvet finery. She also encouraged him to paint his eyelids silver, wrap ostrich feathers around his neck and drape himself in embroidered jackets and swishy satin trousers.

In many ways, Bolan's lurch into androgyny was a continuation of hippie culture's 'Unisex' ideal. It certainly had little to do with bearded Paul McCartney growing his own in his Scottish idyll, or John Lennon's belated engagement with the rights of political prisoners and the cause of Irish republicanism for that matter. Inevitably, it was used as yet another stick to beat the counterculture's diminutive defector. "Once he was fair and had stars up his nose," they whispered. "Now he just wiggles his bottom."

Marc was surprised and privately the abuse hurt him. Publicly, though, he spoke with a new bullishness. "I don't really care what people think," he said. "If the thing works, it works. Elvis Presley wore eye make-up for years. People thought he had dark, sultry eyes. Mick Jagger has wonderful skin embellishment. People are really works of art," he continued as if drafting a Glam Rock manifesto, "and if you have a nice face you might as well play about with it."

Ever since he was Mark Feld, Bolan's tireless reconstruction of himself had always been played out on the field of subcultural style. Since the mid-Sixties, he'd broadly allied himself to movements – Folk, Beat, hippie – that were antagonistic to the mainstream, but more important than that was the opportunity they gave him to sensationalise his own life. Sub-cultures were like elitist clubs, with their own uniforms, argot and sound-tracks. Glam Rock wasn't sub- anything; it was universal and insidious and, in time, transforming everything and everyone in its wake. Between mid-1971 and 1974, few across the rock and pop spectrum were impervious to it – as contemporary photographs of Jimmy Page and The Osmonds ably testify.

In its earliest stages, though, Glam Rock proved controversial precisely because it struck deep in the heart of rock orthodoxy. Privileging 'The Star' above all else, it rejected the community aspect of rock, which had been rooted in subcultures. Returning to the referents of vintage rock'n'-roll – sex, style and simplicity in songwriting – it was deemed counter-revolutionary for shunning the technical advances and artistic ambition of the previous 15 years. And in aiming itself squarely at the younger singles market, it was an affront to those who had grown up with pop and seen it shake off its adolescent tag. But pop had become complacent and Marc's answer was simple. "If there is going to be any revolution in pop, it must come from the young people," he insisted. "If you ignore them, you are cutting yourself off from the life-supply of the rock music force."

The appearance of the third T. Rex single, the eagerly awaited 'Get It On', at the start of July, intensified the controversy. The song itself had been transformed, or at least given a Glam Rock makeover, since the basics had been committed to tape back in Los Angeles. Bill Legend remembers Marc complaining that 'Get It On' needed around ten mixes before he and Visconti were satisfied with the results.

After much control-room endeavour, the breathtaking but baggy groove on the original backing track had been carefully honed into a remarkably polished slab of rock'n'roll revisionism – complete with honking sax (from Ian McDonald), excited piano trills (courtesy of Rick Wakeman) and, thanks to Tony Visconti's last-minute intervention, a small string section. Marc hadn't envisaged strings on the song until the producer happened to mention that both 'Ride A White Swan' and 'Hot Love' had utilised strings. "His eyes widened and he said, 'We'd better have strings on this one, too,'" Visconti remembers. "From then on, the use of strings on singles became a near superstition for Marc."

Flo and Eddie's backing vocals sparkled, especially when they hit those falsetto notes during the chorus. Marc excelled himself, too, delivering at least two lyric darts – "You're dirty sweet and you're my girl", "You're built like a car/You got a hub cap diamond star halo" – direct into rock'n'roll mythology. It was a third utterance, half-whispered over the fade out, that most incensed his critics. Marc's "Meanwhile, I'm still thinking" kiss-off was an obvious tip of the hat to Chuck Berry's 'Little Queenie' – unquestionably the template for 'Get It On'. No matter that The Rolling Stones had been counterfeiting the founding father of rock'-n'roll for years with little adverse opinion.

Neither voltage nor Marc's new-found fame seemed to bother John Peel – at least in the early stages. "Peel cried with joy when he heard 'Hot Love' was number 1", ran one magazine headline. And he proceeded to state the case for Marc's defence. "The great thing about Marc, whom I regard as a dear friend, who comes round, plays rock'n'roll records, watches TV, drinks tea and keeps the hamsters company, is that he has stayed completely true to his principles. People say he's sold out by having hit records, but that's just because they like to be part of a cult."

Three months later, John Peel received his customary advance copy of Marc's latest record. It was 'Get It On'. And he couldn't wait to get it off. "I said to myself, 'If this wasn't Marc I wouldn't play it . . . so I mustn't play it." It was a decision that cost him his friendship. "It seemed to prompt a fairly sudden rupture," says Peel philosophically. "I phoned him up and someone else answered the phone. 'Hey, man, Marc's busy. He'll phone you back.' And he never did. I was disappointed, because Marc had been somebody I liked and spent a lot of time with."

John Peel followed Steve Peregrine Took into Marc's 'Past Sell-By Date' box. The pair rarely spoke again. "This is not a criticism of Marc," the DJ continues, "but he did have this harder side to his character, and there's nothing that's more calculated to activate this kind of dark side of people than success. There aren't that many people who survive it. Most people become monsters. Marc didn't become a monster but he didn't have to be Mr. Nice Guy any more. I suppose it was rather like the electorate's rejection of Churchill after the war. They associate you with the difficult years, and so they move on to someone else."

That someone else was Bob Harris, Marc's second invaluable ally at Radio 1. The DJ first met Bolan when he turned up to interview John Peel in 1967 and found Marc there too. The pair's friendship slowly blossomed during the late Sixties, and when Harris, as John Peel's disciple, also began to broadcast on *Top Gear*, Marc recorded sessions for his shows too. While Peel soon tired of Marc's electric work, Harris' enthusiasm grew with each release. "I think Marc was desperately underrated, particularly once T. Rex got going," he maintains. "I still think the early T. Rex records match any of the great pop that we've heard over the past thirty or so years, yet at the time they were dismissed as fluffy pop singles." For Harris, the apotheosis of Bolan's career was 'Get It On'. "He really peaked with that. It was a magnificent record."

Some thought Marc was making brilliant pop records; others that he was cynically reviving a tired old formula. Beyond any doubt, though, was his pop idol status. 'Get It On' bagged the number one spot in Britain within three weeks of release, just as every magazine reviewer had predicted. Though none could exactly agree why. "If anything, 'Get It On' is nearer the old Tyrannosaurus Rex," claimed Nick Logan in *New Musical Express*. "Not as instantly hitworthy as 'Hot Love'," suggested *Melody Maker*'s Chris Welch, "but positive and likeable." "No point in getting detailed about it," sidestepped Peter Jones in *Record Mirror*. "It's instant and it's a giant hit." 'Get It On' also shared a rhythmic affinity with Cliff Richard's 'Move It', but only Marc would have made that connection.

Talking to Welch in August, Bolan expressed surprise that 'Get It On' had given him a second number one hit. But he made no apologies for becoming famous on the back of a string of hit 45s. "You can sell all the albums you like, but until you get a hit single, you don't *feel* success-ful," he said. But, he added, its lustre wasn't as glamorous as it seemed. "I always wanted to be a rock'n'roll star. But even when I was young and used to go to the TV studios I could see Cliff Richard's pink jacket was a bit tatty and it was a 12s 6d. black shirt." Later on, he suggested that he was merely reflecting the mood of the times. "I never lost that feel for pop. It was always there."

There was something of the *Don't Look Back*-era Dylan in the way Marc was now taunting his adversaries; and there were other parallels too. Six years earlier, Bob Dylan was cast in the Judas role, infuriating folk purists by abandoning acoustic, protest music for an electric rock combo backing. Neither did Dylan simply create art. It lived through him, which meant that his waste-bins and fluffed on-stage lines, his change of clothes and his fantasies were as eagerly dissected as songs such as 'Like A Rolling Stone' or 'Mr. Tambourine Man'. Marc, too, regarded himself – and soon became – worthy of similarly close inspection.

Such was the divide between rock and pop values during the early Seventies that the founding fathers were excused their own plagiarising, revivalist tendencies. When Dylan crossed over, he too returned to elec-trified 12-bar rock'n'roll: Chuck Berry's 'Too Much Monkey Business' was to 'Subterranean Homesick Blues' what Berry's 'Little Queenie' was to 'Get It On'. Even Chuck, whose riffs have been recycled by every person who has ever called himself a guitarist, famously regards his own music as "nothing new under the sun", and openly admits to plundering the styles of Charlie Christian, T-Bone Walker and Carl Hogan.*

According to conventional wisdom, the artifice and commercialism so despised by the hippies were, for the Glam Rock star, something to celebrate. However, *Rebel Rock* author John Street insists that the Bolan-inspired break, though significant, was nowhere near so orderly. "Glitter replaced the rhetoric, sequins replaced beads, and decadence replaced politics," he affirms, but "while styles and tastes changed, the search for sensations continued."

Marc, who had now started to pepper his conversations with fame-by-association references to The Beatles, Mick Jagger and Bob Dylan, saw little difference between his own sensational arrival and the Dylan effect that swept through pop during 1965. "At that point, while he was very

---

* By the mid-1960s, he'd even started to plagiarise himself, 'No Particular Place To Go' being a straight rewrite of his 1957 hit 'School Day'.

beautiful and incredibly important, most of (Dylan's) songs were just great namedrops," he claimed in *Rolling Stone*. "That's no downer, because at the time it was dynamite, but it was still namedrops. I could write you *Tarantula* in five minutes," he added, a reference to Dylan's 'Surrealism on speed' prose-poem from 1966.

That didn't sound like the luminous hippie who, back in April, had plugged 'Hot Love' on *Top Of The Pops* concealed behind a mess of hair and shared the stage with the bikini-clad Pan's People dance troupe. By mid-1971, all restrictions had been lifted. Promoting 'Get It On' that summer, Bolan played the part of the rock'n'roll star to the full. His body draped in satins and velvets, and his face aglow with glitter, Marc romped through a series of mimed performances with a new-found agility and a long-suppressed theatricality. Duck-walking around the stage like a demonic Chuck Berry, he pouted, tossed his flying curls and raised his hand above his head pointing a finger towards the sky as if to emphasise the hotline between himself and the almighty. He faked his Berry-derived riff with a look of studied ecstasy. Even his feet, clad in women's open shoes that highlighted a pair of red socks, appeared to be an invitation to dream.

"I see no reason why freaks shouldn't be in the charts," Marc told *Zigzag*'s Pete Frame at the time of the single, "but then they turn around and resent you for it." And 'they' got their last great opportunity on Sunday August 29, 1971, when T. Rex headlined the Weeley Festival Of Progressive Music in Clacton-on-Sea over the August Bank Holiday. The group had been a late addition to the bill, which also included music press darlings such as Rory Gallagher, Lindisfarne, Quintessence, Colosseum and original bill-toppers The Faces.

There was no love lost backstage, where the rival managements argued over top billing, and the mood in the crowd was no less belligerent. "Do you want to see The Faces?" asked the MC earlier in the day. "Yes!", the crowd chorused loudly. And what about T. Rex, he asked provocatively. A chorus of booing and "No!"s ensued. The Faces, notorious for their convivial, booze-fuelled good-time performances, were "show-stopping", according to Roy Carr in *New Musical Express*. The decision to fight for headline status had backfired on T. Rex. The band strolled out, and the tiny singer stepped up to the mike and said, disarmingly: "I'm Marc Bolan. You've probably seen me on *Top Of The Pops*." The joke was lost on some of the crowd, which continued to heckle him so badly that he was forced to bite back. "Why don't you fuck off," he complained. ". . . If you don't want to listen, then I'll leave."

"T. Rex are a strange band," Carr declared. "When electrified, they encompass the basic rudiments of rock . . . They emit a naïve enthusiasm one would expect from a bunch of blokes who had just acquired their first instruments and were having a good old blow down the local church hall or in someone's front room." His description of Bolan as a "20th century schizoid rock man" was particularly astute. "He draws on all the traditional mechanics of rock (and is) suddenly transformed into a reincarnation . . . Chuck Berry as he duck walks across the stage, Eddie Cochran as he belts out a repetitive riff, Pete Townshend playing at human windmills, Hendrix doing his sexual symbolism sequence."

Where the Class of 1963 and '64 (and, of course, 1967) had been making it up as they went along, Bolan – and Bowie and all those other camp followers – seemed to draw their inspiration from pop itself. DJ Bob Harris was smitten and he too saw T. Rex in terms of consolidation. "(Marc's) a very beautiful man, and his songs are tremendously communicative to young people," he said. "They represent not a polarisation but a drawing together of sympathetic ideas." Harris, presenter of BBC-TV's *The Old Grey Whistle Test* (on which, ironically, T. Rex were deemed too 'pop' for inclusion) and a rooter for progressive rock and earnest singer-songwriters, went even further, claiming that, "No one has captured the spirit of these times like Marc has. I think Marc and T. Rex have got to be the next Beatles, if they're not already."

Two obsessions dominated the music press during summer 1971: 'Selling out' and 'hype', which as a two-page special report in *Melody Maker* in August made clear, was an "Abb. of 'hyperbole – to exaggerate for emphasis'". The amount of press coverage Bolan was receiving seemed like an overdose of hype, but the awful truth of rock and pop magazine publishing was "TEN YEARS AFTER AND YES HIT THE ROAD" or "BEATLES TO REFORM?" headlines in the former and photographs of Tony Orlando's Dawn and Hurricane Smith in the latter.

Even Ringo Starr, who'd seen it all before with The Beatles, was thrilled by the band. "I think T. Rex are fantastic," he said at the end of July. A little later, he elaborated: "I like the showbiz in showbiz, yet everyone was getting so crazy they were all trying to deny it. But whatever you want to think, it is showbiz. When we get up there on stage, we're just the same as Hedy Lamarr."

Nina Myskow, editor of the mass circulation girls' weekly *Jackie*, instantly recognised Marc's appeal. "He was on *Top Of The Pops*, and he was in *Jackie* as soon as we could get him. We went to inordinate lengths to

Marc and Steve Peregrine Took as Tyrannosaurus Rex, photographed in the garden of Hermione Farthingale's parents' home in Edenbridge, Kent, in 1968. Hermione was David Bowie's girlfriend at the time and David, who was present, was displeased that this social visit turned into a photo session. (*Rex*)

John Peel, Bolan's friend and early champion, in 1968. "I liked Tyrannosaurus Rex initially because I've always been drawn to extreme voices," said Peel, whose companion in this shot has adopted Marc's Medusa-like locks. Note Tyrannosaurus Rex's *Prophets...* album in the background. Marc and Peel's relationship ended abruptly shortly after the release of 'Get It On' in July 1971. (*Rex*)

Steve Peregrine Took, Marc's Tyrannosaurus Rex partner, eternally drifting along Ladbroke Grove in a Tolkienesque haze. (*Rex*)

Marc with his wife June, nee Child, pictured in 1971. After they met in 1968 June became Marc's biggest supporter, eventually handling his business affairs during the T. Rex glory years. (*Rex*)

Marc goes electric. On the cusp of T. Rextasy, Marc poses coyly with his favourite Gibson Les Paul guitar. (*LFI*)

Marc with T. Rex partner Mickey Finn in October 1970. Though musically inexperienced, Finn provided a perfect visual foil for the main man. (*UPP*)

The T. Rex band pictured backstage at *Top Of The Pops*, in 1971. Left to right: bass player
Steve Currie, Mickey Finn, drummer Bill Legend and Marc. (*Rex*)

Marc Bolan – guitar hero. "There were times he wanted to be a musician, and there were times he simply wanted to be a star," said Tony Visconti. "That was his main internal struggle I think. Unfortunately most of the time he wanted to be a star." (*LFI/Rex*)

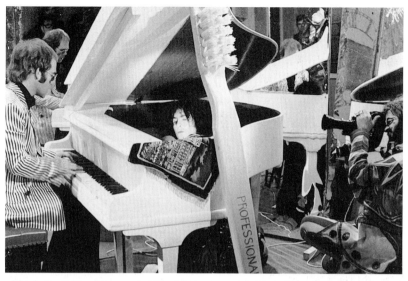

Marc's tousled head pops up in Elton John's piano while Ringo Starr, dressed as a clown, shoots this surreal scene from 1972's *Born To Boogie* film. (*Ronald Grant archive*)

Marc with Ringo Starr in 1972. The former Beatle is holding a copy of his hit single 'Back Off Boogaloo', inspired by the sound of T. Rex. (*Mirror Syndication*)

Heavily made up, Marc swaps electric for acoustic during a scene from *Born To Boogie*. (*Ronald Grant Archive*)

An unusually relaxed Marc pictured backstage at the peak of T. Rextasy, the only frightening aspect of which was that so many of the girls came armed with scissors with the intention of getting a lock of his hair. (*LFI*)

print three-page pin-ups of him," she recalled in 1997. "Little girls like non-threatening, not overtly sexual boys (and Marc had) that boyish quality, that cute cheekiness . . . in spades."

"The record industry needed someone at that point and Marc was the right person," says Bob Harris. "With bands like ELP, Yes and Led Zeppelin around, it wasn't hip to be making singles any more and that part of the market had suffered as a consequence. I loved what Marc was doing in 1971 but because he'd come in the opposite direction, from the underground to number one in the charts, he was an easy target for the critics."

The rock audience tended to shun latter-day Hedy Lamarrs in favour of Cecil B. De Mille types capable of overseeing the script, the cast, the costumes, the whole epic in full widescreen, Technicolor glory. It wanted *Tommy* across four sides of an LP, not songs that lasted no longer than the time it took to roll a joint; it sought the proverbial 'Stairway To Heaven' without having to 'Knock Three Times'; it demanded denim, robust and hard-wearing, not satins that split as soon as you looked at them. Even Deep Purple, Family, Ten Years After and Black Sabbath got caught up in the great sell-out debate for daring to succeed with hit singles. The abuse hurled at Marc was, at times, cruel and unmerciful.

But, in the succinct words of B.P. Fallon, publicist during T. Rex's thrilling months of transition: "Marc changed everything".

★ ★ ★

In his first major *Rolling Stone* interview, published in September 1971, Marc tried to lay the old Tyrannosaurus Rex image to rest. "I don't wanna be James Taylor," he explained, mindful that American journalists – and concert promoters – were still using the old group name. "I'm feeling a lot more aggressive in my outlook towards the world."

Gloves were off; history was swept aside. "There was the quiet period, flowers and peaceful," Marc told Chris Welch in August, "but I don't feel that way anymore. It's not a very peaceful world. I want to boogie, but with good words as well." The 'Bopping Elf' hitched a ride back to Never-Never Land. The efflorescence of Marc Bolan required a more apt, imposing epithet. On September 24, 1971, it arrived in the form of the second T. Rex album, *Electric Warrior*.

June Bolan had the initial idea, Kieron 'Spud' Murphy took the photograph and Hipgnosis designer Aubrey Powell fashioned what was perhaps the first iconic image of the Seventies – the *Electric Warrior* album sleeve. It was a remarkable transition from the ghostly hippie fop on the front of the *T. Rex* album, and all the more remarkable for resisting the commercial pull towards Bolan's face and curls. Instead, the diminutive, novitiate electric guitarist was recast as an incandescent virtuoso of heroic proportions, sculpted – with his huge amp and speaker stack – from the matter of modern mythology. The image was further reinforced by the unprecedented use of a colour picture label, featuring Marc and Mickey, and a fold-out poster of the band.

Electric Warrior was the first T. Rex album recorded as a four-piece, but, said Bolan, "As far as I'm concerned, it's the first album I've ever made. The others were just ideas, but in this one I spoke about me and you and all of us." It wasn't idle puff: the acoustic-based 'Cosmic Dancer' and 'Life's A Gas' chimed perfectly with Bolan's new celebrity, private meditations writ large.

In many ways, *Electric Warrior* was a descendant of John Lennon's *Plastic Ono Band* album, issued the previous December. It echoed Lennon's hunger for simplicity, for basic truths, for a no-frills rock'n'roll sound, for instant, unmediated communication. However, any comparison between this pair of remarkable records ends there. The ex-Beatle delivered an intimate and revealing coming of age album on which he re-evaluated his childhood, his idols, his fame, in short his entire being. Marc's return to simplicity was angst-free without recourse to Primal Scream therapy or rigorous self-examination. Where Lennon had described God as "a concept by which we measure our own pain", for example, Marc preferred to see his God – "High in your fields above Earth/Come and be real for us" – as a saviour machine.

Lennon directed his lucidity inwards. Marc wore his externally and spectacularly – the visual aggression of the *Electric Warrior* sleeve mirroring the blitzkrieg approach of the music within. Claiming that the album was his 'first' was obviously hyperbole but, on an emotional level at least, not without honesty. No other Bolan record had been recorded like this – with a four-piece band, at makeshift recording sessions across two continents, and against a fast-changing backdrop that increasingly suggested that the material was destined for a large audience. All of this contributed to Marc's intuitive belief that, more than ever before, the record should speak in a universal tongue.

When the band returned from the States with the rough tapes for the album, there was little time for deliberation. "We'd worked in different studios, all with different sounds," says Tony Visconti, "but we realised this had to be it; there was no time to make an album, this is the album. It was only at the later overdub stage that we realised we had such a lot of good stuff. I think what we were probably doing was amassing singles. It all happened very innocently."

Back in London, Marc and Tony had squeezed several overdub sessions into T. Rex's hectic spring schedule, as well as recording at least one more new song, 'Rip Off', at Advision on May 12. Written in Los Angeles, towards the end of T. Rex's American sojourn, its attacking, vitriol-filled mood was different, containing a cynicism absent from the rest of the album. "I wrote that for America," Marc tellingly explained in December. "That was such a last-minute track," says the producer, "though I wouldn't say it was haphazard. It was an unconsciously made gem!"

'Rip Off' raged – obscurely it must be said – against the iniquities of the music business. Everything else on *Electric Warrior* thrilled and soothed with a seemingly effortless grace, though numerous overdubs and post-production techniques were used to pull the material together. "Marc and I had a long list of sonic tricks and musical signatures in our arsenal by now," says Visconti. "We were using tape flanging and phasing, unrealistic reverbs, backwards guitars, cool guitar pedals, plugging the guitar directly into the console and overloading the mike pre-amplifiers, even tape loops. Some of the original material was rough, but we kept on refining it with overdubs."

A number of session players including pianists Blue Weaver and Rick Wakeman, Burt Collins on flugelhorn and sax–player Ian McDonald were brought in. 'Fixer' David Katz organised a string section, according to Visconti "a band of gypsies who would play any wacky thing I wrote down . . . Marc and I loved the strings on The Shirelles' 'Will You Love Me Tomorrow'. All those string lines on *Electric Warrior* are reminiscent of early Sixties string pop." Bolan was often required to record a new lead vocal because he rarely sang loudly enough on the live takes. While his original guitar tracks were retained, the sound was fattened with several guitar overdubs, both acoustic and electric, and additional solos too. Visconti made full use of Trident Studios' new 16-track recording equipment.

As early as May, soon after returning from America, Marc stated that, "Practically everything on this album are 12-bars – all blues – but they don't sound like it to me." Revivalism was written all over the record, prompting critics to trip over themselves with trainspotting glee. 'Jeepster'? That was Howlin' Wolf's 'You'll Be Mine' with shades of Presley's 'My Baby Left Me' and one of Marc's lesser-known rockabilly idols Sleepy La

Beef. 'Get It On'? Chuck's 'Little Queenie', of course. 'Monolith'? None other than Gene Chandler's 1962 doo wop hit, 'Duke Of Earl'.*

Visconti's suggestion that *Electric Warrior* was composed of potential singles is – 'Rip Off' aside – borne out by the joy that emanates from each song. Even the opening 'Mambo Sun', which hung on one of those mantra-like rhythms Marc had been using for years, and threw in sinister strings and spell-like "oohs and aahs" towards the end of the song, sounded like a hit despite its obvious flouting of Tin Pan Alley etiquette. There was something deliciously diabolic, too, about the rhyming couplets used on the first two tracks, a surfeit of moons, croons, wombs, tombs and soons. That second cut, 'Cosmic Dancer', a delicate melody drenched in references to Bolan's 'lord of the dance' destiny, neatly employed a subtle backwards guitar effect much used on Jimi Hendrix's posthumous *The Cry Of Love* album, issued that March.

Electric Warrior was awash in raw delights and golden, studio enhanced touches. So many of the record's pleasures reside in the details – the two cellos and bassoon that accentuated the descending line on 'Jeepster' and turned up again on 'The Motivator'; Bill Legend's earthy snare; Flo and Eddie's flying falsettos; Marc's inspired use of the wah-wah pedal; his blues-rock voice thrillingly emasculated yet full of sexual suggestion; the unscripted sound of Marc's Cuban heel stomping on the floor during 'Jeepster'; and a jewellery box of lyric gems. Joy, inspiration and confidence radiate from every song – confidence especially. At one point during the New York session, Marc introduces an early take of 'Jeepster' and says, "I wish Otis Redding was around. He could do backing vocals on this." He didn't sound as if he was joking.

Typically, the between-song banter at the studio sessions tends to reveal that there was rather more of the electric than the warrior about Marc Bolan in mid-1971. "The first year I was with him, he was very pleasant, almost affectionate at times," recalls Bill Legend. Others, who had known Marc during the difficult times when he'd turn up at gigs with a battered acoustic under his arm, sensed that success had activated a wholly different aspect of his personality.

"He was obviously interested in spiritual things but as the materialistic side took off all that took a back seat," remembers Pete Sanders. "I was seriously looking and had gone off to India. When I came back, I asked

---

* Marc wasn't shy about it, either. When Visconti requested the title from the control booth Marc, clearly amused, replied, " 'Duke Of Monolith'."

him about it and he said, 'I'm gonna make it first and when I'm rich I'll buy an island and then I'll get into the spiritual thing.' It was like something he decided to shut off until later."

After the success of 'Ride A White Swan', Marc and June had uprooted from Blenheim Crescent to the more salubrious northern side of the Westway, in leafy Little Venice close to Maida Vale. The rented flat at 31 Clarendon Gardens was better suited to Marc's growing concerns for his privacy and spacious enough to warrant a large music room for his rapidly expanding portfolio of guitars (nine by the autumn), his Brennel home recording equipment and the record collection that sometimes grew by 20 or 30 titles per day. Like a fan, Marc stuck Jimi Hendrix posters on the walls, while June played hippie homemaker draping richly coloured tapestries over the antique armchairs and expansive sofa, laying thick Eastern rugs across the floor and filling any available wall-space with oversized mirrors.

The property came with its own garage which, by autumn 1971, housed an AC sports car and a gleaming white Rolls-Royce purchased secondhand for £2,000. The Roller – the classic four-wheel symbol of British wealth and respectability – was an odd choice. Marc couldn't drive, but that wasn't a problem because June – now indulging her penchant for fur coats – could. It was strange because his love affair with American cars ("works of art", he once described them), chrome-covered machines that were almost as big in real life as they'd seemed in the movies, showed little sign of abating in song.*

"In a way, I suppose he did betray something, because he had the possibility of finding out a lot more about himself," laments Pete Sanders. "Instead he turned into something I didn't imagine him to be." Unlike John Peel, deemed superfluous to Bolan's requirements after a professional spat, the photographer simply found himself with little in common with Marc anymore. "No one minded him being successful, and I think he dealt with the fame in the early days very well," he maintains.

According to Chelita Secunda, "Marc wanted to be a Star and you have to be careful of what you dream of." Pete Jenner, the co-founder of Blackhill Enterprises who had sensed Bolan's ambition as early as 1968, took a wholly less charitable view. "Bolan was a complete arsehole, the way he turned over Peel and everything else," he said. "Quite clearly he

---

* He'd recently written, but not yet recorded, a song called 'Cadilac' [sic].

was just a very ambitious little kid who wanted to become a pop star . . . He'd sussed that the way through for him was by being a little hippie. He used me and he used John Peel."

The estrangement from Peel was the most public indication that it wasn't only music that was changing in Marc's life. On December 8, 1970, Marc had joined *Top Gear* stalwarts such as Rod Stewart & The Faces, The Soft Machine, Curved Air's Sonja Kristina, Ivor Cutler and Bridget St. John at the BBC's Maida Vale studios for a seasonal performance of Christmas carols. Even June Bolan was roped in for a verse of 'Oh Come All Ye Faithful'. Two days later, he was back at the Beeb's Paris Theatre recording for John Peel's *In Concert*. It was the last in a series of four separate BBC session airings for 'Ride A White Swan' since October, an important factor in the single's success. *In Concert* producer Jeff Griffin remembers Marc offering grateful thanks to Peel, Bob Harris and himself in front of the Paris Theatre audience for helping him achieve his success. He never recorded for – or worked with – John Peel again.

Unlike Peel, whose reputation continued to flourish long after his friendship with Marc had faded, Steve Took had floated further towards the margins. After leaving Tyrannosaurus Rex, Took had immersed himself in the politics of ecstasy, occasionally getting himself together to make a return to recording. Shortly after the split, Took had co-founded The Pink Fairies, together with ex-(Social) Deviant Mick Farren and one-time Pretty Things drummer Twink. The band débuted at Manchester University in October 1969.

"I sat down on the drums and started banging away," Twink told Nigel Cross. "Mick was trying to sing, Steve Took was playing guitar and my girlfriend Silver Darling was on keyboards even though she'd never played them before. There was no music as such, and the concert ended up with us standing in the middle of the audience talking to people, pulling down our trousers and farting in their faces!"

Two Steve Took songs, 'Three Little Piggies' and 'The Sparrow Is The Sign', were recorded for Twink's 1970 solo album, *Think Pink*, on which Took contributed guitar throughout. He also appeared on Mick Farren's solo record, *Mona The Carniverous Circus*, credited as Shagrat the Vagrant. On one track, 'Carniverous Circus Part II', Took recited his unpleasant experiences inside the Ashford Remand Centre, where he'd been sent after his drug bust.

After The Pink Fairies adopted a marginally more serious attitude to their work, and Steve fell out with Mick Farren, Took split in spring 1970 to form Shagrat with Larry Wallis and Tim Taylor, lead guitarist and bassist with the Entire Sioux Nation, and drummer Phil Lenoir. Once again, Took had dived deep into Tolkien's *The Lord Of The Rings* to find the group name though, tellingly, Shagrat was not a hero Hobbit but an evil Orc captain.

That April, the group recorded several songs including Took and Wallis' 'Peppermint Flipstick', apparently inspired by Pink Floyd's 'Astronomy Dominé' and a phallic Cadbury's Flake television ad. Nearly six minutes worth of stoned aggression, fuelled by dread, wah-wah-driven chords that teetered on the edge of feedback, and rammed home with a malevolent Took vocal that wavered in and out of key, 'Peppermint Flipstick' – and other tracks cut at the session, including 'Boo! I Said Freeze' and 'Steel Abortion' – represented the darker underbelly of Ladbroke Grove alternative culture.

Took and Wallis continued to work together and during 1971, recorded an acoustic-based session at Wallis' house with ex-Chicken Shack drummer Dave Bidwell on tambourine. One track, 'Amanda', was deliciously tender, inspired perhaps by Took's hero-worship of Love's Arthur Lee, though his lazy drawl was reminiscent of one-time Quicksilver Messenger Service vocalist Dino Valenti.

Took was all about "chromium-plated cosmic supertripping rock'n'-roll neon sex fun," claimed Larry Wallis, so much so that his projects rarely got past the rehearsal stage. This was confirmed by Mick Farren who told *Mojo* magazine in 1995 that Took "wrote songs and cut tracks, but every time he was poised to lay his creation before the public, some manifestation of what could only be fear of failure would bring his efforts to a screeching halt. He'd injure himself or plunge into a personality crisis. Sessions would abort in a chaos of pills or vodka."

When Shagrat ended messily, Took sheepishly performed a series of solo concerts, including an appearance at The Pink Fairies' Christmas Party at Chiswick Town Hall. It was around the time of T. Rex's summer tour, and the performances couldn't have been more different. In an echo of Tyrannosaurus Rex, he sat on a stool, accompanying himself on acoustic guitar and mesmerised the crowd. Still there was no offer of a record contract.

It was a different story entirely to that of his old partner-in-rhyme. The Promethean leaps made during 1971 – two successive number one hit singles and *Electric Warrior* in the starting-blocks – put Bolan in a strong position to renegotiate his contract with Fly. After the years spent virtually pleading for support, he was able to turn the tables and start making his own demands.

According to David Platz, who as boss of Essex Music, Straight Ahead Productions and Fly Records owned a significant stake in Bolan's career, Marc had promised him that he would remain with the label if Platz could make him famous. "We'd thrashed the renegotiation of Marc's contract out at the Venezia restaurant in Soho one Friday," Platz recalls, "and after four hours, everyone – Marc, David Enthoven and ourselves – was happy." But trouble was afoot.

"Over the weekend, I received a phone call at home from Tony Secunda (ex-husband of glitter queen Chelita) who told me, 'I've taken over as Marc's manager and Marc tells me you're renegotiating the contract.' And I said, 'As far as I know, we've negotiated it and it's being typed out ready for his final approval and signature.' Secunda said, 'Listen, I'm in charge now, and what I require on Marc's behalf is not what you've negotiated.'" Secunda then demanded a royalty figure that exceeded what Fly/Straight Ahead had been receiving from EMI. "I told him that was impossible," Platz remembers.

Marc's new hard man was also seeking to restrict the territories so that Secunda and his corkscrew-headed client could make a series of licensing deals throughout the rest of the world. "We discussed it at length and it got more and more difficult," Platz says. "I told him, 'You don't seem to understand. What you're asking is something that would actually cost us money.' We may have been getting something like 15% from EMI and he was asking a figure higher than that. I said, 'How the hell are we going to negotiate a deal whereby we were going to lose money?' Secunda couldn't see that."

Starmakers And Svengalis' author Johnny Rogan describes Tony Secunda as "one of the great sensationalists of the Sixties". Like Rolling Stones image-maker Andrew Oldham before him, Secunda courted scandal throughout his management career, most spectacularly with The Move. Having encouraged the group to smash televisions on stage, he then produced a lewd postcard that cast libellous aspersions on the relationship between Prime Minister Harold Wilson and his secretary Marcia Falkender. Designed to promote The Move's 'Flowers In The Rain' single, the prank backfired with hideous consequences for the group's songwriter Roy Wood. Wilson successfully sued for libel, and as part of the settlement, royalties from the song – a Top three hit in autumn 1967 – had to be donated to charity . . . indefinitely.

Tony Secunda had first met Marc Bolan in the offices of Essex Music/ New Breed Productions shortly after The Move debacle. His relationship with The Move had necessitated close contact with Denny Cordell and David Platz, but both Cordell and Secunda fell out with the publisher, which partly explains Secunda's aggression four years later when Bolan employed him to strong arm the optimum deal for T. Rex.

"I never felt that Tyrannosaurus Rex were really worth managing at that early stage," Secunda says. "After all, I had The Move and Procol Harum, two top chart acts. Instead, Marc took up with David Enthoven and Mark Fenwick, two rich kids who wanted to get in on the music business. That was very convenient because he could manipulate them; Marc was a born manipulator. Eventually, he ran his course with them. Marc had a class complex too, and though he liked to be around that middle-class stuff, it used to get up his nose."

By mid-1971, the Enthoven relationship had soured. Success had made Marc increasingly insecure about his financial affairs, as he explained to *Sounds'* Penny Valentine in May. "The one thing is I'm not a breadhead," he mused. "And in the end that is probably going to be my downfall . . . That's why when there was a mild accusation of selling out it hurt me. Because that's the one thing that would never occur to me. I'm not shrewd enough, you see." Within weeks, that vulnerability had prompted him to seek out a fearsome protector.

"After he'd decided to do a Dylan – stand up, uncross his legs and go electric – and had a couple of hits, I found out he'd been trying to get in contact with me," Secunda continues. "I went to visit my ex-wife Chelita one night, and he was there. She'd set it up in her typically Machiavellian way! Marc was with June, and some crazy French guy appeared with some pure amphetamine sulphate that he laid on the table for our pleasure. We did some of this stuff and we sat and talked for something like 14 hours. He told me how pissed off he was with Platz, and he knew I was the ideal person to go in and clear up the mess."

The conspirators met again over lunch, and Marc handed Secunda a pile of advance copies of 'Get It On' to pass on to influential contacts like DJ Murray the K in the States. Meanwhile, Bolan kept his options open, even toying with the idea of using Chas Chandler, who was just breaking Slade with 'Get Down And Get With It'. Early in September, he'd made his decision and while in New York to organise a winter tour and discuss the promotion of *Electric Warrior* with Reprise Records, Marc formally enlisted Secunda's services.

"All the agreements had run out," recalls the manager, "so it was a perfect situation for me to walk into and really do what I do best – negotiate good deals. I cut out the middleman, which is basically what Platz and Fly Records was, and went straight to the top of the mountain – EMI Records."

By the end of 1971, Secunda and Bolan had formed the T. Rex Wax Co. label, the Wizard Artists and Warrior Music Projects Ltd. publishing companies, and struck a tape-lease deal with EMI giving Marc control over what could be released under the T. Rex name. This aggressive new team renegotiated with Warner/Reprise in America, and Secunda put in place licensing deals in several other territories, including CBS in France and Ariola in Germany.

The label was, in truth, little more than a vanity affair – unlike The Beatles' Apple, Rolling Stones Records or The Beach Boys' Brother outlet, the T. Rex Wax Co. had no use for anything other than Marc's own releases. "It was set up to make the most mileage out of his life," says Secunda. "We grossed something like six million dollars in six months on worldwide record deals alone," he claims, "and most of that was upfront. It was one of the great rock deals of all time and we had great fun doing it.

"We did a deal with the German company Ariola and it reached the point where we were almost ready to sign. And I said to the guy on the phone, 'Naah, it's still not enough. We need more, in cash and upfront. And we want it in a suitcase – today!' This was around 11 in the morning. He called back 15 minutes later and said, 'I'm getting on ze 12.15 from Frankfurt and I'll be viz you by two o'clock viz ze money in ze briefcase.' It was like a fucking Bugs Bunny movie, man! By three o'clock he was there with all the money laid out on the table with Prince Wilhelm de Earwig's face on it. It was a wonderful moment."

Faced with the pent-up wrath of Secunda and an artist who'd desperately been waiting for the tables to turn in the struggle for power, David Platz did something he'd never done before. He washed his hands of one of his artists and pulled out of the negotiations. "That literally ended my association with Marc," Platz says. "I never saw him again; he never contacted me again. Whether it was a guilty conscience I don't know." Platz thought it ironic that Marc had ended up back on EMI, the company that had been distributing Bolan's work since 1968. "I remember talking to one of the heads there and asked him, 'How could you do that? Couldn't you, as a matter of decency, have told us that you'd been approached to sign Marc Bolan?' But that's not the way the music industry works.

Highest bidder wins." It was, of course, a working practice that Platz, master of his own vast empire, understood all too well.

The years he spent enduring managers, agents, journalists and friends advising him how best to improve his act had taken its toll on Bolan. Success had vindicated him and Marc no longer needed to listen to the advice of those who told him what he didn't want to hear. "A lot of young artists get ripped off in various ways," explains ex-*New Musical Express* journalist turned PR man Keith Altham. "And they realise that the most self-protective way of looking after that situation is to do everything yourself. I think it's more a defensive mechanism than being about control." It probably was, at least for the time being.

Back from America, and with Secunda now acting on his behalf, Marc returned to the business of promoting *Electric Warrior*. Despite the controversy he'd whipped up, the album received some guardedly favourable notices. "Marc's music is getting better all the time," claimed Chris Welch in *Melody Maker*. "He has developed the knack for writing good, original pop, and with the aid of producer Tony Visconti, is developing an amazing studio sound with its roots in the Fifties." *New Musical Express'* Nick Logan was similarly complimentary about T. Rex's contemporary take on vintage rock'n'roll values, but warned that Marc may have "been a little too clever . . . I began to feel towards the end that the diligent pursuit after the quintessence of rock and roll had robbed a lot of the songs of their initial funk."

Logan's complaint would have been lost on Marc's younger constituency which, as the pandemonium that surrounded the *Electric Warrior* UK tour during October and November, now represented the vast majority of his audience. Speaking to *Beat Instrumental's* Steve Turner that autumn, Marc claimed that 'Mambo Sun' had been inspired by a six-year-old girl who lived in the flat below him. "She laughed so much when she heard it," he said. "It was the way the words popped and moved. If I'd have sung 'The Scenescof Dynasty' to her she'd have gone out and played frisbee or something."

Few six-year-olds made it to the ABC Plymouth or to Birmingham Town Hall that winter, but the scenes on the *Electric Warrior* tour far exceeded anything witnessed earlier that year or, for that matter, since The Beatles' heyday during 1964. T. Rex needed a police escort in and out of every town they visited; Bolan's claim to be the 'Prophet Of The New Generation' was no idle boast.

For the tour, which opened at the Portsmouth Guildhall on October

19, 1971, T. Rex were accompanied by the softly spoken MC Bob Harris who was forced to spin his set (that invariably included Rod Stewart's 'Maggie May' and Lindisfarne's 'Fog On The Tyne') against a din of constant clapping, footstomping and, above all, piercing screams. The response, a state of what was now being referred to as 'T. Rextasy', stunned Harris, a veteran of Marc's Middle Earth days. "During that tour, the entourage travelled in five big, gas-guzzling Vauxhall Crestas," he says, "and after that first gig at Portsmouth, we waited backstage for a while, enjoying a drink and meeting one or two of the prettier girls that had been chosen by the roadies to join us.

"When we headed for the stage door, the attendant said, 'I'd wait if I were you. There are quite a few people out there.' When we opened the door, we were absolutely stunned. It was as if the entire audience had shifted from the auditorium round to the back! The local police eased the situation, but the most frightening aspect was that so many of the girls were armed with scissors with the intention of getting a lock of Marc's hair."

As the entourage made its way towards the fleet of cars, the extent of the hysteria-induced damage became clear. "Everything had been ripped off the cars and taken as souvenirs – registration plates, windscreen wipers, hub caps, the lot all gone. After we'd got into our vehicles, we began to edge forward, despite the mass of faces pressed up against the glass and people on the bonnet and the roof. Then there was this almighty crunch as the whole suspension gave way under the weight."

Three of the five cars were written off that evening. "That was the night they came up with the idea of letting the last guitar chord resonate while the band made their getaway before the crowd could get at them," Harris says. "Otherwise, it would have been complete madness."

This sort of behaviour hadn't happened in August at the Concert For Bangladesh in Madison Square Garden, New York, where George Harrison fronted a bearded muso supergroup. Nor did that year's other newcomers The New Seekers and The Carpenters inspire anything like such rabid devotion. Audiences at James Taylor, Cat Stevens, Carole King and Randy Newman concerts would have baulked at the sound of a cigarette being lit. Black Sabbath, Deep Purple and Hawkwind concerts were rowdy, but by the end, they'd usually pummelled their fans into delirious, stoned submission. "I wish the scene would change and people would get young idols," complained 'Hype of '71' Elton John. "It's crazy – Rod Stewart's in his mid-twenties, Dylan and Lennon are thirtyish,

Presley's an old man and even I am 24!" Bolan was 24, too, but then he looked a good ten years younger than Elton.

That's why, by winter 1971, *Jackie* magazine was receiving around 800 letters per week from Bolan fans, many of whom increasingly expressed their concern for his health. They'd heard that he was dying of leukaemia and had just three months to live. That he had cancer. Rarely washed his hair. Practises black magic. Neither Chairman Mao nor the Dalai Lama could inspire such love and devotion. It was 'Paul Is Dead' all over again – multiplied ten thousand fold. "The fans? The fans were insane," remembered Chelita Secunda.

The cult of 'MARC' demanded, and usually got, the most minuscule details pertaining to his life. Mysterious tales from his past (the 'Wizard', busking in Hyde Park, those hippie years) were recycled, each time gaining in outlandishness as the newly invigorated teenage magazine market was swamped by a range of new titles such as *Popswop*, *Music Scene* and *Superstar*. Once in a while, Mickey Finn was wheeled out to relieve the stress on Bolan, but even his affable, laid-back manner and film star looks couldn't compete with the corkscrew-haired Superstar with a penchant for inventing words such as 'Jeepster'.

This (pre)pubescent identification with Marc can be explained by his androgynous beauty, his peculiar outfits and mannerisms and that aspect of his narcissism that revealed itself as childlike vulnerability. Still metaphorically pinching himself with delight for having defied the doubters, sometimes Marc's eyes would fix on the camera lens for a split second too long, prompting a brief self-conscious smile before he'd compose himself again. Rolling Stones guitarist Brian Jones, who, too, was overly preoccupied with – and never really managed – his own celebrity, left himself similarly unguarded during the mid-Sixties.

At the peak of his fame, Marc told *Jackie*: "I don't see Marc Bolan of T. Rex. I see a little boy of a year old. In a sense, I am still waiting to grow up. I am still waiting to be a man and see some hairs on my chest." Despite the showy displays, there was an inherent sense of the innocent abroad in Marc's performances. The cast-offs may have already been mounting up, and the business matters kept firmly under control, but this doesn't prove that Marc's apparent naïvety was necessarily bogus. "There was always an air of innocence about him, a childlike quality that made it very powerful and very honest," explains Keith Altham. "A child's vision can be much clearer than an adult's. Sometimes, I found it quite disturbing. He could express a profound truth very simply."

And sometimes he could dress the simplest things in life, sexual desire for example, in the most bafflingly obscure ways. 'Jeepster', though, was a more obvious metaphor than many suspected. Far from being a word conjured from Bolan's increasingly fertile mind, a Jeepster was indeed a car. And the song, lifted from *Electric Warrior* by a slighted David Platz at Fly Records, ensured that T. Rex became the best selling singles artists in Britain of the year when it peaked at number two throughout December. Once again, Marc had been pipped by a characteristic overdose of seasonal nonsense, on this occasion the innuendo-ridden 'Ernie' sung by comedian Benny Hill.

Despite his unrelenting schedule, Marc continued to write new songs at a prolific pace. "There's an easy-to-grasp feeling about them," he told *Beat Instrumental*'s Steve Turner. That's probably why plans to release 'Sailors Of The Highway', a song entirely lacking in any 'Bolan Boogie' and premiered on *The Bob Harris Show*, were shelved. Even prior to the release of 'Jeepster' on 45, T. Rex had returned to the studio to perfect an even more refined version of the group's sound.

"I have a very high energy level at the moment," Marc told Michael Cuscuna during a short trip to America in December. "So I don't feel any wear on my spirit or my body. There comes a time when you get worn out . . ." he added. Something had to give, though, and Marc admitted to Cuscuna that his grand conceptual epic, *The Children Of Rarn*, loosely based on his 1968 writings and more properly conceived during 1970, had been temporarily shelved. "It's a pretty historic story," he continued, "which was gonna be the album before *Electric Warrior*, a science-fiction album.

"It's about prehistoric earth before the dinosaurs were heavy creatures," he'd tell anyone who'd listen. "There were two races of people then, the Peacelings and the Dworns. Now the Dworns were soulless people, very bestial. Dworn is actually a two-sided word – it's a man, but it's also a machine, which in fact was a prehistoric motorbike which worked on solar power. It has solid ivory wheels, a golden base and two gazelle horns to steer it. It could go about 800mph. Anyway, there were a lot of these creatures called the Lithons . . ." And so the saga continued.

"It was going to be our *Tommy*, our *Sgt. Pepper*, our big rock opera," recalls producer Tony Visconti, who got 15 minutes of the project's key elements down on tape some time during 1971. It was an unprepared session, with Marc using the producer's nylon-stringed classical guitar to outline his key musical themes. Mournful cries of "Rarn, Rarn" were juxtaposed with incongruous, 'One Inch Rock' type boogies, with Marc holding it all together with some narrative links. With all the grandeur of a Glam-baiting Pomp Rocker, Marc had big ideas for *The Children Of Rarn*, which just 12 months earlier he envisaged as a double-album with a book, a radio show, a stage production and, of course, a big-budget film.

Surveying the epic landscapes of his own life, which had changed dramatically during 1971, he admitted to Cuscuna: "I don't know when we'll record it now." Marc knew that an 80-minute fantasy suite would be lost on his new audience. Besides, his greatest challenge now was to keep creating and refining those three-chord, three-minute anthems that had transformed the pop world over the course of the previous 12 months. That, and of course, conquer America.

9

Superstar

"It's very important for me to keep in contact. That's why I send the roadies out to buy all the music papers."
> – Marc Bolan, *New Musical Express* (August 1972)

"Marc had a catchphrase: '300,000 in five days, number 1 in two weeks'."
> – Ringo Starr

"The whole thing was Marc Bolan. It was never T. Rex. He was T. Rex."
> – Steve Currie, bassist, T. Rex

"Being around the band in 1971 was fun," remembers Mick Gray, who was Marc's executive road manager and Personal Assistant between 1971 and 1976. "It was like a family. Before every show we would form a circle, hold hands and chant ending in a yell! There was no sign of any drugs apart from Mickey having the odd smoke. Marc seemed to have a genuine rapport with the audience, he seemed gentle, almost fey and June was always there to listen like a big sister."

During 1972, that began to change. Marc Bolan celebrated his newly conferred Superstar status by developing a taste for cocaine washed down with copious libations of champagne. He stopped listening to the advice of those around him and, fortified by the ego-swelling stimulants he'd previously eschewed, increasingly commanded his own hermetically sealed paradise. Within months of achieving success, Marc Bolan had become an untouchable on the cusp of surrendering himself to his public image, and the private habits that made it seem all the more believable. It was the realisation of a dream, and as long as the hits kept coming, as long as Marc's face continued to dominate magazine covers and as long as the crowds still chanted his name – all of which continued throughout 1972 – Marc Bolan: Superstar saw no reason to halt the celebrations.

Marc Bolan's Shea Stadium moment came on Saturday March 18,

1972. T. Rex played two concerts at the Empire Pool, Wembley, to a total of 16,000 roaring, adoring fans, shows that prompted *Melody Maker* to declare: "BOLAN MANIA HITS NEW PEAK". It was the first time the venue had been used for a major single artist concert. Ringo Starr brought along a small team to film the event for a project that started life as a documentary and ended up becoming a full-length feature film. 'Telegram Sam', released in January, had already given T. Rex their third number one hit single, and while the group spent much of February touring America, that spring Bolan and the 'Glitter Rock' phenomenon became a national obsession.

Around the time of the Wembley show, Charles Shaar Murray was granted an audience with Marc in his new West End office. Bolan, dressed in an expensive black velvet suit, sipped Scotch and Coke, and emitted a string of grand thoughts ("There's very little that I don't know about rock'n'roll – on any level. Or pop music, for that matter") that caused the journalist to depart with deep reservations about him, both as a human being and as a musician. Nevertheless his piece published in *Creem* magazine under the title, "Hello. I'm Marc Bolan. I'm a Superstar. You'd better believe it," wasn't coy about Bolan's current status.

"Marc Bolan, Superstar," it began. "A star is someone who we know about, but a Superstar is someone everybody knows about – your parents, the milkman, your bank manager, everybody . . . To the most important group of people in the country – the adolescents and pre-adolescents – Bolan is more than a Superstar, he's a Superhero . . ." At the same time, Pink Floyd advertised their latest tour by posing with their backs to the photographer.

Apart from a one-off performance at the Starlight Rooms in Boston, Lincolnshire, on January 15, the Wembley concerts were the first domestic T. Rex shows since the *Electric Warrior* tour ended the previous November. Initially, the gigs were envisaged as a stepping stone to similar, large-scale one-off ventures abroad, but the extraordinary response – and subsequent immortalisation in the *Born To Boogie* film – has enshrined the day forever as the apotheosis of Bolan's career. It marked the moment when Rexmania genuinely rivalled Beatlemania and an entire movement – Glam Rock – piggybacked it to create a sense of pop reborn and bopping. It was just like 1964, or 1956, again.

In the studio, Visconti and Bolan were close to patenting a 'T. Rex sound' that would echo the Bolan persona – extravagant, magnificent, unmistakeable. But it was the magnitude of that persona that was in such evidence at Wembley. Dressed (for the second show) in a sparkling, champagne-coloured jacket and a T-shirt that bore his own image, Marc dominated the stage, the vast hall, the movie cameras and the headlines that followed the shows. He strutted and swaggered, pouted and shook his mane of hair, letting out a stream of excited vocal whoops and shrieks that prompted the same from an audience already close to derangement. He played the part of a guitar hero, albeit one who preferred to use the instrument as a prop rather than a substitute for masturbation.

Any cock-extending tendencies centred on the image of Bolan. Giant backdrops of himself hung behind him and the mass identification with the Star, which became a distinguishing feature of Glam Rock, was in evidence elsewhere too – on the scarves that bore his name, on the pin-up 'Supersize' posters that fluttered above the heads of the crowd and in the stars and glitter that many of the – predominantly female – audience wore on their cheeks and their clothes.

Iggy Pop, who was in London to boost his flagging career, described the show as "kinda Chipmunky". He wasn't the only American who failed to succumb to T. Rexstasy. "America is very important whether you like it or not," Marc admitted back in May 1971. He'd returned there in December for a short promotional visit, giving several high profile radio appearances that appeared to pay off when 'Get It On' entered the US Top 10 in January 1972. The title caused some headaches at Warner Bros who changed its title to 'Bang A Gong (Get It On)'. A euphemism for fuck, 'Get It On' was also deemed too close to the title of a recent hit, 'Get It On In The Morning' by Chase. Many insist that the confusion robbed T. Rex of an even higher chart placing.

After a short series of dates in Germany and Scandinavia at the end of January, T. Rex were back again, flying into Los Angeles on February 14 for a two-week US tour designed to build on the momentum of 'Bang A Gong' and to promote *Electric Warrior*. For the first time, the group were headliners, and the series of dates in mid-sized venues was well attended in the wake of considerable advance publicity. "T. Rex are the new Beatles," declared one concert programme, "the teen idols of the Seventies and the biggest pop sensation in years."

Reviewers didn't always see it that way. Playing sets that lasted just 45 minutes including encores didn't help and Mick Jagger, who was in the 5,000-strong crowd at the Hollywood Palladium in Los Angeles on February 15 advised Bolan as much. Nevertheless, he managed to summon up the enthusiasm to dance in the wings in his white suit, and attend the aftershow party at the band's hotel, where he discussed cricket with Bill Legend and signed an autograph for Steve Currie. Marc Bolan began his recording career just two years after the Stones, but to the old guard he still had much to learn.

The *Los Angeles Times* was reasonably enthusiastic, praising the band's "enormously accessible, driving rock and roll sound" and Marc's "certain star quality". Detroit, a city always more in tune with rock'n'roll basics, was even more smitten by the show on February 19. "Bolan had the audience in the palm of his hand," reported John Wiesman in *Melody Maker*. "Then the band left the stage. Bolan grabbed an acoustic guitar and sat on the floor," he continued. "Unbelievably, the house shut up. He played 'Spaceball Ricochet' and they screamed. When he played 'Cosmic Dancer', they screamed and whistled and screamed for more. It was . . . a killer concert."

It was a rather different story five days later in Chicago when T. Rex found themselves following support band Uriah Heep, hard rock hairies from England with a distinct smell under their collective nose about Glam Rock. The evening began with a backstage row over top billing. Bolan won, but it was a Pyrrhic victory because he hadn't reckoned on Heep's significant following (nor the fact that their US outlet, Mercury Records, was based in the city).

Uriah Heep's Mick Box says, "It was an unfortunate night for Marc Bolan because his decision not to allow us to do an encore upset the audience so much that they continued to shout throughout the entire T. Rex set. Their management locked us in our dressing room so that we couldn't come back on, but we could hear the uproar in the hall because there was a speaker in the room. Marc went out there and was greeted with a bit of booing and jeering, but he thought he'd found a way round it. He said, 'What about Jimi Hendrix?', and a big roar went up. 'What about Eric Clapton?' Same again. Then someone shouted out, 'What about Uriah Heep?', and the place went mad. He really had a hard time that night."

"The sequins he had pasted on his cheekbones sparkled more than his music," concluded the *Chicago Tribune*.

The tour climaxed on February 27 with the first T. Rex headline show in New York, at the prestigious Carnegie Hall. Earlier in the day, Marc, June and manager Tony Secunda prematurely celebrated the imminent conquering of America by dropping handfuls of dollar bills from their seventh floor terrace in the City Squire Hotel. Days later, when Marc gave British journalists his rose-tinted verdict on the American tour, he'd suggest that his Carnegie Hall performance had been "incredible" and that even Paul Simon was spotted dancing in the aisles. Eyewitness accounts and contemporary reports beg to differ.

Marc walked on stage dressed in a sequined silver satin suit and with two silver stars beneath his eyes. The audience sat, dressed in denims and T-shirts, waiting to be impressed. A shaky version of 'Cadilac', with which T. Rex had been opening sets since the Weeley Festival in August 1971, was greeted by mild applause – and that was for one of the hardest sounding songs in the group's repertoire. 'Jeepster' died a similar death, prompting Marc to distract the audience by dancing wildly. His customary, three-song acoustic interlude, featuring 'Cosmic Dancer', 'Girl' and 'Spaceball Ricochet', gained a smattering of polite applause. Only a ten-minute 'Get It On', followed by an encore of 'Summertime Blues', got the crowd on its feet.

"Smoking spotlights on 57th Street, virtually non-stop radio announcements, heavy newspaper advertising – the aura surrounding T. Rex's first Carnegie Hall concert had all the elements of hyped Superstardom," wrote Don Heckman in the *New York Times*. "Too bad the results couldn't justify the means."

Some insist the band were simply exhausted. Tony Secunda rests the blame more firmly on Marc's shoulders. "Carnegie Hall was the final straw," he recalls. "It had been pretty much the worst tour I'd been on in my life, and Marc just wasn't the same guy any more. The cocaine was getting to him – I think he was using very bad quality stuff in America – and he'd become almost impossible to communicate with. I'd taken him to the hall several weeks earlier and I'd stood at the back and had a conversation with him just to show him how acoustically perfect the place was. I said, 'When you play here, you're not gonna need that Marshall stack, baby.'

"We'd set up this hot media blast for the gig – searchlights lit up the Manhattan skyline, heavy faces were there to see the concert, and what does Marc do? Locks himself in the toilet with two bottles of champagne and gets out of his brain. He walked on stage wearing a T-shirt of himself and fell flat on his face during the opening number. It was so loud that no one could hear a damn thing – it was awful. I walked out and sat on the steps outside, and Paul Simon came running out after me and said, 'What the fuck are you doing, man? This is fucking bullshit, man.' He gave me shit and then he ran into the night. I thought, this is where it comes to a close. I went off and stayed the night with friends.

"The next day, I took off with Mickey Finn – who was more

embarrassed than anybody because he had to stand next to Marc on stage – and a friend for a Valium holiday in Acapulco where we tried to pretend it hadn't happened. Mickey then flew on to Paris, where T. Rex were due to start recording *The Slider*, and I followed a few days later. But I knew it was the end of the line and told Marc so in no uncertain manner. The embarrassment was just too extreme. Still, I made a lot of money and got a nice Ferrari out of it."

Other sources indicate that Secunda was sacked. His work – to disentangle Marc Bolan from the David Platz empire and set up various deals and companies that Bolan would staff with his own gofers – had been completed. After the split, the T. Rex offices were moved from Secunda's 7 Charles Street premises in Mayfair to 16 Doughty Street, just off Gray's Inn Road near Holborn. Both Marc and June were directors of Warrior Music Projects Ltd, while Chelita Secunda – who enjoyed a brief liaison with Mickey Finn during 1972 – was given an official post as Merchandising PR and Personal Assistant to Marc Bolan.

The new offices were situated on the first floor above the office of Bolan's solicitor Peter Carroll. It had two main rooms, a reception room at the front that overlooked the street and a conference room at the back that was partitioned by folding wooden doors. On a day-to-day basis, Chelita would run the office – deal with correspondence, fan mail, PR and liaise with Marc's costume suppliers – with June or Mick Gray also popping by regularly. "Marc would come in when he needed to or when he felt like it," says Gray, "and this always caused problems because fans – including one (Boy) George O'Dowd – would hang around outside."

A real life sighting of Marc Bolan, who was ubiquitous except in the flesh, was a remarkable thing in 1972. Potential rivals such as Slade, Elton John and Rod Stewart had been threatening to steal some of his thunder for several months, but Bolan eclipsed them all. A face, a record company (Marc's head formed a significant part of the T. Rex Wax Co.'s red-and-blue label logo) and, increasingly, embodied in a recognised sound, Marc Bolan seemed to offer more than was expected from 'ordinary' stars.

When he'd been interviewed by LWT's Humphrey Burton on December 8 for a television special, *Music In The Round* (broadcast on April 23, 1972), Marc cut an ephemeral figure as he sat crosslegged in his purple-and-blue smock top, trousers with an ornate peacock feather design, girls' brown shoes, with his hair cascading majestically around his neck and with glitter on the sides of his cheeks. Asked where he found inspiration for his lyrics, he said, "I don't really know. I personally believe that I was . . . a previous life or something . . . a previous reincarnation, a bard of some sort, because most of the things I write about are descriptions of places I've never been to." It wasn't the usual rock'n'roll answer. As he sat back and sang 'Spaceball Ricochet', the corners of his mouth turned downwards in a gesture of infinite sadness as he declares, "It's a pity that I'm like me". Critics scoffed that Marc's lyrics were essentially meaningless, but sometimes his delivery of the simplest of phrases could cut as deep as Christian Barnard's scalpel.

'Telegram Sam', the first T. Rex single of 1972, was a word feast of a quite different kind, a succession of fleeting, unrelated images that, like Warhol's pop art, still appears wholly in tune with today's cultural hypermodernity. Full of nonsense characters – 'Purple Pie Pete' and 'Golden Nose Slim', 'Jungle Faced Jake' and the quixotic 'Telegram Sam' – the single also managed to mythologise Bob Dylan and of course ("I ain't no square with my corkscrew hair") Bolan himself.

'Sam' performed its own publicity. Bolan teasingly claimed he'd written it in New York "about a man who does little services for me". Fingers inevitably pointed towards an unnamed drug dealer. Tony Secunda maintains otherwise. "It's about me," he says. "I was his main man. 'Jungle Faced Jake' was Sid Walker, my assistant, who was a black guy."

Ultimately, those were ephemeral matters. 'Telegram Sam' was crucial in that it finally fulfilled Marc and Tony Visconti's aim to create music as distinctive as Phil Spector's 'hit factory' or the Motown sound. Utilising a simple, fuzzed-up Chuck Berry guitar riff (and another one of those mournful passing tones that underscored the chorus), the pair concocted their own wall of sound based on past pop glories. It was a footstomping boogie beat augmented by saxes, strings and backing vocals – into which they fed the fantasy world of Marc Bolan. The result, a highly personalised pocket symphony, was an instant success, so much so that Bolan would find it virtually impossible to break the habit.

★   ★   ★

In the run-up to the Wembley shows, early in March 1972, the T. Rex entourage were travelling to the Chateau D'Hérouville, also known as the Michel Magne or Strawberry Studios, just outside Paris. Bolan had been advised to record out of Britain for tax purposes, and the Chateau came on the recommendation of Elton John, who'd recently recorded his forthcoming album, *Honky Chateau*, there.

"We were on our way there in a limo," remembers Tony Visconti. "I'm sitting in the back with Marc and Mickey, and Steve and possibly Bill too. Marc is drunk. He's swigging from a bottle of Cognac, and this is in the morning. All of a sudden, he breaks into a song, 'I'm an old boon dog from the boon docks'. He tries to get us to sing. There's an element of fear in the air. The leader is out of control.

"I was often confrontational with him, but I knew this was the wrong time. 'C'mon everybody, sing!' he says. 'C'mon Mickey, you cunt.' Marc's howling like a dog and he's slobberingly drunk. It's like a scene from *A Star Is Born*, or Elvis. To keep the peace, Mickey starts singing, and Marc put his arms around him. That's how *The Slider* began.

"When we arrived at the studio, it turned out that Marc was not able to have the master bedroom. The owner's clothes were in there, although he wasn't around himself. While we were having dinner, Marc instructed his roadie Mickey O'Halloran to throw the guy's clothes out. Mickey showed some reluctance, so Marc shouted at him, 'Do it now!' Mickey's a big guy, and before long, he returns and he's furious. 'You're not gonna talk to me as if I'm a fucking animal, and I'm not gonna treat other people like they're fucking animals. I'm not gonna do it,' he says. They ended up nose to nose, before Marc says to him, 'Let's talk this over.' He was really embarrassed at losing face in front of all of us. And after all that, when Marc returned with the situation resolved, he turned to us and said, 'Don't worry guys, it's just an ego thing.'"

The Slider, the long-awaited follow-up to *Electric Warrior*, was recorded swiftly and, for Marc at least, with near instantaneous inspiration. Ever since Marc had started to earn big money, early in 1971, he preferred to record on the road or abroad. The basics were put down in just five days, with further sessions taking place in Copenhagen's Rosenberg Studios in Denmark at the end of the month, with an overdub session for Flo and Eddie's talismanic backing vocals taking place at the Elektra Studios in Los Angeles in April.

One of the tracks recorded at the Chateau sessions was 'Metal Guru'. Casting aside funky rock'n'roll for the three-note descent that under-scored so many of Marc's effervescent anthems with melancholy, it also fed into the Bolan mystique by giving the erstwhile Electric Warrior a new epithet. 'Metal Guru', its rhythm reminiscent of Buddy Holly's 'That'll Be The Day', was a remarkably simple affair – reeking of casual abandon, and with wonderfully decadent, swelling vocals, it epitomised Glam Rock's pop disposability and for that reason has good claim to be its defining anthem. Inevitably, the song – which hinged on its oft-repeated title in what was two minutes-plus of verseless paradise – opened old wounds concerning Bolan's musical formula.

Even Marc's staunch supporter Bob Harris was forced to rethink his own attitude towards his friend's music in the wake of the single. "I never actually told Marc that I didn't like 'Metal Guru'," he remembers, "but that was the record which made me think, 'Hang on, what's he doing?' I was never that keen on his music after that one."

Reviewing the singles in the May 13, 1972 edition of *Melody Maker*, unfunny alternative jokers Cheech & Chong gave the view from across the Atlantic. "If I was marking this on a scale of one to ten, I would give it minus three," said Cheech. "It sounds like the drummer mixed it," claimed Chong. "It's nothing. It sounds like early Small Faces around the time of 'Itchycoo Park'," added Cheech. "Is it pre-Beatles? The arrangement sounds like it was done by a deaf and dumb Phil Spector," concluded Chong. At least Bolan and Visconti's Spector aspirations had been noted.

Marc, now undoubtedly the most famous man in pop, was even beginning to get up the noses of his peers. Having compared himself to Bob Dylan and John Lennon in an earlier issue of *Melody Maker*, he found himself receiving a public ticking off from the ex-Beatle at the start of April. "I ain't never heard 'Jeepster', though I heard and liked 'Get It On' and his first hit," Lennon wrote in a personal response to the paper. "Anyway, we all know where those 'new' licks come from, right, Marc? . . . By the way, Marc's checking us out, not vice versa! He's called us, babe! Anyway, he's OK – but don't push yer luck. Love Lennon, Ono." Ironically, Lennon himself was moved to revisit the rock'n'roll music of his youth when he commenced sessions in 1973 for what was to become his *Rock'n'Roll* album, produced by none other than Phil Spector.

Marc found The Rolling Stones easier prey. "They're just not that important anymore," he claimed on May 6. "I think they're finding it difficult to live within the context of 16-year-old kids. That's who they were important to, that's what they were about and that's what Mick still wants . . . The beginning of 'Tumbling Dice' is a bit like 'Get It On'. In fact they played it to me and watched my reactions . . . But maybe they've left it a little late." Two weeks later Jagger countered: "There's nothing happening here. The music is negligible. There's a lack of originality, and that's why I don't care about it. I'm not interested in going back to small English towns and turning on all the ten-year-olds. I've been and done all that."

Marc Bolan knowingly swam against the tide of critical opinion, believing that his art – for he always saw his music as such – was at its most potent when it was kept simple and reached the widest audience. Poet Pete Brown, who was sceptical of the whole notion of hippie culture anyway, remains a dissenting voice from the frowning faux-underground critical establishment. " 'Metal Guru' sounds far more honest to me than his published poetry or his lyrics with Tyrannosaurus Rex," he says. "It had a very strong identity which seemed perfectly valid and entertaining. And it wasn't pretentious. Everyone who's been really successful in British rock'n'roll has assumed a persona, and the lyrics Bolan wrote later on support his persona."

Marc later elaborated on the importance of repetition in the music of peak period T. Rex. "I wasn't deliberately trying to be obscure," he said. "It's just that I think in an abstract way. My songs fit my personality and my lyrics are very important to me. I like my songs to be durable to the ear and exciting to the mind. Repetition comes into my songs a lot because I think my lyrics are so obscure that they need to be hammered home. You need to hear them eight or nine times before they start to make sense. I don't see anything wrong with that. Some artists repeat the most simple lyrics about 40 times over. Look at 'I Want To Hold Your Hand' or 'All You Need Is Love'."

Throughout 1972, each successive T. Rex record fanned the debate concerning the originality of Bolan's music. His revival of electrified rock'n'roll in 1971 that had been grudgingly accepted by the rock cognoscenti was now deemed to have been supplanted by a cynicism that dressed up the most basic rock'n'roll chords and lyric nonsense in a flash, formulaic production. Charles Shaar Murray was, like Pete Brown, not a convert to Bolan's earlier work (excepting the *Unicorn* album), but he too offered a dissenting voice. "T. Rex's music is not derivative," he wrote, "in the sense that, say, Grand Funk's is, because though you can see where it's coming from, it is a synthesis, and all creative rock music has been a synthesis."

Marc's most vociferous cheerleader was fourth Beatle Ringo Starr, who'd already compared T. Rexstasy to Beatlemania and Marc to Hedy Lamarr. Ringo had been the ex-Beatle least likely to succeed, but a surprise hit in 1971 with 'It Don't Come Easy' and roles in *Candy*, *The Magic Christian* and Frank Zappa's *200 Motels* ensured he was not destined for oblivion just yet. A passionate film buff, he was also the self-appointed Managing Director of Apple Films Ltd, for which he was devising a series of television documentaries profiling celebrities like Elizabeth Taylor, George Best and Richard Burton. At that point he heard about T. Rex's Wembley shows. After discussions with Bolan and Secunda, who sought assurances that the Beatles' heavyhanded business manager Allen Klein would not be involved, the project soon outgrew the small screen.

Over the next few months, what was originally going to be a concert movie developed into what Marc later described as "a film with surrealistic overtones". Others less kindly regarded the non-musical elements as just plain silly. The finished 65-minute movie took months to complete, thanks to a poorly recorded soundtrack which required much over-dubbing, and the inclusion of various scenes recorded in and around John Lennon's Tittenhurst Park estate in Ascot, which Ringo was housesitting for the New York-based Lennons.

The central sequence was a variation on the Mad Hatter's Tea Party, which featured a heavily made up Marc performing an acoustic medley of 'Jeepster', 'Hot Love', 'Get It On' and 'The Slider', accompanied by a string quartet conducted by Tony Visconti. Meanwhile, Geoffrey Bayldon (better known for his role as the children's television character, Catweazle) recited some Bolanic verse ("Beatles, Stones, Zep, Rex'n'all/Keep on rockin' at the Union Hall"); June and Chelita got to dress up as nuns and chew burgers; and a vampiric Mickey Finn gorged himself on blood-red strawberry jam.

Other moments were rather less successful. A scene with Ringo Starr on an aircraft runway, where the pair tried unsuccessfully to deliver a line each from Elvis' 1957 hit, 'Party', might have raised a smile after a few glasses of Dom Perignon, but it failed to work on any other level.* Perhaps the inclusion of the sequence was the result of a much needed injection of spontaneity, because the pair spent several tiring weeks editing 52 hours of material at Twickenham Film Studios into a 65-minute movie intended to hit the screens in time for Christmas.

More captivating was a supersession featuring T. Rex jamming at Apple Studios with Ringo on a second drum kit and Elton John at the piano. Two songs from the session survived the ruthless editing process and made it into the final cut – a new Bolan song, 'Children Of The Revolution', and a thundering version of Little Richard's 'Tutti Frutti'. A unique Marc and Elton version of 'The Slider' remained on the cutting-room floor.

---

* The 1948 Cadillac that Marc was seen driving – legally; it was on private land – had been pur-chased from Ringo.

While Bolan spent more time with Ringo Starr – which included a sailing holiday accompanied by George Harrison and June in the south of France in May – some among his inner circle began to drift. Bernard P. ('Beep') Fallon, who'd successfully hyped up Bolan for the past two-and-a-half years and spent many hours in his company, but was left behind when T. Rex toured America in February, announced his departure in a note that playfully paraphrased Dylan – "It's Alright Marc, I'm Only Leaving".

Bob Harris also made his exit from the inner sanctum around this time. "Marc was a strong self-promoter," he says, "and was extremely astute in terms of where he placed himself. But I think this ability evaporated during the 1972–73 period as he increasingly began to believe all the publicity and lose sight of where he sat. It was a shame because I really liked Marc a lot. He was so energetic, and never less than interesting to be with. You'd forgive the moments when you saw the harder, nasty streak coming through because that had always been outweighed by the enjoyment of being with him.

"Suddenly, Marc saw himself as the most important thing in pop music and a great poet too, and I found it all rather unpleasant and unnecessary. I thought the records stood on their own merits without him having to constantly remind everyone just how great he was. The posing really did get out of hand, whereas before, it had only been limited to the concert stage or photo sessions. I'd go round and suddenly I found I wasn't talking to Marc any more. He'd be sitting back pouting his lips, and I thought, 'No! Remember me?'"

Asked by *Melody Maker*'s Richard Williams and Michael Watts whether success had changed him around this time, Bolan replied: "Well, I'm still the same little boy I was. I still get off reading music papers. I still get off on guitars. There's this great block, you see, between the kids and the pop star, which doesn't exist, man, in reality. I don't think I've changed since I was four years old. I think I was hipper when I was born than when I'll go back. You just get sadder. You see more pain and suffering. Life is loving people, screwing people, mentally having affairs with people, seeing old friends, going back to your old home where you used to live, going to school . . . but," he concluded, "you end up disliking yourself most of all, probably."

Despite all the hyperbole, its ubiquitous, iconic cover – a memorable monochrome image of Bolan playing Twenties vamp Theda Bara playing the Mad Hatter – and the glittering pair of singles that preceded it, there was more than a touch of the vulnerable inner child sailing close to self-loathing on *The Slider*. The essence of the title track itself, though heard as a chugging, rock'n'roll sexual metaphor, was unequivocal: "And when I'm sad/I slide," Marc sang. And the song ended with an ominous "Watch now, I'm gonna slide". 'Mainman', more obviously melancholic, was, said Marc at the time, "a song about me . . . I've never cried so much in my whole life as this last year."

Success laid Bolan emotionally bare. His attempts to exorcise his fears, and his loneliness met with incredulity, which only made filling the void with the staple diet of a successful rock star – drink, drugs and rampant egotism – all the more inviting. Claiming that *The Slider* was the first record on which he'd been frank and truthful about himself (which was at least half true), and then watching someone like Charles Shaar Murray describe the record as "close to a total artistic collapse" hurt. Even Rosalind Russell in *Disc* blithely claimed, "I don't know why 'The Slider' was chosen as the title track because there doesn't seem to be anything extra special about it." No one, it seemed, bothered to listen to what Marc had to say.

The Slider was *Electric Warrior* polished and refined. Slow songs were interspersed by boogie numbers; several of the cuts could have been lifted off the record as singles; only the sad songs got sadder and the self-satisfied ones sounded more proud than ever. There was even another token heavy rock number, 'Buick Mackane', the bastard offspring of the as-yet-unreleased 'Children Of The Revolution' and Deep Purple's 'Black Night'. Reactivating 'The Walk' riff yet again (for 'Baby Boomerang') was pure incitement, and despite the addition of some Dylanish, 'Subterranean Homesick Blues' style scanning, the song was definitely boogie-by-numbers without the customary sprinkling of magic.

But, as Bolan kept insisting, it was the personal songs that made *The Slider* worth listening to. 'Spaceball Ricochet', its title an uncanny echo of Tony Visconti's Tibetan Lama friend Chime Rinpoche, was extraordinarily touching, its opening acoustic strums and vocal hum reminiscent of David Bowie's 'Space Oddity'. But only Bolan could make a line such as "With my Les Paul/I know I'm small/But I enjoy living anyway" sound like the utterance of an enlightened Zen master. 'Rabbit Fighter' was less pointed in its subject matter, but no less tender – and boasted some impressive double tracked guitar lines that Bolan was particularly proud of.

Prior to *The Slider*'s release, on July 21, the tide of T. Rexstasy had been maintained by the appearance of Fly's cash-in *Bolan Boogie* compilation album (which effortlessly topped the charts), a slew of magazines serialising 'The Marc Bolan Story', sometimes in special one-off issues, and a short four-city tour of Britain. Morrissey caught the 'supershow' in Belle Vue, Manchester, on June 16. "It was just a complete mess," he said on Granada TV's 1997 documentary *Dandy In The Underworld*, "a very exciting mess. But you could not hear the music because of people screaming."

That mess prompted a rash of "T. REX FANS IN TICKET RIOTS" headlines, with Marc claiming that security considerations were making it "almost impossible to tour". He also suggested that he might "become a recluse". (Almost exactly a year later, David Bowie/Ziggy Stardust did exactly that.) A little later that year, in mid-October, Marc and June purchased a country residence on the Welsh borders with exactly that in mind.

The Bolans' new rural retreat was an old, 13-roomed vicarage in Weston-under-Penyard, outside Ross-on-Wye near the Forest of Dean, for which they paid £67,000. June was the motivating force behind the purchase, though Bolan – mindful of a time when his pop idol days would inevitably pass – was able to envisage a creative life in the wilds, with his own home studio and peace for his writing and composing. By the end of the year, there was no question of the Bolans spending much time in their country idyll in the immediate future, and so a Mr. and Mrs. Doug Stapleton were employed to look after the residence, complete with stables and outbuildings. A pack of Lurcher dogs, a pony called Spotted Dick and Colin the hedgehog basking in the tranquillity of country life, awaited their absentee landlords. Like the fans who constantly stalked the building, they were to be disappointed.

Further disruption to the Bolans' life occurred after a national newspaper published Marc and June's private address. The Maida Vale flat was besieged by fans and the couple moved to a high security rented flat at 47 Bilton Towers in Great Cumberland Place, just behind Marble Arch. Black-tinted windows were installed in the Rolls-Royce and the Jag ("the runaround" according to Mick Gray) was sprayed an oddly conspicuous purple. The protective trio of roadies-cum-minders Mickey 'Marmalade' Gray and Mick O'Halloran, together with Marc's chauffeur Alphi O'Leary, provided a buffer between Marc and his public, but their presence meant that real privacy – solitude – had become a rare thing in Bolan's life.

The release of *The Slider* marked the pivotal moment in Marc's career. Despite the immediate rush of sales, reputed to be 100,000 copies in the first four days, the album failed to reach number one, failed to sustain the momentum of *Electric Warrior*, and as sales soon tailed off, failed to find a place on the end-of-year Top 10 best-sellers lists. Marc Bolan: Superstar was in danger of becoming a victim of his own success. Publicly over-exposed, privately troubled and increasingly threatened by a host of aspiring Superstars in waiting, he began to withdraw from Britain and concentrate on other markets. Marc never had another chart-topping record at home.

★ ★ ★

Back in autumn 1971, 'Superstar' was little more than the title of a minor hit for The Carpenters. By mid-1972, anyone with a penchant for a bit of on-stage razzmatazz and one or two hits under their belt was a potential candidate for Superstardom. The epithet was quickly adopted by magazines keen to capitalise on the reawakened teenage pop market, and a handful of virtual pop veterans – Rod Stewart, David Bowie, Elton John (who'd tellingly changed his name to Elton Hercules John by deed poll in the spring), The Sweet, Slade and token American Alice Cooper – basked happily in its glory. So too did singer Paul Gadd, the oldest newcomer in town who, as Paul Raven, had recorded a handful of unsuccessful rock'n'-roll 45s at the start of the Sixties and later became the warm-up man for *Ready, Steady, Go!*

Gadd had buried Paul Raven in a much-publicised stunt on the River Thames and, with Marc's ex-arranger Mike Leander writing and arranging his songs, reinvented himself as Gary Glitter. By June 1972, he was riding high with a footstomping, handclapping, thoroughly irresistible instrumental called 'Rock & Roll (Parts 1 & 2)'. His new persona was a gloves-off challenge to Bolan's supremacy. Considerably less handsome than Bolan, Glitter took the role of the Glam Rock idol and ran with it, squeezing into costumes that made Liberace look underdressed, and stomping uncomfortably around the stage to his reductionist musical anthems in his high-altitude platform boots.

"Marc didn't go as far with it as I did with Glitter," says Mike Leander, "but what he did with the eye make-up and looking sharp was fantastic. It was a time of great spectacle. That was what it was really about, and the records were geared to that. In the Seventies, the music was constructed to be seen; during the previous decade it was made to be heard, preferably with a joint dangling from your lip. The audience became part of the show too: they dressed up the way the star dressed. Every show was like a party."

Unlike Bolan, whose emergence during 1971 opened up a can of ideological worms, Gary Glitter was unequivocal about his appeal. "The Glam
thing was great fun," he says, "and Marc, David Bowie, myself, Slade and
Sweet would always be thinking visually. When we did *Top Of The Pops*,
which was our major outlet, we were basically trying to create a video in
one live take."

Glam Rock had brought a revived spirit of competition to the singles
market. "We all tried to outdo each other," says Glitter. "I was more
glitter than Glam but it was glamorous. We rebelled against the late
Sixties, where all the bands wore beards and jeans; we wanted to see show
business. Our heroes were Elvis and the early rock'n'rollers. The Sixties
became the great message era, so we tried to bring a bit of theatre back
again."

Someone else who was stretching Glam Rock's new found theatricality
was American shock rocker Alice Cooper who, like Bolan, had been an
underground maverick since the late Sixties. His summer holiday anthem,
'School's Out', topped the singles chart in August, and his stage show – a
riot of dismembered dolls parts, a real live python and a bloody mock execution – hogged the headlines. "There's got to be more theatre," Cooper
insisted. "It's been too still for too long. Groups have got to go out and
form an image. Images are fantastic: The Beatles had an image, The Stones
had an image . . . I see something more than most people see in rock. I see
something artistic, and although I hate to say it, cultural."

Marc Bolan wasn't particularly unsettled by Gary Glitter or Alice
Cooper, or even by the summer crop of 'weenybopper' idols – David
Cassidy, Donny Osmond and Michael Jackson – who were prompting the
same hysterical scenes of fandemonium that he'd inspired at Wembley
earlier in the year. But there was another pretender to Marc's jewel-
encrusted crown, a determined starseeker who, like him, had been waiting
in the wings for the best part of a decade. Now, with a hit single,
'Starman', and a critically acclaimed album, *The Rise And Fall Of Ziggy
Stardust And The Spiders From Mars*, it was David Bowie's turn to shine.

No one was keener, or more perfectly poised, to bring theatricality
into popular music than Bowie. As early as February 1971, a profile in
Rolling Stone magazine was titled 'Pantomime Rock'. "There's enough
fog around," Bowie told John Mendelsohn. "That's why the idea of
performance-as-spectacle is so important to me." He concluded that pop
music "should be tarted up, made into a prostitute, a parody of itself. It
should be the clown, the Pierrot medium. The music is the mask the

message wears – music is the Pierrot and I, the performer, am the message."

His words were incredibly prescient, and even before his records started selling, America responded favourably to Bowie's intellectual take on pop, parody and pancake. "David Bowie is the most singularly gifted artist creating music today," the same magazine claimed around the time of the *Hunky Dory* album at the start of 1972. "He has the genius to be to the Seventies what Lennon, McCartney, Jagger and Dylan were to the Sixties." In the view of the *New York Times*, he was simply "the most intellectually brilliant man yet to choose the long-playing album as his medium of expression".

Bolan's epiphanic defection from the underground symbolised the gulf between the pop and rock categories; David Bowie was seized upon to paper over the cracks. According to *Glam Rock* author Dave Thompson, "The people who followed could not help but take (Bolan's) lead, and with it a facet of his own personality. Gary Glitter took the primeval stomp, Slade took the terrace chant simplicity, The Sweet took the pre-pubescent awareness and David Bowie took the sex." And some of Marc's audience, too.

Having disappeared from view after the success of 'Space Oddity' in 1969, Bowie had floundered for a couple of years, only forging a convincing new musical direction during 1971 after dropping his quirky English-ness and looking towards American mavericks such as The Velvet Underground and Iggy & The Stooges for inspiration. Bolan's success had irked, excited and inspired him, and he began 1972 by taking Marc's androgyny line a significant step further. "I'm gay and I always have been," he told *Melody Maker*'s Michael Watts in January 1972, "even when I was David Jones." The declaration prompted front-page headlines in the rock press, which despite its easy acceptance of hippie-era unisex values, maintained a stiff upper lip when the sexual politics got serious.

Marc responded to news of Bowie's forthcoming *Ziggy Stardust* concept album in April 1972 with a pre-emptive, "I've written a film about a messiah who visits Earth. He expects to find a race of Gods and what he finds is just a mess." Bowie, still the underdog at this stage, was more generous, including several neat, Bolan-inspired touches on the *Ziggy Stardust* album – the one-note backing vocals, simple, T. Rex (circa 1970) beat and Bolan-like guitar break on 'Soul Love', for example, and the "smiled sadly", minor key melancholy of 'Lady Stardust' (performed at the Rainbow in August while an image of Bolan was projected behind the band). He also name-checked T. Rex on 'All The Young Dudes', the hit Bowie gifted Mott The Hoople that summer.

Bolan was less charitable, dismissing Bowie's artful persona-play that had so tickled critical sensibilities with a curt: "I believe the ultimate star is the star who makes it by just being themselves." In the same issue that *New Musical Express* ran a live shot of Bowie on its cover with the head-line "Bowie Zowie – Britain's high-priest of Camp Rock", Bolan swept aside claims that he was about to be usurped. "They said Dave Clark was gonna topple The Beatles – it's as bullshit as you can possibly get," he laughed.

Gary Glitter had taken the fun, fashionable end of Bolan's Glam Rock. Bowie seized what Iain Chambers memorably describes as its "sensational-ist aesthetic of the strange" and eclipsed the smiling, vaguely camp Bolan with his declaration of bisexuality, his odd-eyed gaze, the dead, translucent skin that covered his painfully gaunt body accentuated by weirdly con-trived skin-tight costumes and dyed, toilet-brush hair. Bowie was strange, sensationalist and, more than Marc ever could be, an aesthete.

The old Mod-era rivalry went into overdrive as the pair competed for magazine cover stories. Bolan and Bowie had spent years exaggerating their presences so that someone, anyone would notice them; now, they'd become spectacular works of art in themselves. Rejoicing in the idea of the Star (Bowie, via the investigative ruse of Ziggy, at a distance), the pair refuted both the apparent enlightenment of the late Sixties and the working class puritanism of their childhood environment.

Glam Rock has often been denigrated as a vulgar, simplistic escape from reality; but it was probably more concerned with accepting the reality of the facade. Bowie understood this more than Marc Bolan who, though studied in the artifice of self-construction, steadfastly believed in the divine right of the artist. "It's much more of a realism for me to think that this (clothes, hair, gestures, the room) is all me; that there's nothing else in here. It's all outside. I prefer that way of existence," claimed Bowie in his best Andy Warhol accent.

It was another of those contradictions that makes a comparative study of Bolan and Bowie so intriguing. The cerebral Bowie claiming spiritual emptiness; and Marc, who hung his thoughts in the wardrobe, continuing to claim a spiritual, 'magical' dimension to his life and work. In an echo of his late Sixties interviews, he told *She* magazine, "It's up here floating around, and if I don't pull it out of my head and make the record, then it won't exist. Whereas in one second I can pull it out, tape it and it exists, and you sell one million records. If I don't pull it out of my head, if I don't weave that dream, nothing will happen."

That almighty sense of his own inspiration goes some way towards explaining the haste with which T. Rex recorded during these months. In the face of the interminably long-winded progressive rock artists, Marc's no-nonsense attitude was exhilarating and did much to nurse pop back to full health. But sometimes it added to the frustrations of the backing musicians – Steve Currie and Bill Legend in particular, who were still on a basic wage of £40 per week plus £26.50 for each recording session. "We were hired hands, really," admits Legend. "Steve and I were in the same boat, though he resented it more than I did. He was always on the verge of leaving. I think Tony managed to hold it all together marvellously under the circumstances."

While Marc waved the wand, dropping a seemingly endless quantity of star-shaped melodies, Tony Visconti was the magician who dropped them into a hat and pulled them out, one by one, in gilt-edged, three-minute bites. But even he was beginning to tire of the routine of a T. Rex studio session. "After *Electric Warrior*, there definitely was no innocence anymore," he says. "We were making calculated T. Rex recordings. There was a formula; innovation was secondary." Bill Legend concurred. "When we were recording *Electric Warrior*, there was a direction. Then all of a sudden we were speeding. Marc was getting a lot of stuff done for the sake of it."

At the start of August, T. Rex had returned to the Chateau d'Hérouville to record a new single, 'Children Of The Revolution' and put down some provisional sketches for a follow-up to *The Slider*. They also emerged with a second single, 'Solid Gold Easy Action', apparently written in strict accordance with Marc's 'Do it NOW!' dictum. "We'd stopped what we'd been doing and Steve and I started playing around with that shuffle beat," remembers Bill Legend. "Marc came along, asked us to play it again, scribbled down some words and ten minutes later we had 'Solid Gold Easy Action' in the bag." "As easy as pickin' foxes from a tree," bragged Marc throughout the song – though the emergence of several outtakes in recent years reveals Bolan and Visconti's painstaking expertise in transforming something as simple as an ordinary shuffle beat into two-and-a-half-minutes of pop greatness.

The June 3 edition of *The Weekly News* carried one of several articles that year titled "Marc Bolan Superstar", and included a typical piece of Bolanic hyperbole: "Today I'm not making £40 a week but £40 every second," he bragged. The deals that had been set up with Tony Secunda were lucrative, although since Secunda's sacking, June Bolan had been overseeing the contracts and important paperwork. A protracted wrangle during the summer over the release of some old demos dating from the Simon Napier-Bell/Track era prompted Marc and June to seek out new staff.

The imminent appearance of the 20-track *Hard On Love* collection angered Marc even more than Fly Records' shameless milking of the old Tyrannosaurus Rex catalogue. He had already watched helplessly as *Bolan Boogie* stole some of *The Slider*'s thunder, the 1968 single 'Debora' enjoyed an unlikely Top 10 chart placing in April, and the four Tyrannosaurus Rex albums were repackaged as two strong selling 'double-packs'. He drew the line at these cheaply recorded demos from 1966 and 1967 that were never intended for release in the first place.

On June 22, 1972 Track Records and Polydor, the label's distributors, were successfully injuncted and *Hard On Love* was consigned to record collectors' heaven.*

Marrying his artistic temperament with a desire to stay on top of T. Rex business proved too much, even for Marc Bolan. Back in February, he justifiably aired his misgivings about the business of rock'n'roll. "I just didn't trust anyone," he said. "I trusted the kids, but I regarded myself as having been screwed so many times. I've mellowed towards that now."

He mellowed even more when June appointed Tony Howard, who had previously worked for the NEMS agency (who booked T. Rex in Europe) to manage Marc and the group. "June felt she had done all she could for the band," says Mick Gray, "and she wanted to spend more time with Marc and her own project, the Rectory on the Welsh borders."

"He gave the image of being dynamic and not being afraid to be ruthless," Gray adds, "but I don't think he was strong enough with Marc." Howard's first act was to drive a further wedge between the master and his apprentices. "The first thing he did was to appoint Alphi O'Leary, the brother of a friend, as Marc's bodyguard/valet in an attempt to keep the band and crew away from Marc when we weren't working," says Gray. "Alphi treated Marc like a young son and smothered him. It made Marc worse rather than better, and it made my life hard having to go through Alphi to get to Marc for answers."

---

* Two years later, when Bolan's circumstances had altered considerably, Napier-Bell and Kit Lambert hammered out a deal over lunch with Marc at the Savoy Grill and the record trickled out to an uninterested public as *The Beginning Of Doves*.

"A man that doesn't look after his own affairs is basically a fool," Marc said at the end of the year. "You owe it to yourself to have some idea of what's going on. I like to know what's going on, but it doesn't mean I can't have people working for me. But I can't get behind the conventional management bit because it was built for puppets and Pinocchio didn't do too well, did he?" He didn't, but that's because his every whim and fancy was indulged on Pleasure Island, which existed only to ensnare the weak-willed. Marc was making his way there at a pace quicker than even his close confidantes could have imagined. But first there was America.

T. Rex flew into Montreal, Canada, on September 5 to begin a six-week north American tour oblivious to the fact that when they returned, in mid-October, T. Rexstasy would have lost a little of its lustre, the band's spirit would be broken and the leader out of control. "We were beginning to make mistakes and no one was seeing it," says Mick Gray. "We should have toured Britain and supported *The Slider* and 'Children Of The Revolution' because we still had not established ourselves on our home turf. We were still regarded as a teenybopper singles band."

Things didn't start too well. In Montreal, Bolan admonished the audience by saying, "I feel that we're working damn hard up here and not getting much response." Backstage, he was already dispirited, and confided in a reporter that, "We're not hoping to achieve anything from this tour . . . Basically we came here because we want to work . . . We want to get in shape for our Christmas gig in England." His defeatism was uncharacteristic and indicative of cracks in Bolan's armour.

The following night's show in Toronto's Massey Hall piled on the agony. "T. Rex is undoubtedly the worst excuse for a rock'n'roll band to hit Toronto since the golden days of The Monkees," claimed Ian MacDougall of the *Toronto Star*. "Rock music could be set back five or six years." And things seemed to go downhill from there. Reviewing the last night of the tour, at the Civic Auditorium in Santa Monica, *Melody Maker*'s Richard Cromelin concluded: "This was supposed to be the tour that would plant T. Rexstasy into a previously resistant America, but that hasn't quite been the way it's worked out . . . The live T. Rex is a terrific disappointment," he conceded, blaming Bolan's "long, boring guitar solos", too much between song time wasting, a lack of spontaneity and Marc's stage manner; "His movements are repetitive, empty and forced," Cromelin claimed.

Mick Gray cites four main reasons why the tour was such a disaster. Marc's attitude: "In his mind he had already conquered America, and now he was going to show them he was a guitar hero." Tony Howard agreeing to let The Doobie Brothers support T. Rex: "They were a goodtime band who gave the punters what they wanted – short songs without too many frills. They stole the tour and got a hit single ('Listen To The Music') out of it." T. Rex's US label, Warner Brothers: "They were too soft on Marc. They should have told him to play to the audience instead of to himself. They seemed to give up on the band halfway through the tour." And the band's sound: "It was too thin when exposed to sophisticated PA systems. We needed another musician to fill out the sound."

Actually, T. Rex had gained four additional members towards the end of the tour. At the penultimate show at Winterland in San Francisco, on October 13, they were joined by Julia Tillman, Stephanie Spruill, Omah Drake and Gloria Jones – the same Gloria Jones who'd first encountered the dog-baiting Bolan in the Hollywood Hills in August 1969.

By September 1972, the fortunes of both had changed dramatically. Now an in-house Tamla Motown songwriter, working with The Four Tops, The Jackson 5, Gladys Knight & The Pips, Marvin Gaye and Diana Ross, Gloria was also a well-travelled session singer who'd sung with Ry Cooder, Delaney & Bonnie and Ike & Tina Turner.

"Marc had used two of Aretha Franklin's singers for the Academy of Music dates in New York earlier in the tour," Gloria says, "but when they came up to the West Coast he decided to look for other singers. Bob Rehger, an executive at Warner Brothers, recommended me for the job. I called the girls to the Beverly Hills Hotel where Marc had a bungalow. He went mad. He loved our sound, our energy. He found what he was looking for."

Omah only lasted one show "because she decided to wear a pink afro on stage and she was close to 300 pounds," Gloria remembers. "Marc said we can't have that; there can only be one star on stage."

Earlier that summer, in June, Gloria Jones had been in Europe as one of The Sanctified Sisters, part of the massive Joe Cocker entourage that rolled in to London for the open-air Garden Party at the Crystal Palace Bowl. That's when she encountered Marc Bolan for a second time. "Joe took the four of us – me, Viola Wills, Beverly Gardner and Virginia Ayers – to the Speakeasy," Gloria says, "and as we arrived Marc was coming out. As we teased Joe, 'Why aren't you running around in a Rolls-Royce?', Marc said, 'You've gotta be careful with those girls.' I said, 'Joe's with these chicks from California, darlin'.' Marc looked at me as if to say, 'I should kick her ass!' We kept seeing these kids with tall hats and cloaks during the day. It was explained to us it was the Marc Bolan and T. Rex cult."

Cocker was another Denny Cordell discovery, who broke in Britain during 1968 with his extraordinary take on The Beatles' 'With A Little Help From My Friends'. After an equally memorable showing at the Woodstock Festival in 1969, he conquered the States with his never-ending Mad Dogs And Englishmen tour, an experience so gruelling that the singer retreated to Laurel Canyon in the Hollywood Hills where he remained until spring 1972.

While Marc Bolan had definitely been adding an occasional twinge of Americana to the refined Englishness of his voice (particularly noticeable on 'Telegram Sam'), Cocker's earthy vocal rasp had prompted many to dub him 'the white Ray Charles'. It was a raw, gritty sound that Americans particularly welcomed. Its lived-in hoarseness suggested 'soul' – a quality that was apparently missing in Bolan's music.

It was an awful misjudgement indicative of the prejudices of the time but, frustrated that his own voice wasn't deemed a proper vehicle to vocalise genuine feelings, Marc partially bought into it. By augmenting T. Rex with black American backing singers, he was responding to two myths: that his music was more artificial than, say, Cocker's; and that black musicians necessarily add authenticity. That said, his slow, growing attachment to the contemporary soul sounds of black America soon gave new impetus to his music.

Within days of returning to Britain, T. Rex were abroad again, back to the relative calm of the Chateau d'Hérouville putting down songs for the follow-up to *The Slider*. But the atmosphere had changed dramatically. The building had become a little run-down, friendly staff had been replaced by unfamiliar faces, and then there was the dispiriting legacy of America.

"Recording *Tanx* was not a happy experience because of Marc's behaviour," maintains Mick Gray. "It was full of his tantrums and ego!" he says with mild affection. "And Tony Visconti was frustrated by Marc and his inability to progress. He was talented when he wanted to be, but he was ruled too much by his ego and the influence of substances."

It didn't help that Marc didn't have many songs ready. "It's something new for me because we went into the studio and I didn't have a clue as to what we were going to do, so all the material was written in the studio," he confessed weeks later.

Mick Gray and Tony Visconti aren't alone in portraying Marc at the mercy of his own tried-and-tested formula; it's the stock response of virtu-ally everyone who knew Bolan during 1972 and 1973. The *Tanx* record-ings sounded like *The Slider* in defeat but parts of it at least were dressed in the cast-offs of Marc's victors. There was greater variety than on either of the previous hit albums; the songs were more richly textured and with dynamics that broke out of the Bolan boogie mould; additional instru-mentation, including Mellotron and saxophone, gave greater depth; and at least two tracks featured a new, more soulful-sounding Marc.

The American experience had bruised Bolan. So, too, had the torrent of criticism that kept coming his way in the British music press. In July, Atomic Rooster's Vincent Crane summed up the view from the progres-sive rock fraternity when he complained: "I feel Marc Bolan is totally mediocre in every respect. He can't sing very well, he can't play very well and he can't write very well, but everyone's raving about them and that upsets me . . . I don't think T. Rex is anything new at all." Even Slade's Dave Hill stuck his ludicrously high silver platform boot in: "I like his songs, but there doesn't seem to be much going on as far as the group is concerned."

Slade were certainly T. Rex's biggest rivals as far as the younger, female end of his audience was concerned, and for a while there was keen com-petition between the two camps. "Bolan said in a *Melody Maker* interview that Slade was no competition and I had it in for him from that day on," says Slade's bassist Jim Lea, who with singer-guitarist Noddy Holder wrote almost all of their material. "The records he made were tremendous but I still had it in for him."

"After a while we got to know Bolan," says Slade drummer Don Powell. "He suggested that we coordinate our singles so that we didn't release one at the same time. That way we'd each have been certain of getting to number one. Chas [Chandler – Slade's manager] told him to fuck off."

On a purely statistical basis Slade did win out chartwise over T. Rex – at least after 1972. Bolan's 11 Top 10 hits between 1972 and 1975 were beaten by Slade's 13; Slade had six number ones to Bolan's four; and Slade singles went from nowhere to number one on three occasions, a feat that T. Rex never accomplished. But in every other way imaginable – except-ing perhaps in live performance – Slade could never be the equal of Marc Bolan and T. Rex.

In the first days of November, and with the basis of over half the album on tape, Marc had James Johnson from the *New Musical Express* over to the

Doughty Street offices to discuss his new musical strategy. Each fresh glass of white wine was chilled with an ice cube, and each of Johnson's questions was met by an aggrieved, touchily defensive response. Marc was adamant, though, that T. Rex had changed. Radically so, he insisted.

"The album is totally a heavy rock album," he said. "I used a lot of black chicks on it, also Lesley Duncan. I feature a pianist very, very heavily and I play slide guitar on every track. It's a gospel album in fact. Like, the title track (sic) is seven minutes long. There's a lot of ooooooooeeeeeee on it . . . I'm using a lot of brass and a couple of saxes doing solos." Then came Marc's revealing Pinocchio moment, adrift and alone on Pleasure Island. "I don't know how radically different it'll seem to other people," he confessed, "but I think it's different."

Perhaps it needed to be – although it is equally possible to see in Bolan's determination to break out of type a hasty tampering with a winning formula. After the stinging attacks on *The Slider*, the last two T. Rex singles of 1972 had stalled at number two. Despite being thrilling variants on the Bolan formula, this modest dip in fortunes was seized upon by cynics as evidence that Marc's star was already waning. When Bolan promoted 'Children Of The Revolution' at the start of September, just prior to flying off for the north American tour, there were small visual clues that change was imminent. The wildest ends of his hair – Marc's crowning glory – had been trimmed, the gentle curve of an incipient belly (under an unflattering green smock) was just visible, and while glitter still lit up his eyelids, Marc's foppish, fedora-topped look showed a willingness to distance himself from the shininess that Gary Glitter was now making his own.

The performance veered towards high camp, but the song – propelled by a splendid, jaw-juttingly crude, two-chord motif straight out of the 'Louie Louie'/'You Really Got Me' mould – provoked much debate. "What revolution?" asked the moaners. Wasn't Bolan simply debasing a Sixties concept by applying it to a new generation for whom revolution meant boys in make-up and girls in hot pants? Bolan, who had recently sanctioned a new line of fan club T-shirts bearing the legend 'SUPERMARC' was unconcerned, claiming that it was the sound and not the words that were now his main priority. "You can quote words of lyrics but they're not poems, they're songs," he told *Beat Instrumental*'s Steve Turner. "The music is foremost because the chords are what capture the essence of life."

The chords were heavier and more strident than on previous T. Rex 45s, and though reviews spoke of the "familiar riffs and refrains" and claimed that the song was "scarcely revolutionary in concept", 'Children Of The Revolution' was regarded as a step in the 'right' (rock) direction. The two flipsides amplified the new bite to the T. Rex sound. 'Sunken Rags', a boogiefied reworking of a song Marc had already recorded in acoustic form late in 1971 and donated to the Glastonbury Fayre fundraising album earlier in the year, was also a subtle dig at the press monkeys constantly on his back. 'Jitterbug Love' went even further, its soulful hard rock feel topped with some of the most histrionic backing vocals yet heard on a T. Rex record and some spidery lead lines from guitar hero Bolan.

'Solid Gold Easy Action', the hit single conjured up during that ten-minute session in August, was Bolan at his most brazen and blasé. The "Chugga-chugga-chugga-chug Hey! Hey Hey!" riff – a virtual war cry that anticipated the Adam & The Ants sound a decade later – made Gary Glitter hits seem unduly fussy, the lyrics toyed knowingly with The Rolling Stones' '(I Can't Get No) Satisfaction' ("I can't get no satisfaction/All I want is easy action!") and the record still achieved a number two placing in December 1972. Less happily, the slapdash methodology was extended to the product: 'Solid Gold Easy Action' was the first T. Rex single not to carry two songs on the B-side (the perfunctory 'Christmas message' at the start of 'Born To Boogie' hardly counted).

A sense of abandon that the late Sixties Marc Bolan would never have tolerated was beginning to creep into his career. New songs were less likely to be inspired by Marc's Guardian Angel or, indeed, his pretty 'Poon' statue, than by drunken nights on the town with Ringo Starr and writer Terry Southern. ('Tenement Lady', recorded during the October sessions at the Chateau, was the product of one such liquid night at the Park Lane Hotel in New York.) There was now a bullishness in Marc's behaviour (evidenced too in his increasingly aggressive singing voice) that suggested he was partaking a little more regularly in that favoured pursuit of the early Seventies' rock community – cocaine.

While others testify to Marc's occasional coke snorting during 1972, Mick Gray cannot remember seeing Marc openly taking the drug that year. "In fact, he went mad with me when he found out that I'd taken some at a party in Montreal in September," he says. "Ironically, I was bollocked but Tony Howard and others got away scot-free." Cocaine became a more open fact of Marc Bolan's life during 1973, especially when June wasn't around. But the writing was already on the wall by the winter when, says Gray, "Marc was becoming everything he hated in Steve Took."

Weeks earlier, in September 1972, Steve Took had been back in the news. He'd signed a deal with Tony Secunda ("Say the contract is worth a million," he suggested conspiratorially to Charles Shaar Murray), and the pair gained some publicity on the back of Marc's success. Secunda paid for some demos at Olympic Studios; Took was anxious to counter Bolan's recent claim that he was "in the gutter somewhere". However, the press coverage gave no indication that Took was anything other than a day-dreamer in leather, shades and stubble with an appetite for Mandrax.

Secunda's management was hardly likely to reform him. "Steve used to call him Tony Suck Under," says a close friend. "That relationship didn't really do Steve much good at all. So much cocaine went up his nose during that time, and Steve became so paranoid that he ended up being a total recluse living in a flat behind Secunda's office in Mayfair. He became convinced that, because he was with Secunda, Marc's lot was going to have him kneecapped or run over. He sat in the flat and listened for noises all day long." The association didn't last much longer than the flurry of press articles, though Secunda did issue some typically diabolical threats to David Platz at Essex Music which secured Took some royalties from the Tyrannosaurus Rex recordings.

"Those Secunda sessions were much more rock-oriented," remembers Mick Wayne, the ex-Junior's Eyes guitarist who'd collaborated with Bowie and had known Took and Bolan since 1968. Pink Fairies' Russell Hunter (drums) and Duncan Sanderson (bass) joined Wayne (on the cusp of becoming a Pink Fairy himself) and Took at the session. "He was trying to re-record 'Amanda'," Wayne remembers, but the trouble with all that dope-induced thinking was that he was always questioning the results. Nothing ever got finished."

Took waited in vain for an audience, though earlier in the year, he had made an effort to re-establish contact with his old Tyrannosaurus Rex partner. On January 15, as T. Rexstasy was reaching its peak, T. Rex played a one-off show at the Boston Gliderdrome, a massive new venue that held 6,000 people. The television cameras were there to film the group for inclusion in a forthcoming documentary *Whatever Happened To Tin Pan Alley?* (screened in March). Also in attendance was a party from the underground magazine *Frendz*, amused at the prospect of watching their old underground renegade entertain a crowd of screaming girls from the provinces. Among those passing round copious spiffs on the coach to the concert was Steve Took.

"Steve said to me, 'Do you think I ought to go to his dressing-room and see him?' " remembers one of his intimates. "I said, 'Yeah,' so we trotted round and knocked on the door. Marc nearly fainted. They just fell into each other's arms, hugging each other tightly. At an instant, you could see there had once been this really close relationship."

That's not how Mick Gray remembers it. "Steve was out of his head and Marc was not pleased to see him or his friends. During the show Steve tried to join the band on stage and Marc ordered me to throw him out of the gig. Steve was gentle and went of his own accord."

After 1972, Took slid away, his whereabouts the subject of the occasional rumour pertaining to self-destruction but little in the way of hard fact. "He knew he had the talent," says a friend, "and so did we. He was an extraordinary performer and it broke my heart that he couldn't just get up and do it without getting out of his head. It was as if he never could believe that anything good would ever happen in his life. It was a total death wish trip and eventually he achieved his wish."

It was the arrival of one of Steve Took's rare royalty cheques that prompted his death. "About two days before he died he had been given four mushrooms," Mrs. Valerie Billet, 27, who lived with 31-year-old Took in Kensington, told Westminster Coroner's Court. "And the night before he died we injected ourselves with powder morphine." On the night of October 27, 1980 Stephen Ross Porter awoke from his stoned slumber, reached for a cocktail cherry and attempted to swallow it. The cherry jammed in his vocal cord, and Marc Bolan's first fabulous musical collaborator choked to death. Pathologist Dr. Michael Crompton recorded a verdict of accidental death.

Back in October 1972, while Steve Took still harboured dreams of following his ex-partner into the big-time, Marc too was beginning to attract the odd bad vibe. The number one spot was no longer Marc's divine right, America was proving a tough nut to crack and a degree of panic had set in at recent studio sessions. That month *New Musical Express* printed a letter so extraordinary that one wonders whether it had been sent anonymously by an insider. "You have knocked Marc Bolan, criticised him and abused him," complained 'A T. Rex Fan'. "He has now been driven to drink and if it wasn't for his wife, June, he'd be dead by now . . . Yes, he's going to die soon. It'll be YOUR fault."

The autumn newsletter of the T. Rex Fan Club sought to quash any unseemly claims. "We have had a lot of letters from people who have heard various and sometimes quite disturbing rumours about Marc," it began. "Well, to put a few minds at rest, Marc is a perfectly HEALTHY and

HAPPY person. He does not wear a wig, he has beautiful soft hair which he washes twice a week with a really good herbal or protein shampoo, he does not have any serious diseases and he's really a perfectly ordinary 5′ 7″ tall guy!" Privately, though, it was a different story. "Really, we were all doing too many drugs," admitted Chelita Secunda in 1997

"The coke was not so obvious yet," says Mick Gray, "but the champagne was always there. It was Marc and June's poison." And the champagne corks popped noisily at the launch of *Born To Boogie* on December 13 at the decidedly unglamorous Oscar 1 cinema in Brewer Street in London's Soho. However, the fizz didn't last long. The film, which had taken Marc and Ringo the best part of a year to complete, was a critical failure. After an initial Christmas rush, the movie stalled in the suburbs, and failed to secure American distribution.

To the large rump of fans that had remained loyal to Bolan through all the sniping and the competition he was now facing, *Born To Boogie* was – and remains – perhaps the final glorious moment before T. Rexstasy passed into history. The Wembley scenes were every bit as frenzied as they'd imagined; the 'surrealistic' linking material offered a rare and fascinating glimpse of a pop mystic behaving madly, and then there was the all-star studio footage, glimpses of Marc in Wonderland, the opportunity to ogle at the Superstar for 65 minutes at 24 frames a second.

The film was a typical product of Bolan's sensualist approach to his work – if it felt good, do it. Smitten by rock'n'roll cinema from an early age, Marc was all too aware of the impact of the Star on the screen, and he milked it for all it was worth. There's rarely a frame in the movie where Bolan doesn't feature. From the opening still of the 10-year-old Mark Feld, with a magnificent quiff and a guitar strapped, Presley-like around his body, *Born To Boogie* presented Marc Bolan as he'd always imagined himself to be – the pop idol who was different from the rest.

"*Born To Boogie* is a pop film, of course, and I'm very pleased with it," Marc told reporters at the time. "I think it works well," added the man who had started referring to himself – only half tongue-in-cheek – as "Cecil B. de Bolan". He also claimed that the movie validated all those 'T. Rex: the new Beatles' claims made earlier in the year. "I can't think of any likely comparison to us except Ringo and the dudes," he deadpanned.

"It's one of those total-personality efforts," complained Nick Kent in *New Musical Express*. "(Its) only saving grace is in giving the viewers a chance to see Bolan as he wants us to view him," he added, before suggesting that Marc had shot himself in the foot by including an acoustic scene where he "strums the most blatantly out-of-tune guitar I've possibly ever heard and whines obnoxiously for over five minutes." Kent, whose own heroes were debauched and/or decadent figures such as Syd Barrett, Brian Wilson, Keith Richards and Iggy Pop, was not aware that Marc Bolan was well on his way to joining them.

"*Born to Boogie* was the apex of Marc's career as he saw it at the time," remembers Mick Gray. "It was intended to keep the fans happy while he concentrated on America, Japan and Australasia. But it was disjointed and too egotistical. Marc was trying to be too clever for his fans who just wanted to see the man sing."

Publicly Marc refused to acknowledge the film's poor notices. Privately, though, "he was gutted inside", Gray claims. "Behind the façade, Marc was a lonely person who lacked confidence. This was the Mark Feld few ever saw. He had lots of associates but few real friends who told him the truth. The happy side was often an act prompted by several brandies but he could soon turn if he had too many."

That could mean turning angry, or else turning to that old refuge of the forlorn – the comfort of childhood habits. Donovan remembers visiting Marc at Bilton Towers in December 1972, shortly after T. Rex had returned from a short ten-day tour of Japan, and watching him amuse himself with "two toy Tyrannosaurus Rexes that puffed out talcum powder and made horrific reptilian noises while they battled on the glass table." Marc had brought back dozens of toys from the trip. Perhaps this rediscovery of the infant Mark was what he meant when he started claiming that he was "leaving the image behind . . . I'm becoming more like the old Marc Bolan."

The private descent into an existence where Cognac, cocaine and champagne had ousted Poon, Marc's totemic symbol of creativity, from his mantelpiece was, in the words of the usually affectionate Jeff Dexter, fast changing his old Mod mucker into "a monster". A sternly self-denying ascetic during the late Sixties, Marc Bolan: Superstar had by the end of 1972 cast off all restraint. He was even contemplating his own mortality. "I don't know whether I'm going to be around for much longer as a human being," he told James Johnson in *New Musical Express*. "We had about four near-death plane crashes on this last tour. That's why I can't take everything seriously." His apocalyptic talk was a licence to live for the moment.

Without belittling the 'monster' judgement, there is more than a touch of theatricality about the accusation, not least because it was tempting to invoke if only to counteract the dreamy, benevolent mystic that was still being sold to readers of *Jackie* and *Popswop* magazines. These younger fans didn't witness Marc railing about David Bowie and threatening revenge on unsympathetic journalists. Instead, those with tickets for the 'Rexmas' shows in London on December 22 and 23 (which some claimed had taken almost a month to sell) witnessed a carnival atmosphere with mounds of fake snow; an expanded T. Rex line-up that included three English backing vocalists and a sax player; a huge neon sign that flashed the group's name; and a more robust set that included two heavier numbers, 'Buick Mackane' and 'Chariot Choogle', both premiered live on the American tour.

Another song unveiled – and recorded – in America was 'The Jean Genie'. It was David Bowie's latest single, and Marc was watching its progress with teeth bared. By mid-January 1973, the song had replaced 'Solid Gold Easy Action' at number two in the British singles chart. More distressingly, though Bowie wasn't yet selling anywhere near as many records yet, he had begun to knock Marc off the front pages of the music press. Worse still, he enjoyed a critical kudos that had always eluded Bolan – and he'd made a reasonable stab at conquering America on his first proper visit, winning favourable notices in the *New York Daily News* ("A star is born," declared legendary rock critic Lillian Roxon) and making an impressive showing at New York's Carnegie Hall, where Marc had stumbled back in February.

The Christmas issue of *Melody Maker* was a virtual love letter to Bowie. "The Man Who Sold The World?" was the question posed by the front page headline. "Well, not yet, but David Bowie was certainly THE main man of 1972, just as we predicted when we front-paged him back in January." *Ziggy Stardust* was nominated pop album of the year, and there was considerable excitement about the artful one's forthcoming British tour.

Marc was having none of it. "With no disrespect to David, it's much too soon to put him in the same class as me," he said. "I'd give Slade that credibility but, without being arrogant or unfair, I certainly wouldn't give it to David. He's still very much a one-hit wonder, I'm afraid . . . Really, I've always thought Mott The Hoople were bigger than David." After claiming never to have heard a Bowie album, "or at least any of the last four", Marc then dispensed a little paternal advice. "I think maybe he's been sucked into something that's unhealthy for him. You can't create an image, it's only what you are. The whole pop star machine thing is a heavy one to handle. Maybe David can cope with it. I suppose I managed . . ."

The rivalry was keenly felt on the other side of the fence, too. According to Bowie's in-house photographer Mick Rock, "I wasn't allowed to photograph Marc Bolan because he and David weren't talking at the time. Marc wanted me to do stuff for him because he liked my work and wanted to stick his finger up to David! But David would have been very upset and I respected this. That was cute, their dispute. They were young and close for a long time, then something went wrong. But when David got big he felt generous towards Marc."

"Marc was pissed off when David started to take off both at home and in the elusive USA," Mick Gray remembers. "They had a love/hate relationship; they were very similar people, both control freaks out of control."

There was no greater evidence of Marc's fighting mood than '20th Century Boy', the first T. Rex single of 1973 and an extraordinarily powerful restatement of Bolan's pop ingenuity. More impressive still, Marc had produced the basic track himself at EMI's studio in Tokyo while touring Japan back in December 1972. From the bellicose brace of blocked E chords that announced the song in electrifying fashion, '20th Century Boy' hung on a two-note hook straight out of The Rolling Stones' late Sixties songbook, now given a definite Seventies hard rock feel. Bolan's voice accentuated the aggression, while saxophonist Howie Casey and four backing vocalists – Vicki Brown, Barry St. John and Sue & Sunny – overdubbed by Tony Visconti back in London, piled on the intensity. The memory of Marc's bizarre 'Life's A Gas' duet with Cilla Black – she wearing a red feather boa and blue eye shadow, he sporting an embarrassed grimace – on her BBC television show in January was quickly forgotten.

Despite all its power and glory, '20th Century Boy' stalled at number three and enjoyed the shortest chart run of any T. Rex single thus far. On its way down, in the second week of April, it was overtaken by a new Bowie single, 'Drive-In Saturday', as calm and understated a 45 as Bolan's latest had been agitated and thrillingly combative.

By now, the fruits of Bolan's new musical direction had been unveiled on *Tanx*, the follow-up to *The Slider* that was released to considerable fanfare in March 1973. The title was mawkish and trite; the cover image poorer still. In contrast to the iconic dignity of the sleeve for *The Slider*, Marc was now reduced to blatantly asserting his sexuality with the aid of a suggestively placed toy tank, its gun-barrel pointing proudly towards the viewer. Cynics sniggered that it was final confirmation that Marc was indeed shafting his audience.

The tank, and the lifeless silver-grey tones of the sleeve, did nothing for Bolan's image. Those who bothered to take a closer look beyond the feather boa wrapped under his chin, and beneath the mass of hair and generous lashings of eyeliner, saw that Marc Bolan was becoming bloated. His chest had filled out, his eyes were puffy, his cheeks ever widening. His tank was full all right – of booze.

There was nothing extraordinary about a successful rock star feasting on the fruits of his success. Even at his most desperate, during the mid-Seventies, Marc Bolan's habits were not uncommon for someone living the lifestyle of a rock'n'roll gypsy. What was most surprising, though, was how quickly the strain of success was revealing itself physically on someone who, for much of his life, had been the proudest peacock in the rock business.

Despite the boldness of the cover image, *Tanx* was musically torn between traditional T. Rex and forging a more mature 'rock' feel. Nowhere is this better illustrated than on the opening 'Tenement Lady' which, after a deliberate false start (symbolic of Bolan's tentativeness, perhaps), undercuts its Bolan boogie stride with Mellotron and phased vocals. Midway through, it mutates into something different entirely, almost soporific and Moody Blues-like. It was different, but whether it was enough to assuage the critical rock audience is debatable.

Much the same could be said for most of the record. The instant hit of pop cool of the previous two T. Rex albums had been replaced by a half-hearted move into more sophisticated territory whether the hooks were less obvious and T. Rex's heavily orchestrated wall of sound had been replaced by a greater reliance on studio trickery. The T. Rex boogie-machine rode roughshod over 'Shock Rock', a robust 'Mad Donna' (introduced in French by the young daughter of the boss of CBS France) and 'Born To Boogie', which sailed dangerously close to self-parody. 'Highway Knees', 'Broken Hearted Blues' and 'Life Is Strange'; ballads in the vein of 'Girl' and 'Life's A Gas', fell somewhat short of either.

Just three of the 13 songs on the album suggested that Bolan remained an artist of genuine significance with ability to develop. 'The Street & Babe Shadow' had a streetwise funkiness that had been missing from T. Rex's work since *Electric Warrior*, its insistent rockaboogie rhythm undercut by a heavily treated guitar. 'Electric Slim & The Factory Hen' was a rare moment of genuine tenderness, a gentle shuffle offset by rousing orchestration and an impassioned vocal that even made a suggestion such as "Me I'm loose/Like a golden goose/You can have my juice" sound like sweet nothings.

The song also hinted that Bolan was heading into a different direction geographically as well as musically. "Frozen feet on a winter street, man that ain't your fate/Greased in the sun, California fun, man that's more my style", raved the man now more than happy to expose his once porcelain skin to sunlight.

The key track, though, was the closer, 'Left Hand Luke', the only evidence to back up Bolan's assertion that *Tanx* was a gospel record. Unnamed backing singers whom Marc claimed had worked with Aretha Franklin feature strongly in a nod to The Rolling Stones' use of Clydie King and Vanetta Fields on their sprawling, inspired 1972 set *Exile On Main Street*. The singers' soulful choruses tended to obliterate the new, lordly tone with which Marc delivered his wordiest song on the record (and that extraordinary "Myxomatosis is an animal's disease" lyric turn).

There was no hiding the song's denouement, though, a hideously inebriated scream that zeroed in towards the mike, before tailing off with a loud, climactic groan as if Marc had just passed out on the studio floor. His final words had been "No one's gonna fool me, baby". But as the last moments of *Tanx* continued to resonate with mild discomfort, there was a sense that Marc was staring into the abyss of a self-inflicted hubristic disaster. But at the same time, the personal adventures he would pursue with such gusto over the next couple of years also freed him to embark upon a risky, though often thrill-packed musical journey that resulted in some of the most misunderstood work of his career.

10

Reelin' And Rockin'

"Whatever happened to the Teenage Dream?"
> – Marc Bolan, 'Teenage Dream' (1974)

"Cocaine and flattery was exactly what Marc didn't need."
> – Jack Green, guitarist (2002)

"I'd have thought he was in much more of a fantasy world during the period when he was a star than he was in the Tyrannosaurus Rex days."
> – John Peel (1992)

Success had transformed Marc Bolan from a softly spoken child starlet with ascetic tendencies into a VIP whose Faustian pact with fame threatened to rob him of his dignity. It was, he'd always believed, a deal worth making, and there is not a shred of evidence to suggest that he rued the day when 'Ride A White Swan' carried him, reborn and bopping, into the public arena. But success, and worse still the threat of it being snatched away from him, played havoc with Marc's psyche. On every level, simply being Marc Bolan – or, when he cared to remember, Mark Feld – was, by winter 1972, becoming a struggle. His fame had been achieved incrementally, via a series of stages that had seemed almost premeditated, perhaps even pre-determined. Now head of state in the realm of stardom, Bolan floundered without obvious direction. He'd had the hit records, made the movie, banked the cheques and proved the Jeremiads wrong. With only himself left to impress, he began to cut himself adrift from all that he'd known and embrace new levels of recklessness in the pursuit of creative inspiration and personal development.

This leap into the unknown was always a possible outcome for sensation-seeking Marc Bolan. Whether it would further jeopardise his career and tear a huge hole in his already precariously balanced personal life was, on one level, of no interest to him. He was Marc Bolan:

Superstar, strong enough to deal with the consequences of inevitable change. Or so he thought. Staring into the abyss of musical confusion and emotional stasis, he sought solace and a new impetus to his life. Gloria Jones, the T. Rex backing singer who once forgave him for kicking Jobriath's dog, provided both – though during the darkest moments ahead, when Marc's private conflicts threatened to consume him, he would call upon her forgiveness on many an occasion.

Born in Ohio on September 19, 1945, the daughter of a Pentecostal minister, Gloria Jones grew up to the sound of gospel music. "I was raised in a very religious home, but my parents soon realised that I had talent," she says. "I performed my first solo when I was four, at seven, I began to study the piano and at ten I became the pianist for my dad's church choir. My father moved from Ohio to California so that I could be in movies."

During the mid-Sixties while at college, Gloria teamed up and sang gospel with Billy Preston, Edna Wright and Blinky Williams. "Hal Davis from Motown heard our group and said, 'I've gotta have you girls come in and do a session for me.' At the time, Brenda Holloway had just signed to Motown, The Supremes were breaking and Martha Reeves too, so there really wasn't any place for Gloria Jones." However, Davis did introduce her to Ed Cobb.

"Ed had recorded an instrumental song, 'Heartbeat', with Billy Preston, but he decided to do the track with a vocalist and called me to do the session." The pair then began working on a new song Cobb had been playing around with. "When Ed sang 'Tainted Love', it wasn't working, so I changed the song to work for me," she says. Neither 'Heartbeat' nor 'Tainted Love' made any impact at the time, though both became fixtures at Northern Soul all-nighters in England during the early Seventies.

Meanwhile, Gloria Jones had become an in-demand LA session singer, appearing on classic key records, notably 'Silent Night' for *Phil Spector's Christmas Album*, and The Rolling Stones' 'Salt Of The Earth' on *Beggars Banquet*. "That was Merry Clayton, Brenda and Patrice Holloway and myself," she remembers. Prior to her involvement with T. Rex, Jones also worked with Delaney & Bonnie, The Supremes and Ike & Tina Turner.

At the turn of the decade, Jones had been spotted playing piano by the British-born lyricist Pam Sawyer, and over the next couple of years, the pair became in-demand songwriters (Gloria writing under the pen name LaVerne Ware), freelancing for Jobete Music Co, the music publishing wing of Motown. Their work was covered by many major names including The Jackson 5 ('2468'), Gladys Knight & The Pips (the Grammy-nominated 'If I Were Your Woman'), Diana Ross and Marvin Gaye ('My Mistake [Was To Love You]') and The Four Tops ('Just Seven Numbers [Can Straighten Out My Life]'). When, in early June 1973, she received a call from Marc's manager Tony Howard asking her to join T. Rex in Munich for a week's recording, Gloria Jones was working on a solo album for Motown.

"It was clean," she insists of her relationship with Marc at the time. "We were friends. When we played with T. Rex in Los Angeles in the fall of 1972, Marc took a limousine and came to my home to meet my family and my friends and everyone told me, 'We think he's attracted to you.'" Mick Gray confirms that when T. Rex decamped to the Musicland Studios in Munich to start sessions for the follow-up to *Tanx*, Marc and Gloria were "not an item". That was despite the fact that the pair had met again in April when the expanded T. Rex line-up filmed a hastily arranged sequence in Hollywood for ABC-TV's *In Concert*.

Some among the entourage even had their suspicions that Gloria might have been closer to Tony Howard – and that Marc had taken a shine to backing singer Pat Hall. "He didn't have a fling with Pat," counters Jack Green, who was recruited as a second guitarist for the forthcoming American tour. "She was a big, lovely, funky woman! But I can't see that at all." Discussing the origin of the Big Carrot moniker used by Marc, Pat and Gloria for a sideline single later that year, Jones jests that "he might have been looking at Pat's breasts!" That's more likely to have been a smokescreen for the real inspiration for the name – mighty Marc's appendage.

When Bolan arrived in Munich on June 17, the only thing on his mind was music, and the great strides he was taking with it. T. Rex had spent much of the early part of the year touring the continent with a new, harder rock sound, exemplified by 'The Groover', recorded in March at Rosenberg Studios in Copenhagen and released as the follow-up to '20th Century Boy' in June. A self-referential feast, 'The Groover' opened with a battle cry of "T. R.E.X!", namedropped 'Jeepster' and lauded a stud and a star at whom "the kids yell for more, more, more".

However, combining the robustness of the previous 45 with 1972-style Bolan boogie, 'The Groover' tended to undermine Marc's claims that T. Rex were moving on musically: "Why make *the* T. Rex single again?" complained Steve Peacock in *Sounds*. In retrospect, plucked from the context of the inexorable T. Rex hit factory, 'The Groover' sounds – like the majority of early Seventies T. Rex singles – difficult to fault. Back in 1973 though, Bolan's voice (which virtually stayed on the same note throughout) and Tony Visconti's production were starting to sound rather too familiar and the pop audience was growing restless. 'The Groover' hit the Top five, but it was Slade's 'Skweeze Me Pleeze Me' and Wizzard's 'See My Baby Jive' that were going straight in at number one.

'The Groover' *was* Bolan-by-numbers – albeit iced with wailing, wah-wah guitar and backing vocals – that neither won new converts nor disappointed the faithful. But when heard in conjunction with the flipside, a scorching, tub-thumping slice of Hendrix-like hard rock titled 'Midnight'*, it was clear that Marc – who'd now dropped the mid-show acoustic slot that had been a feature of T. Rex concerts since 1971 – was ploughing his energies into capturing the muso-inclined rock market.

As further evidence of this, Marc had begun sitting in on sessions with other musicians. A London jam with Alice Cooper the previous October, featuring Nilsson, Keith Moon, Flo & Eddie and bassist Rick Grech was high spirited but, according to Alice, comprised little more than some "old Elvis songs, and a half-hour version of 'Coconuts' – a dirty version". None of it was releasable.

Even though it's still not entirely clear whether he played on the record, Marc had been the inspiration for Ringo Starr's March 1972 single, 'Back Off Boogaloo'. Round a dinner table one evening, Bolan – no doubt in his 'best selling poet' mode – launched into some verbal improvisation: " 'Back off boogaloo, ooh you boogaloo, do you want some potatoes, ooh, you boogaloo'," remembered Ringo in 1998. Fired up by the single's success, Marc dashed off an untitled demo for his Beatle buddy at Air Studios on 7 April, which may or may not have been utilised on the *Ringo* album that was being recorded at Sunset Sound Recorders Studio in Los Angeles around the same time. Marc *did* play guitar on one track, a cover of Randy Newman's 'Have You Seen My Baby'.

His much rumoured collaboration with the Electric Light Orchestra around this time can be better substantiated. According to ELO archivist Rob Caiger, paperwork and master-tapes at EMI confirm that Marc played on three songs recorded at Air Studios in April 1973 during sessions for the band's *On The Third Day* album. 'Dreaming Of 4000' (provisionally titled 'Mambo' on the tape box) and 'Ma-Ma-Ma-Belle' (lifted off as a single in March 1974) were included on the album at the end of the year. A third, 'Everyone's Born To Die', which features separate solos from

---

* A similarly raucous Jimi song of the same name had appeared on the posthumous *War Heroes* album in 1972.

Bolan and ELO frontman Jeff Lynne, has just been released on the re-mastered *ELO 2* album. Contrary to rumour Bolan does not appear on ELO's 1973 hit, 'Showdown', though Jeff Lynne did play the solo on Marc's Gibson Firebird.

More unusual still, Marc joined ELO for the encore at the group's April 10, 1973 show at Watford Town Hall. Incredibly, it was his last public performance in Britain that year. Around the same time, just when everyone from Mick Jagger to Little Jimmy Osmond was slipping into rhinestone-studded jumpsuits, *Melody Maker* broke the news: "GLAM ROCK IS DEAD! SAYS MARC". It was, perhaps not entirely coincidentally, one of the last significant cover stories of Marc Bolan's career.

Glam Rock wasn't dead; if anything, with Roxy Music and Lou Reed, Suzi Quatro and The Carpenters stretching its parameters to incredible lengths, it was about to peak. But Bolan, the architect of the movement who knew a good headline when he uttered one, felt compelled to distance himself from what *Music Scene*'s Gordon Coxhill had disparagingly dubbed "The Powder-Puff Bandwagon". "I think glam rock/sham rock is as dead as a doornail, and I want to wait until people are ready for the next phase," he insisted.

Unlike David, Rod and Elton (whose recent *Don't Shoot Me, I'm Only The Piano Player* album included an affectionate nod to Marc on 'I'm Going To Be A Teenage Idol' ["I sit cross-legged with my old guitar/ Going to get electric and put a silk suit on"]), none of whom seemed to give a tinker's cuss about Glitter or Cassidy or Sweet or Wizzard, Bolan protested a little too loudly. His old hero Cliff Richard was back with a comradely 'Power To All Our Friends', but Marc – who'd even seen his Marie Antoinette locks hijacked by Mott The Hoople's Ian Hunter – was unable to feel anything other than a grudging envy that the whole shabby lot of them had hitched a ride on his basic idea and had debased it.

Unsettled by mood swings that alternated between bullishness to feeling bruised and abused, Bolan ploughed himself into his work. "I'm spending a lot more time on recordings now," he said just prior to the Munich sessions, adding that he intended to re-do most of the Copenhagen recordings. "In the past I would have just kept it and worked on it," he confessed. He also expressed a greater interest in the production process. "I've become much more critical about smaller things like the hi-hat sound or getting a good bass drum sound as opposed to just getting drum sound," he said. Mindful of the tax situation in Britain (which, pre-Thatcher, had been a useful tool in spreading the nation's burden more equitably), Bolan also suggested he was going to move to France and equip his new home with a 16-track studio. He was going to become a producer.

That Marc no longer spoke about *The Children Of Rarn* didn't necessarily mean he'd lost his appetite for big ideas. "I've just formed two bands," he continued. "One is a very heavy band and I'm going to concentrate very much on space music (with) probably very little in the way of lyrics. I'm prepared now to just take some people in the studio and let them do what they want – if I like them obviously. The things that I produce probably won't be singles."

By the time T. Rex got to Musicland Studios, situated in the basement of the Arabella Hotel opposite the Munich Sheraton, the heavy band and space music had conflated into something Marc called "Spaceage funk/interstellar super soul"; at least according to his hieroglyphic scrawl on work-in-progress session sheets. The two bands plucked from Marc's mind metamorphosed into one – Zinc Alloy And The Hidden Riders Of Tomorrow, a half-hearted alter ego for Marc Bolan and T. Rex. But in truth T. Rex was already two distinct entities – an omnipotent Marc Bolan, who wrote the songs and was becoming more dominant in the studio, and the musicians, producer, engineers and entourage, all of whom felt increasingly alienated from their master.

"I don't think Marc was a good tactician," Bill Legend explains. "We all wanted to contribute more but it was frustrating when we spent so little time working on things in the studio. He tended to take everyone for granted and didn't really know how to motivate people. I always gave him my best but it wouldn't have taken much for him to give us the occasional word of encouragement." On the eve of the Munich trip, the band opened that week's music press to find an announcement from Marc that *Born To Boogie* had marked the end of T. Rex as a four-piece and that he was now putting together a "cosmic ensemble". "When Marc started to talk like that, I took his comments literally and that also affected me badly," says Bill.

Outtakes from the sessions occasionally reveal glimpses of a more grateful Marc Bolan. "I like the drums on that, Bill," he says at the end of one rough take. More often, though, as those same tapes reveal, Bolan's dominance of the sessions is both exhilarating and exhausting. His voice, once angelic and seductive, leers boisterously. His guitar playing, once tentative and subdued, is now irrepressible. It was inevitable that, while Marc overdubbed his umpteenth guitar part, the rest of the band would rue the fact that they'd barely had more than a small handful of takes to perfect their own parts.

The attention to detail that Mark Feld once paid to the quality of the stitching on his lizard-skin shoes was back. Only now, the recording studio had become an extension of Marc Bolan's body. His own celebrity no longer a novelty, he turned his inherently obsessive behaviour on his work. No longer able to exercise control over the wider musical world, Marc narrowed his attentions to his own domain. No longer content to be merely a musician (or even a virtuoso), he aspired to become a sculptor of sound, able to see a piece of music through from inception to the final cut. He'd write the song, rush the band through a take, then agonise over the mixing desk for hours, flicking switches and sliding the faders in a bid for perfection. But, like a child with his first butterfly net, Marc spent so long in thrall to the ritual that the pursuit became more important than the catch.

"Marc isolated himself in Munich," says Mick Gray. "Everyone used to go to clubs after the sessions but not Marc; he just wanted to listen to that day's mixes in his room." Under siege and fighting for his creative life, Bolan had the future of T. Rex at his meddling fingertips. Only he could resolve the battle between creative satisfaction and continued success that had now reached its most critical point. Not even Tony Visconti, his studio partner for almost six years, could be entrusted with the responsibility.

"Marc and Tony seemed to be cold towards each other in the studio, mainly because Marc 'knew best' about every aspect of recording," remembers Mick Gray. "He was pretty together in Munich, with no obvious problems with drink or drugs, but he was at his arrogant best! Yes, Marc was taking coke but it was not resulting in all-night recording of rubbish as it did later on. Tony suffered more than most during this period because Marc was challenging his authority as producer. Maybe it was the drugs that made him do it, but to me it was ego."

"There were times I would sit up with him all night just doing a 15-second guitar solo," Tony Visconti told Ted Dicks in 1978. "There were times he wanted to be a musician, and there were times he simply wanted to be a star. That was his main internal struggle I think. Unfortunately most of the time he wanted to be a star."

At this point, there was only one producer in the studio and that was Tony Visconti. "Tony had to go back into the studio on his own to clean up takes after Marc had gone without telling him. That's the way it had to be," says Mick Gray. "There were times when Tony even retuned Marc's guitar because it was out of tune – even when Marc insisted it was in tune!"

Gloria Jones remembers the album being "the last one that Marc and Tony worked on", but maintains that she "never saw the blow-out because Pat and I were never around when business was discussed. We were either in our rooms or waiting for the call to come to the studio." Marc was still closer to his producer than to his backing singer, although one night the trio – joined by Pat Hall – did meet socially for langoustines in the hotel restaurant. "We'd never had those before," Gloria says. "We were really excited." Big Carrot was still strictly off the menu.

Around 20 tracks were recorded during the week-long session, nearly all of them utilising Pat and Gloria's backing vocals. If Marc and Gloria hadn't yet fallen in love, he'd certainly been seduced by the contemporary black America dimension that the singers gave to T. Rex. Where Flo & Eddie's voices had sounded serene, slightly camp and complementary to Bolan's slightly fragile tones, Gloria and Pat sang it loud and proud. On new songs such as 'Liquid Gang', 'Interstellar Soul', 'Nameless Wildness' and 'Hope You Enjoy The Show' (an abrasive collision of strutting hard rock and shrieking soul), Marc's voice – for so long the defining element of the T. Rex sound – was in danger of being reduced to a bit part.

Bill Legend was definitely feeling as if he'd gate-crashed someone else's party. "He'd really got into black music by this time, but I think he tried to force it unnecessarily. Marc had a lot in his head, but at the same time he was so bloody impatient and trend-conscious. He couldn't see the wisdom of building on it. It was all like, 'It's gotta happen now.' I loved tracks like 'The Avengers (Superbad)', 'Liquid Gang' and 'Carsmile Smith & The Old One', but I don't think those influences always worked."

With the basis of a quite different record in the bag, T. Rex returned to London. 'The Groover' – promoted with a video that was more Judy Garland than Jimi Hendrix – had stalled at number four and was beating a hasty retreat down the chart. Marc, who was determined to oversee all aspects of his empire, spent some of July attending to business matters in his new office at 69 New Bond Street.

The T. Rex operation had relocated there in the spring, taking over the lease for the entire building and subletting parts of it to Pink Floyd and Peter Rudge, a leading tour manager who worked with The Who and The Rolling Stones. More formal than the Doughty Street premises, the T. Rex office was situated on the first floor. As visitors reached the top of

the first flight of stairs, they would be met by Sandy Campbell at reception. To the rear was a general office for administration staffed by, among
others, an accountant named Ian Taylor, and Eve Slater, secretary to
Marc's business manager Tony Howard. The front office – the one that
housed the gold discs and the famous rocking-horse – was shared by
Howard and, when he was in, Marc. Other office regulars included solicitor Peter Carroll and journalist turned publicist Keith Altham. (But not
Chelita Secunda – no one seemed to tell her that the office had moved.)

On the face of it, these appointees were handpicked flunkies who,
unlike June or Tony Secunda, David Platz or Andrew King, David
Enthoven or Simon Napier-Bell, were there to cater to Marc's every
whim. "I've never been a pop puppet," Bolan proudly declared. He had
been, of course – and sometimes, when there was someone else taking
care of his business, it worked better that way.

"He totally trusted Tony," says Gloria Jones. "Tony was like a big
brother besides being a manager. He wanted Marc to be happy and
successful. Yes, Marc was the boss, but Tony was there for him 100%."
According to Mick Gray, "Tony Howard was everything. June didn't
have a say after he came on the scene. But Tony had a difficult time with
Marc, especially after June went. I do not think he was strong enough to
deal with him. He tended to look for a consensus decision rather than
being strong with Marc. Tony would not try and talk Marc out of his
excesses – the booze, the drugs and the egotistical guitar solos." According
to Jeff Dexter, this apparently conciliatory approach was deceptive. "Tony
was a rock; he was not a yes man. He'd say yes to Marc just to shut
him up."

From this mixed picture, another one emerges in the light of some
crucial financial decisions made in the T. Rex offices during the summer
of 1973. In a bid to maximise the Bolans' finances, and alleviate the
burden of the British tax system, Marc, Tony and their advisors created a
series of offshore companies. But what may have looked extremely bene-
ficial back in 1973 acquired a more sinister aspect after 1977. That's
because the Marc Bolan Estate – a faceless edifice that hid behind a wall of
solicitors – continued to reap the benefits of the Bolan legacy while Marc's
dependents were left in the dark and unrewarded. It's a situation that
remains unresolved to this day.

Then as now, there were huge sums of money involved. Warrior Music
Projects Ltd (WMPL) (formerly T. Rex Ltd in the days of 'Telegram
Sam'), in which 'Mark Feld' had a 60% stake and June 40%, received

around £100,000 from EMI on the back of record sales in Britain during 1972. That figure was based on the unprecedented 12½% royalty rate struck by Tony Secunda late in 1971. Bolan's earnings from publishing royalties would have been even higher. Add in income from similar deals struck in many other territories (including a particularly lucrative arrangement with Ariola in Germany, Switzerland and Austria which netted him in excess of £100,000 that year), plus concert fees and sundry other income, including all royalties from his pre-1972 recordings, and it's likely that Marc Bolan would have earned around £2 million in 1972.

In the midst of all this, Marc's lawyers Carroll & Co wrote to Tony Visconti on July 12, 1972 offering the producer a new deal. Instead of the 2% royalty rate he'd been on since the Straight Ahead days (which based on the British figure alone would have earned him at least £16,000 in 1972), he was offered a paltry £10,000 per annum plus £100 per day in the studio and expenses. He rejected this and in August settled for a 1% royalty rate, a compromise that greatly upset him at the time. From today's vantage point, though, it means that at least one person involved with T. Rex's music is still benefiting from it.

Whatever the walk of life – despite the arts sponsorship, the charitable donations and, in Marc's case, the value-for-money maxi singles and kindly demeanour – the wealthy go to great lengths to avoid paying their share of their tax burden. Many loopholes exist that can be legitimately exploited by accountants and solicitors, and one of the most popular is to form an offshore company. Between July 1973 and February 1974, Marc Bolan and his advisors did exactly that on several occasions, forming Wizard (Bahamas) on July 19, 1973, Wizard (Jersey) on or around August 6, 1973, Wizard (Delaware) on August 10, 1973 and Wizard Publishing on February 11, 1974. Another company, Wizard Artists, was set up in the UK during 1972 – though by July 1973, in a move inspired by the breakdown of Marc's marriage to June, its share capital had been transferred offshore to Wizard (Bahamas).

After Marc and June's marriage collapsed ("on or about 26 July 1973" according to the paperwork), the assets of WMPL were transferred to Wizard Jersey and Wizard Publishing (in Delaware, USA), and June was instantly disenfranchised. She sued the estate for compensation in 1979, and it's believed she reached a compromise pay-off.

In October 1973, Marc Bolan also made out his will, leaving £10,000 apiece to Gloria and June, a similar figure each to Tony Howard and Mickey Finn and £20,000 to his parents Sid and Phyllis Feld. Tony

Visconti, Terry Whipman and June Child's parents were each left £5,000, with the remaining monies – a huge, incalculable sum – left to various charities.

Some blame the messy legacy of Marc's finances on Tony Howard who, as Marc's business manager, should have foreseen the potential pitfalls. Others wag fingers at the faceless legal eagles that set up the operation. What's certain is that Marc's son Rolan receives only a token benefit from his father's work, and Bolan's most treasured asset, his master-tapes, have been sold on and split up on several occasions to the highest bidder. Inevitably, Bolan's music and reputation has been devalued as a result, with shoddy product and bad vibes tarnishing a rich heritage.

It's ironic that a man who expended considerable time and energy in protecting himself, by maintaining control over his publishing and his tapes, died leaving a vacuum that has meant that Marc Bolan's posthumous career has endured a precarious, prestige-threatening existence.

★　★　★

June Bolan had declined to go to Munich. Her idea of success was to sit in the garden of Eric Clapton's house in the Surrey stockbroker belt, a glass of bubbly in one hand, a joint in the other. Marc had enjoyed the wilderness of wildest Wales, but he felt complacent and uncomfortable simply basking in the relaxed lifestyle of the English rock aristocrat. He'd barely visited his country mansion on the Welsh borders, purchased the previous autumn. Besides, he was simply too unsettled to rest; the recording studio was becoming Marc's home, the American stage his holiday destination.

Unstable and insecure, Marc Bolan inevitably began to view June through different eyes. Her occasional absences from his side were an indication that they were growing apart. From the time they'd first met, early in 1968, June Bolan had been a powerful force in Marc's life. "June kept Marc on the ground in the early days when there was much to do," says Mick Gray. "She was his wife, lover, his mother and his best friend. When she relaxed her hold the troubles started and so did the excesses."

June Bolan was not, adds Gray, "against fun. She smoked, drank and participated in social drugs." But by 1973, even Marc's most vociferous supporter – the one who'd introduce him to writers and bounce ideas off, who had the nous to suss out those who could be helpful to his career and those who were sycophants – was feeling neglected. And sometimes worse. "It was after *The Slider* album when it started," she told Ted Dicks. "We were on tour and he became incredibly violent. He was never a violent person really, and if he became cross he used to hit himself on the head. I mean, he never hit me. He usually did it when gigs went bad." And, by all accounts, there were quite a few of those.

Publicly, Marc was ostentatious and self-aggrandising. In private, he agonised over his music, his career and his life, papering over the hurt with a bottle of brandy or vodka and the bags of cocaine that increasingly became part of the entourage's luggage. A temporary fix to cure his loneliness and self-doubt, his use of drink and drugs to bolster his confidence also began to undermine June's role. "I love June very much," he told John Blake in the *Evening News* in May 1973, "but people are weird. Things change and I never know." It was a revealing slip that he sought to cover up immediately. "But I'm very happy at the moment," he insisted. "Marriage is a great basis for sanity. I'd have opted out years ago without June."

In that same interview, Marc also admitted: "The pressure is fantastic. I'm a million pound industry but I'm only a kid really." He sat round a table discussing his financial future with serious men in suits. He wielded power over every aspect of T. Rex. He was recognised, fawned over and treated like a king wherever he went. And he was bombarded by images of himself, from magazine covers and billboards to television and T-shirts. As his heart rate pounded furiously with every generous hit of coke, as he stumbled around his flat at 47 Bilton Towers with a large iced vodka slopping around in an outsize glass, he cared for little but the fact that he was Marc Bolan, a boy from nowhere whose genius had now been recognised around the world – and that he could do just what he pleased.

One day in 1973, Tony Visconti made a rare visit to Bilton Towers. "He was coked out of his brain a lot by now," says the producer, "and he was drinking. He said, 'Get some champagne out of the fridge.' I opened the fridge door, and there were like ten bottles of champagne and one big, cold boiled chicken, which was a staple Jewish dish. I said, 'What's this!', because I was still a vegetarian and he said, 'I'm into chicken now, man. June says I need chicken.' Marc always thought it was immoral and unhealthy to eat flesh from a dead animal, but drugs make your body and your soul very dense. There's no capacity for subtle thinking any more. Marc was super-conscious for most of his career; now he's a step away from being asleep from the booze, the coke is doing something to his nervous system and he's eating greasy chicken. He was talking gibberish, too."

Mick Gray also remembers the switch from juices and pulses to burgers and junk food. "I was amazed as anyone else when Marc started eating meat. For the whole time he was with June he was a vegetarian, then all of a sudden he was eating meat. He did not do it gently, either, starting with a bit of fish or chicken."

Pete Sanders, who'd photographed many of Bolan's earliest record sleeves, has fonder memories of the last days at Bilton Towers, though he sensed that much had changed. "I remember visiting him in that block of flats off Edgware Road, and while it was all very nice – I think we had tea or something – I felt there was a door closing, that we were both pursuing totally different goals. I think the fame really got to him. He began to believe the myth and moved away from the person he once was."

Marc, by now describing himself as a "street punk", had no immediate wish to retire to the Welsh borders and develop *The Children Of Rarn* into a huge mythological epic. The sense of urgency he now felt about his career had made him grow contemptuous of his past, a fact confirmed in an incident recalled by John Peel's manager Clive Selwood. "I was with Bridget St. John at the BBC's Television Centre and I bumped into Marc and Harry Nilsson there," he recalls. "Both of them were having great difficulty remaining vertical, and Marc introduced Bridget to Nilsson as 'You know, one of those Peel proteges'. I thought that was extremely unkind. The whole affair was a bit of a downer because Marc – whom I'd known since the Tyrannosaurus Rex days – had become quite fat and was obviously drinking too much by that time."

Marc Bolan had made his final break with the self-denial that had become fashionable in the late Sixties and for which he'd been such a good advert that David Bowie praised him for his hermit-like austerity in interviews. Fame had toughened Bolan up. The hard side was already there, of course, a legacy of the Stamford Hill survivor who'd been bruised many times on his slow, inexorable path to stardom. Asked later about his newly discovered taste for meat, his answer illustrated the underlying change in his philosophy. "I didn't object to eating animals because, given the chance, I'm sure they'd eat us," he explained. "It was just that I didn't like the thought of putting something of a lower intelligence inside myself. I'm much more perceptive now than when I was in a macrobiotic state." The one-time Utopian now preferred to see life as a state of war.

Keith Altham, who'd taken over from B.P. Fallon as Marc's PR in mid-1972, and who has worked with some of the biggest egos in rock, sees this transformation as a simple fact of life in the world Bolan now inhabited. "Marc was obviously a very self-centred person," he recalls fondly, "but if he hadn't been, he wouldn't have been a star and he wouldn't have got where he was. All stars have to be selfish to survive."

Unlike Altham's other charges over the years, who have included The Rolling Stones, The Who and Rod Stewart, Marc Bolan's selfishness was actively hampering his chances for survival. His band and entourage mistrusted him, his management indulged him and his fans – who were seeing increasingly less of him – were beginning to slip away. Marc couldn't see that. He saw only the promised land, America, that had once succumbed to Beatlemania and was always just one tour away from embracing Rexmania. "One more tour, Tony!"

Liaising with Warner Brothers, Tony Howard agreed that T. Rex would accompany American bozo rockers Three Dog Night on a coast-to-coast stadium jaunt that took in Canada and the deep south, the midwest and all the major cities. It was ill-matched and a decision that cost T. Rex dear, for the fraught, cataclysmic two months left the band drained, the record company exasperated and Marc Bolan hopelessly estranged from his wife. That's because within days of starting the tour, some time between July 27 and 31, 1973, Marc had begun an affair with Gloria Jones.

"We were in Miami performing at the Sports Auditorium (on July 27)," she remembers. "That night, Pat and Marc and I were riding around in the limo. He said, 'What would you like to eat?' I said seafood. He went in and ordered everything on the menu. When we got back to the hotel, there were over 129 boxes of seafood! We were still friends at this stage. Then we went on to Shreveport, Louisiana (July 31), and that's when he actually said that he liked me. We were very discreet . . ."

June Bolan had flown out for the tour, which began on July 20 in Milwaukee, Wisconsin, but within days, she'd been called back to England on business. According to Mick Gray, "Gloria was making up to Marc, but his interest was less obvious at first. Once June was off the scene, they seemed to get closer. At first we just thought they were flirting. Marc was never a womaniser so his flirting was just accepted. I never thought it would develop the way it did; a lot went on behind closed doors."

Marc, who refused to entertain groupies and had strayed from June on only two occasions, was remarkably loyal – at least by rock'n'roll standards. "He never really went adrift, maybe two or three times that I know of," Mickey Finn confirms. "He was very much a recluse." But things were different now. Stability had become the scapegoat in Bolan's battle to hang on to success and develop creatively. Incredibly, to everyone that knew him, Marc was now even prepared to gamble with June, the rock that instinctively knew how to steady the Superstar's cradle.

The affair came to a head when June rejoined the tour and confronted

Marc in Seattle on August 15. "She gave him an ultimatum and it threw him," Mick Gray remembers. "She'd done this before with Marsha Hunt and with Terry." This time Marc deliberated for too long and June flew home in a temper. "Had she stayed, Marc would have returned like a naughty schoolboy," Gray reckons.

The ramifications of the disastrous six-week American tour were lost on Marc, who partied hard with Gloria behind closed doors and numbed himself to the fact that Three Dog Night (who usually headlined) invariably took the plaudits with showy displays of instrumental virtuosity, often fuelled by booze or cocaine. Bill Legend remembers one awful night at the Paramount Theater in Portland, Oregon. "It was a disaster," he says. "I think Marc was coked up or speeding and in the middle of 'Jeepster', he stopped playing and began to tune up, just as the dry ice engulfed the stage. Then, still trying to tune his guitar at full volume, Marc fell to the floor, so Steve and I prematurely ended the song.

"Meanwhile, these whining notes could be heard coming out of the dry ice, though nobody could see where from. Then Marc got up, walked towards Steve and I and said, 'You're fired! FIRED!' He walked off stage, up a gangway that led to a dead end, threw his guitar off, fell down on his knees and banged his fists against a radiator. It was a terrible night." There may have been mitigating circumstances. It was August 14, the day before the big bust-up with June in Seattle.

Not everyone thought the fourth T. Rex north American tour a disaster. "Overall it was very good," Marc claimed later. "It was strange playing with Three Dog Night. Although they're very nice people, musically we weren't that compatible; we did tend to wipe the floor with them a bit. The audiences were fantastic, so that's the only thing I can judge the tour by." Jack Green, the ex-Sunshine guitarist who'd been hastily recruited to flesh out the sound days before the tour, saw the biggest cocaine mountains he'd seen in his life. As he looked out from the stage, he also saw only smiling, clapping crowds. "We went down really well every night," he insists. "It was the record sales that were poor."

That was true. *Tanx*, which the group were ostensibly promoting, was represented by just one song in the set, 'Born To Boogie'. And like 'The Groover' it had stiffed, too. But it hadn't been all doom and gloom in America. In fact 'Telegram Sam' and *The Slider* both charted, the latter cracking the Top 20, though the full-scale rout of the market that Bolan and Warner Brothers had hoped for failed to materialise. A few months later, in spring 1974, T. Rex were quietly dropped, joining Back Door and Roxy Music in the label's long list of great British mistakes. "Promoting Marc in the States cost a fortune," explained a Warners spokesman. "We just haven't made enough money off him to justify what we were having to spend."

June Bolan's assessment that "America wasn't good for him; it destroyed him" might be expected in light of events out there, but it's a view that's borne out by others in the T. Rex entourage – and by contemporary reviews. "T. Rex played for almost two hours with a cumulative effect of massive Novocain injections," complained Judith Sims of the show in Santa Monica, one of the band's few American strongholds. "Bolan's songs tend to sound alike anyway, each one based on a catchy, repetitive theme – but catchy for three or four minutes on record. Extended to 10, 20 or 30 minutes in concert, those songs go way past boredom."

"Marc thought he was a guitar hero playing solos no one wanted, often out of tune," Mick Gray explains. "The long solos came from Marc's ego and what he perceived the fans wanted to hear. Needless to say, he was out of touch with what they wanted, and he could not understand their reticence to respond." Gray adds that Jack Green's skills were wasted on the tour. "I was asked to play rhythm so that Marc could concentrate on playing lead," says the second guitarist. T. Rex feigning Led Zeppelin on stage cut little ice with Americans whose suspicions were already aroused by Bolan's teenybopper image in Britain.

In spite of the private upheavals and the occasional public execution, T. Rex did manage some impressive performances. One, filmed for NBC's *Midnight Special* on September 3 at the end of the tour, shows the group in hyperactive mode. During 'Get It On', one of two songs broadcast at the end of the month, Marc, Pat and Gloria trade "Oh yeahs" with gusto, Jack Green fills the sound out perfectly, Marc plays up to the cameras, and midway through the performance the audience is on its feet and dancing. Unfortunately, through a combination of sloppy shows and confused expectations, this reaction was the exception rather than the rule.

Marc's masturbatory guitar marathons were accentuated by more openly sexual behaviour on stage. "He even shoved the neck of the guitar through the legs of one of the backup singers," noted one reviewer, "an elementary bit of symbolism indeed." Other nights, he'd throw his boa in Gloria's direction. America may have been disappointing in terms of business, reputation and intra-band camaraderie, but – when he wasn't reading the reviews – Marc Bolan was regularly hitting the button marked T. Rexcessive.

"Up until then, Marc hardly drank and virtually never touched drugs. But once Gloria got possession of him, he was like a different man," says Mickey Finn. "Soon he began to experiment with drugs of every sort, and his drinking became really worrying." Certainly, the crisis precipitated by the split with June, and the illicit thrill of a transatlantic, crosscultural relationship that had the potential to jeopardise and/or transform his life accelerated Bolan's substance abuse. Diving headlong into the unknown, Marc was too preoccupied with the ramifications of change to notice the problems piling up around him – least of all his own self-destructive tendencies, which by now were revealing themselves in his physical appearance as well as in his ever-changing moods.

On September 4, Marc Bolan flew into London and went to see June, whose pride had taken a severe battering after their public altercation in Seattle. "As I understood it, Marc tried to make amends but June stood her ground," says Mick Gray. "Marc seemed gutted for a while. I do not think he intended the relationship with Gloria to become permanent at first." June moved out of Bilton Towers to stay with friends, then rented her own place.

Marc had always been resistant to change in his personal life, and any rift with June meant more than the end of a relationship; it marked the final break with a way of life that he'd outgrown. A week later, he jetted off to Nassau in the Bahamas for a tryst with Gloria. "That was a little sneak holiday, you know!" she admits. "Marc called me up and said, 'I'm going to the Bahamas, will you meet me there?' He teased me and said, 'If I go out there and get a suntan, I'm gonna be darker than you!' We took a boat ride, and every day we would go out on the beach. And Marc would be getting darker and darker and darker. By the time we got back to London, no one recognised him!"

It wasn't just the suntan. As if to make a total break with the past, June's final act (of revenge perhaps?) had been to cut Marc's hair. It was like Delilah dispossessing Samson of all his power, the tight, middle-aged ladies' perm look – offset by an unappealingly oily suntan – did Bolan no favours whatsoever. For someone whose appeal was so heavily reliant on visual magnificence, the removal of the corkscrew curls gave the faithful another reason to stop buying his records.* While critics complained that T. Rex were impervious to change, Marc Bolan was moving so fast that

---

* When magazines asked readers whether they preferred the 'New Marc' to the 'Old Marc' or, the result was always a resounding "No!".

few could – or bothered to – keep up with him. In contrast, David Bowie was still sporting the same 'cockade *orange'* he'd maintained since the emergence of 'Ziggy' in mid-1972.

The suntan, the haircut – both were visible manifestations of the dramatic changes that had taken place in previous weeks. With June out of the flat and Gloria thousands of miles away, Marc was prone – privately at least – to revealing a sensitivity he'd not needed to consult in years. Ace session bassist Danny Thompson, who'd worked with Tyrannosaurus Rex on the Joe Boyd session towards the end of 1967, did some work on the forthcoming *Zinc Alloy* album on October 13. "There was a problem with some of the bass parts," he recalls, "so Tony Visconti, with whom I'd worked on a Tom Paxton album, invited me up to Advision."* One evening around this time, Thompson was invited up to Bilton Towers.

"Marc and I had a lot of fun babysitting for Tony (Visconti) and Mary (Hopkin)," he remembers. "When he shut that door, he forgot all about that star trip. I thought he was really sweet and I remember him laughing about Gary Glitter and all the hype. Of course he used to brag about writing 14 songs a day, and I loved that about him, but I don't think he really believed it. To see him as an egomaniac is to totally misread him," he suggests, adding, "If anything, he seemed a bit lonely at the time."

The image of Marc as a sad elf-like character adrift in a fantasy entirely of his own making may be difficult to accept, but undoubtedly a private hell co-existed that counterbalanced the public displays of megalomania. One night, Marc read some of his poetry into the cassette recorder that always stayed with him. Typically, the words gave little indication of his emotional state, but he signed off with a curt, revealing "Marc Bolan, summer 1973. And I'm lonely."

"Marc was never one of the lads," adds Mick Gray. "He spent a lot of time on his own. In Japan, everyone hung about in clubs and entertained groupies. I passed his room one day and he'd bought a load of toys. He was sitting on the floor playing with his toys. I thought it was pretty sad."

After Bermuda, Gloria Jones had returned home to Los Angeles. "Every night Marc would call and the phone bill got so high that he said it would be better just to fly me over here!" Some time during November 1973, Gloria moved into Bilton Towers but wary of the flat's past associations, the pair soon moved to a third floor apartment in The Avenue, one

---

* According to a surviving memo, "Marc forgot to bring his cheque book to a session." The producer had to pay the studio out of his own pocket.

of the most exclusive roads in St. John's Wood.

"He brought his jukebox with him," Gloria remembers, "so we had a few problems conditioning the neighbours to the idea that there would be music." But his main concern was, she insists, privacy. "He needed to become a human being. That's where the song 'Change' comes in. It was a different environment. That was Marc understanding and dealing with change." But at least one thing stayed the same. "We spent a lot of time at the zoo," says Gloria. "He loved that gorilla Guy. He always felt that Guy communicated with him. Marc would look at me and say, 'Look, he knows me! I *know* he knows me!'"

Although the coincidence of his relationship with Gloria and Marc's fascination for contemporary American soul music suggested a musical meeting of minds, Gloria Jones doesn't remember it that way. "They released my album (*Share My Love*) on Motown, I had new management, a billboard in Hollywood and they were going to put a big campaign behind me. But then Marc asked me to come to London. I sent a telegram to the management that said I will not be able to continue my career because I'm in love!" Marc paid the record a backhanded compliment: "It's a very nice album, although I'm sure I could produce a better one for her."

Despite the union of musical talent, the pair rarely ever wrote together. "The only thing I did was the background," Gloria says. "When he wrote songs, I never interfered." Marc nevertheless encouraged her especially during their early days together. "One day, he walked into the living room in Avenue Road and he handed me his guitar. He says, 'Write a song.' I'd never played a guitar in my life! He tuned it for me and I just started strumming. That's when I wrote 'High'."

'High' was one of the last songs to be recorded for the first of Marc's much discussed production projects. From mid-November through to March 1974, he'd been amassing tracks for a Pat Hall solo project – at Music Recorders Inc. in Los Angeles and various studios in London including Scorpio and Apple. This venture into a new sound dimension was significant. Bolan was the first major British solo artist to embrace contemporary US soul (long before Bowie and Lennon); it was a notable diversion from the T. Rex hit factory; and it confirmed that Bolan was a remarkably different beast to those who'd hitched a ride to fame on his shirt-tails. Unfortunately, few ever got to hear about it.

Earlier that year, he'd made a tentative move into production with a single issued under the Big Carrot moniker. 'Blackjack'/'Squint Eye Mangle' had been recorded with some small input from Pat and Gloria,

but, essentially, it was little more than a T. Rex instrumental jam that provided a showcase for Marc's playing. The Pat Hall album marked an
authoritative leap into territory that was reflected in the inclusion of Eddie
Kendricks' 'Keep On Truckin'' and Betty Wright's 'Clean Up Woman'
among Marc's Top 10 records towards the end of the year. (His passion for
vintage R&B was well represented, too, with Clyde McPhatter and The
Drifters' 'Money Honey', Fats Domino's 'Ain't That A Shame' and The
Cadillacs' 'Speedo' also in the list.)

Pat Hall, who once claimed she'd done so much session singing that
"I'd go on into the next day if I had to recall the names" (Ray Charles was
one), had an extremely powerful voice. "Marc really loved Pat's voice and
she had such a range," admits her singing partner. "He really had fun
recording her and writing for her." However, the project was shelved after
an emergency sent Pat back to the States, though a collection of working
mixes was released as a curio in 1996. Discussing the sessions with *Record &
Radio Mirror*'s Roy Hill during a break from mixing in March 1974, Marc
took umbrage at the writer's comment that the material bore many
familiar Bolan trademarks. "I don't think it sounds remotely like me," he
countered justifiably.

The trio of Marc, Pat and Gloria then indulged in a bit of mutual back-
slapping which proved that at least some of Marc's influence was rubbing
off on what the piece called his "Blackbirds". "Pat is a really fantastic
singer with a five octave range," claimed Gloria Jones. "Getting into
Marc's music has really inspired me," said Pat. "Do you know I literally
had to beg him to play on a few numbers on the album. He's so modest."
"He's very dedicated," added Gloria. "You know, he's very hardworking
and he's always writing." More revealingly, the reporter noted that Marc
was munching on a cheeseburger.

At least half of the aborted Pat Hall album consisted of Bolan originals –
two T. Rex B-sides, 'Jitterbug Love' and 'Sunken Rags', 'Sailors Of
The Highway', the 'lost' single from 1971, and a new song, 'City Port'.
Marc's guitar and voice inevitably made themselves heard (including some
overamped rhythm on 'Tell Me'), though the sessions were notably unlike
T. Rex, with superfunk backings, Bohannon-style handclaps and Pat's
Labelle-like vocal gymnastics. Two of the strongest songs came from the
pen of Gloria Jones – 'When I Was A Child' and the wistful 'High', which
inspired Pat to new heights of delicacy. ('High', with lyrics by Bolan, was
one of only two known Bolan/Jones co-compositions. The other was
'Cry Baby', and both songs featured on Gloria's 1976 solo album, *Vixen*.)

In contrast to Pat's spirited, at times histrionic performances, were sessions for Gloria's brother Richard Jones. Jones was, in Bolan's words, 'a dude', an imposing, larger-than-life character with at least as much front as Marc and similar aspirations to carve out a singing career of his own. "He loved Richard," Gloria says of her brother with the cool baritone voice. "He felt that Richard could be another Barry White."

Richard Jones became a regular fixture at T. Rex's sessions at the Music Recorders Inc. (MRI) studios in Hollywood, where he'd sometimes arrive with a small entourage of musician friends who would invariably sit in on sessions. "He was a big, mean-looking LA hustler type, though I remember him being a nice bloke," says Jack Green.

Within 24 hours of jetting into Los Angeles, on November 12, 1973, Marc was overseeing a Richard Jones session at MRI. One song, 'Power Of Love', was a strong, gospel-flavoured performance that featured some distinctive organ-playing uncannily similar to Gloria's childhood friend Billy Preston's contribution to The Rolling Stones' 'Melody' on their 1976 *Black And Blue* album. In fact, the pianist was Sylvester Rivers, who was joined on the session by guitarist Ray Parker Jr., Scott Edwards on bass and drummer Ed Green. 'No No No', also taped that day, was an impressive, silky smooth arrangement with Jones playing his superfly sex god role perfectly. Marc's 'Big' Richard Jones album was still being put together in September 1977 and it remains unfinished and unreleased.

Bolan was never likely to challenge the supremacy of Kenny Gamble, Leon Huff and Thom Bell, the architects behind the emerging Philly Sound of Harold Melvin & The Blue Notes and The O'Jays. However, his immersion in contemporary US soul, nurtured further by Gloria and Pat and the US soul stations the trio tuned into while riding around the States in Marc's touring limo, was genuine and would leave an imminent and indelible impression on his own music.

★ ★ ★

While Marc was in love and immersed in new musical distractions, T. Rex were in disarray. Steve Currie and Bill Legend had finally secured a wage rise after three enormously successful years, though the rise from £40 to £50 hardly placated them. Steve Currie regularly jested that the band ought to buy Marc a giant papier-mâché ear. The band members' lack of voice and economy class treatment – in every facet of life from plane tickets to onstage respect – irked, and after T. Rex's two-week tour of Japan and Australia during October and November, Bill Legend left the group.

According to Bill, there was no big bust-up. The drummer simply asked Tony Howard for his passport after the final concert at Brisbane's Festival Hall and took the next flight home back to his family in Essex. Like so many of Marc's former associates, Bill never heard from him again. But the truth behind his departure was that he was fired by Tony Howard on Marc's orders. "Marc was convinced that Bill's playing was being affected by his diminishing hearing, that he could no longer keep time," says Mick Gray.

The departure of Bill Legend signalled the final demise of T. Rex as a rock'n'rollin' four-piece. But when Tony Visconti finally threw in his towel with Marc, some time around October 1973 after some fraught overdub sessions for the new album at Air Studios in London, he took with him history, stability and that distinctive T. Rex production sound. Marc Bolan, who'd struggled to extricate himself from his past throughout 1971, and who had been virtually omnipresent over the next couple of years, finally had *carte blanche* to construct the future according to his own vision. That same month, the release of *Great Hits*, a splendid summation of the past two years' successes, represented another closure – though its lowly number 32 chart placing confirmed the domestic market's growing rejection of its errant, and increasingly erratic idol. So much for the 'By Great Demand' claimed in the adverts.

Tony Visconti was the last survivor from the early Ladbroke Grove days, but his friendship with Marc had been under strain for many months, both socially and professionally. The disagreement over royalties in July 1972 had stunned him. "At that stage in his career, Marc felt he didn't have to pay a royalty to anybody," says the producer. "And to top it all, the lawyer asked me, 'What does a producer do anyway, Mr. Visconti?' I went home very upset, and later received a call from a sobbing June, who came over to smooth it out. She explained that the most Marc could afford was one per cent. Bullshit! My manager couldn't get it any higher than that, so I actually dropped my earning power by 50%."

Visconti produced *The Slider*, *Tanx* and *Zinc Alloy* albums under those terms, though even more galling than the new financial arrangement had been Marc's changing attitude. Matters reached a head in Munich back in June, though Visconti agreed to finish work on the album when T. Rex returned from America in October. "After 'Truck On' (taped in Munich), I saw the writing on the wall," he says. "Marc's songs weren't getting any better and he couldn't break free from the formula. It took half an hour to mix T. Rex songs. I'd EQ the drums in a certain way, compress the bass and put a slap-back echo on Marc's voice or ADT it to make it sound like two voices, because he'd become too lazy to double-track his vocals. I remember mixing a song very quickly one day, and Marc turned to me and said, 'Cheap isn't it?' We both laughed, but that was the sad truth. It was getting very cheap, it was easy to do, and it was no fun any more. We were drinking more than we were working."

That was all true, but worse still, Marc's determination to assume total control of everything – which accelerated during 1973 – was an affront to Visconti's professionalism. "Tony was ignored when he gave advice," says Mick Gray, "and Marc was often drunk or coked out and aggressive." There had been a formula, but it was the interminable late nights slaving over an out-of-tune overdub by a paymaster who didn't know when to stop that finally wore Visconti out. Besides, a new challenge had come his way in the summer.

"David (Bowie) called me in the middle of the night," the producer told Bowie biographer David Buckley. "I could tell he was on something, probably cocaine, because he was speaking quickly, rambling really. He said could we get together soon?" Visconti agreed, and that winter the pair hid themselves away in the producer's new 16-track home studio in France and mixed Bowie's apocalyptic, futuristic space-age soul epic, *Diamond Dogs*, issued in April 1974. Bolan's *Zinc Alloy* album, almost 12 months in the making, pipped it by a month – but the reception that would greet both records contrasted wildly.

With Marc out of sight and often out of the country during much of 1973, Bowie ably filled the vacuum. As a singles artist, he couldn't touch the remarkable run of success that T. Rex enjoyed during 1971 and 1972. But his understanding of the rock market, explained with an artfulness that Marc could never do so convincingly, won him huge album sales and credibility. While Marc quietly retired to the recording studio and spent most of his time abroad, Bowie was 'retiring' in spectacular, hold-the-front-page fashion. On July 3, 1973, at the climax of his sell-out British tour, he made a dramatic announcement from the stage of London's Hammersmith Odeon. "Not only is it the last show of the tour, but it's the last show that we'll ever do," he uttered breathlessly to audible gasps. Ziggy broke up the band, just as Bowie had predicted on the *Ziggy Stardust* title track.

Bowie's fascination for art, in particular the work of Andy Warhol, was reaping dividends; his life was indeed mirroring his art. Marc's preference for poetry and Ray Bradbury's science fiction writings suggested not the studied depersonalisation favoured by his rival but a gentle drip feed of fantasy. Only now the reality of Marc's fantasy was every bit as dramatic as David's, and with no *doppelgänger* device to protect him as the drip feed became a gushing torrent of pills, thrills and belly-swelling, significantly more perilous. Marc got fat. David got thin. Marc got soul. David got America.

The changes that were taking place in Bolan's life were not reflected in 'Truck On (Tyke)', the last T. Rex single of 1973 and the least successful since the days of Tyrannosaurus Rex. The voices of Gloria and Pat were almost as prominent as Bolan's but the repetition of the song title 63 times in little more than three minutes became the major talking point.

"It grieves me to report that 'Truck On (Tyke)' is a curiously lifeless and colourless offering, and one wonders whether this particular space-age cowboy isn't last year's space-age cowboy," said John Peel. "Perhaps it is significant that I took all the T. Rex singles out of the box I use at the village youth club because they never get played anymore." Desperate to find something positive to say, he noted that Marc pronounced the word 'dinosaur' just like The Hollywood Argyles did on their doo wop classic, 'Alley Oop'. "At least Marc's sources are good," he concluded.

'Truck On (Tyke)' was not one of Marc's most memorable songs. Briefly, he'd considered releasing another single from the *Zinc Alloy* sessions, 'Venus Loon', a far more brutal slice of punkoid funk recorded at Electric Ladyland midway through the American tour. It would have sent out a message more in tune with Bolan's new direction but, he declared later, the song was "far too '74 to be '73, dig?"

The gulf between his own musical ambition and his faith in his audience's ability to move with him became even more evident late in January 1974 when T. Rex undertook their first British tour in 18 months. Billed with barely concealed spite as the 'Truck Off' tour, the six dates (which strangely avoided London) unveiled an impressive-looking ten-piece T. Rex but – with the exception of a new single 'Teenage Dream' – no hint of new material or direction.

More than six months after Bowie had buried Ziggy, the posters proclaimed ham-fistedly that Marc Bolan and T. Rex would be "On Tour As Zinc Alloy And The Hidden Riders Of Tomorrow". Inevitably, Bolan's return inspired scenes reminiscent of 1972-style T. Rexstasy, but while the songs remained the same, his reaction to the chants of "We Want Marc!" hadn't. "It was annoying to hear them scream out for me," he said after the Glasgow Apollo show on January 22.

Bolan wasn't the only aggrieved soul at the shows. The promised "spectacular new stage production" consisted of the old flashing neon T. Rex backdrop; a small extension to the stage on which Marc was able to lie on his back and shake his tambourine to fans within touching distance of him; and a hydraulic, star-shaped dais that raised him, vampire-like, from the ground to face his audience.

"When he used to piss me off, I used to set it a little bit more, give it a bit of kick, and sometimes he'd land a bit further than where he wanted to land," admitted road manager Mick O'Halloran in 1997. A large press contingent had travelled to Glasgow to review the tour, but something must have aggrieved O'Halloran that day. Dressed in outsize flared white trousers, embellished with a musical stave similar to that which greeted visitors at the gates of Presley's Graceland mansion, a sparkling dark cape and an open-fronted, armour-like shirt from which spilled a generously endowed chest, Marc Bolan was as close to Gary Glitter as he'd ever get (a fact emphasised by the twin drum, twin sax, twin backing vocals, twin guitar line-up).* And there was worse to come. As he took an ungainly leap onto the star-shaped prop, Marc fell onto his back and into the drum kit, and had to be helped off stage by Mickey Finn and his two roadies. He made a sheepish return a few minutes later, but the damage had been done.

When promoting 'Truck On (Tyke)' on Granada TV's *Lift Off With Ayshea* a month earlier, he'd looked uncomfortable without his guitar (Jack Green handled Marc's Les Paul on this occasion), and ungainly as a few excess pounds on his short, stocky stature pushed him in the direction – visually at least – of his old Regal Zonophone labelmate Joe Cocker. Christmas in the Bahamas with Gloria hadn't done his figure any favours and the Bopping Elf was now, the press gleefully reported, a "Porky Pixie" and a "Glittering Chipolata Sausage". Marc Bolan had become a strange hybrid of Gary Glitter and Mountain's infamously chubby guitarist Leslie West – and he didn't give a damn.

"The thing is that I know what's going on, and the kids know what's going on, so it really doesn't matter what other people think, what the media think," Marc countered when the less than flattering reviews rolled in. Others were less convinced of the accuracy of his perceptions.

---

* The new-style T. Rex, including second guitarist Jack Green, were augmented by Howie Casey (tenor sax), Dick Parry (baritone sax), Davey Lutton (drums), Paul Fenton (drums) and Pat and Gloria on backing vocals.

"There was a lot of coke," remembers Jack Green, whose services were dispensed with after the tour. "They would go into their raps: 'I'm the greatest guitarist since Jimi Hendrix,' and Gloria would reply, 'Yes you are.' It was almost like a gospel thing and it could go on all night. It was really bad for him. Egos were going wild."

Simon Napier-Bell has said that cocaine was the drug that best fitted Marc's personality; it was a "fuck you" drug. And by early 1974, there was plenty of it in and around the T. Rex camp. "Marc would never put out a line of coke," Jack Green remembers. "He'd open a new packet every time. Our faces would just freeze into a smile. We had so much our jaws couldn't move." Oddly, as his closest rivals grew emaciated on the stuff, Marc simply expanded. Being short didn't help either; nor did the empty bottles. "He didn't eat much, so it must have been the drink," concludes Mick Gray.

Back in 1972, Marc complained that his lifelong idol was stagnating in the showrooms of Las Vegas. "I don't want to hear Elvis singing live now," he said. "I'd just like to see him walk on stage – and walk off again before the performance. I'd hate to be disillusioned." Yet, surrounded by too many willing to flatter and too few brave enough to question, Bolan too was slipping into a Presley-like netherworld. "It did not pay to question Marc or even stand up to him; if you crossed him you were out," maintains Mick Gray, who says he was sacked on numerous occasions only for Tony Howard to reinstate him.

"The band were totally frustrated by Marc but were frightened to question his judgement in case they were sacked. In most cases they were sacked anyway. If Mickey had stood up to Marc early on, perhaps things may have been different," adds Gray.

"He had a nice attitude until he believed his own publicity, and that's not a put-down, that's just the music scene," says Mickey Finn. "You've got to believe in yourself so you've got to believe the publicity. But he did get a little bit OTT in my opinion."

"Marc thought that whatever he did was great," adds Jeff Dexter. "He never felt he was stuck. No one could ever question what Marc did because he was doing it, and he knew he was right. If you questioned Marc, you'd be frozen out."

Everyone is entitled to their 'fat Elvis' moment, where all constraints can be cast out and replaced by an obsessive, depraved dive into an orgy of excessive behaviour. Besides, John Lennon was still midway through his 'Lost Weekend' in Los Angeles (or "Lost Arseholes", as he so delicately put it later). While Marc was whipping out his belt and beating the British stage in a petulant display of frustration masquerading as showmanship, his traumatic private life at last got the soundtrack it deserved.

'Teenage Dream' was Marc Bolan's coming out record; its hookline, "Whatever happened to the Teenage Dream?", obviously rhetorical. Marc never had to play 'blue notes' in order to temper the upbeat Dolan boogie with sadness. His voice, and those trademark, down-the-neck riffs lent his sound a rich undercurrent of gentle despair. But none of this prepared the way for 'Teenage Dream', a Visconti/Bolan co-production so drenched in melodramatic resignation that it was less a lament (Alice Cooper's 'Teenage Lament '74' had recently charted) than a lordly glimpse through the iron bars of an increasingly detached existence.

On 'Teenage Dream', Bolan surveyed the debris of his past (the Silver Surfer is "all sad and rusted", the god from a "rusty world" is broken) in a mocking, decadent tone that began with a cackle and ended over five minutes later in a crescendo of effusive strings and 'Cosmic Choir' chorus. The chord sequence – roughly C–Am–F–G and played with great spirit on piano by War's Lonnie Johnson – was rich in nostalgia, too, both for late Fifties teen ballads and Marc's own songs such as 'Catblack'. Where Bowie tinkered ironically with pop's past, Bolan couldn't help but use it to make a grand statement about himself. "I just wrote that down in the studio without thinking about it," he said, adding that 'Teenage Dream' was his best lyric. He certainly sung it as if it was.

Breaking with type didn't exactly help Bolan's fortunes commercially, though, and the single only peaked at a disappointing 13. Coming hot on the heels of The Sweet's 'Teenage Rampage' and the aforementioned Alice Cooper 45, the title prompted considerable debate in the pages of the music press, not all of it favourable. One teenager, Randolph Angel from Glasgow, told *Melody Maker*: "Bolan's talking about himself. He thinks he is the teenage dream. Years after he's been forgotten, he's trying to make a comeback." It was a cruel assessment, as grand and exaggerated as the song itself, but the feeling that Bolan had had his day was, by spring 1974, endemic.

'Teenage Dream' had been recorded during the eventful American tour in August 1973, and was one of the last songs written for *Zinc Alloy*. Its subject matter, and Bolan's appearance on the accompanying tour, tended to overshadow the LP which, when it eventually appeared in March five weeks after the tour had finished, received short shrift in the press. The delay was partly down to Marc's insistence on a deluxe, multi-foldout latticed cover, an extravagance that matched the record's full title – *Zinc Alloy And The Hidden Riders Of Tomorrow/A Creamed Cage In August*, as unwieldy as any in Bolan's extensive catalogue.

According to Gloria Jones, this elaborate cover was eventually limited to a run of just 1,000 copies because the oil crisis put a drain on resources. There was another possibility; EMI may have decided that the demand didn't justify the expense. It was a judicious decision. The record hit 12 in the album charts, and received the usual mixed, baffled notices, none more so than from Rosalind Russell in *Disc* who wrote that while "the style hasn't changed . . . the songs are all in much the same vein as 'Teenage Dream', which does mark a distinctive change in style."

The style had changed; so too had the intent, the instrumentation, the production, even the billing, now credited to 'Marc Bolan & T. Rex'. A roughly hewn gem forged from frustration and the fear of failure, *Zinc Alloy* remains a remarkable testament to Bolan's resilience in the face of adversity, and its commercial failure an indictment of that era's sloppy prejudices.

To reflect the musical changes he was making (and, less impressively, a belated nod to the Bowie/Ziggy dichotomy), Marc wanted the new album to be called *A Creamed Cage In August* and credited to 'Zinc Alloy & The Hidden Riders of Tomorrow' (a send-up of the two Stardusts Ziggy and Alvin, he insisted). EMI baulked, not only because of falling record sales but because the cover image of Bolan – shorter hair, design studio eyes of blue and a luminous suntan – striking though it was, was hardly *The Slider*. EMI flashed a strip stating 'Marc Bolan & T. Rex' across the corner of the sleeve just in case.

Drawing on sessions that stretched back 12 months, *Zinc Alloy* ought to have been an inconsistent, unmanageable mess. Months later, Marc admitted as much himself: "Although the overall album is very good, one of my best I think, there was no general theme to it." While eclecticism for its own sake isn't necessarily a virtue, as the jet-lagged *Tanx* proved, there was an unwavering confidence about *Zinc Alloy* that makes it possible to overlook the record's obvious flaws and its difficult birth.

It was fairly obvious that Tony Visconti had been held to ransom by Bolan during the sessions. Marc's voice, lower in the mix than at any time since his earliest 45s, was engaged in a virtual battle with Pat's and Gloria's, whose feisty cries sometimes nudged him off his own record. And there was little evidence of that classic T. Rex formula.

To compare *Zinc Alloy* with The Rolling Stones' masterful *Exile On*

Main Street would be a gross error of judgement in anyone's book. But there are parallels. Both albums weren't particularly well received at the time; both inhabit their own unique world, and both meld rock'n'roll abandon with an urgency and directness mistaken at the time for vulgarity. The records are long and unwieldly; the sessions piecemeal and fuelled by spontaneous inspiration. The musical directors on both (Keith Richards and Marc) are out of control, the producers reduced to virtual bystanders.

Discussing the album at the time, Marc was at a rare loss for words. "It's got a lot of spaces . . . kind of intergalactic Neil Young . . . very under-produced in a way . . . I've got what I've been looking for." Bingo! "Unintentionally, it's very different," he concluded, which only confused matters further. What wasn't on *Zinc Alloy*, apart from a few bars of one of the key tracks, 'Painless Persuasion v. The Meathawk Immaculate', was the old Bolan boogie machine. It was an unprecedented omission that heralded a new era of Marc Bolan & T. Rex. In its place was a riot of Marc's "space-age funk" (especially on 'Venus Loon', 'Galaxy', 'Liquid Gang', 'Interstellar Soul' and 'The Avengers [Superbad]'), with diversions into bizarre bubblegum ('Sound Pit', 'Nameless Wildness'), a soul mantra delivered like a Glam Rock John Wayne ('The Leopards Featuring Gardenia And The Mighty Slug') and the rediscovery of Marc's life motor – change.

Simply expressed and delicately executed, 'Change' was not as artful as 'Changes', the theme tune Bowie had written for himself three years earlier. But it was every bit as talismanic. A random word search through a huge document of interviews covering the years 1973–1977, both with Marc and about him, revealed more references to 'change' than to 'T. Rex'. It was an obsession – even though Marc didn't always seem to understand the difference between change and stagnation.

As a harbinger for the months ahead, though, 'Painless Persuasion v. The Meathawk Immaculate' was the album's most prescient song. "I can feel earthquakes inside of me," Marc sang, against an ominous "It's gonna go" backdrop yelped recklessly by Pat and Gloria. "I can sense landslides of devilry/I can be everything that's bad to me," he continued, before all three chorused: "What's goin' on." It was a question that would be raised many times over the course of the next 12 months.

11

Too Pooped To Pop

"I haven't slipped. I'm still number one."

– Marc Bolan (July 1974)

"Long after June left, I did have fits of violence. I still do. It's the poetic side of my nature – kicking television screens in and throwing hatchets at pictures of Elvis Presley."

– Marc Bolan (October 1976)

"It was like Elvis on a bad trip."

– Jeff Dexter (1992)

In spring 1974, Marc Bolan quietly packed his bags and quit Britain. Engrossed in his new role as a soul music producer, in thrall to his new musical companions on the American West Coast and rediscovering the world through the eyes of his new love Gloria Jones, he embarked upon an itinerant life spent jetting back and forth between the south of France, London and the Hollywood Hills. This sojourn, which continued well into the summer of 1975, drew a veil over the career of Marc Bolan: Superstar, though it's never been entirely clear what kind of life he replaced it with.

We know that when he did make the occasional return to London, invariably to promote a new record, this Marc Bolan – overweight and often drunk – looked several shadows of his former Glamglorious self. We also know that his music – spread across a meagre clutch of releases that the press did its best to ignore – had, by and large, veered off in a direction all of its own. What has never been fully understood, though, is why and how Marc Bolan, the man who single-handedly reinvented pop for the Seventies, managed to jettison his career so quickly and so spectacularly.

Marc, of course, never saw it that way – at least not publicly. Gloria Jones knew the hurt behind the bravado. "When you are the biggest star next to the Beatles, you figure that your fans will grow with you," she says. "There was Slade, there was Gary Glitter. Then all of a sudden there were younger groups coming up like the Bay City Rollers. They're kids. His fans didn't follow the growth; they wanted him to stay the same. So what do you do if you're a person who has a gift, is a wonderful composer and poet and a brilliant ideas person?"

Marc Bolan had already rejected his past – several times over. Now, aware that his days as a teenage idol were diminishing with each record, he turned his back on his public. It wasn't, after all, particularly difficult to do. As he admitted in July 1973, a limited shelf-life was simply a fact of life in the teen-orientated pop market. The events of the previous months had only accelerated the process, making any and every change easier to embrace.

"I think that in two or three years' time I'm going to be out of the bag I'm in now," he said. "It takes care of itself in the same way that the Stones are no longer a teenage idol band. It always lasts about five years on that sort of level. Then you become an artist and you just do what you want to do." Pausing for breath, he added, "I wouldn't do anything I do unless it made me happy."

Being the biggest star in Britain and half the western world had been the realisation of a fabulous fantasy, though it hadn't necessarily brought happiness into Marc's life. He had played the part of the Superstar to perfection, but privately, his search went on. The experience had made him cynical, a confirmation that production-line creativity spiced up with a little sensationalism invariably won out over risky artistic endeavour. He'd now done all that. But to accept that the public had decided it had heard enough of Marc Bolan and had taken its affections elsewhere was more difficult. But, he told himself, they couldn't take away the urge to create that had been with him since his mid-teens. Nor could they allay Marc's compulsion to explore his loss of innocence in the manner of a 19th century Romantic searching to extend the boundaries of his existence – irrespective of what he may find.

"It was hard," says Gloria. "Everybody was fighting him because they didn't want him to change and it absolutely broke his heart. People didn't understand he was very sensitive and pure in spirit. So what do you do? Do you make music to please the fans or do you make music to please your soul? And that's what you gotta understand; Marc was a soul man." Using the recording studio as his Good Samaritan, Marc Bolan plunged perilously into a kind of personal anarchy.

"I believe everything I do is a work of art," Bolan claimed in January

1974. On that basis, his year-long exile must be judged as a particularly fertile period, because Marc was in and out of the recording studio wherever he was based – in London, Chicago, Los Angeles, Paris or Munich. As the heaps of tapes that survive from this endless search for sonic salvation attest, Marc met at least as many dead ends as he did new avenues.

Amid the jewels there were rambling instrumental jams (one track, titled '11.15 [Jam]' on the session sheets, was a showcase for Bolan's fiery noodling), uninspired hooks ('Video Drama') and overwrought soul strainings ('Do I Love Thee'). But with Marc's new working methods – turn up at the studio, have a drink and a toot and start playing, sometimes all night – such unreleasable wastage was inevitable. While the criteria for Bolan's judgement had altered dramatically, his decision-making, though invariably more erratic, was vindicated by the commercial releases, which more or less reveal an acute, judicious sifting of material for his next two albums. Unfortunately, despite the inclusion of some of the most stimulating, enduring work Bolan had ever committed to tape, they didn't sell.

Back in 1972, Marc told Radio Luxembourg's Mark Wesley that he had one message: "Just freedom. I came from a working-class background, a straight sort of background. And if nothing else, I've proved that someone from that environment can get a Rolls-Royce or whatever." No longer wanting for material wealth, or even the status that comes with being a star, he now defined freedom as the absence of constraint – any and every constraint.

"Freedom is something that's very hard for most people to understand," says Gloria Jones, "but Marc didn't have a problem with being free. He didn't have a safety net around him. He lived life to the full."

Unfortunately, when Marc exercised his freedom, it inevitably had repercussions for those around him. In April 1974, while he was still holed up in London's Scorpio Studios mixing the Pat Hall album, the remaining members of T. Rex (now trimmed back to a four-piece with just Mickey Finn, Steve Currie and Davey Lutton surviving the *Zinc Alloy* tour) had good reason to question their collective future.

"I've been thinking for a while now about gradually phasing the band name of T. Rex out, because that's really where I'm at," Marc told *Disc* a few weeks earlier. "Now it's me with a few backing musicians and that's how the whole Bolan thing should be developed. Perhaps later, I'll do concerts backed by strings and various musicians who want to work with me."

It was all very well for David Bowie to ditch his Spiders From Mars, which he could claim had been a fictional backing band anyway, but for Bolan to consider dropping the T. Rex name – with which he was synonymous – was a wretched idea, especially at a time when Marc's name had about as much cachet as Roy Wood or Suzi Quatro, at least in pop chart terms. However, as T. Rex's hits-heavy set-lists indicated, there was an element of conservatism about Marc that makes this era of exiled abandon all the more extraordinary. Even when the rest of the band didn't play on T. Rex records – a common occurrence during 1974 – Bolan could never quite make the break and declare himself a solo artist.

In June 1974, by which time Marc and Gloria were living in Los Angeles, the only album credited to Marc Bolan released in his lifetime appeared in the racks. Titled *The Beginning Of Doves*, it was simply the old *Hard On Love* project that had been cooked up by Track Records, Kit Lambert and Simon Napier-Bell and successfully injuncted by Marc two years earlier. Bolan grimaced at the merest mention of it. "Those were demos done when I was 17 or 18 and never meant for release," he complained later in the year. However, over lunch with Lambert and Napier-Bell, he had hammered out a compromise deal whereby he sanctioned the record's release as long as the sleeve and advertising did not mislead audiences. "Now it's alright that they're out because people know what they are," he shrugged. It was a fascinating collection from Marc's wilderness years, but it could hardly have come at a worse time. As *New Musical Express*'s cub journalist Chrissie Hynde put it: "Marc Bolan needs this album right now like he needs barbed wire underpants."

A second relic from Bolan's past was revisited that spring. After a short break in Spain in April, Marc and Gloria moved on to Los Angeles. Ostensibly to visit Gloria's parents and Wally Thurmond, her son by a professional football coach, who was living with them, the trip was extended to take in two weeks at the MRI Studios. The other members of T. Rex were not invited to join them. Marc's hunger for change, his recent work with Pat Hall and the calibre of musicians Gloria and Richard Jones were able to put at his disposal, meant that the May 1974 Los Angeles recordings were conducted as Marc Bolan solo sessions.

As an indication of how elastic Bolan's musical mind had become, the decision to reactivate *The Children Of Rarn* at MRI and develop it into a full-blown funkaboogie epic takes some beating. The idea may have been interstellar soul, but the result, judging by the tapes that survive, was cosmic slop of the third-rate kind. As the 40-minute session limped on towards an inevitable anti-climax, with Marc vainly reprising his 'Ram' overture from the 1970 *T. Rex* album, the effect was akin to Elvis Presley's perfunctory crucifixion of his rock'n'roll hits in a glorified dining-room in Las Vegas.

It was a pointless exercise – and certainly no match for the dynamic, edgy funkadelia that George Clinton was coming up with around the same time – but as he sought to experience life in all its 57 varieties, Marc seemed more than willing to try anything at least twice. And when his endeavours were accompanied by choruses of encouragement from his new companions, and generous quantities of booze and cocaine, everything he committed to tape sounded like the work of a genius – at least until the next morning arrived and he struggled to remember what he'd done the previous evening.

One particularly bright LA morning it was decided that *The Children Of Ram* wasn't working after all and the lacklustre demo joined a mountain of studio recordings made between spring 1974 and spring 1975 that wisely remained in the vaults. "I know exactly what I want in the studio," Marc maintained months earlier. But the reels of tape that document the blind alleys and the unfinished songs tell their own story.

Marc was never particularly comfortable improvising in the studio. He could go off on a solo guitar extravaganza as long as the other musicians stayed in the same key, but once a pattern had been established he was rarely able to break out from it. Surrounded by strangers with whom Marc had little musical rapport, this could prompt a pitifully repeated refrain like 'Video Drama' or, once in a while, something inspired and out of the ordinary. 'Light Of Love', a new song that had prompted the April MRI session in the first place, was one of those moments when everything came together.

Bolan's voice, slight, yearning and loudly shadowed by Gloria's, maintained some continuity with the past. But the clipped handclap and hi-hat intro, the motorik, proto-disco beat, Gloria Jones' distinctive clavinet and the direct, almost vulgarly upfront production, confirmed that Bolan hadn't merely broken the T. Rex mould; he'd buried it. The rudimentary fuzztone of his guitar ought to have been hideously out of context, but its presence only adds to the single's unlikely charm.

By summer 1974, the Glam Rock hangover had kicked in with revivalists Showaddywaddy, The Rubettes, Alvin Stardust and, above all, The Bay City Rollers capturing the teenybop market. Their costumes were as idiotic as Bolan and Bowie's had once been enticing; their music straightened out every last wrinkle of strangeness hinted at by their fore-bears. The Wombles and Abba jostled for the number one single, Pink Floyd and Led Zeppelin mounted huge, lucrative spectacles, and the gulf between rock and pop seemed more hopelessly divided than ever. It was as if Bolan and Bowie had never happened, and mainstream pop's loving embrace with the peculiar had been nothing more than an illicit flirtation.

If 'Light Of Love' was an attempt to introduce the British audience (Bolan no longer had a US deal) to a new American street sound, it failed. If it was an attempt by Marc to kickstart his career with a startling new direction, it failed too. The effervescent charms of 'Light Of Love' had proved incompatible with a Top 20 placing and the song endured much ridicule for its "La-la-la-la-la the light of love" lyric hook. It was nonsense, but top-notch nonsense at that.

A promotional film, shot in Paris and sent to various television stations so that Bolan didn't have to go anywhere he didn't want to, was equally distinctive. Marc's performance was more camp and decadent than before. His hair had grown, and his belt had tightened. The studio setting, transformed unconvincingly into a disco with flashing lights and the group dressed in white, somehow enhanced the feeling that this was just a Bolanic dream sequence and that everything would be all right in the morning. It wouldn't, not for some time.

In July 1974, Marc – as Mark Feld – made a formal request to the French Consulate in London for a visa. Although he never took up resident status, he made several lengthy stays in France over the next 12 months. His preferred playground was the Côte d'Azur, the most expensive stretch of coastline in the world. Not that he ever saw much of the beach.

The first extended stay on the Riviera, for much of August, was a working holiday. The T. Rex line-up had regrouped with a second keyboard player, Peter 'Dino' Dines, in tow and had decamped to the Negresco Hotel in Nice. With another American tour arranged for the late autumn, Bolan rehearsed the band extensively at the nearby Victorine Film Studios. When the day's work finished, usually around three in the afternoon, the rest of the group would meet their partners and head for the beach before retiring to the hotel bar during the evenings. "That was a bit of a waste in such a beautiful city," Mick Gray admits. "I think we got out and saw a festival of flowers one evening, but that was it."

Marc and Gloria usually stayed out of the sun and headed back to the hotel, where they spent most evenings and weekends. Occasionally, Gray would drive them out to a village above the town (the capital of the French Riviera) for a meal. On a couple of occasions the pair ventured into Monaco, the tiny, hideously expensive independent state east of Nice.

Coincidentally, for the region is renowned for its racism, the sojourn was mildly soured when a new driver employed by Marc was deemed hostile to Gloria. "He refused to drive her or do any chores for her unless Marc instructed him," says Mick Gray. The offending character was promptly sacked.

Gloria maintains that she never experienced any racism during her time with Marc. "If that's something he knew, I was never made aware of it," she says. "One time we were walking through the airport in Mobile, Alabama, and he was wearing the hat and these gold high-heeled sandals. My dad would say, 'You be careful down south,' but they just thought it was two chicks walking! I wasn't aware of any prejudice."

According to an interview later that year, in November, Marc insisted he'd not been idle. "Artists go through hot and cold periods so I've just waited for the time when I feel hot." Five books, three screenplays and 95 songs were, he claimed, all ready to go. Between 'Light Of Love' and 'New York City', released the following summer, a paltry 11 songs – most of which had already been taped at MRI in May 1974 – were the only public evidence of this prodigious output.

"I have the good fortune to be free financially and mentally, so I can stop one thing and experiment in other areas whenever I get the urge," Marc admitted in the same interview. It contained far more truth than his earlier boast. Marc was relishing his freedom, but the indiscipline was having a drastic effect on his health – physically, mentally and commercially.

The spur for the American tour had been a new record deal struck with the Los Angeles-based American independent Casablanca, recently established by Neil Bogart and distributed through Warner Brothers. The arrangement had been discussed that spring, when Marc's intention had been to secure an American release for *Zinc Alloy*. Casablanca had other ideas.

"Neil came down to listen and wasn't that excited about *Zinc Alloy*," Marc admitted to Alan Betrock in November 1974. "He didn't feel it was my best and I agreed with him. There's moments of course, and some songs I'm quite proud of, but it was put together over a two-year span (sic) so it's very choppy." Bogart's desire to hear what Marc could come up with in 1974 was the reason behind the hastily arranged MRI sessions in May.

It had been Bolan's intention to return to the Chateau in France to mix the spring 1974 tapes but the studio was closed. Instead, he returned to Los Angeles after the Nice rehearsals finished late in August. Before he left, he told *Circus* magazine that the new material "has a kind of energy like 21st century Chuck Berry".

By the time Marc was back in America, and making some final adjustments to the tapes prior to the album's release in September, he was comparing the forthcoming record to *Electric Warrior*. "I wrote most of the songs in the studio (and) it's also the first one I've produced myself," he said. Marc was rejuvenated and "feeling an excitement about words and music I haven't felt for about a year now". For once, he struggled to describe the record. It was "straight American rock'n'roll"; it was "funky"; it was simply "different and tight". It was also the most controversial, commercially bankrupt and creatively misunderstood album in Marc Bolan's career.

Light Of Love was released (in America only) in time for the tour, an ill-conceived two-month venture blighted by bad organisation and awful reviews that broke even Marc Bolan's indomitable spirit. He would never return to the States on a professional basis again. Mickey Finn insists that the admission of failure destroyed Marc. "Undoubtedly. He just couldn't crack it. I don't know why. It was too massive, and Warner Brothers didn't work hard enough."

Back in Manchester, the teenage Morrissey, who had switched his affections to the deviant, druggy New York Dolls, was delighted. "Marc was too intellectual to really make it in America, and I'm glad that he didn't," he told John Willans and Caron Thomas in October 1991. "His lyrical language was truly only graspable in the cosmic imagination, and consequently he is never considered to be a classic British pop writer in the way that, for instance, Ray Davies is."

But Marc didn't stop trying to shoehorn contemporary American influences into his music. While Eno was patenting a new, sophisticated kind of minimalism in England, Marc's engagement with the street vibe of black America had prompted – perhaps by accident as much as design – a gloriously debauched union of grit and grandiloquence. If Norma Desmond had convinced Joe Gillis to finish that script for her in *Sunset Boulevard*, then this surely would have been its soundtrack.

With Marc handling the production, and with more than a little help from MRI engineer Gary Ulmer, the sound was always going to be harsher than before. Tony Visconti had always given T. Rex records a neat, flamboyant touch, but *Light Of Love*'s chromium production was deliciously devoid of finesse. Even Marc's lyrics, which had been reined in significantly since the verbose Tyrannosaurus Rex days, hit new levels of brevity. The 'Light Of Love' single had set the tone; 'Solid Baby', 'Space Boss', 'Think Zinc' and the faintly ludicrous 'Precious Star' (which hinged on the phrase "Ooh like a precious star you are") took the space-age minimalism to almost comical extremes.

Light Of Love (or *Bolan's Zip Gun* as the reconfigured album was titled for the British market the following February) was Marc Bolan's 'fuck you' album, an extraordinarily ambiguous record that made a genuine leap into the unknown while at the same time plummeting the depths of parody. Neither did anyone realise that, like the music of Faust and Funkadelic, the record would be better understood years after its making. A fabulously flawed sonic crystal ball, at its best *Light Of Love/Bolan's Zip Gun* made a virtue of trance-like repetition years before late Seventies Industrial Music and early Eighties Hip Hop paved the way for the entire dance music explosion.

When Kate Phillips took a hatchet to the album in *New Musical Express*, her delineation of the record's "dehumanised ooh-ooh chorus, the hypnotic masturbatory intimacy of that breathy voicebox (and) the same catchphrase approximately 153 times per track" would, today, constitute a review to die for.

Probably the most powerful example of what *Melody Maker*'s Chris Welch described as "bizarre stomping lunacy with production" was 'Think Zinc'. A mutant, metal-techno refashioning of the vintage T. Rex sound, it opened in the footstomping manner of the Supremes' 'Where Did Our Love Go', then hit the manic button with a demonic, fuzzed up guitar riff, filth-honking horns, and a pulsating backing track overlaid with vocals that sweated and swelled as Bolan repeated the title like an out of control monomaniac. All that just to praise a vitamin.

At the other end of the scale was 'Token Of My Love'. A hideous disfiguration of the old style Bolan boogie, sluggish and emasculated with strained vocals and a backing so leaden as to make the Glitter Band sound as fluid as the Grateful Dead, 'Token Of My Love' is quite possibly the most ghoulish song Bolan ever committed to tape – which makes it a grimly fascinating, voyeuristic listening experience.

The 'wall of sound' that Marc hinted he'd achieved on the record was best evidenced on 'Space Boss', a big production with a huge, two-drum sound that contrasted with the album's other big production number, 'Till

Dawn'. Left over from the last days with Tony Visconti, the song revisited Marc's favourite 1950s teen ballad chord sequence, only this time he'd invested the song with a playfully camp, overwrought passion.

Unfortunately for the remaining rump of his British audience, who picked up the record as an expensive import, *Light Of Love* was diluted by the inclusion of what Casablanca regarded as the best three tracks from *Zinc Alloy*. That didn't matter to the American market which, if it bothered to turn up for a T. Rex show (or, more accurately, caught the group by accident while waiting for Blue Öyster Cult to come on), certainly didn't rush out and buy the record the following day.

★ ★ ★

Prior to the American tour, which kicked off with little ceremony at the Tower Theater in Upper Darby, Pennsylvania, where T. Rex opened for Blue Öyster Cult, Marc and Gloria attended one of David Bowie's Los Angeles shows at the Universal Amphitheater during the first week of September. They left midway after 'All The Young Dudes', which – with its T. Rex reference – was Marc's favourite Bowie song. Ostensibly a continuation of his extravagant *Diamond Dogs* stage show, the tour had changed dramatically since the summer. Once Bowie hit on the sound of Philadelphia (TSOP), he stripped away the props, rearranged his set and transformed the tour into an approximation of a contemporary American soul revue.

"Marc loved soul music, but I think David just went a little deeper into it," Gloria says. "He totally changed over to R&B." That was the key to Bowie's success in the States. Unlike Marc, who'd been dipping a tentative foot into the sound of young black America for the past two years, Bowie's conversion had been tardy but total.★

According to Mickey Finn, "The difference between Marc and Bowie is that Bowie – and I mean this with the greatest respect – changed with the seasons. He upgraded his material to change his style. Marc had this hit formula but he never moved on. He probably did in his head, but not musically. It's more comfortable to put on an old pair of shoes than buy some new ones and break 'em in . . . You can't keep selling something that you've already sold."

★ Ironically, 'Young Americans', the title track of Bowie's self-styled 'plastic soul' album from 1975, was uncannily reminiscent of Bolan's own 'Till Dawn', itself a close relative of 'Ghetto Baby' from the Pat Hall sessions.

While Marc's voice had deepened and lost much of its earlier elfin charm, it was still the defining element of T. Rex. That was misleading, though, because by late 1974, when everything else about the group's sound had changed drastically, even those closest to him hadn't been paying full attention. David became a soul stylist; Marc, who keenly noted that "Black producers are just rediscovering the use of sound like the rock'n'-roll producers did after *Sgt. Pepper*", absorbed the influence more subtly.

These London boys, now grown up and with impeccably powdered noses, had met in New York during the summer, when Bolan claimed to have helped David find musicians for the *Diamond Dogs* tour. Marc told *Circus* magazine that they had sat in David's hotel room and watched *A Clockwork Orange* "about four times . . . We just got back into what we were like when we were kids. David and I have always been the closest of friends. None of the feuding that was reported was real. We sat down in that room and decided our futures." If that was the case, then David certainly got the better deal.

The meeting didn't prevent Marc from taking a cheap shot at his rival in *Record & Radio Mirror* when he declared that Cockney Rebel, a quirky new Glam band fronted by another Dylan-obsessed motormouth Steve Harley, made David Bowie "look tired".

The rehearsals in the south of France had tightened up the T. Rex sound, though no one dared tell Marc that his lengthy, going-nowhere-fast guitar solos still sat uneasily with an audience that refused to regard T. Rex as anything other than a peculiarly British-flavoured bubblegum act. "When he made those decisions, he made those decisions," says Gloria Jones. "True musicians do not cross lines. I wanted to make him happy. *He* made the decisions."

"Last time out (the January 1974 British tour) we had two drummers, a sax section and backup singers, but the whole thing just got too messy," Marc told Alan Betrock in New Jersey during the tour. "Now I don't think that there's any band that can wipe us out onstage!" Unfortunately, Blue Öyster Cult, who headlined the key venues, and occasional support acts Kiss, ZZ Top and Black Oak Arkansas, were invariably better received than T. Rex, whose set was spirited, but to America's majority of unbelievers, turgid and unconvincing. "They didn't believe Marc. They believed Bowie," says Donovan.

According to Vancouver's local newspaper, which reported on the October 21 show, "The excellent record tracks degenerated into thick-textured boogie, rock sludge . . . a few were hostile, and many were leaving." Even the simple stage prop backfired: "The white neon star that lit up on stage seemed to mock him."

Nascent indie maverick Eugene Chadbourne witnessed another Canadian performance, this time in Calgary, two nights later. "Once Bolan jumped off the star platform and started playing his guitar everything pooped out. He had basically mediocre musicians like a conga player and an organist trying to follow him, but they all ended up out of tune and bumping into each other because Bolan wasn't going anywhere. He was standing completely still."

After noting that when Gloria "joined in on the choruses it made the slick little melodies that Bolan writes come to life", Chadbourne described the silence that greets Marc's announcement of 'Teenage Dream'. "What's the matter with you? That's only the number one song in England!" Bolan barked with characteristic mendacity. That was the last straw for Chadbourne. "There was this steady stream of people leaving and I followed them," he admitted proudly.

They were all wrong, insisted Marc, whose intake of booze and cocaine increased sharply as the tour progressed. His entrance, even when it was made in club venues like the Joint In The Woods in New Jersey, was cheesily spectacular, as he leapt off his hydraulic star with the flash-bulb surround. His outfits – embellished with space-age shoulder pads and a rhinestone-studded belt – were starry, Hall of Fame affairs. Sweat poured from his body as he put everything into each performance, which climaxed in a riot of feedback and the ritualistic, violent whipping of his guitar while clouds of theatrical smoke engulfed him. But still no one bought *Light Of Love*.

A sense of frustration intensified as the tour progressed, which wasn't helped by the regular changes to the itinerary. On stage, too, the optimism that had fired Marc up at the start of the tour was fast ebbing away. Gloria Jones blames the drop in morale on the cancellation of a showcase date early in the tour at Long Beach in California. "It was the most important concert for Marc in 1974," she maintains. "He'd sold out the Arena, but he had laryngitis and the doctor told him he couldn't perform. That's when America got angry because there were over 17,000 people there ready to see him."

Marc hid his despair by withdrawing into his own performances, soloing wildly, lost in his own six-string electrical storm. But even that sometimes let him down. "He used to get frustrated with the sound," says Mickey Finn. "He always used to go to his amp and put it up full blast. But Mick

O'Halloran doctored the amp so when it was on, say seven, it was really on four. He thought he was getting the volume but he wasn't. He'd say, 'That was a good sound,' but you could never tell him 'cos he'd go crazy."

The band had witnessed Marc 'going crazy' many times and it wasn't a pretty sight. The futility of the endless tours of America, the declining record sales, the collapse of the domestic T. Rex audience and the sheer loneliness of his self-imposed exile impacted on Bolan badly. The bag of cocaine, ripped open with its powdery contents spilled across the table, and the vodka and brandy bottles half empty and strewn across the floor were a more than adequate testimony to that. The Marc Bolan of 1973 who had confessed into his cassette machine how lonely he was had, by winter 1974, hit a disturbing personal low.

On the face of it, T. Rex's performance at the Agora Ballroom in Cleveland, Ohio on November 8, 1974 was just another show. The band had emerged from four days recording at the Paragon Studios in Chicago during a break in the tour, and their performance was robust and intense. The crowd even responded favourably to the MC's request for "a big scream for T. Rex".

'Jeepster' rambled on for seven minutes. 'Telegram Sam' too. Then Marc announced a song from the new album. It was 'Token Of My Love', and while it was no less ponderous or club-footed than its studio counterpart, the performance was rich in bathos, perfect in its despair. Marc, his face puffed up and Presley-like, rarely sounded so visceral as he bellowed theatrically, swaggering around on his platform shoes, his outside shoulder-pads giving him a tank-like demeanour. Gloria, hiding behind dark glasses and a headscarf, shadowed the melody, her banshee voice growing in intensity as each verse piled on the agony.

As Bolan repeated the song's key line, "Every day/Every single day/ My heart is broken/Oh yeah", the burlesque sense of despair was almost unbearable. It wasn't just his heart that was broken. Marc Bolan: Superstar was miles from home and disintegrating in front of a diminished, largely uninterested audience.

'Teenage Dream' was played out with fatal hubris. Then Bolan announced a new song, 'Zip Gun Boogie', that seemed to chug on for ever. Jamming around on one chord for over nine minutes, it seemed to take Bolan's repetition theory developed in the studio earlier in the year to ludicrous extremes. But the sheer immersion in excess that the performance symbolised reflected perfectly the appalling drama of Marc Bolan's private life that winter.

While in Chicago at the start of November to record at the Paragon Studios just prior to the Agora concert, T. Rex were installed at the Playboy Tower Hotel. One evening, some time around midnight, Mick Gray heard a knock at his door. He had been enjoying the company of a hotel receptionist named Michelle. As Mick answered the door, she hid in the bathroom. The unexpected visitor was an obviously distressed Gloria Jones.

"Her eye was purple and badly swollen," Gray remembers. "They had been drinking again and Marc had lost it and hit her in the eye. I got some ice and made her swab her eye with the ice in a towel. Gloria was too upset to return to Marc, and was feeling threatened, so I let her stay in my room and I slept on the sofa." Evidently, a somewhat disappointed Michelle left soon afterwards, quetly closing the bathroom door behind her.

The occasional lapses into violence that both June Bolan and Marc himself admitted to reached their nadir during November and December 1974. "I believe that Marc was very physical in his relationship with both June and Gloria," Mick Gray asserts. "It certainly sounded like it. Marc and Gloria had a stormy relationship; he beat her up on more than one occasion. She would disappear back to her parents for a day or two then return."

"He wasn't fighting with me. He was fighting with himself," says Gloria Jones, who prefers to call the altercations "disagreements . . . It wasn't that he was angry with me. He would take his frustrations out. I just dealt with it. I understood the hurt of being a number one star and then all of a sudden no one likes what you are doing."

The events of winter 1974 are understandably difficult for Gloria Jones. "I can never really hold any type of memory like that because a minute of stuff like that and then it's all over. Things were not going right. The music was his life. You're sensitive. What does a person do? You're only human."

When the tour ended, late in November, Marc and Gloria realised that they needed some stability to their lives. After a short stay at the Beverly Wilshire Hotel, they moved into a low level property in Del Resto Drive, a cul-de-sac in Benedict Canyon in the Hollywood Hills. Tellingly, the owner, an antiques dealer named John Good who lived down the road, insisted on a full inventory when the pair, together with Mick Gray, moved in early in December.

The house, which was fully furnished, comprised a master bedroom, lounge, hall, kitchen, utility room and a maid's room which was not used. There were two further rooms upstairs where Mick Gray slept. The main feature at the front of the house was a double garage. Behind was a wooded area sloping up to the next property where deer would sometimes come down the hillside to feed in the garden. Outside the lounge was a patio and a swimming-pool (that Marc didn't use) surrounded by potted orange trees.

"The deer used to hop over the fence," Gloria remembers, "and one day Marc says, 'I can't believe it! I see a deer out here drinking out of the pool.' I said, 'Oh Marc, let me take off this green robe. He might think I'm a leaf and try to eat me!'" Bizarre things sometimes happened in Benedict Canyon, scene of the Manson murders five years earlier.

Most of the time, Del Resto Drive was a haven of calm and tranquillity. The only regular visitors were Richard Jones and his entourage. "Marc was around a lot of love and people who loved him," Gloria maintains. "Harry Nilsson was very supportive. We were at the Rainbow, a very famous rock'n'roll club in Hollywood. Marc called Harry and arranged to meet him there. He walks in with Richard, and Harry says, 'Oh, shit, Marc's come in with a bodyguard! He got all paranoid."

Harry Nilsson also hung out with Ringo Starr, John Lennon and Keith Moon, none of whom were known for leaving a glass half-empty. Marc, too, had become part of the liquid gang of ex-pats. The will to self-destruct that he'd hinted at in interviews as early as 1971 had begun to consume him.

"Marc was a lager drinker when I first worked for him," says Mick Gray, who joined the T. Rex organisation in August 1971. He also enjoyed the occasional champagne. It was when he moved on to brandy and vodka during 1973 that Marc's drinking started to become a problem. By winter 1974, it had got completely out of hand. "Things were so bad in Del Resto Drive that I used to hide half full bottles of booze on the flat roof above my room," remembers Mick Gray. "I used to open a skylight, put them on the roof, then clear them away later." Sometimes, when Marc demanded a late night drink, Gray would drive slowly hoping that the liquor store would be closed when they arrived.

This picture confirms what bassist Steve Currie said back in 1978. "He used to drink vodka and wine," he told Ted Dicks. "I've seen him go through 16 bottles of Rosé between two o'clock and four or five in the morning. He couldn't really cope with it. He'd wake up the next morning forgetting what he'd done in the studio."

Obsessive by nature, and in the grip of an endless desire to lose himself, Bolan was like a child when it came to drugs and alcohol, according to Currie. "He didn't know when to stop. I'd get pissed, but he'd be lying on the floor still asking for the siphon to be put in his mouth . . . (And) he got very heavily into drugs, unfortunately cheap ones, not good quality coke."

One night in December 1974, soon after they'd moved into Del Resto Drive, Mick Gray went out for the evening leaving Marc, Gloria and Richard Jones back at the house. "When I returned, at about two in the morning, I found Richard wiping Marc's face with cold water. He was coming round after knocking himself out chasing Gloria. He had lashed out at her in a drunken rage, hitting her in the face." Gray was later told that as Marc began to chase Gloria up the stairs, he grabbed hold of a large wooden figure about six foot tall to swing himself round. It fell on him and knocked him out. "Gloria spent that night with her parents, but she returned after a few days," Mick remembers.

Gloria Jones also recalls the incident. "That evening, Marc had to deal with some spiritual issues. I phoned my father and I asked him to come up to Del Resto. And he gave Marc a cross. Marc held on to the cross and dad just said, 'Son, everything is gonna be alright.' Marc hadn't given up, but he was just devastated with everything."

Gloria refutes the suggestion that Marc was an alcoholic. "I never saw him act like an alcoholic. When alcoholics cannot get a drink, they shake, they sweat and you have to give them sugar and water to stabilise the blood. I've never seen Marc in a state like that. If you drink too much and you lose your temper, that's different. But an alcoholic is someone who's in real trouble."

Neither does she see herself as a victim. "If you're together, you're together through thick or thin," she believes. "It doesn't matter if someone is violent or unhappy. The point is, if you're there, you're there through it all. You're not gonna sit there and let someone destroy themselves. It was a disagreement, not a fight.

"What people fail to understand is that Marc was a human being. He was human, *and* a good person. No matter what he went through he always kept that love in his heart."

That love might still have been there, but it was certainly getting more difficult to locate as Marc sought to mend his broken heart by assaulting his nostrils and his liver. "It was a tough time to love Marc," says Tony Visconti – and he was talking about 1973, before the empty bottles really started to pile up.

"I know people say he turned into a complete monster, but the Marc Bolan I knew was nearly always nice," says Jack Green. "Then again, he was having hit singles, enjoying cocaine and brandy and all the fame. Walking around in that cocooned way it's gonna affect you – it's a classic scenario."

Mark 'Flo' Volman is quite clear about the source of Bolan's problems. "The downfall of Marc was not lack of record sales, or the problems he was having with the addictions that get into everyone's life but get blamed on rock'n'roll. I think that it was Marc Bolan, it was fame, and fame skirting away is what scared him."

"There were a lot of issues," says Gloria Jones, including a crisis within the band that tends to get overlooked. "He was trying to win. If you have one player on the team and the rest are like, 'Do we jump on the train or don't we?', it's hard. Marc was thinking internationally; the band was British. He was doing a lot of travelling, listening to a lot of different music on the radio and working with fantastic musicians at MRI. He realised that he could keep up with Ray Parker Jr., and with Ed Green on drums, who was Barry White's drummer. He's playing with these great people, and then he goes back and plays with his band. Marc was asking himself: 'Am I regressing? What am I doing?'"

As he often did when he needed to focus on something other than his relationship with the rest of the world, Marc returned to the studio. The sessions in Chicago had, he said, yielded enough material for a new album – "12 tracks in four days, and it's like nothing I've ever done before at all," he said, adding that "it's very, um, hard rock."

There would be no new T. Rex album for at least another year. EMI weren't in any particular hurry for one; neither, it seems, was Marc. He was now so removed from the routine of day-to-day stardom that he was able to convince himself that, like Gloria Swanson or perhaps even Syd Barrett, his self-imposed exile might even enhance his mystique.

The events of November and December 1974 had done nothing to settle Marc's creative nerve. One week he was recording rock-type material in Chicago with the five-strong T. Rex line-up. The next, he was in MRI with percussionist Bobbye Hall Porter and other top Los Angeles session players recruited by Gloria and her brother Richard.

"MRI was a state-of-the-art LA studio that was little used by any major artists," says Mick Gray. Situated just off Hollywood Boulevard opposite Grauman's Chinese Theatre, it was run by engineer Gary Ulmer. "He was a nice guy and a bit like Tony Visconti in that he cleaned up after Marc left the studio. He was a very patient man!" However, the studio was also a haven for strangers, including some of the hangers-on that would come in tow with Richard Jones. This tended to unsettle the sessions. "I always had bad vibes there because of the drugs," says Mick Gray. Nevertheless, Marc, who rarely complained when someone arrived at the studio bearing gifts in little packets, seemed to thrive on the atmosphere. Before the year was out, the bulk of 1976's *Futuristic Dragon* was already down on tape, much of it utilising non-T. Rex musicians.

Two keynote, late-era Bolan songs were recorded at the MRI sessions. 'New York City' was pure bubblegum and an obvious choice to blow away the memory of 'Zip Gun Boogie', which had failed to crack the British Top 40 when it appeared to little fanfare and much critical abuse in November. "Ugly, banal and with all the panache of Uriah Heep," complained Steve Clarke in *New Musical Express*. "I flopped in good company," said a defensive Marc a couple of months later, citing similarly disappointing sales figures for recent John Lennon and Stevie Wonder singles. By 1976, he was a little more forthright: "I hated it," he admitted.

There is pleasure to be had with 'Zip Gun Boogie', but it's an illicit one that matches its dumpy riff with Marc's shuffling gait; that equates its banal repetition with the air of ossification that T. Rex seemed to represent during the mid-Seventies; and that delights in the sheer nerve of releasing a 45 so forced and flawed that it defies conventional critical judgement. 'Zip Gun Boogie' redefined the rock'n'roll single as all pose and bluster long before the Britpop boys came along and repeated the joke.

In the end-of-year singles tables, T. Rex fared worse than here today, gone tomorrow acts like The Pearls, Andy Kim and Peppers. Commercially, at least, Marc Bolan was probably no more popular than he had been at the time of the first Tyrannosaurus Rex record.

The other song, first taped at MRI and again in France in spring 1975, went under the provisional title of 'You Damaged The Soul Of My Suit'. According to Gloria Jones, the cut concerned Marc making his peace with his public ("He was telling them, 'If you don't support me, I understand'; he felt that the industry had damaged his soul because they were against his music"), or his imminent divorce from June Bolan ("It's that one line, 'You're not a bad girl'," she says).

It's the latter option that's most likely. Months later, interviewed on London's Capital Radio, he confessed that the song had been written about "a woman who had bruised my ego". Bolan's marriage was over,

Marc as Zinc Alloy, his alter ego for the January 1974 UK tour. By this time Marc's career was suffering and fans were beginning to desert T. Rex after the band's three years at the top. (*LFI*)

Marc with producer Tony Visconti in late 1973, towards the end of their six-year working relationship. Visconti was one of several collaborators who began to desert Marc at this time. (*Redferns*)

Gloria Jones first met Marc in 1969 on tour with Tyrannosaurus Rex. She became his constant companion from July 1973 until his death. (*Redferns*)

Marc backstage at *Top Of The Pops* promoting 'Teenage Dream' in February, 1974. Bolan fans were distraught by his California tan and shorter hair that some compared to a style worn by middle-aged women. (*Harry Goodwin*)

By early 1974 the press was starting to dub Marc 'the Glittering Chipolata', an unflattering reference to his increasing girth, the result of a diet that comprised too much cold chicken washed down with champagne. (*Redferns*)

With T. Rextasy on the wane, Marc kept a lower profile for much of 1974 and '75, spending large amounts of time travelling between London, Los Angeles and the south of France. The lifestyle of a jet-setter was not conducive to his health. (*LFI*)

Marc poses with Gloria, cutting an unlikely pair in the mid-Seventies. (*Redferns*) Inset: The proud parents with Rolan Bolan, who was born at a private nursing home in St John's Wood, London, on September 26, 1975. (*Rex*)

Marc's T. Rex band around the time of the *Futuristic Dragon* tour, clockwise from top left: Gloria Jones, Marc, Steve Currie, Dino Dines and Davey Lutton. "It was the saddest spectacle I'd witnessed in years," wrote Allan Jones in *Melody Maker*. (*EMI Records*)

Marc sports a black eye following an unprovoked attack by a David Bowie fan in Manchester on February 24, 1976. "One moment Marc was talking at the guy, the next he was in a drunken heap on the floor nursing a damaged eye," remembers tour manager Mick Gray. Marc later said the black eye was caused by a mass charge of fans. (*Rex*)

The final T. Rex line-up in Spring 1977, left to right: bassist Herbie Flowers, guitarist Miller Anderson, Marc, keyboard player Dino Dines and drummer Tony Newman. (*PA Photos*)

By the summer of 1977 Marc had cleaned up his act, slimmed down and become an unlikely champion of punk rock. "I consider myself to be the elder statesman of punk," he claimed in February 1977, "the Godfather of Punk if you like." The punks – among them Siouxsie Sioux and The Damned – agreed. (*Relay*)

David Bowie and Marc Bolan performing together during Marc's last ever television appearance, filmed on September 7, 1977. It was the climax to a 12-year-old relationship that encompassed both respect and rivalry. (*LFI*)

Marc and Gloria on stage together for the final time for *Supersonic* in March 1977. (*Relay*)

Police examine the wreckage of the Mini GT in which Marc died in the early hours of September 16, 1977 after the car hit a tree on Barnes Common. (*Popperfoto*)

Tuesday September 20, 1977: Fans and stars alike attend Marc's funeral at the Golders Green Crematorium in North London. David Bowie, top right, seemed particularly distressed. The centrepiece of the floral tributes was the white swan, below, from Marc's last manager Tony Howard. (*PA Photos*)

but with June's firm, protective hand no longer there to curb his wildest excesses, Marc's inner fragility sometimes struggled to cope with his wild embrace of freedom.

Gloria was supportive but less inclined to wag an admonishing finger in Marc's direction. She preferred to encourage him to work things out for himself. "Sometimes you have to go within your self and start loving yourself again," she says. "Marc had to go back within his soul, within his life and just clear up some things. Maybe he thought he made the wrong decision by trying to experience something new. I had to be strong to understand that he had to deal with this.

"The most important thing was that he pulled through. After my dad gave him the cross, he realised that, 'Hey, these people are my friends.' We didn't leave him. We let him go through whatever he wanted to go through, but we were by his side. He had to do whatever it was to get straight internally, and after that he said, 'Let's go and have a rest.' That's when we went to the health farm in the south of France."

Between January 1975 until some time in 1976, Marc leased an apartment on the 14th floor of the résidence l'Estoril B, in Avenue Princesse Grace, Monaco. A tax-free haven for the rich, famed for its Monte Carlo Casino and the dubious glamour of the autocrat Prince Rainier and his wife Princess Grace, formerly the ice-cool American film star Grace Kelly, Monaco is also impeccably located. The front of Marc's flat overlooked the Mediterranean; the Swiss Alps were visible from the back. Tennis star Bjorn Borg had an apartment and tennis shop in the same block, and Ringo Starr lived elsewhere in the principality.

The l'Estoril residence was intended as more than just a holiday home. Marc had his Rolls-Royce and furniture transported there from London but, says Mick Gray, he never really settled there. "They were happier in Los Angeles," he says. Marc and Gloria rarely ventured out much in Monaco, buying most of their meals from a bistro at the bottom of the block, with occasional sojourns to a fish shop behind the famous Casino and very occasionally entertaining Ringo Starr and his PR man. Gloria occasionally went to the Salon at the Casino, but only to play the machines, never the tables."

Shortly before the move to Monaco, Marc said: "I don't want to get into that complacent, laid-back kind of Dylanesque atmosphere. I'm a rock'n'roller." But whenever he was there – in January 1975, again in April and May, and short stays during the summer and winter period – he did little more than put his feet up.

"At that time there were a lot of changes and Marc was growing older and ready to settle down," says Gloria Jones. "A lot of people don't understand the period between '74 and '75 when he gained weight; he was finally just living. He had worked ten years without one proper holiday. He relaxed and went with the flow."

However, at least one project was discussed almost as soon as Marc moved there. It was an acting part in a thriller movie, *Obsession*, starring David Niven. "It's a very dramatic script," Bolan told Jan Iles for *Record & Popswop Mirror*. "I play a psychotic who has sexual problems and sells dope. I kill three people and end up in a nuthouse. It's quite a lovely role which is certainly gonna screw a lot of heads up." To prove it, he threw his script into the writer's lap.

Most people assumed the tale was another Bolanic fable but, says Mick Gray, the project did get beyond the fantasy stage. "The man behind it was John Marshall who produced *The Wicker Man*, but nothing ever came of it. Marc had problems learning his lines anyway."

Bolan had boasted to Iles that, "I'm the star and it all revolves around me which is really nice," but, says Gloria Jones, "Every time they showed Marc the drawing of his character, he always thought the guy looked like Mickey Finn. I said, 'Maybe they're confused!'" The project was abandoned when no financial backer could be found.

One month in Monaco was hardly sufficient time for Bolan to clean up. He wasn't ready for that anyway. Stopping over in London *en route* back to Los Angeles at the end of January, Marc checked into the Carlton Towers Hotel in Knightsbridge. When Roy Carr from *New Musical Express* came to interview him, he found a fallen star. Marc's portly frame looked awkward in a pair of American moon boots, and he had a tell-tale early morning beer in his hand. At one stage during the meeting, Bolan caught himself in a mirror and uttered, "Oh God, just look at the state of me," an admission that at least he was beginning to see himself as others saw him.

Typically, Marc put his usual spin on things. His fall from grace had been deliberate; he was bored, he said. The great American mistake? That wasn't poor performances, that was over-hyping! It hardly mattered anyway because – yes, like Bowie, who'd just been offered a part in Nic Roeg's *The Man Who Fell To Earth* – Marc was going to be big in the movies.

The nearest Marc Bolan ever got to Hollywood was MRI Studios, his virtual home whenever he was out in California. By the time he was back in there, on January 30, 1975, Mickey Finn, his sidekick and visual foil since autumn 1969, was no longer in the band. Apart from Marc, now only Steve Currie remained from the classic T. Rex line-up.

"I got tired, Marc got tired. We all came to the end of our tether with each other," Finn insists. "There wasn't an argument. There was just an atmosphere and lots of evil rumours flying about, and I started losing interest and not turning up. It just went off the boil. It was a mutual thing. He was upset, I was upset. It was very sad."

The truth is sadder still. "Marc told Tony Howard to sack Mickey," says Mick Gray. "Mickey Finn was sacked by Tony while we were mid-air *en route* to Los Angeles on January 29, 1975." Finn, whom Marc had always affectionately referred to as 'Fingers', was never mentioned by his long-time partner again.

Mickey Finn looked good in those centre-spread posters that were a regular feature in *Jackie* during 1971 and 1972, but as a musician, he'd been a passenger for much of his time in T. Rex. Asked if he'd ever learnt to play the bongos, he admits, "I don't know. It's debatable!"

A near-silent presence by Marc's side, Mickey Finn added a more traditional touch of glamour to T. Rex though Marc liked to tease audiences about the true nature of their relationship. "Did you know Mickey and I are married?" he'd say between songs. (As late as January, 1975, Bolan was still being questioned about his sexuality. "I'm bisexual," he told Jan Iles, "but I believe I'm more heterosexual 'cos I definitely like boobs. I always wished that I was 100 per cent gay, it's much easier.") Now, the wedding was well and truly off, and Finn instantly found himself alone, abandoned and, after a lengthy binge of women, booze and a costly drug habit, poorer to the tune of – by his own calculations – £1 million.

Sue Worth, his partner at the time of Marc and June's marriage in 1970, had left him during the glory years because of Finn's persistent infidelity. However, after his departure from the group, they were reconciled and married in 1978. Like Mickey's antique business, it didn't last. By the early Eighties, Finn cut a lonely figure on the south coast of England, dipping into small-time band management and propping up bars on the post-punk club scene in Bournemouth.

A brief return to the public eye in 1983, on a television tribute to Marc Bolan, revealed him as a somewhat wizened character, and two years later, The Blow Monkeys briefly requested his bongo-bashing services. Since then, Finn, an avuncular if elusive man who lives frugally in south London, occasionally resurfaces in the tabloid supplements, usually around the time of a Bolan-related anniversary. "I've got no responsibilities because I've got no money at all," he admits.

Whenever Bolan's beautiful balloon looked in danger of crash landing – an increasingly likely outcome since 1973 – someone inevitably was bailed out in order to keep the operation aloft. The departure of Mickey Finn was a likely response to the deep crisis Marc faced at the end of 1974. In strictly musical terms, losing Finn was meaningless. Since 1972, his presence in T. Rex had been largely talismanic, but now Bolan could no longer afford to be sentimental.

"1974 was not a good year for me or a lot of people, but then it wasn't a good year for the world," Marc said at the start of 1975. With the British release of *Light Of Love* (repackaged with three new songs as *Bolan's Zip Gun*) imminent, and a stock of impressive material in the can at MRI, Bolan had cause for optimism. "This is gonna be a good year; I can feel it," he said. "Last year I was so apathetic because everything was wrong; the timing, the crazy vibes, everything. This year will be a gas, it's gotta be!"

It was – but not for Marc Bolan and T. Rex. 1975 belonged to David Essex and Tammy Wynette, to Mud and Elton John, Shirley Bassey and The Bay City Rollers. Life was no longer a gas for Marc Bolan, his band or those among his fans who didn't happen to live in minor seaside resorts. The records dried up, but Bolan failed to dry out. He did, however, finally turn his back on America and head for home.

After a brief flurry of press interest at the start of the year, Bolan returned to his life in exile, dividing his time between Los Angeles and Monaco for the first half of the year. The first evidence that he'd survived the critical lashing heaped on the 'Zip Gun Boogie' single came in February with *Bolan's Zip Gun*. But it didn't bring good news. For the first time, an all new T. Rex album – not that you could tell from the anonymous sleeve – failed to chart, an unthinkable event just 12 months earlier.

Of course it hadn't helped that all but three of the songs had already appeared on the *Light Of Love* album. But Bolan himself was uncharacteristically sniffy about the record after its release, describing it as "completely over-produced" and "the worst record I made". It was an odd way to treat what was in many ways his most radical extended musical experiment, but once he'd begun to wash Los Angeles out of his hair, Marc Bolan beat a hasty retreat to the security of a more conventional rock'n'roll sound.

Prior to the album's release, Marc was full of the joys of living and working in Los Angeles. "I've found a recording studio that I really like which has its own computer desk," he said. His claim that he already had a follow-up album half finished – one with "a much bigger sound" than the current one which he dubbed "simplistic" – was no idle boast. Neither was his insistence that he still intended to produce albums for Gloria Jones, her brother Richard and the so-called Cosmic Choir which included the Joneses and a few mates. He was, however, still insisting that "T. Rex as such doesn't really exist any more . . ."

Bolan's existence, too, was under threat during the early months of 1975. "I was advised to give up drugs because I was developing high blood pressure. I could have killed myself," he said in April 1977. "That's been one of the problems in my life, the urge to self-destruct. Many great artists suffered from it and had tragic lives."

In a bid to avert a potential tragedy, Marc and Gloria installed themselves in a fashionable health clinic for two weeks in the hills behind Cannes in spring 1975. "The first day we had a Russian masseuse," Gloria recalls. "Before they give you the massages, they put you against a wall and hose you down with waves of water. Marc said, 'I'm not doing that!' "

He was rather more cooperative when the doctors checked out his heart rate. "He had the heart rate of a 70-year-old man," says Gloria Jones. "That's when he realised he'd not stopped working. He was absolutely exhausted. He knew that he had to change his eating habit, his lifestyle, everything."

It wasn't going to happen overnight. "I thought it was an attempt to dry them both out," remembers Mick Gray, "but it was a complete waste of time because neither kept to their diets when they were there. They both came out the same weight as when they went in, and the day they came out they went for a big meal with plenty of wine in the bistro under the l'Estoril B apartment."

While they were at the clinic, the doctor stopped the pair on the elevator and said he had some important news for them. "We were looking at each other going, 'Oh God, what's going on?' " Gloria remembers. "Next morning, I went to the doctor's office and he told me I was pregnant. I went back to our room and said, 'Marc, I have some news to tell you. I'm expecting.' He jumped up, grabbed me and started screaming! When he let go of me, he said, 'I thought you were gonna tell me that I was gonna die!' It was an accident, but a lovely accident. Marc told me, 'I have achieved everything in life that I wanted, but to have this child, that is something I never thought would happen to me.' That new life gave him meaning to his own life."

It wasn't all sweetness that spring, though. In March 1975, Marc decided to return to the Chateau d'Hérouville for the first time since autumn 1972. The sessions, which produced two fairly perfunctory recordings, 'Billy Super Duper' and 'Depth Charge', were disastrous.

According to Mick Gray, the engineer Clive Frank, who was Elton John's sound man, was not impressed at all by Marc's attitude. "Coke was the master and it prompted an horrendous marathon session complete with an excess of brandy. Most of the takes were rubbish, and Clive Frank walked out in disgust."

Despite Marc's insistence that T. Rex no longer existed, the regular Currie, Dines, Lutton, Bolan and Gloria Jones line-up attended the Paris sessions. When he wasn't aggravating sound engineers, Marc used the time to lay down plans for a new project. The failed attempt to revive *The Children Of Rarn* the previous year hadn't yet quelled Marc's enthusiasm to put together a grand concept album.

His latest idea was *Billy Super Duper*, a "teenage punkoid opera" loosely based on the life of a street kid living in the 25th century. Other songs tipped for inclusion and recorded elsewhere were 'Brain Police', 'Metropolis' and 'Dynamo', none of which gave any real indication of the project's narrative structure. Billy was likely to have been conceived as a pseudo-religious space-age fantasy ("Maybe us and God will truly meet", Marc sang on 'Dynamo', possibly intended as a concluding part of what was probably nothing less than an old-fashioned rock opera). Over the next 12 months, *Billy Super Duper* would be superseded by what Marc grandly titled *The London Opera*.

The following month, in mid-April 1975, Marc and T. Rex were back in Musicland Studios in Munich. On the day of the flight to Germany, Bolan woke up in Browns Hotel complaining of chest pains. "I called the doctor who diagnosed high blood pressure caused by heavy consumption of cognac the night before," remembers Mick Gray. "Marc took a day's rest, then flew out to join the rest of the group and started drinking again."

One night, Steve Currie returned from a night club at around three in the morning and found Marc wandering the corridors alone. "He was standing there in tears because he could feel the vibes of all the people that had been massacred by the Nazis in the Second World War. I took him back to his room and made him coffee all night."

"The sessions were pure anarchy with Marc at his worst," remembers Mick Gray. "Mac the owner/engineer barred Marc from ever returning." But not before T. Rex nailed a half-decent version of 'The Soul Of My Suit'.

On the final day of recording Donovan dropped by with his step-son Julian and taped a new version of his 'Lalena'. "Marc was living in the hotel above the studio," he remembers. "He was very enthusiastic, very hyper and had begun to put on a bit of weight on his cheeks and around the hips. He looked like the Artful Dodger with his little waistcoat as he strutted around his hotel suite with an enormous breakfast."

Donovan also remembers Marc being "very enthusiastic about a musical that he and David Bowie had been working on, a futuristic fairytale . . . but David had soared off to the States and was very busy." More intriguingly, he adds that, "At one point a doctor arrived and gave him a B12 shot. Marc dropped his pants, the doctor took out his giant needle, gave him a shot in the arse, and Marc pulled up his trousers and the doctor left. And Marc didn't stop talking once." Perhaps that explains why Bolan was beginning to compare himself with fleet-footed guitarist Mahavishnu John McLaughlin.

By the end of May 1975, Marc and Gloria had made a surprise move back to London, renting a house at 25 Holmead Road in Fulham. As well as providing the couple with some stability that had been lacking from their lives since early 1974, there were at least three other reasons why Marc 'came home'. "Marc really wanted the baby to be born in London," says Gloria Jones. "That was the beginning of our settling down." She also maintains that, "Marc's heart was back in England. He wanted to recapture the success that he'd had before."

A third reason is more prosaic. "Marc could not cope with his own company for long," adds Mick Gray. "Abroad, there were no audiences, no matter how small, for him to play up to. In Monaco he was a nobody in a town of somebodies. In Los Angeles, no one took any notice of Marc on his rare public trips. He was driven everywhere and never walked down the sidewalk. He became even more isolated from the real world because he never tried to integrate himself into his new homes."

Just six weeks after his return, Bolan was back in the charts with a new single, 'New York City', a delightfully inane "boogie mind poem" based on the 'One Inch Rock' riff that once took Tyrannosaurus Rex within a whisker of chart respectability back in 1968. Bolan basked in his first genuine success since 'Teenage Dream' 18 months earlier, and the song's basic appeal – just three lines of verse: "Did you ever see a woman/ Coming out of New York City/With a frog in her hand" – achieved a new peak in Bolanic minimalism. The distinctive vocals of Flo & Eddie marked a second reacquaintance with Bolan's past, which had been largely expunged during Marc's lengthy spells in Los Angeles and Monte Carlo.

Bolan embellished the song's limited subject matter with a characteristic mix of fantasy and namedropping as he publicised the single, which appeared in late June 1975. "I was walking with David Bowie in New York City," he said, "and we saw this 90-year-old lady who is part of Andy Warhol's Factory and who claims to be a witch. She was walking down Park Avenue with this enormous toad in her hand." Sources close to Bolan suggested that the real inspiration for the song came from a toy Kermit the Frog that he'd given to Gloria. "A fan gave him Kermit the Frog and I was getting out of a limo with it in New York," she confirms.

The pair had a ball shooting the video. Both piled on the pancake, with Marc's thatch of hair decadently swept to one side, his heavy rouge, powder and lipstick suggesting that he wasn't quite ready to surrender his passion for extravagance just yet. Gently tilting his head, he gave a wonderfully emasculated performance that owed much to silent screen goddess Gloria Swanson, particularly his playful moues and hand gestures. The bizarre frog and harlequin props only enhanced the mood of conviviality that had long been sorely lacking from T. Rex's public life.

Perhaps conviviality was behind the bizarre idea of packing the group off to play four concerts in faded seaside resorts during July 1975. Wary of the negative publicity of playing to half-empty venues in major towns and cities, Bolan's mini-tour took in Douglas on the Isle of Man, Great Yarmouth, Hastings and Folkestone. It was a low-budget venture with the group arriving at their holiday destinations in a minibus, and Marc and Gloria pulling up outside venues in a slick black limousine.

"He can certainly wriggle," wrote Martin Hayman in *Sounds* of the Hastings show on July 25. "And thrust, and pouted, opened his mouth in orgasmic soundless groan, jumped and bumped, and thrust and ground up against his guitar, kneeled and stuck it out from his crotch, and leapt up and down." All that despite carrying a few too many extra pounds.

Within the T. Rex organisation, the venture was regarded with raised eyebrow incredulity. "The seaside tour was an unmitigated disaster with no reason or game plan," maintains Mick Gray. "We seemed to be clasping at straws, and Tony Howard seemed to have no control over our destiny." The fans, those impassioned small pockets that remained from the hundreds of thousands who had eagerly charted the course of T. Rexstasy just two or three years earlier, had a ball. Marc entertained small groups of them in the hotel lobbies and bars, instantly making himself the first Superstar who truly fell to earth.

From this point on, Marc Bolan's relationship with his audience acquired an intimacy that's virtually unique in the pop world. T. Rex concerts became celebratory carnivals, almost fetishistic in their devotion to Bolan the icon, even if that figure was starting to look a bit worn round the edges.

After some 18 months in the wilderness, Marc Bolan had gained weight and regained some of his audience. Now measured in hundreds rather than millions, the loyal crowds who would wait at the stage door were crucial to Marc's recovery, providing him with loyalty and a sense of self-worth that had been bruised and battered by the American experience. Now operating from a new base in London, Marc Bolan was ready to reignite his career.

12

Go, Johnny Go

"Listen, I was the originator of Punk Rock. We had a big sign on the Strip that read 'The Cosmic Punk Comes' and no one got it."

– Marc Bolan, *Record Mirror & Disc* (June 1976)

"Marc was considering some big decisions. It was about changing his life and his career. I think he wanted to get back to his roots."

– Jeff Dexter (2002)

"A new age of Bolan – T. Rex Unchained".

– Slogan on badge (spring 1977)

When the transformative zeal of the Sixties gave way to the individual hedonism of the early Seventies, Marc Bolan had been perfectly poised to clean up. He'd made a convincing hippie, and was reasonably rewarded for his efforts. But as the pipedreams dissipated into dope-induced defeatism, solace was sought in spectacle. Glam Rock provided a moment's pleasure, and Bolan, who instigated and epitomised the form, was implicated when its moment was deemed to have passed.

By summer 1975, rock culture had become hopelessly self-referential. In the absence of any epochal change able to reach beyond the readers of the music weeklies, or any stars worthy enough at least to pretend that something important was happening, it had begun to re-excavate its own history. It was no coincidence that, as harsher economic and social realities kicked in, it was the primitivism of original rock'n'roll and Sixties garage rock, and the abrasive sonic violence of Iggy & The Stooges and The Velvet Underground that was being eulogised in lavish retrospectives long before the arrival of punk rock.

Shortly after settling in London that summer, Marc too paused for reflection. "Tyrannosaurus Rex was very relevant to flower power and '67 because everyone else was into the Hendrix and Cream thing," he told

Beat Instrumental. "The only way I could get noticed was to do the exact opposite." Giving a neat twist on contemporary trends had been the key to Bolan's success. He'd done it again in 1971 by shunning the singer-songwriter route and instead dressing up the era's self-obsession in stardust, adding a rock'n'roll beat. By 1975, though, he was still masquerading as a star when stardom had been debased by Johnny-come-lately glam imposters, and when the new disco culture demanded floor-filling beats not faces.

It had been three years since Bolan commanded any real kudos, and almost two since his records stopped selling. When asked what he'd been doing since leaving the country the previous spring, Marc replied, "I went off the scene because I wanted a low to make the highs higher." On that basis, Marc Bolan – with a minor bubblegum hit ('New York City'), a small but appreciative audience and a home in London again – was back on a high. Exile had numbed him to the realities of fading stardom, and never having been properly forced to confront it, any minor hint of a high was enough to rekindle the old flames of fame. It was a little fix that would keep his spirits up for the remainder of his life.

A virtual nobody on the streets of Monte Carlo and Los Angeles, Marc Bolan was still a figure worthy of comment in London.* Unfortunately, that comment was usually along the lines of 'What has he done to himself?' However, some kind of stability beckoned. When Marc and Gloria moved into the house in Holmead Road, just off the Fulham end of the King's Road in west London, Sid and the doting Phyllis Feld, who'd visited their son out in Monaco, weren't too far away in Putney, where Sid was a janitor in a block of council flats. And there were always the Bolanites who'd often congregate in small groups outside the house in Holmead Road or the offices in New Bond Street.

In her rambling, run-down mansion in Sunset Boulevard, Norma Desmond received piles of fan mail every day. Unbeknown to her, each letter, invariably requesting a signed photograph, had been written by Max, madame's butler, ex-husband and keeper of dreams. According to his publicist Keith Altham, Marc too had his Norma Desmond moments. "He went through a period of being quite Howard Hughes-like, to the extent that he even imagined that fans were bothering him. One day, my colleague knocked at his door and there was no answer. As he walked back

---

* Designer Ossie Clark deemed a sighting of Marc in the King's Road on October 6, 1976 important enough to note in his diary.

down the path, Marc peered out from an upstairs window and whispered, 'Are they still there?' The road was absolutely deserted. 'There are about 20 of them. They're hiding under the bridge. Get down by the gate, and when I open the door, make a run for it.' It was a real performance of paranoia."

Essentially, though, being in London did allow for the return of a little reality in Marc's life. He had even begun to feel like a fan again himself. "One day, when I was expecting Rolan, we were in Earl's Court and we ran into Peter Green," remembers Gloria Jones. Just five years earlier, Green had been the chart-topping guitarist and frontman with Fleetwood Mac. A spiritual crisis, prompted by a massive LSD binge, had sent him – another short, fat Jewish East Ender with dark flowing locks – on a down-ward spiral and out onto the streets of the capital. Marc recognised him instantly. "He said, 'Peter, how are you?' Peter replied that he was fine. Marc said, 'I'm gonna go buy you a pair of shoes!' And he bought Peter a pair of shoes. After we left, I said to Marc, 'Did he know you?' 'Yeah,' he said, 'I think so!' Peter had some difficulties, but that was Marc. He just said, 'That's one of the greatest guitarists in the world.'"

On August 28, 1975, Bolan and a heavily pregnant Gloria were record-ing at Scorpio Studios, in Euston, London. A small group of fans had con-gregated outside and were trying to eavesdrop on the session through a letterbox. In the past, Marc might have ordered his road manager Mick O'Halloran to gently ask them to leave their idol in peace. This time, Marc's voice suddenly appeared from the other side of the letterbox and after a short conversation, the teenage Bolanites were invited in to watch the day's work. When the session was finally wrapped up, in the early hours of the morning, the teenagers returned home – thrilled but exhausted.

Someone else who believed in the power of old-style, larger-than-life pop stars was television producer Mike Mansfield. He'd been commis-sioned to make a new Saturday afternoon TV pop show for the autumn and among the first names he called up were Gary Glitter, The Sweet, David Essex and, of course, Marc. That show was *Supersonic,* an un-ashamedly gaudy affair with elaborate, over-the-top stage sets that always looked as if they were on the verge of falling apart. Not unlike its stars, of course, a retinue of has-beens in the eyes of anyone over the age of 14.

Nevertheless, *Supersonic* provided a lifeline for Marc, who appeared on the show many times between September 1975 and April 1977, when it was taken off the air. Supplemented by occasional appearances on LWT's

Saturday Scene, his renewed television exposure tended to give the impression that the international captain of insterstellar soul was in fact a parochial, cabaret-like entertainer suitable for children and very little else. Unfortunately, Marc's addiction to adoration was such that he gave little cause to think otherwise.

Among the songs recorded at the August Scorpio Studios session was 'Silver Lady', based on a home demo titled 'I Could Have Loved You'. By the time it was issued on single on September 26, 1975, it had been transformed into 'Dreamy Lady', and Mike Mansfield invited Marc to perform the song on *Supersonic* – twice. On the show's launch edition, on October 4, Marc mimed to 'Dreamy Lady' – a glorious revival of his favourite C/Am/F/G chord sequence that effortlessly utilised a soft disco backing – and ended up being smothered in bubbles, a not uncommon feature of the programme.

His second appearance, broadcast on October 18, remains one of the most remarkable in a career already rich in dramatic entrances and theatrical display. Rising from the floor on the five-pronged, hydraulic star that had been all around America with him, Bolan leapt off the platform looking every inch an impeccable extra from *Carry On Screaming*. Or the glam rocker who'd been through it all and had arisen from the dead. (Which, unknown to the viewers, wasn't too far from the truth.) His blue zip-up cat suit was one size tighter than it should have been and his big, streaked hair had been crimped into sharp, dagger-like strands. He wore a black feather choker around his neck, and his face, deathly white, resembled a canvas for a visibly challenged trainee make-up artist, an explosion of rouged cheeks, blood-red lips, panda-like eyes and bright blue eye shadow.

Perhaps it was all a ploy to divert attention away from his excess pounds, but Marc Bolan's second *Supersonic* appearance has to go down as the day the Siouxsie Sioux punk rock look was patented. That this creature from the black and blue lagoon, who prowled the stage portly yet magnificent, was miming to a song that was light, infectious and undoubtedly one of his most outstanding later recordings, makes it all the more bizarre. *The Rocky Horror Show* and *Cabaret*, both of which presaged the chic appeal of decadence that later informed aspects of punk fashion, may have unwittingly inspired Bolan's sartorial transgression, and he never repeated it. But this performance alone justifies the 'Godfather Of Punk' tag that he shamelessly wrapped himself in several months later.

The single, credited to the 'T. Rex Disco Party', was only marginally less remarkable, yet it failed to maintain the commercial momentum of 'New York City'. Despite the distinct absence of Bolan boogie on 45 for at least two years, reviewers seemed to suggest that 'Dreamy Lady' had at last broken some kind of mould. Guest reviewing the singles in *Sounds*, Heavy Metal Kids' vocalist Gary Holton went so far as to liken the single to Bolan's work with Steve Took. "I used to be really into Tyrannosaurus Rex," he enthused. "I've got all their albums and this sounds like the old Marc coming out again." Its lowly chart placing – number 30 – may have been reminiscent of the Steve Took era, but nothing else was.

Backed by perfunctory cover versions of Otis Redding's '(Sittin' On) The Dock Of The Bay' (sung by Gloria) and a nostalgic cover of Bobby Freeman's 'Do You Wanna Dance', a number two hit for Cliff Richard back in 1962, 'Dreamy Lady' was released to a surprising lack of public enthusiasm on September 26, 1975. That same day, Marc had been rehearsing for his first *Supersonic* appearance. "I started to have pains and I went to the doctor," Gloria remembers. "He told me I should go to the clinic. I said, 'I can't have the baby now because Marc is doing the television show! He *has* to be here.' I phoned Marc and told him I was going to the clinic. He said, 'I'll finish taping and then I'll be over.' He said, 'You must hold the baby!'

"When Marc arrived, he scrubbed and put on the hat and gown. For a natural birth it was quite an easy one. Before the last push, I said, 'Marc, I really don't think I can make it.' He said, 'What are you going to do? Walk around with the baby hanging out of your pussy all of your life!' When Rolan came into the world, the first thing Marc said was, 'Oh look at those little balls!' " Rolan Seymour Feld Bolan was born in a private room at a hospital in St John's Wood.

Like his parents, Rolan's astrological star was Libra, a sign of strength, determination and success, which pleased Marc enormously. Like Bowie's son Zowie, his rhyming name was a 'whatever next' conversation piece. "Bowie called his child Zowie Bowie so I thought I'd call mine Rolan Bolan," Marc explained, blissfully unaware that he was increasingly sounding like the world's biggest David devotee. "We chose the name a few weeks earlier when we were staying at the Blake Hotel in Roland Gardens in South Kensington," says Gloria. "That's what inspired Marc." Unfortunately, the couple's stay was rudely interrupted when David Cassidy demanded their suite, the best in the hotel. "They kicked us out and we went to the Portobello," Gloria remembers.

While plans were being made to re-establish T. Rex in the New Year with the release of a new album, supported by the band's first extensive tour of Britain since 1971, fatherhood and being back in London prompted Marc to reminisce on his own childhood. Writing songs such as 'I Believe', 'It's My City', 'Bombs Out Of London' and 'Petticoat Lane', he developed a new idea, *The London Opera*. Meanwhile, two further city-inspired songs, 'London Boys' and the urgent-sounding 'Funky London Childhood' (an uncharacteristic John Lee Hooker-style boogie), were taped at Scorpio in October and, unusually, premiered on Thames TV's *Today* show later that month.

Marc had been a guest interviewer on the show ever since upstaging the programme's anchor Alan Hargreaves back in July, when he constantly quizzed the other studio guest, *Kojak* star Telly Savalas. It was a role he enjoyed immensely. "It's fun doing interviews because they can't bull me," he explained in October, adding, "I'm the biggest bullshitter of all time." Among his small screen guests that autumn were *Marvel* Comics boss Stan Lee, Keith Moon,* John Mayall, Angie Bowie and Roy Wood.

Whatever role he played, Bolan never once put the brakes on his imagination. He'd been offered a late-night chat show, he claimed, and among the guests lined up for it were Greta Garbo, Ingmar Bergman, Orson Welles and Salvador Dali – only four of the 20th century's most wonderful Superstars. Of course, this weekly legend-on-legend summit meeting never happened.

Marc wasn't shifting many records, but he was inexorably drifting into the nebulous role of celebrity without portfolio. "People would interview Marc even when things weren't going well because they knew they could get good copy from him," says Keith Altham. "The media really liked people like Marc, and he made my job easy. I'd phone him up and say, 'There's a page going in *The Mirror*.' And he'd say, 'What shall I be this week? Bisexual? Trisexual? Shall we say I take a gold bed with me on the road?' He loved a bit of outrage."

Altham compares Marc's understanding of the media with that of arch-manipulator Mick Jagger. "Mick's more cynical in the way that he employs it to his own advantage," he adds. "Jagger is premeditated; Marc was instinctive, and I think people warmed to him because of that."

Bolan's new found ubiquity prompted him to rethink his public role. Admitting that T. Rex had turned into a moneymaking machine, and that

---

* Moon's cruel humour concerning Marc's dwindling fortunes actually reduced Marc to tears on screen.

some of his recent records had been "below par", he now predicted the arrival of a "huge art medium, an audio-visual art form" that would replace rock'n'roll.

Those misplaced ideas for the David Niven film and the all-star chat show were soon swept aside. All thoughts turned to this exciting new space, which would be filled by Marc's latest epic production, *Billy Super Duper*. It was, he claimed, "a very intricate science fiction story full of more imagery than you've heard on any album ever. It's a combination of *The Children Of Rarn* album, which in fact I never recorded, and *2001* and *A Clockwork Orange* all sort of squashed together. It's got some amazing characters, places, worlds, planets, galaxies . . . everything's stuck in there. It'll take you days to get through it. It's an immense work. It's not a concept album as such, just a story set to music with lots of images. I think it will be important."

By spring 1976, Marc's plans for his fictional intergalactic street punk had become even more elaborate – and confused. "I've just completed this amazing piece called 'Billy Super Duper' which is like a 15-minute jive – incredible – I've written it for a sci-fi show that's being planned," he told one interviewer. "It's going to be an audio-visual experience lasting three hours," another was informed. It was, in fact, merely the latest in a long line of big Bolan ideas that never came to fruition.

The two singles excepted, 1975 had hardly been a vintage year for Bolan recordings, and a plethora of unexceptional outtakes confirms this. However, some public embarrassment was spared when 'Christmas Bop', a seasonal 45 worked on in view of those fans at Scorpio in August, was pulled. A clutch of (much coveted) surviving labels bearing the MARC 12 catalogue number shows just how close the song came to spelling a seasonal disaster. The song was a ham-fisted take on the old Conway Twitty standard, 'It's Only Make Believe', taken at twice the speed and no match for his old pal Roy Wood's Phil Spector-sounding 'I Wish It Could Be Christmas Everyday' issued two years earlier.

Marc, Gloria and Rolan spent their first Christmas together in Los Angeles where the newborn was proudly exhibited to the extended Jones family. On his return to London Marc, together with Keith Altham, drummed up enthusiasm for the next stage in Bolan's rehabilitation: the release of the seventh T. Rex album, *Futuristic Dragon*, and an 18-date tie-in tour. "The idea of Marc Bolan is still a big Superstar, whether people like it or not," Marc boasted unconvincingly. He also claimed to *Super Star* magazine that 1976 was also going to see a new, clean-living

Bolan. "I'll be getting my kicks from playing to the kids again for the first time in three years," he said excitedly. "I suppose you could say I've re-discovered my original dream all over again."

A couple of months later, during the Scottish leg of the tour, he reiterated the point to fan Andy Gardiner. "I've no longer got manic death wishes or the urge to overly abuse myself with drink or drugs," he told him. "I've been through that and to come out on the other side in one piece and a better person is an amazing feeling . . . Drink and drugs are a musician's worst enemy."

Unfortunately, the boast simply wasn't true. Marc was frequently drunk during the *Dragon* tour, and often belligerent with it. He got into scrapes, put his hand through a plate glass window, berated his audiences, frequently forgot his lyrics and received a predictable slew of poor reviews. He also appeared to be in poor health and was badly dressed. Still, the exposure did put Marc Bolan back in the charts: *Futuristic Dragon* spent one week at number 50.

Once again, the tour was ill-conceived, combining essential shows at major venues with dates in smaller provincial towns such as Folkestone and Withernsea. To cover the expense (and Bolan didn't come cheap), the smaller venues were compelled to price tickets accordingly, with the result that T. Rex played to a handful of half-full houses during the four-week tour which lasted throughout February and into the first week of March.

The original plan was to extend the *Dragon* theme with an elaborate stage set, but Marc Bolan wasn't David Bowie and the idea soon got whittled down to a simple dragon backdrop. Marc also donned his own worsted *Futuristic Dragon* suit (in a choice of scarlet or green), comprising a figure-hiding double-breasted jacket and baggy trousers trimmed with leopard-skin patterned velvet. A thick blond streak had been dyed into the front of his hair ("We were going to Vidal Sassoon at that time and colour was coming in," Gloria explains), crowning one of the least appealing images of Bolan's entire career.

The band, now with Tyrone Scott (backing vocals and keyboards) joining drummer Davey Lutton, Dino Dines (keyboards), bassist Steve Currie, Marc and the returning Gloria Jones, was well-rehearsed. The 15-song set, one of the longest in Bolan's career, was a strictly crowd-pleasing catalogue of hits with only the two singles, 'New York City' and 'Dreamy Lady', representing the new album. But Marc's discovery of his original dream quickly turned into a nightmare. "That was my last tour with Marc and it was hell," Mick Gray maintains. "His drinking was bad and he came close to upsetting many people with his tongue – both in the party and the fans."

On the third date, at the Lea's Cliff Hall in Folkestone, Bolan was particularly loquacious. After admitting to his audience that being a superstar "only gave me problems", he came over all misty eyed about his "flower child" days as he introduced 'Debora' during the acoustic interlude, back in the set for the first time since 1972. This part of the show was one of the tour's few plus points, when ecstatically received singalong versions of 'Ride A White Swan', 'Life's A Gas', 'Conesuala' and 'One Inch Rock' provided an intimacy that had been missing from T. Rex concerts for four years.* This informality was a welcome contrast to the sickeningly slick performances of his contemporaries, a defiance of 'professional' values that would be taken to new extremes by a new generation of anti-rock iconoclasts later in the year. But it didn't always save the shows.

Having claimed prior to the tour that he was "bionic", Marc spent much of the five weeks on the road nursing wounds as well as the obligatory hangovers. The February 14 show at Withernsea Pavilion, Humberside, had been billed as a St. Valentine's Day Dance with no hint that T. Rex were to perform. It was intended as a night for love and romance, not live revivalism. Midway through the set, the overwhelming mood of indifference prompted a "How do you expect me to play when you're walking around eating fucking hamburgers?" outburst from the stage. The atmosphere hotted up afterwards, so much so that the stage was invaded, and Marc was pulled over in the mêlée. Throwing his guitar down, he ran off the stage and promptly punched his fist through a glass door. Marc was rushed to casualty where he received stitches to a badly lacerated right hand. The press was later told that a bottle of champagne had been tossed through the dressing-room window by a fan as a mark of admiration.

Ten days later, while the group were in Manchester to play the Free Trade Hall, Marc was attacked by a youth who screamed, "Bowie's much better than you!" before punching him in the face. "One moment Marc was talking at the guy, the next he was in a drunken heap on the floor nursing a damaged eye," remembers Mick Gray. "I picked him up and he was feeling very sorry for himself. It was probably the first time he'd been in a fight with a male since his schooldays." Marc later passed off the black

---

* At the Floral Hall, Southport, on February 12, he dropped in an impromptu verse of 'Mambo Sun' during the acoustic set. Incredibly, it was the first time this classic Bolan song had been acknowledged in concert, proving just how inflexible the T. Rex set-list had been.

eye as a hazard of the job, caused by a mass charge of fans.

Some true believers hired vans and travelled from gig to gig savouring every moment with their touchable Superstar. Most neutrals didn't see it that way at all. "Marc Bolan played London's Lyceum Ballroom last Wednesday," wrote Allan Jones in *Melody Maker.* "It was the saddest spectacle I'd witnessed in years. There were no more than a thousand people there to see him and he paraded himself before them like a faded old tart looking for one final trick before fading into obscurity." It got worse. "He jerked and grimaced about the stage like an obese puppet . . . his band was dismally inept and uninspired and at times he seemed to realise that it's virtually all over." The tour ended with a whimper as Marc developed a heavy cold in Scotland forcing the Motherwell show to be cut short and the final date at Kilmarnock to be cancelled.

As a measure of Marc's self-delusion, he wriggled out of questions pertaining to the tour's less than flattering attendances by stating that, "I did this tour without any publicity just to get the feel of things again. Now I want to do more live shows. I was the first artist to play Wembley and I did it twice with 20,000 there each time. I feel like doing it again and I know that they'd sell all the tickets in a day." As Jeff Dexter, who had begun to see a bit more of his old Mod mate since the previous autumn insists: "Marc was never a has-been in his own eyes. He didn't hear other people. His world just wasn't that real."

The tour was bad enough. *Futuristic Dragon*'s hammy title and equally ludicrous cover artwork, a painting by *My People* . . . artist George Underwood depicting Marc astride the fire-snorting mythological creature, was an open invitation for cynics to quip that Bolan was now the cartoon character he'd always threatened to become. That was a pity because despite much of the material being over a year old, the record featured the strongest set of songs Bolan had put together in one place since 1972's *The Slider.* Songs such as 'Chrome Sitar' and 'Dawn Storm' (an unrecognised 'plastic soul' classic) restored much of the sense of purpose that had been missing from the more experimental T. Rex productions of the previous couple of years. And the return of the Visconti-era styled strings, strident backing vocals and a prominent horn section marked a determined retreat from the minimalistic glory of *Bolan's Zip Gun.*

That Marc felt a distance from the material was evident in interviews around the time of its release. He preferred to discuss the records he was producing for Gloria and Richard Jones (now three years in the making), his forthcoming book of poetry, *Wilderness Of The Mind* and fantasy plans such as *Billy Super Duper* or *Future Man Buick* ("Incredible, it may be done as a movie") than to dissect the record track by track as he used to do back in 1972 – or 1968 for that matter. He did, however, regard the album as a literary achievement. "You'll find that the lyrics of at least four of the tracks are very complex," he told Geoff Barton in *Sounds*. " 'Casual Agent' is like the equivalent of 'The Scenescof Dynasty' from the early days. Sometimes I get into words, sometimes I don't."

Much of the record had been recorded during the dark days of winter 1974, which was probably another reason why Marc seemed to keep *Futuristic Dragon* at arm's length. The aforementioned highlights, 'Dawn Storm' and 'Chrome Sitar', were dense productions and two of the most emotionally charged songs in Bolan's career – although few at the time understood just how low Marc had to go in order to achieve those end-of-tether performances. 'Jupiter Liar' (which had been EMI's pre-ferred choice as the first T. Rex single of 1976) was a joyous, only faintly pastiche-like retread of prime-time Bolan boogie, while – yes – 'Casual Agent' did feature some of Marc's most mischievous lyrics in years.

Most poignant, though, was 'All Alone'. It had been written in 1974, Bolan said, while "sitting indoors with 1,000 kids outside, watching myself on *Top Of The Pops*. I was so lonely I cried my heart out. The song totally sums up my life at that time." Inevitably, perhaps, 'All Alone' was another of those cuts committed to tape at MRI during December 1974.

There had been talk of another late 1974 soul-influenced cut, 'Sanctified', being reworked as the follow-up to 'Dreamy Lady'. Unfortunately, that idea was shelved in favour of 'London Boys', no doubt due to the fact that Marc had become obsessed with his birthplace again since returning home the previous summer. Musically slight to the point of insignificance, and with a painfully trite chorus – "Oh yeah! We're the London Boys" – the single plummeted new depths that nostalgic name-checks for Petticoat Lane and the London to Brighton scooter run did nothing to save it from. It failed to secure a Top 30 placing.

" 'London Boys' is about me when I was 14 and king of the Mods," Marc admitted, adding that the lyric also dates from that time. The truth was that he'd written them rather more recently than that. A line such as "Changing life patterns to get to the top" is an obviously retrospective take on Marc's Hackney Mod days; so too is the uncertainty he sings about once he gets there. It's a pity that Marc never devoted enough time to projects such as the *London Opera* which, coming from the capital's biggest ever pop name, could have worked with a bit of nurturing. Instead, he posed with an oversized Benelli motorbike for the publicity pictures; presumably the oversized Marc would have looked pretty daft perched on a scooter.

Months later, Bolan insisted that 'London Boys' "should have been Top five. I think it was great but maybe it was wrong for the time." He was right: maybe it was made for 1961.

For the first time in his life, Marc seemed to be in the grip of nostalgia. Having pulled himself back from personal ruin out in Los Angeles, he no longer seemed willing to put himself at the mercy of the unknown. He recorded a version of Little Richard's 'Rip It Up' in private, and performed the old Frankie Lymon/Marty Wilde hit, 'A Teenager In Love' in public (for a Capital Radio broadcast in March 1976). Invited to choose 'My Top 12' records for the Radio 1 series in May, he spoke lovingly of Elvis' visual flair, contrasting it with the 20-minute guitar solos favoured by the metal bands ("Not heavy metal, heavy boring!", he joked). Rick Wakeman on ice "doesn't rock me at all", he added. And Marc Bolan? "I incorporated a lot of Hendrix, Townshend and Elvis' wiggle, put it together and came up with something quite interesting," he concluded. Quite rightly, of course.

During the *Futuristic Dragon* tour, he dropped in on Roy Wood for a boozy trip down memory lane, jamming their way through rock'n'roll favourites such as the Isley Brothers' 'Twist And Shout' and Buddy Holly's 'Oh Boy'.*

These regular reruns of his funky rock'n'roll childhood inevitably lit fires in Marc's mind. He was, he insisted, going to put together a rock'n'-roll revival show. "I'd avoid the overdone things like 'Blue Suede Shoes' and 'Johnny B. Goode'," he said, instead inviting the interviewer to "Imagine 'A Teenager In Love' with Cat Stevens, David Bowie and myself doing the three-part harmonies. I'd have Gloria and Tina Turner in there too." Of course there was no chance of such a project ever happening, but Marc's back-to-basics attitude was genuine enough and at the end of April 1976, he asked Jeff Dexter to find him the cheapest studio in London. He was ready to throw in the towel with hi-tech American studios and recapture the grit and grime that had been the breeding ground of rock'n'roll in the first place. Jeff found him Decibel, a small

---

* The session, which is of little musical value, does include some fascinating Bolan quips. During a brief discussion about plagiarism, Marc admits, "I nicked ('Jeepster') off a Howlin' Wolf song." In virtually the same breath, he adds, "I never stole anything in my whole life."

studio just off Marc's old Stamford Hill catwalk, and booked him in there for several days during May.

While Marc prepared to record the most revivalist song of his career, on May 3 he and Gloria witnessed probably the most admirably arrogant display of rock'n'roll futurism of the decade. Filling the Empire Pool, Wembley, for a remarkable six-show run as part of his 'Station To Station' tour was David Bowie, now recast as an austere, ultra-European Thin White Duke. Four years earlier, the venue had played host to those incredible scenes of T. Rextasy at its optimum moment. In 1976, Marc was only half filling theatres in Folkestone and St. Albans while David, now the most critically acclaimed rock artist in the world, was selling out a huge world tour.

Earlier that day, Marc had seen his hairdresser and attended a photo session at EMI House in Manchester Square, and – despite his claim earlier in the year that he might actually perform with Bowie – danced behind the stage during the evening. Bowie's cold wave performance was light years away from the cosy rock'n'roll simplicity that Marc had now embraced after his long, fraught excursion into interstellar soul. Yet despite the gulf that had grown between them, both commercially and critically, for the first time Marc seemed almost proud of the achievements of his old adversary. After all, as he reminded Andy Gardiner in March, he'd virtually created Bowie.

That conversation on a tour bus in Motherwell formed the basis for so many of those Bolan/Bowie collaboration rumours. Marc claimed that David played on 'Casual Agent' and contributed something to 'I Really Love You Babe'. He, of course, helped out his struggling pal on the lengthy coda to 'Memory Of A Free Festival' (which also featured the Woolworth's organ that had earlier been used on Marc's 'Organ Blues'), 'Black Country Rock' (the song with the neat Bolan pastiche) and 'Ting A Ling'. 'Space Oddity', too. "I helped him with it a little bit," Marc said with feigned coyness. He also admitted to a sneaking admiration for 'Karma Man' and 'In The Heat Of The Morning', two lesser-known Bowie songs from the late Sixties, though David's best he reckoned was 'Wild Eyed Boy From Freecloud', the fantasy-laden B-side of 'Space Oddity'.

Later that spring, Marc was full of enthusiasm for a new film project that the pair had apparently been discussing. "We've written a script and we need two million to make the film," he said. Then with uncharacteristic restraint, he backtracked a little, mindful of Bowie's increasing guardedness regarding his own projects. "Like, we're working on a script, put it like that, you know." He did give some insight into the difference between the pair's working methods, claiming that Bowie could spend 12 hours in a studio just twiddling with a drum machine, while he himself works "very fast". Nevertheless, "we're mates, we think very similar, read the same kind of books, probably had the same kind of background . . ." And not a hint that this year's model, Fox perhaps or Slik, made David "look tired".

For years, Marc, like most pop and rock musicians, had based his riffs on blues-inspired rock'n'roll and his chord sequences on Tin Pan Alley traditions. As Tony Visconti remembers, "Marc never stole; he was always influenced by!" The line was a thin one as George Harrison discovered when the publishers of The Chiffons' 'He's So Fine' successfully sued him for plagiarism on 'My Sweet Lord'. Marc had already sailed close to the wind on countless occasions.

"'I Love To Boogie' was written in ten minutes in the studio after putting together these nine rockabilly LPs in my head," Bolan bragged to a *Record Mirror & Disc* reporter in June 1976. "'Hot Love' I did the same. The middle eight is from 'Heartbreak Hotel'."* Bigmouth had struck again, but this time others were willing to strike back. On the same day, *New Musical Express* reported that a bunch of aggrieved rockabilly enthusiasts had planned a 'burn-in' of the latest T. Rex record at a pub in the Old Kent Road, south east London. They claimed that Bolan had ripped off an obscure rockabilly recording from 1956 by Webb Pierce called 'Teenage Boogie'. A spokesman for the Teds, disc jockey Geoff Barker, complained that, "The records are so alike it can't be coincidence. He's kept the basic melody and simply changed the chorus lyrics . . . even the guitar solo is a rip-off."

The last thing Marc needed was a time-consuming and costly lawsuit, so he quickly backtracked and claimed that he was simply trying to rework Carl Perkins' 'Honey Don't'. Meanwhile, a heated flurry of correspondence was exchanged between Pierce's publishers and Bolan's London office. At one stage, it looked as if 'I Love To Boogie' was going to be injuncted but, according to Jeff Dexter, Marc's manager Tony Howard employed a musicologist to analyse both songs and his findings were sent to the complainants. The parameters of the debate were sufficiently

---

* In fact, Mick Gray maintains that 'Boogie' had been written in Monaco in January 1975 and first recorded a month later at MRI.

widened to cast doubt on Marc's alleged plagiarism, and it was pointed out that 'Teenage Boogie' was itself based on a riff that had been around long before the song was written. The matter ended there.

Marc went home and celebrated in the most mischievous way he could. Spinning the Webb Pierce song on his stereo, he then launched immediately into his own song on his guitar. His cassette recorder was running, too, capturing the obvious similarity between the songs for posterity.

Despite his return to Decibel and Air Studios that spring, not to mention the stockpile of material he had that dated back to the winter 1974 sessions in America, Bolan again dipped into his distant past for the B-side. ('London Boys' had been paired with 'Solid Baby' from Bolan's *Zip Gun*.) This time 'Baby Boomerang' from *The Slider* was reactivated, a choice that adds some weight to the rumour that the song had been written about New York poet/singer Patti Smith, who'd recently crossed over into the rock mainstream with her extraordinary début album *Horses*.

Blissfully oblivious to the controversy that surrounded the single, one enthusiastic Bolan fan dashed off a letter to *Record Mirror & Disc* stating that, "'I Love To Boogie' sounds so fresh compared with all the current chart sounds, which proves Bolan is a true original". Nostalgia did indeed appear to be the new novelty because Bryan Ferry, The Shangri-Las, The Beatles and The Beach Boys were all finding success with songs first popular back in the Sixties. However, despite Charles Shaar Murray's insistence in *New Musical Express* that 'I Love To Boogie' was "terminally vapid, totally devoid of hooks and cursed with a production as flimsy as a wet Kleenex", Marc's minimalist rock'n'roll venture at least had something in common with the new wave of unrefined R&B groups that had been nurtured on the pub circuit.

Also doing the rounds, but as yet still fairly unknown outside their own circle were The Sex Pistols, fronted by another north Londoner whose face would eventually define an era and a style in much the same way that Bolan's had. That was Johnny Rotten and it was he, not Marc or David, who possessed the answer to rock's current malaise.

★　★　★

The Punk underworld had yet to touch the life of Marc Bolan, who had only belatedly embraced the deviant appeal of Lou Reed. Encouraged by the relative success of 'I Love To Boogie', which reached number 13 in July, he prepared for a *Supersonic* TV special, *Rollin' Bolan* and briefly turned his attentions to matters of a more domestic nature.

At the end of June 1976, June Bolan sued for divorce, citing Gloria Jones as the third party. Marc, who had made contingency plans back in 1973 in a bid to prevent June from making a huge claim on his finances, was unhappy at the prospect of battle over a settlement, though the hearing on October 5 passed with little ado. Deputy Judge Donald Ellison declared: "I am satisfied that the husband committed adultery with the co-respondent, and that the wife finds it intolerable to live with him," and granted a decree nisi. Twelve months after that date, it was to become a decree absolute thus severing the Bolans' matrimonial ties forever.

"The facts are that she initially left me, and we just grew apart," Marc explained after the ruling. "There were no great scenes, no smashing things up. It just suddenly happened one day. We weren't a couple anymore." He also used the opportunity to shed a little light on his sexuality. "Anyway, I'm gay," he only half-jested. "I can't say I was a latent homosexual – I was an early one. But sex was never a great problem. I'm a great screwer . . ." Asked about the institution of marriage, he replied: "Gloria doesn't want to get married and neither do I. If I ever marry anyone again, I'll put in a clause that when it ends you're on your own – and that means financially, too."

Meanwhile, he'd finally got round to completing work on the album he'd been producing for Gloria Jones since 1973. "After the baby was born, Marc suggested that I should restart my recording career," Gloria says. "One night Gonzalez, who had a deal with EMI, were performing at the Nashville and they asked me up to sing a number. So I did." After securing her own deal with the label, Jones released her version of T. Rex's 'Get It On' in April. Taken at a breakneck pace that even Tina Charles would have had difficulty keeping up with, the single won reasonable reviews and Gloria was invited to join Gonzalez as a guest singer on their European tour supporting Bob Marley & The Wailers.

"I went on my own, but Marc surprised me in Manchester (on June 27, 1976)," she says. "Marc took a train up there and went straight to the auditorium. When he arrived Bob Marley was sitting on stage just playing his guitar. Marc told me he just sat on stage and watched him play."

Although much of Gloria's Bolan-produced album, released as *Vixen* in December 1976, had been recorded at MRI over the past couple of years, Gonzalez helped out on a couple of tracks, notably 'Go Now' and a reworking of 'Tainted Love' at Scorpio earlier that year. However, it was the mark of Bolan that was most obvious. As well as producing the record (skilfully avoiding the most obvious T. Rex trademarks and delivering a hard-sounding soul record not unlike Chaka Khan's early work), Marc wrote several songs and played guitar on many tracks.

'High', 'Sailors Of The Highway' and 'Drive Me Crazy (Disco Lady)' (originally titled 'Ghetto Baby') had been salvaged from the aborted Pat Hall LP tapes; 'Get It On' (parts one and two) was obviously a T. Rex song; 'Cry Baby' was a reworking of a 1975 outtake; 'Savage Beethoven', and 'Tell Me Now' had been specially written for the record. *Melody Maker* reckoned the material wasn't as convincing as the songs Gloria had co-written with Pam Sawyer in her Motown days, though Robin Smith in *Record Mirror* was delighted when he spotted "more than a few T. Rex influences", concluding "I bet Marc's proud". He was, but *Vixen* got quietly lost amid the Christmas rush.

With both his parents working musicians, it was inevitable that Rolan Bolan's upbringing was going to be somewhat unconventional. However, with Gloria occasionally working away and Marc seeking to rebuild his career, Sid and Phyllis Feld were more than happy to become active grandparents. During the first two years of his life, Rolan regularly slept over in their flat at 9 Inglis House, Whitnell Way in Putney, which came with Sid's job as caretaker of the council-run block. Marc had given his parents the opportunity to transform their lives on several occasions, offering to buy them a detached house with a garden of their own, but Sid and Phyllis were happy to stay where they'd been since the early Seventies.

"They never wanted to change their lifestyle," says Marc's brother Harry. "They were so proud of Marc when he really made it, but it never affected the way they lived. Dad put his heart into that job. He'd do the bins at six in the morning, get all his work done early, and from opening time to closing time he'd meet his friends in the Angel or the Green Man pub." The only luxury the Felds allowed themselves was when Marc gave his Rolls-Royce to his father for his birthday one year.

Although Gloria Jones insists that "he gave all that up" when Rolan was born, referring to Marc's bad habits, it was obvious from the drunken 'Dragon' tour that Bolan still enjoyed more than a few drinks when he needed to. Nevertheless, he had great plans for his son. "He always wanted Rolan to have a good education because he felt that if he'd been educated he would have conducted his business better," Gloria says. "Marc was a good father, and Rolan also had Marc's parents. He had the love of the family, a real family environment."

Back in March 1976, Marc insisted to Andy Gardiner that Rolan's birth "has changed me . . . made me realise there is more to life than music 24 hours a day." This new maturity may have taken some time to filter through, but by the summer, Marc had begun to take control of himself; he seemed sharper, mentally more robust and happier.

It was the relative success of 'I Love To Boogie' that had prompted Mike Mansfield to float the idea of a Marc Bolan television special for *Supersonic*. On July 13, T. Rex – now without Gloria Jones – filmed five songs that were broadcast on August 28 as *Rollin' Bolan*. It was the final T. Rex performance with Davey Lutton (who was sacked) and Steve Currie (who quit) in the line-up. Currie had remained with Marc far longer than anyone had expected. Never the most animated of musicians, Steve Currie was burnt out by the end of his tenure. Apart from some work with Chris Spedding in 1977, he followed Steve Peregrine Took, Bill Legend and Mickey Finn into obscurity. Like Took, he was destined for one final notice in the music press. That came in May 1981, when the news pages reported that Currie had been killed in a car crash in Portugal.

Unlike Took, Steve Currie had been rebuilding his life. After splitting up with his wife, he moved his new girlfriend Peta Heskell into his Twickenham home in 1979. The pair emigrated to Portugal the following year. Some time around midnight on April 28, 1981, Currie was returning to his home in the village of Val Da Parra when, half-a-mile from his destination, his car veered off the road. He died instantly. No other vehicle was involved.

The *Rollin' Bolan* show wasn't notable just for being Steve Currie's swansong. With his hair now considerably shorter, and his voice decidedly warble-free, Marc seemed to have turned back the clock a decade in what probably was a subconscious bid to play the part of the 'London Boy' with conviction. Only his fuller face, and the band, a motley collection devoid of anything resembling style or panache, gave any indication that this was the mid-Seventies. In his black-and-white costume, an 'I Love To Boogie' badge pinned to his lapel, and his cherished orange Les Paul around his neck, Bolan seemed to be a stranger at his own party.

It wasn't the most confident of T. Rex performances, not least because it was the inaugural outing for second guitarist Miller Anderson, who'd played alongside Dino Dines in the Keef Hartley Band in the late Sixties before joining Savoy Brown. Unusually, three as yet unreleased songs were performed that day in addition to 'I Love To Boogie' and 'New York City', the band's two biggest hits in recent months. 'Funky London Childhood' and 'The Soul Of My Suit' had been around for a while; the third was 'Laser Love', the next T. Rex single. The riff was a weak take on The Rolling Stones' 'Brown Sugar', a comparison enhanced by Anderson's slide-playing, picked up perhaps from his recent jams with ex-Rolling Stones guitarist Mick Taylor.

By the time Bolan was promoting 'Laser Love' on *Top Of The Pops* and *Supersonic*, Currie and Lutton had been replaced by ace session players – bassist Herbie Flowers (who, as a sideline, had co-written Clive Dunn's winter 1970 hit 'Grandad') and drummer Tony Newman. Both had been veterans of Bowie's 'Diamond Dogs' tour and, says Gloria, "They really had a great sound and a great energy. Some nights they'd hit something really special. Herbie was a great bass player, and Marc was able to play off Dino's organ playing and Miller, who was a strong guitarist." One new song, 'Life's An Elevator', the flipside of the forthcoming single, featured some neat, un-T. Rexlike guitar interplay.

"It was my idea to get good session musicians," insists Jeff Dexter, "and I convinced Marc that the band David Bowie had used was the right one. It was good for him, and everyone hoped it would make him work harder with that calibre of musician behind him. By that time Gloria was working with Gonzalez and doing her own thing, and it seemed right that he should be one of the boys and make it with a boys' band. Of course, he said the whole band was his idea, but that's the way he was."

Nostalgia for his teenage days had been evoked on his previous two singles, 'Laser Love' was more typically flat mid-Seventies fare. As if to make up for the record's lack of sparkle, Marc dreamed up a "Marcos Bolantino" look to promote the song. The image – dark suit, wide art deco tie, brilliantine hair and made-up eyes – was inspired by silent screen Latin matinée idol Rudolph Valentino, and though it bore no relation to the record's leaden sound, 'Bolantino' was lapped up by the press. Badges were circulated proclaiming "A new age of Bolan – T. Rex Unchained". It was a different story in record shops up and down the country where the new Bolanic age simply meant "Boxes of T. Rex Singles – Unopened". 'Laser Love' stalled at number 41.

On October 5, 1976, Marc promoted 'Laser Love' on *Supersonic*. Mike Mansfield also found time to include a newly recorded version of 'Ride A White Swan', which Marc mimed to from within a large polystyrene swan that was pulled shakily around the studio floor on a fork-lift truck while feathers rained down on the sorry spectacle. There were, it has to be said, better ways to inspire public confidence in Marc Bolan. The new age of Bolan was looking decidedly kitsch.

The new-look T. Rex – Newman, Flowers, Dines and Anderson – were the most accomplished group of musicians Marc Bolan ever had around him. But the pull towards children's television, enhanced by appearances on The Bay City Rollers' *Shang-A-Lang* and a short-lived show hosted by half-hit-wonders Arrows (whose drummer Paul Varley was June Bolan's new beau), had a dispiriting effect on those musicians. While Marc puffed and pouted out front, in a brazen attempt to convince his pre-teen audience that he was the most thrilling sight they'd ever set eyes on, Herbie and his mates would sometimes giggle and bounce incredulous looks off each other.

Marc was just pleased to be back on television. He didn't even baulk when, on December 19, he played second fiddle to Gary Glitter for *Christmas Supersonic*, filmed at the Theatre Royal in London's Drury Lane and organised in conjunction with the *Daily Mirror* Pop Club. The presence of Princess Margaret and her children, as well as hosts Joanna Lumley and Russell Harty only added to the preposterousness of the occasion which concluded with Marc sandwiched between Twiggy and Marti Caine for the all-star finale of 'We Wish You A Merry Christmas'.

It had been a busy autumn for Bolan who, in addition to breaking in a new band, had bought a spacious Victorian residence in west London, a short drive away from his parents' flat in Putney. The house at 142 Upper Richmond Road, East Sheen was a stone's throw away from Richmond Park, and Marc and Gloria spent many days walking Rolan through its vast green spaces, feeding birds and marvelling at the herds of deer that roamed freely there.

It was a quiet, secluded property set back from the main road but the 12 months that Marc and Gloria shared there were hardly peaceful ones. "We had to renovate the house," Gloria remembers, "and Marc really wasn't comfortable with builders all around the place hammering and wandering around. It was a funny period. You could never really relax." One story has it that the state of the floorboards was so bad that one day Marc fell right through the floor

Because of the upheaval, Marc and Gloria spent most of their time confined to one large room, where Marc would conduct his business prostrate on a bed, write songs, play music, watch videos (when virtually no one else had a VCR) and entertain Gloria and Rolan surrounded by unpacked boxes and builders' materials. That was another reason why Rolan spent time at his grandparents. It wasn't easy, Gloria admits, but "we did relaxing things. You know, the tears would come along sometimes, but we became homebodies."

Christmas 1976 was disrupted when T. Rex were booked to perform live on a seasonal television show in France. The group flew out to Paris on December 23, but after lengthy rehearsals, problems with filming meant that Marc sang solo to pre-recorded backing tracks. Once again, a stage prop backfired when the platform intended to raise him up to stage level stalled, prompting some hasty action by studio technicians who yanked him up physically – leaving him nursing a damaged shoulder.

Marc was back in France in February 1977 for a short tour with T. Rex. He used the opportunity to revisit a few of the places he'd first seen with Riggs O'Hara back in the mid-Sixties, including the Louvre art gallery where he headed straight for the statue of Hercules. It was, he told his tour diary, "just the artistic inspiration to key the Bolan brain for boogie". Other influences that spring included reading Gore Vidal's *Myron* and jamming with Steve Harley, but the key impetus to Marc's renewed enthusiasm for music was the invigorating sound of punk rock.

When punk broke towards the end of 1976, Marc's initial reaction was typical of those from the established rock community – confusion bordering on outright hostility. "This so-called punk rock thing. It's not selling. The kids don't want it," he complained in September, the same month that the 100 Club put on the infamous Punk Rock Festival. What they needed, he suggested, was Marc Bolan, pop's first great iconoclast for whom punk meant early Sixties American girl group The Angels, maverick film director Federico Fellini, pop falsetto Frankie Valli and Hollywood outsider Orson Welles. The list at least revealed that Marc understood the new wave's urgent need to reject conventional icons.

Bolan regarded himself above and beyond 'Old Fart' status, a conceit that was eminently justifiable. He had been getting up the noses of the rock cognoscenti for years and, besides, the whiff of faded pop glory was infinitely more appealing to punk sensibilities than the earnest dullards that featured on the cover of *Rolling Stone* every second week. Marc may have mistrusted its new ambassadors, but he welcomed punk's ability to shake up the old order – one that always had trouble accepting him. His understanding of it was somewhat suspect. After repeating a line from 'Laser Love' – "My love is as strong as the raging sea" – he turned to his interviewer and said, "You can't get any punkier than that, can you?"

Most of all, punk rock gave Marc an opportunity to pontificate in the pages of the music press. While most of his contemporaries sneered scathingly at this apparent *coup d'état* by a cabal of cloth-eared, shockingly clad musical heathens, Bolan's gradual warming to the new wave was a mixture of instinct and opportunism. Its attempt to tear up the old rock rulebook encouraged Marc to reposition himself within the new scheme of things – "I consider myself to be the elder statesman of punk," he claimed in February 1977, "The Godfather of Punk if you like."

Age alone – not to mention beards, cheesecloth shirts, bad jeans, even worse haircuts – excluded most of Marc's generation from punk rock approval. But Bolan's long-term affinity with street culture, his continued faith in youth as rock and pop's primary audience, plus his insistence that punk's new anti-stars were the children of his revolution grown up, created the perfect conditions for a mutual appreciation society.*

Never one to miss a good PR opportunity, Marc held the launch for his new album *Dandy In The Underworld* on March 2, 1977 at London's premier punk Mecca the Roxy Club in Covent Garden. Various Sex Pistols, Damned and Generation X members were in attendance, though the presence of Paul and Linda McCartney and Alvin Stardust tended to dilute the impact.

Marc cut a dashing figure as he darted between his old friends and the new wavers. Slimmer than he had been at any time since 1973, he turned up in a pair of tight, straight leg trousers and a fitted, canary-yellow jacket, his ringleted hair cut back to a more acceptable length. Never mind the kids' TV, here's the new Bolan. "I have stopped using drugs. I stopped drinking six weeks ago. I just want to work," he confessed days earlier. "The way I was going, I could have been forgotten about completely in about five years. And my ego just couldn't have taken that. This is going to be my year."

Taking pride in his appearance was the most obvious indication that Marc had started to take control of his life. "He had a new jacket tailor-made for that *Dandy* press party," remembers Gloria Jones. "It was gorgeous, and he definitely didn't want anyone touching that yellow jacket. Throughout the evening, he'd look across at me and make gestures if anyone came close to dirtying up that jacket! It was a running joke that lasted all night."

It was an item of clothing that led to The Damned being added to the T. Rex tour as support band. "He saw me wearing a Bolan T-shirt in a music paper photo, and I think that did it," says the band's Captain

---

* He was in good company: Iggy Pop, Lou Reed, Syd Barrett and David Bowie were among the few other recipients of punk goodwill.

Sensible, who first saw T. Rex in concert at the Weeley Festival in 1971. "He had a bit more perception at the time. He saw through the shit that the *News Of The World* and *The Sun* were saying, namely that punk rockers were just a bunch of boneheads.

"At the time, there were a lot of people who'd stop you in the street and punch you in the face because you dressed in punk gear. So it was quite good for anyone to say anything nice about the groups at that time. When Bolan said we were all right, that something was happening around the punk thing, it was very controversial."

Sensible also confirms that most new wavers regarded Bolan as quite separate from the rest of the old guard. "His music said it all," states the Damned's bassist-turned-guitarist. "He was out on a limb, destined to make weird records with weird lyrics, doing something that nobody else could understand. Bolan wasn't the seen-it-done-it-all merchant. He had fresh ideas."

Marc's first record of 1977 didn't quite live up to the Captain's assessment. A cover of 'To Know Him Is To Love Him', Phil Spector's old Teddy Bears' hit from winter 1958, it was a public declaration of Marc's love for Gloria Jones, a surprisingly enjoyable and affectionate gesture but one that was hardly going to inspire the pogo dancers in London's clubland. The single – credited to Marc Bolan and Gloria Jones – was backed by a vigorous new version of 'City Port', originally taped for the Pat Hall album. Writing in *Melody Maker*, Caroline Coon did spot one punkish element about the performance, though. "Somebody's singing in the wrong key," she carped, adding that, "this is less a duet than Marc sounding as if he's singing to himself, about himself, naturally . . ."

The favourable notices that Marc had been coveting for years now finally began to roll in almost the moment the 'Dandy In The Underworld' tour got underway. *Melody Maker*'s Allan Jones, who'd cruelly suggested Bolan was ready for cabaret after witnessing the Lyceum show in February 1976, was at Newcastle's City Hall for the tour's first night. "Much of the old zip and rush has been restored," he enthused. "Hell, 'Jeepster' still sounds great, even to these jaded ears." He had come, he said, expecting disaster. He left with the sounds of "a beezer" 'Get It On' ringing in his ears. "One has to congratulate the old campaigner for coming through," he concluded.

Jones' assessment was typical of the response that greeted the tour. It was probably the most accomplished set of T. Rex performances since Marc first enlarged the group from a duo into a four-piece early in 1971. Instead of relying again on a set crammed with baggy versions of the hits, the choice of material – a judicious, disciplined blend of old and new – reflected Marc's new-found confidence. Only on 'Hang-Ups' and the predictable 'Get It On' finale did Bolan pay lip-service to the rockist tendency.

If anything, The Damned demanded that Marc loosen up even more. "We'd go up and tell him what we wanted to see him do, which was play more guitar solos and do an album of really raw stuff. He'd say, 'That's interesting, guys, I'll have a word with my manager.' He was doing a really wild version of 'Debora' on the tour, but I think the management were against releasing it."

The 'Dandy' tour, more often than not greeted by screams, certainly proved that Marc Bolan could survive, and possibly even thrive in the new climate. The wildest excesses of those old American tours had been curtailed and the 13- or 14-song sets were tight, uptempo and impeccably held together by the exaggerated presence of Marc Bolan. There was more than a touch of parody in Marc's performances now, his Liberace camp laced with punkish panache. It was rude – the pay-off line in 'Jeepster' was now "I'm gonna fuck you, babe!" – robust and, just occasionally, rather silly. The main culprit in that department was Dino Dines, whose single-note synthesizer parts could reduce songs like 'The Soul Of My Suit' and even 'Debora' to a nonsense.

The tour ended with a high-spirited, 13-minute act of vandalism on 'Get It On' at the Portsmouth Locarno where T. Rex were joined by The Damned, hopelessly drunk and utterly disorderly. Marc rattled off a fiery flurry of solos, then took the tour bus to Putney Bridge where he got out, put a coin in a nearby telephone box and called his father to take him home. Presumably, he got a good night's sleep, happy that Marc Bolan and T. Rex had finally turned a corner.

For four years, Marc had been fighting a losing battle with the prevailing tendencies towards soft rock, predictable metal overkill and classically inclined epics. He no longer had the power to alter matters single-handedly as he'd done in 1971. Something else had to happen. "I have been sitting around waiting for the pop climate to change," he admitted in February 1977, "for something like punk rock to come along." Bolan now scented real success again, and that hunger replaced his hitherto unquenchable desire for fatty foods and alcohol. He pulled on a tracksuit and trainers for his daily exercises. Perrier and lemon replaced beer and brandy, and greasy fry-ups were substituted with omelette or grilled fish with raw vegetables. It was a commitment he maintained, more or less, for the rest of his life.

Captain Sensible remembers Bolan's daily routine and the high-spirited mood of the T. Rex camp during the March 1977 tour. "Marc was chirpy and happy to be out touring," he says. "There was no sense of him being a has-been at all. He actually paid for The Damned to go out with him, and we all travelled together on the same coach. While we were stuffing our faces with egg and chips in the service station, we'd see Marc jogging past our window every few minutes. He didn't smoke, drink or do drugs, though he was still a little bit portly at that stage. I've still got the copy of the *Dandy* album he gave me. He signed it: 'To the Captain. Keep it clean. Marc'. He was very together."

In truth, Marc probably still dabbled occasionally with coke or speed, both of which would have helped him maintain a trim figure as long as he ate and drank sensibly. "There might have been the odd digression on the 'Dandy' tour," reckons Jeff Dexter, "but it wasn't like the madness you'd normally find on the road. Everybody tooted in those days, but it certainly wasn't serious stuff."

"When Marc got slim again, we laughed because he said after all the money he'd spent going to a health farm all he had to do was change his diet," Gloria remembers. "He was very sensible. He went more or less back to a vegetarian diet, only eating vegetables." He also took up cycling. "He loved his bike. He'd often ride it over to his mom and dad's," she remembers.

Dandy In The Underworld issued to coincide with the start of the tour, was similarly fit and lean but no way was it a punk rock record. In fact, much of it had been recorded the previous autumn before the shock of the new wave had fully sunk in. The material was more tightly focused than on any Bolan album since *The Slider*, the production more direct and the sleeve a punkish portrait in black-and-white, but *Dandy* still vacillated between the grand gestural flourish and pub rock bubblegum. It did, however, give Bolan his first Top 30 album since *Zinc Alloy* early in 1974.

Tapping into the anger and alienation of the Blank Generation just wasn't possible as the old pro put his session musicians through their paces in the refined space of Air Studios in central London. The results, then, were rather mixed and didn't quite live up to Marc's claim that he was "sounding marvellous again". Most of the songs were preceded by a maxim ("A fool's lament is the wise man's milkshake" is how Marc introduced 'I'm A Fool For You Girl') or a signpost ('Jason B. Sad' was "a distant boyfriend of Johnny B. Goode"), but any conceptual unity was, as always, cosmetic.

The 'Dandy' of the album title might have suggested a possible rewrite of 'Billy Super Duper', but there was little to link the songs together. 'Funky London Childhood' (rewritten as 'Visions Of Domino'), a faintly youthful vibe on the otherwise pedestrian R&B of 'Groove A Little' ("The first punkoid track ever done," claimed Marc farcically) and a hint of urban strife on 'Teen Riot Structure' all lent the record a fashionably social dimension. However, *Dandy* was far too polished a product to rival the first great punk records, such as The Damned's 'New Rose', The Sex Pistols' 'Anarchy In The UK', and The Buzzcocks' *Spiral Scratch* EP.

The album's finest cut was its first. The title track, four-and-a-half minutes of pure Bolan melodrama at its best, found Marc revisiting the Greek mythology that had inspired him back in the days of Tyrannosaurus Rex. His favourite C-Am-F-G chord sequence was back, too, majestically restated despite the cheesy, pomp rock synth.

'Dandy In The Underworld' was 'Teenage Dream' all over again, with Marc surveying the debris of his fractured career – only this time, with lessons learned, he was on his way back up not down. "Distraction he wanted, to destruction he fell," he intoned over a big, confident backing, before inquiring, "When will he come up for air?" and, more to the point, wondering "Will anybody ever care?" The song's final verse moved further away from the discourse on death of the original Orpheus legend on which the song was based, and towards a restatement of the overriding theme of Marc's life. "Change is a monster," he declared, "changing is hard." But Marc had managed to move on, closing the 'plastic soul' chapter of his career and reacquainting himself with the simple rock'n'roll rhythms of his youth.

In a way, the title implied that Marc was a dandy highwayman living off a punk rock underworld, but with the new wave still strictly a minority taste, Marc's guarded affiliation only further confused the marketplace. By the time he filmed what was to be his final appearance on *Top Of The Pops* in March, Marc had got his cheekbones back. But when the new single, 'The Soul Of My Suit', stalled at number 42, it confirmed that Bolan's difficulties were far from over – at least commercially. And there were other problems to deal with that month, too.

Mick Gray had left the T. Rex organisation temporarily due to a car accident in 1976, but he could already see that Marc was becoming suspicious of some of the characters involved in the day-to-day running of his financial affairs. The cash flow problem was one indication, the unsound investments in fine art and Benjiboards, a company set up to exploit the trend for skateboards, was another matter altogether. From March 1977 through to the summer months, Marc Bolan made a series of emphatic moves to root out the bad apples.

Jeff Dexter agrees. "There was not as much money around as there should have been. A lot of it had supposedly been invested wisely but it was filtered away by accountants and lawyers and Marc had begun to realise that. In a funny way, I think he might have held Tony (Howard) responsible, but he was also annoyed with himself for believing the so-called professionals." After discovering that a lot of the investments had been worthless, Bolan began to dispense with the services of several advisers who had been involved in the T. Rex organisation since 1973, around the time the offshore companies were formed.

Many intimates of Marc's during the Seventies are convinced of the existence of a second will that rendered the one drawn up in October 1973 obsolete. But where it ended up, and why it was suppressed, remains a mystery. A Jersey-based trust fund to benefit Rolan Bolan was definitely set up, which tends to support claims that Marc would have drawn up a new will at the same time to also take account of his son. "We will never discover the whole truth now that Tony Howard is dead, but I am certain that he knew more than he let on," says one.

While heads rolled behind the scenes, Marc Bolan became increasingly visible during spring and summer 1977. Acutely aware of the ideological shifts taking place, he began to play his peculiar yet populist card. "Let's face it, I'm unique. Nobody wiggles their bum the way I do," he told *Record Mirror*'s Robin Smith in April. "But seriously, I talk to my fans. I've never set myself on a lofty pedestal; I'm willing to talk to anybody. I also advocate freedom, not only sexually but in every aspect of life." He railed against censorship. "Sex is an art and in 'X' rated movies people are only trying to express their feelings. Why should a minority of people say that the majority of people shouldn't see things?"

Buoyed by the success of the tour, Bolan went into hyperbolic over-drive. "I've given a real kick in the pants to the people who'd written me off," he started quite reasonably. Then he lost it completely. "My band is so strong at the moment it could blow the likes of Queen, Led Zeppelin and The Who right off stage." In truth there were probably a thousand other bands up and down the country that could give the new T. Rex a run for their money. But Bolan, who admitted that the 'Dandy' tour made his ego "bigger than it is already", had once again succumbed – as he did so easily – to fantasy.

A little reality crept back in when, disappointed by Marc's preference to mime on children's television programmes rather than continue going out on the road, second guitarist Miller Anderson quit at the end of June. Ironically, his last appearance with the group was a live-in-the-studio performance for Granada's *Get It Together* filmed on June 22. After the demise of *Supersonic* in March, television outlets became more difficult to find, though Anderson's swansong performance remains one of the finest pieces of T. Rex footage from Marc's later career.

Technically, the group were pretty hot; but it was the visual spectacle of Bolan – slim with chiselled features, his electric hair now uncannily close to that of errant Pink Floyd man Syd Barrett – which was most striking. Marc looked every inch the elegant, decadent cult hero his punk rock cheerleaders wanted him to be. Not that this helped record sales. 'Dandy In The Underworld', remixed and with a new vocal part, was the first T. Rex single to miss out on a chart placing. It's a fact that still beggars belief.

The failure of the single was a setback, but Marc was handed two lifelines early that summer. The first gave him the opportunity to capitalise on his hip elder statesman image by contributing a monthly column for *Record Mirror* (ghostwritten from Marc's notes by his publicist Keith Altham). It allowed him to pontificate on the contemporary music scene, peppering his affection for punk rock with the inevitable lapse into self-mythology.

Pictured only half-mockingly with a crown and sceptre, Bolan kicked off his first missive with a verbal outburst equal to the '20th Century Boy' intro. "I love the raw-edged energy and freshness new wave has brought to the British rock scene. The music of now is NOISE, be it beautiful, elaborate, complex, clean or bestial, primitive, political or raw." He then compared the impact of punk rock with the R&B boom, Led Zeppelin and the birth of heavy metal, and of course glam rock, which was "me, Bowie, Alice Cooper and a couple of other people". He was a little sniffy about punk fashions, though, advising the bondage trousers brigade to vary the styles a bit: "I had imagination," he teased.

His imaginative gifts were capable of moving in truly mysterious ways. In his second column, published in July, he unveiled his ideal supergroup: Leslie West (lead guitar), Steve Jones (rhythm), Marc Bolan (vocals), Billy Preston (organ), Chick Corea (synthesizer), Bob Dylan (harmonica), David Bowie (sax), Iggy Pop and Lou Reed (backing vocals), with Sid

Vicious and Captain Sensible providing "Stereophonic Spitting". It was a hilarious, wholly unworkable ensemble.

The choice of Leslie West was out of character, and so were Marc's comments regarding matters from beyond the world of rock'n'roll. After bemoaning the media's role in provoking the violence between Teds and punks, for the first time in his life, he acknowledged music as a force for social – and not simply individual – change. "'Anarchy In The UK' and 'God Save The Queen' are going on all around us," he wrote. "Just pick up a newspaper and read about Grunwick, Enoch Powell or the Jubilee celebrations. The Pistols are a bloody good mirror. Anyone who thinks things are not in a mess just does not look around."

Bolan recognised that punk rock operated on a different level to his own, but he increasingly envisaged a role for himself as part of it. After catching the still-unsigned Siouxsie & The Banshees at the Music Machine earlier that summer, he entertained the idea of producing them. There were at least three good reasons why his interest had been aroused: Siouxsie's 'Dreamy Lady' make-up; the band's Bolan-like sense of drama; and the inclusion of '20th Century Boy' in their set.

By the time of Marc's third *Record Mirror* column, published in the first week of August, he had met Muriel Young and Mike Mansfield for lunch in Rags restaurant where they discussed a fresh concept for a television pop show. Marc loved the idea, especially when Young, the producer, suggested it should be a six-episode series called *Marc*. He immediately accepted the proposal and, with the help of Jeff Dexter and manager Tony Howard, began to draw up a list of potential guest artists.

Initially, he told his *Record Mirror* congregation that Presley, Sinatra, Vera Lynn, The Rolling Stones, Parliament, David Bowie and Iggy Pop might be worth approaching. But for a 4.15pm light entertainment slot aimed at children returning home from school, *Marc* was more suited to Stephanie De Sykes, Showaddywaddy, The Bay City Rollers, Mud, Rosetta Stone and a regular dance troupe called Heart Throb. Bolan kept his own slots fairly lowbrow, too, mixing new versions of his hits with recent singles, chucking in the occasional teenage favourite such as the old Marty Wilde hit, 'Endless Sleep' and Chris Montez's 'Let's Dance' to vary it a bit. Oddly, at the same time, he wrote in his column that, "I hope you'll feel I'm moving with the times 'cos I gave up doing remakes of Sun record oldies with 'I Love To Boogie'."

What made *Marc* different was the outlet it gave for new wave acts: Generation X, The Jam, Boomtown Rats, The Rods, and a group of old wavers dressed up as new, Radio Stars, fronted by his ex-John's Children colleague Andy Ellison, all received invaluable exposure on the show.

"I was jogging down the King's Road towards the studios where the band were rehearsing," Ellison remembers, "and I heard this Mini hooting at me. The window went down and it was Marc and Gloria. We talked about Radio Stars, and he told me about his television series starting soon, and said that I must come and do it. I never thought he'd get back to me, but not long afterwards, we were invited to do the show."

"With the programme it felt like he was almost starting again, and he seemed to identify with what was going on at the time," said Siouxsie Sioux in 1997. Part of what was going on at the time was informed by a new playfulness in terms of sexual orientation. In the sixth and final episode, *Marc* – who often dressed in pink or in leopard skin for the programme – says, "There is a new group called Generation X. They have a new singer called Billy Idol, who's supposed to be as (takes a pink rose to his nose and sniffs it) pretty as me."

"Marc would often make camp remarks," Mick Gray maintains. "He'd talk about Mickey and him getting married or comment about 'Reg' and John Reid having the honeymoon suite at the Chateau. Although I never experienced or observed a gay side to Marc, he had a feminine side which was obvious. And he still hung out with gays, but that was part of the scene. Even Gloria seemed to have quite a few gay friends."

For much of the filming of *Marc*, which took place at Granada's television studios in Manchester, Gloria was away in America recording what was to become her *Windstorm* album. His confidant while she was away in Los Angeles was Jeff Dexter. "I spent six weeks with him constantly. Sometimes Eric Hall was with us. Otherwise, the only other idiot on the block was Steve Harley. When we were on our own, we were a couple of oiks from London. It was good for him, and good for me to be with him. We hadn't been so close since 1972."

Gloria kept in regular contact with Marc by phone. "The show gave him a new lease of life and exposed his music to a new market," she says. "He was very happy about the two or three million viewers he'd get each week." But really, genuinely happy? Neither Mick Gray nor Jeff Dexter thought that Marc Bolan was ever truly happy – at any time during his life. He wasn't necessarily miserable either, but the more he let his front slip, the more confused he seemed to become.

Friends were in short supply, too. "Ringo and Marc were close for a while but stopped seeing each other after the split with June," says Mick

Gray. "Harry Nilsson was a big pal of Ringo's really. Alice and Marc were nodding acquaintances who hardly knew each other. Elton was another friend but he too went with the split with June. Jeff Lynne and Roy Wood were ships in the night that came and went. Steve Harley hung in there for a while but Marc and him were not that close." Gray maintains that Marc's only close friend was Jeff Dexter.

"I supposed we had so much shared history," Jeff says, "and that meant I didn't have to bullshit with him." Marc and Jeff picked up again properly during T. Rex's visit to France over the Christmas period at the end of 1976. "Christmas Eve was a turnaround really. That was the first time we had spent two whole days together without anybody else around."

Jeff admits that his close pal of 15 years could be "unbearable for much of the time", but, he says, during August and the early part of September 1977, Marc had "become a more real person than he had been during the previous five years. He opened up." Even though Bolan had cleaned up his act considerably since returning to London in mid-1975, the Marc Bolan who took his television show incredibly seriously, who went to bed early each night and who rediscovered his passion for reading was a new man.

Despite the calm exterior, there were several deep vibrations erupting in the pit of Marc's stomach. And not always good ones. "There were going to be some changes," Jeff insists, without being specific. Mick Gray, too, had heard that Marc was re-evaluating his life. For starters, although it's not being suggested that there was anything in it other than reopening old channels of communication, both are fairly certain that Marc had met June Bolan on more than one occasion that summer.

"June was adamant that she and Marc met quite regularly during 1977 for lunch and talking through things," says Mick Gray. "She insisted that they both visited Mick O' Halloran, who was in intensive care in hospital in Portsmouth that summer. June told me that she made Marc go, because he was squeamish about sickness and had refused to visit (his driver) Alphi when he was in intensive care." Marc apparently left a metal Buddha by Mick's bedside.

How many times they met and for what reason remains a mystery, but Jeff Dexter also believes it happened. "Twice," he says. But how does he know? "Just a hunch," he says. June Bolan maintained until the very day she died that she had meetings with Marc during 1977.

There was nothing necessarily suspicious about the trysts. Gloria Jones maintains that she and Marc were blissfully happy in their new home that last summer. "We finally got the rooms painted. We had a lounge in the bedroom, we had a piano room and Marc had a room for his guitars and things. We were just getting settled, and though they were still renovating the house, Marc was hoping that everything would be ready for January when we planned to get married. We had planned to grow old together."

"I'd heard that too," says Jeff Dexter. Marc, though, had always been pretty coy on the subject. As late as August 1977 in a profile in the *TV Times*, he said, "We have no intention of getting married. Marriage is such a juvenile thing. Rolan is our bond; our common interest in things like music, sex, watching the telly is what is keeping us together. Gloria and I don't need anything else."

However, privately, Marc was a man with – as his song says – hang-ups. He was, it seems, reaching another crossroads in his life, just as he had done in 1970 and again in 1973. "Everything is sweet, babe/Then everything is the pits," he sang in 'Hang-Ups'. Another song, 'Pain And Love', that ended with the words, "Don't make my life so lonely", was equally doubt-ridden. So often happy on the outside, it's quite likely that Marc was prone to depression whenever he was alone and forced to confront himself. And that summer, with his lover away, his son with his parents and he alone with an old mate filming in Manchester, Marc was forced to face himself rather more often than he might have preferred.

Perhaps he'd had too much time to think. According to Dexter, "Marc wanted to do some things that I didn't think were very good. It wasn't real enough. Yes, I suppose it was about a life and career change. I think he probably wanted to get back to his roots."

Marc also felt remorseful about some of his actions that had been prompted by his drink and drug nadir. "I think he felt more sorry for himself than for anyone else," Dexter says. "It made me think: when I first got to know him, he actually pretended he was a fighter then." But by September 1977, Marc had become a changed man. "He was a parent, a father, he was always very responsible and he was there for people," Gloria adds.

The climax to this long, strange summer took place on Wednesday September 7, 1977. David Bowie, who had a new single to promote, had agreed to fly in from Switzerland to film a segment for the final edition of the *Marc* show. Months earlier, Bowie had said, "I never had any competition except Marc Bolan back in England . . . I fought like a madman to beat him. Knowing theoretically there was no race. But wanting passionately to do it."

That balance between comradeship and competitiveness was severely tested shortly after Bowie pulled up in his limousine outside the Manchester studio, with an entourage that included Coco Schwab, his publicist Barbara de Witt and a bodyguard. "Stars are a pain," sighs Jeff Dexter. "We hadn't had one problem in five weeks apart from a few dodgy fans. It had been a great morning. Marc had been as sweet as a nut.

"I'd driven down to the station to pick Tony Howard up from the airport, and as we walked through the studio back door, a guy stops us and says, 'Sorry, it's a closed session.'" Apparently, several journalists had been invited by Keith Altham to witness the historic spectacle of Marc and David sharing a stage together for the first time, but Bowie's camp was not amused. That Tony Newman and Herbie Flowers still had some scores to settle with David over pay dating back to the 'Diamond Dogs' tour only added to the powder-keg atmosphere.

"I walk in and go screaming at the security man," Dexter continues. "Of course, this happens with stars all the time. David may simply have said that he didn't want people at the rehearsals. Anyway, the guy from the record company and David's management and minders threw everyone out of the TV studio, even the union floor manager. The union called a meeting, and that's why the show never got properly finished."

Marc offered David a guitar as a peace offering; another guitar got smashed to smithereens. The producer Johnny Hamp went hopping mad when he heard what had happened. And after the filming had finished, there were plenty of tears all round. On screen, though, the summit meeting of the two glam dames appeared to be a masterclass in Superstar diplomacy.

Having filmed their respective individual performances earlier in the day – Bowie premiered '"Heroes"', Marc turned in a convincing revival of 'Debora' – the pair returned around tea-time to record 'Standing Next To You', in essence a riff with no tune to go with it. Due to the problems encountered earlier in the day, the production crew threatened to stop filming dead on 7pm. With the seconds ticking away, Marc – dressed in tight faded jeans and a similarly figure-hugging white T-shirt – hopped onto the stage to join his guest, who was hiding, Presley-like, behind a big pair of shades. Exasperated by earlier events, there was a forlorn look in Marc's eyes as he delivered an abrupt "Thank you and goodbye" to camera in the exaggerated camp style he'd been cultivating throughout the series.

Bolan then bade a second, more convincing farewell, the last one he'd ever give to a public that had ignored and adored him several times over during the course of the past decade. "From all of the boys in the band, David, everybody, all the cats, you know who they are. This is a new song." Bowie counted the group in and the ascending eight-note riff similar to the one the Beatles used for 'Lady Madonna' burst into life. But, even though they'd rehearsed the song several times earlier in the day, Bowie missed his vocal cue. Finding his way in, a split second later, David yelped, "What should I do?" at precisely the same moment that Marc tripped into his microphone, off the stage and out of public life forever. The cameraman zoomed in on Bowie's huge grin before the aggrieved technicians switched the equipment off. It was an ungainly exit for Marc Bolan, and an extraordinarily apt denouement to an infamously puzzling pop friendship.

★   ★   ★

The television show gave Marc something else to think about other than Gloria's absence and the failure of T. Rex's latest single, 'Celebrate Summer'. He'd claimed once again that the song epitomised the new wave sound, but apart from a few seconds of blistering white noise guitar, 'Celebrate Summer' was merely a quirky piece of upbeat pop. But there were other signs that suggested a Bolan renaissance was on the cards. Cube Records (which had inherited the Fly catalogue) had plans to release three songs – 'Ride A White Swan', 'Jeepster' and 'Monolith' – from T. Rex's first brush with fame, plus a previously unreleased song, 'Demon Queen', on an EP titled *Bolan's Best + 1*. Marc's plans for a limited edition 12" of 'Celebrate Summer', backed by 'Solid Gold Easy Action' "at the request of Joey Ramone" never materialised.

Though Marc was eminently newsworthy throughout 1977, there was little evidence that his raised profile was helping him sell more records. With 1973's *Great Hits* long deleted, EMI decided to put together a retrospective collection in time for Christmas. Colin Miles, who was handling the budget price NUT series where the record was destined, had a meeting with Bolan early in September at EMI's Manchester Square offices. "He arrived brimming with confidence," recalls the A&R man, "a wonderful elf-like character who played the part of the camp glam rock star to the hilt. Working on the assumption that artists aren't necessarily the best judges of their own work, I had already drawn up a provisional track listing. But there was a problem. Marc desperately wanted 'Jitterbug Love' (the B-side of 'Children Of The Revolution') on it, whereas I had pencilled in 'The Soul Of My Suit'.

"When I told him I disagreed with his choice, he became very animated and took off on this Nureyev-like ballet routine, complete with sweeping arm gestures and much spinning around on the floor. It was mind-blowing. There was Marc Bolan dancing round my office telling me I'm crazy because I don't like 'Jitterbug Love'. I quickly concluded that the song really ought to go on the record after all and he calmed down."

On Friday September 9, Marc returned to EMI's offices dressed in his fake leopard-skin suit for the photo shoot for what had been provisionally titled *Solid Gold T. Rex*. Earlier that day, he'd entertained a fan who had travelled from Birmingham in order to catch a glimpse of his hero. "It was in my office in Victoria," remembers Keith Altham, "and before the fan arrived Marc was going through his 'Do I have to?' routine. But typically, when it came to it, instead of just spending half-an-hour with him, Marc stayed with him for a couple of hours – even taking him out in his car round London."

The fan, Dave Rooney, arrived brandishing a 'Marc Bolan Is God' badge which delighted Bolan. So did news of an event due to take place at Earl's Court early in October to celebrate Marc's 30th birthday. Both badge and party had been cooked up by two London-based fans, Ros Davies and Colm Jackson. They'd met Marc during the 'Dandy' tour and several times outside the New Bond Street office and, surprised at his accessibility, had published the *Hard On Love* fan magazine with a view to becoming the officially sanctioned British-based branch of the fan club.

The 'Bolanites Unite' event was intended as a hopeful first step, and when Rooney brought the subject up, Marc immediately volunteered to turn up and play. "I shall make a conscious effort to go through what I consider to be the Marc Bolan song book . . . my best songs," he promised. He even floated the idea of calling up Mickey Finn and Steve Took for the occasion.

Marc discussed many topics that afternoon, enthusing proudly about his new version of 'Debora', describing the cratefuls of poetry he'd amassed and declaring his intention to record a live album on the next T. Rex tour. He also gave a curt, though telling insight into the fractured state of the modern mind, the kind of mind that had seen Mark Feld become Marc Bolan, a repository of ideological contradictions, of conflicting drives and desires. "People don't understand you can be five people at the same time," he said, knowing that he'd concealed many facets of his own character in his bid to become Marc Bolan: Superstar. It was a persona that had tended to cloud many subtleties in his thinking, especially during the past few years, although the hint of a personal crisis that summer suggested a potential deepening of Marc's imaginative gifts.

A revival in Bolan's fortunes had been underway since the 'Dandy' tour in March. Marc, had been extremely prolific throughout the year, both publicly and at home, where he recorded informally with Gloria Jones, Steve Harley and even David Bowie. Marc and David, together with what sounds like Gloria (even though she has no recollection of the jam), worked on an incredibly intense – and punkishly vicious – collaboration titled 'Madman', which marked a real shift towards a more anguished, hyper-electric sound. In September 1977, as Marc's 30th birthday approached, he was no more certain of which direction his life and career was going to take than he had been in September 1970 when he excitedly waited for the first pressings of 'Ride A White Swan' to come back from the record plant. But he was pleased when Gloria rang to tell him she was about to come home.

EPILOGUE

"If I Could Have Grown . . ."

"It's a great loss to us. I had a life with this man. I loved this man. I lost my man, you know."

– Gloria Jones (2002)

"It would have been nice to have met up again as a couple of 50-year-olds."

– John Peel (1992)

"I still feel really sad when I see him on television. He was a real giant. What a tragedy his death was."

– Danny Thompson (1992)

Some time around lunchtime on August 16, 1977, Elvis Presley collapsed in his bathroom at his Graceland mansion just outside Memphis. The moment Marc heard the news, he called Gloria in Los Angeles. "Elvis is dead," he mumbled through floods of tears. That singing, dancing demigod who had entered the life of nine-year-old Mark Feld in 1956, and never really left it, was dead at 42. It marked the end of a 21-year-long relationship that had seen Mark grow from fan to contemporary. More painful still, Presley's demise was a rude reminder of Marc's own mortality. "I'd hate to go now," he whispered to Steve Harley. "I'd only get a paragraph on page three."

★ ★ ★

Almost a year earlier, the September 18, 1976 issue of *Record Mirror* saw fit to print a remarkably insignificant piece of pop tittle-tattle. Marc Bolan had been sighted in Morton's restaurant in Berkeley Square, an upmarket locale in central London. What's more, it gushed, he'd signed the visitors' book twice simply to please the receptionist. So Marc Bolan made time for people who showed an interest in him. Big deal.

In the early hours of Friday September 16, 1977, Bolan was back there again. He was celebrating with old friends and new acquaintances, his lover and her brother, his manager and a few strangers eager to make his acquaintance. Then they could go home and tell the folks they'd spent an evening sharing the high life with Marc Bolan – you know, T. Rex, the curly haired one. Used to be famous, didn't he?

Marc was in a convivial mood to put it mildly. Richard Jones had been in the country for a matter of days. Gloria, who'd been away for several weeks working on her record in California, had only recently returned. They had much to celebrate. Bolan was already in talks with Muriel Young for a second series of *Marc*. Earlier in the week, he'd met *Supersonic* producer Mike Mansfield in Morton's where they knocked around a few ideas for a small-screen 'pop opera'. Herbie Flowers had handed in his notice, but Marc had already approached Hawkwind bassist Adrian Shaw about stepping in for a late autumn T. Rex tour of Britain with a view to staying on for some German dates early in 1978.

The route to the late-night rendezvous at Morton's restaurant had been convoluted but nothing out of the ordinary for a back-in-favour pop star. Especially for someone who'd recently been living a subdued existence while keeping fit and well for the duration of the *Marc* show. It was an ordinary day; Thursday September 15. Marc had kept his appointment at the dentist, where he'd arranged to have a bridge inserted. He was so keen to celebrate Gloria's return that he convinced his dental surgeon to share a bottle of wine with him.

Later that afternoon, Marc was picked up by his regular taxi firm to meet up with Gloria and Richard. The trio found a place to eat and drink before Marc remembered that he'd arranged to meet Jeff Dexter at the Speakeasy, the popular music business hangout. Jeff was checking out The Lightning Raiders, a new power-punk band fronted by Andy Allan (son of *Ready, Steady, Go!* producer Elkan Allan), and Bolan, who had heard a rough demo in the T. Rex office, expressed an interest in producing the young singer.

Unfortunately, by the time Marc had arrived at the 'Speak', he was in no fit state to pass judgement. "He was totally pissed, uncontrollably pissed," says Jeff Dexter. "He was loud, aggressive and full of himself. He was even too drunk to eat." Jeff was mildly surprised, but more than that, he was gravely disappointed. "It had all gone pear-shaped. Gloria had only been back for two days and Marc had turned into a lush."

After briefly sitting in with Alfalfa, who were playing a Thursday night residency at the Speakeasy, Marc, together with Gloria and Richard, drove on to Morton's. "I called Tony (Howard), who was already there, and I said, 'Tone, watch out, Marc's on his way and he's arseholed,'" says Dexter. "They were going there to meet Eric Hall. I was supposed to go there too, but I wasn't gonna carry on with the drunks."

Shortly after midnight, the trio arrived at the restaurant, a popular haunt for celebrities, particularly Jewish entertainers. Eric Hall, the EMI promotions man who had known Marc since the Stamford Hill days and had pranced around in a frog suit with T. Rex at the *Rollin' Bolan* special, told Ted Dicks that, "We had planned a welcome home meal for Gloria." It had been a lovely evening, Hall added, though by 1am, he'd gone.

According to Morton's secretary Jennifer Sharp, Marc and his small group of friends ate in the upstairs restaurant, where a blonde singer called Victoria serenaded them with some gentle songs on the piano. Richard Jones took a particular interest in her performance, and when the eight- or nine-strong party adjourned to the bar downstairs, where a light music quartet of saxophone, trumpet, bass and piano continued to play, Victoria and a few other stragglers joined them.

"It was just a wonderful evening with all of our friends," says Gloria Jones. As the night wore on, the mood became more intimate, and Marc persuaded Gloria to sit at the piano and play a few songs. "I got up and I did a number and then everybody asked for more," she recalls. "Marc was telling me how much he loved me; I was telling him how much I loved him. It was a glorious, glorious time. We all had a beautiful night."

Despite the fact that Marc kept an account with a taxi firm that he used regularly, the party left Morton's at around 4.00am in the early hours of Friday September 16, and decided to make their own way home. "We didn't have a driver that night," says Gloria. "It was just one of those things. It was just a strange evening. Before we had the tragedy it was a wonderful evening with everybody who was involved in our lives. We were all together for Marc for that last night not realising . . . He was happy, he was pleased with his television show and he was in a really good frame of mind."

It was still dark, but at that time in the morning, the roads were empty. Two cars made their way through the streets of South Kensington and Fulham, back to Marc and Gloria's house in Upper Richmond Road West. Without the London traffic, they thought, they'd probably make it home in less than 20 minutes. Gloria drove Marc in a purple Mini 1275 GT. Richard Jones, who had persuaded Victoria the pianist at Morton's to join them, followed close behind.

Minutes before 5.00am, the two-car convoy had crossed Putney Bridge and was on the final stretch home. Richard Jones remembers seeing the tail lights of the Mini vanish over the humpback bridge along Queens Ride, a treacherous B-road that skirts the southernmost part of Barnes Common. The tree-lined road was still engulfed in darkness, but as he approached the bridge, Richard saw clouds of steam rising.

The next thing he saw was the wreckage of the Mini. The front of the small car had almost completely caved in, having crushed on impact as it careered off the road at the bend that lay immediately beyond the bridge. The car had smashed into a tree and the passenger's side had taken the brunt of the collision.

Leaping from his own car, Richard Jones' fears were immediately confirmed. Inside, he saw his sister caught between the steering-wheel and her seat. The car engine had trapped her foot under the clutch, and though Gloria Jones was barely conscious at least she was breathing.

Marc, whose longstanding fear of machines had dissuaded him from ever learning to drive, was still in the passenger seat. But such was the force of the impact on the left-hand side of the car that the seat had turned 180 degrees and was now wedged in the back half of the vehicle. Richard was in no doubt that Marc Bolan, his lifeless body dressed in a pair of orange glitter lycra trousers and a fluorescent green-and-white top, was dead.

Barnes Police Station logged the incident at 5.58am. Shortly afterwards, Marc Bolan was pronounced dead on arrival at Queen Mary's Hospital in nearby Roehampton. By 7.30am, his death was being reported on radio news bulletins. Maria Callas died later that same day, but it was the legendary opera singer who was relegated to page three. "MARC BOLAN KILLED IN CRASH" was the story all the papers led with.

At the inquest, held at Battersea Coroner's Court on November 24, 1977, the cause of death was recorded as "shock and haemorrhage due to multiple injuries consistent with road traffic accident. Passenger in a private motor car which collided with a tree. Accidental."

At one stage, it seemed likely that Gloria Jones would face prosecution charges "for driving while unfit through drink and possibly for driving with excess alcohol in her blood", according to Inspector William Wilson. While this fact tended to hog the headlines, serious attention was also given to the state of the car she was driving. The Mini had been serviced either one or two days (depending on which account you believe) prior to the accident. It had been taken to a garage in Sheen, close to Marc and Gloria's home, where the car's wheels were balanced and a tyre had been replaced.

When the Mini was examined after the accident, the pressure in the offside front tyre was only 16lbs, 12lbs less than it should have been; one of the rear tyres was marginally down; and two nuts on one of the front wheels were not even finger tight. There was also talk that the vehicle may have been one of several used by Pink Floyd's management company, and that it had been 'souped up' in accordance with the band's thirst for high speed motor-racing.

★ ★ ★

On Tuesday September 20, four days after the fatal accident which had left Marc Bolan dead and Gloria suffering from facial injuries and unable to speak because her jaw had been wired up, Marc's manager Tony Howard visited her in hospital. She'd been inundated with flowers and messages from well-wishers, but the news that Marc had been killed had been kept from her until she was off the danger list. It had fallen to Tony Howard to break the news.

That same day, a huge gathering of family, friends, fans, music industry associates, and assorted voyeurs flooded through the gates of Golders Green Crematorium to pay their respects to Mark Feld, to Marc Bolan and to a 20th Century Superstar.

The lure of many big-name stars – David Bowie, Rod Stewart, Steve Harley, Linda Lewis, The Damned, The Brotherhood Of Man, Alvin Stardust, and Tony Visconti and his wife Mary Hopkin – brought out the autograph hunters, which particularly sickened Marc's one-time producer. "It was making a mockery of the whole thing," Visconti says.

That the event was a spectacle of the grandest order was rather apt. Eight limousines filled with staff from EMI Records filed by. There were floral tributes from Elton John, Gary Glitter, Keith Moon, the members of T. Rex and the man Mark Feld once aspired to become, Cliff Richard. A huge white swan, four feet tall and five feet long, had been painstakingly constructed with chrysanthemums. Marc's name was spelled out beside it in flowers of red, green, blue and grey. The accompanying card from Tony Howard contained a simple message: "In life, in death, in love".

The sombre atmosphere was inevitably inflected with a sense of disbelief. No one there expected to mourn the death of someone so young, an enormous presence who had been a fixture of domestic and international life for almost a decade. Many had come to say goodbye to someone they'd never met. But they too felt that they knew him. After all, the public Marc Bolan was no less real than the private Mark Feld; Marc himself believed in Bolan more than he ever believed in Feld. The reality of the fans' collective imagination remains an essential part of Marc Bolan's life story. Located in it are the same drives, and the same transgression of rules and obstacles that compelled Mark Feld to choose the kind of life he lived.

Predictably, Rabbi Henry Goldstein spoke of two Marc Bolans: "The real one – a good-natured boy who loved his parents – and the image projected on stage. Now those who knew him as one or other are united to mourn his death," he said. There were other Marc Bolans, too: the creative spirit who immersed himself in weird and wonderful worlds and who refused to conform; the fame seeker who desired to become public property and then found himself trapped by it; the pained man who sought solace in drink and drugs and then found a kind of peace again without recourse to either. Marc Bolan, whose songs celebrated seagulls and swans, Jeepsters and Cadillacs, had been forever on the move. It was shocking to accept that he'd been stilled, and so suddenly and violently.

As his body was prepared for cremation, it was wrapped in his favourite pair of black velvet trousers, with the red and green diamond pattern down the sides of each leg, and a silk top with the letters M-A-R-C emblazoned on the front. However, in accordance with the Jewish faith, they were probably removed prior to immolation. It was something the ex-Stamford Hill Mod would have appreciated.

In an extract from his 1966 diary, Marc Bolan wrote: "I make it to sleep and dream of going to Heaven, and seeing Big Daddy and having some scenes. You know when I get to them pearly gates, they were old and rusty and deserted. I made it through only to see weeds and darkness everywhere. When, then in the distance, I saw a huge temple of gold. I ran up but once more it was real rusty. Inside was much the same, must have been cool once upon a time, but now it was as if the great God of Heaven and Earth were dead and I hadn't noticed it before . . . Guess it was a bad dream."

A bad dream: that was exactly what so many people felt when they woke up to the news on the morning of September 16, 1977. Marc Bolan dead? Well, what's that I hear on the radio then? "Catch a bright star and place it on your forehead/Say a few spells and there you go . . ."

Whatever Happened To . . .?

Marc Bolan is dead – and, as the following grim roll call reveals, so are an extraordinary number of his friends and associates. Thankfully, a few are still alive and well . . .

June Bolan
After her split from Marc in 1973, June lived with Arrows drummer Paul Varley, giving birth to their daughter, Iona, in 1978. She suffered a fatal heart attack on September 1, 1994 while holidaying in Turkey.

Rolan Bolan
Marc's son was brought up in California by his mother, Gloria Jones, and, after leaving school in the early Nineties, has attempted to follow his father into the entertainment world. He has recorded and performed as Rolan Bolan and the Brothers Bounce, and is currently modelling for Tommy Hilfiger.

David Bowie
The death of his old pal and rival hit Bowie hard, and he continues to speak about Marc Bolan with respect and affection. He performed Bolan's '20th Century Boy' at the Brit Awards alongside Placebo, and remains a Superstar, albeit one with distinctly 21st century hues.

Denny Cordell
The New Breed/Essex Music/Regal Zonophone whizz kid beat a slow retreat from the music business after his Sixties heyday and eventually moved to Ireland where he died on February 18, 1995.

Steve Currie
After leaving T. Rex in 1976, the bassist played on a number of sessions, most notably for guitarist Chris Spedding, before moving to Portugal. He was killed in a car crash on April 28, 1981.

Jeff Dexter
Still pint-sized and sartorially as sharp as ever, Jeff occasionally dabbles in rock management and continues to work on his own magnum opus.

Harry Feld
Marc's elder brother carries the torch for Marc and the immediate Feld family. He is happily married and living on the south coast where he works in the local transport department.

Phyllis Feld
Marc's mother died on January 11, 1991.

Simeon Feld
Marc's father died on September 19, 1991.

Mickey Finn
Finn has guested with The Blow Monkeys, and even Bolan tribute band T. Rextasy. But apart from infrequently selling his tales of life in rock'n'-roll's fast lane to the tabloids, he remains a quiet, reclusive character.

Tony Howard
Little was heard of Bolan's ex-manager until he died in 2002.

Gloria Jones
In the wake of Marc's death, Gloria left England and attempted to rebuild her life in the States. She has released several albums, and continues to work with new artists. Jones is currently living in South Africa where she devotes much of her time to working with children living with Aids.

Richard Jones
Gloria's brother continued to work in the music industry throughout the Eighties and Nineties in a variety of capacities – musician, manager, record importer. At the time of his death, on April 13, 2001 from a heart attack, he was advising his nephew Rolan on his career.

Mike Leander
The arranger/producer/songwriter behind Gary Glitter, Leander amassed a considerable fortune during the Glam Rock years. He died on April 18, 1996.

Bill Legend
Bill continues to play drums when he can in and around the Essex area and occasionally guests with T. Rex-related bands.

Simon Napier-Bell
After a relatively quiet Seventies, the impresario finally came good with Japan, and then Wham! during the Eighties. He has written two volumes of memoirs and still dabbles in pop management.

Riggs O'Hara
'The Wizard' is alive and well and living in West London where he remains deeply committed to community theatre.

John Peel
Peel remains Radio 1's premier DJ and his championing of everyone from Bolan and Bowie through punk rock and beyond has made him arguably the most influential man in British music.

David Platz
The publishing mogul continued to expand his empire after Bolan quit his organisation in 1971. He died aged 65 from motor neurone disease on May 20, 1994.

Chelita Secunda
The flamboyant T. Rex publicist moved in quieter circles after her time with Bolan, though still with characteristic grace. She died of a heart attack on March 7, 2000.

Tony Secunda
After a brief spell managing Steve Took during 1972, Secunda worked with Steeleye Span and later Marianne Faithfull, though he never regained the foothold he had in the pop market during the Sixties. He moved into publishing and uprooted to Anselmo, California, where he died of a heart attack on February 12, 1995.

Ringo Starr
Despite a very public battle with alcoholism, Ringo has survived two of his ex-Beatles colleagues and continues to tour with his All-Starr Band.

Steve Peregrine Took

Having parted from Bolan in autumn 1969, Took never quite managed to find his way out of Ladbroke Grove. After a series of aborted attempts at reactivating his career, he died on October 27, 1980 after choking on a cherry stone, having blown his final royalty cheque on a variety of illicit substances.

Tony Visconti

The producer split with Bolan late in 1973, and returned to David Bowie, with whom he went on to record a string of pioneering rock albums throughout the decade. Now widely recognised as one of the world's top record producers, Visconti has recently been reunited with Bowie after a 20-year hiatus, producing David's summer 2002 album, *Heathen*.

Discography

MARC BOLAN & T. REX: On Vinyl and CD

Marc Bolan's recorded legacy is a rich, though sometimes hazardous terrain. There are two important elements to this discography: to highlight the original vinyl records (and one or two posthumous goodies), and to provide a judicious guide to what's available on CD. Much money has been wasted on shoddy, unnecessary Marc Bolan and T. Rex releases that confuse the marketplace and do endless harm to his reputation. Happily, matters have improved greatly since 1992 – at last the T. Rex albums are out there in their original sleeves, with decent notes and appropriate bonus tracks, for example – which has done much to rescue Bolan from slipping into some kind of Gary Glitter pantomime figure.

ORIGINAL VINYL RELEASES

Singles

As Marc Bolan

The Wizard/Beyond The Risin' Sun
November 1965; Decca F 12288

The Third Degree/San Francisco Poet
June 1966; Decca F 12413

Hippy Gumbo/Misfit
December 1966; Parlophone R 5539

With John's Children

Desdemona/Remember Thomas A'Beckett (Bolan on A-side only)
April 1967; limited number with picture sleeve; Track 604 003

Midsummer Night's Scene/Sara Crazy Child
June 1967; release cancelled, though some 25 copies were apparently given away at the John's Children club in Leatherhead; Track 604 005

Come And Play With Me In The Garden/Sara Crazy Child (Bolan on B-side only)
August 1967; limited number with picture sleeve; Track 604 005

Go Go Girl/Jagged Time Lapse
October 1967; A-side is a version of Bolan's 'Mustang Ford' and features Marc on guitar; Track 604 010

With Tyrannosaurus Rex

Debora/Child Star
April 1968; some with picture sleeve; Regal Zonophone RZ 3008; No. 34

One Inch Rock/Salamanda Palaganda
August 1968; some with picture sleeve; Regal Zonophone RZ 3011; No. 28

Pewter Suitor/Warlord Of The Royal Crocodiles
January 1969; Regal Zonophone RZ 3016

King Of The Rumbling Spires/Do You Remember
July 1969; some with picture sleeve; Regal Zonophone RZ 3022; No. 44

By The Light Of A Magical Moon/Find A Little Wood
January 1970; Regal Zonophone RZ 3025

With T. Rex

Ride A White Swan/Is It Love/Summertime Blues
October 1970; picture sleeve; Fly BUG 1; No. 2

Hot Love/Woodland Rock/King Of The Mountain Cometh
February 1971; Fly BUG 6; No. 1

Get It On/There Was A Time/Raw Ramp
July 1971; Fly BUG 10, picture sleeve; 7/71; No. 1

Jeepster/Life's A Gas
November 1971; Fly BUG 16; No. 2

Telegram Sam/Cadillac/Baby Strange
January 1972; T. Rex Wax Co. T. REX 101; No. 1

Metal Guru/Thunderwing/Lady
May 1972; T. Rex Wax Co. MARC 1; No. 1

Children Of The Revolution/Jitterbug Love/Sunken Rags
September 1972; T. Rex Wax Co. MARC 2; No. 2

Solid Gold Easy Action/Born To Boogie
December 1972; T. Rex Wax Co. MARC 3; No. 2

T. Rex Christmas Record
December 1972; flexidisc free to Fan Club members

20th Century Boy/Free Angel
March 1973; T. Rex Wax Co. MARC 4; No. 3

The Groover/Midnight
June 1973; T. Rex Wax Co. MARC 5; No. 4

Truck On (Tyke)/Sitting Here
November 1973; T. Rex Wax Co. MARC 6; No. 12

Teenage Dream/Satisfaction Pony
January 1974; T. Rex Wax Co. MARC 7; No. 13

Light Of Love/Explosive Mouth
July 1974; T. Rex Wax Co. MARC 8; No. 22

Zip Gun Boogie/Space Boss
November 1974; T. Rex Wax Co. MARC 9; No. 41

New York City/Chrome Sitar
July 1975; T. Rex Wax Co. MARC 10; No. 15

Dreamy Lady/Do You Wanna Dance/Dock Of The Bay
As T. Rex Disco Party; September 1975; T. Rex Wax Co. MARC 11;
No. 30

London Boys/Solid Baby
February 1976; T. Rex Wax Co. MARC 13; No. 40

I Love To Boogie/Baby Boomerang
June 1976; T. Rex Wax Co. MARC 14; No. 13

Laser Love/Life's An Elevator
September 1976; T. Rex Wax Co. MARC 15; No. 41

To Know Him Is To Love Him/City Port
as Marc Bolan & Gloria Jones; January 1977; EMI 2572

The Soul Of My Suit/All Alone
March 1977; T. Rex Wax Co. MARC 16; No. 42

Dandy In The Underworld/Groove A Little/Tame My Tiger
May 1977; picture sleeve; T. Rex Wax Co. MARC 17

Celebrate Summer/Ride My Wheels
August 1977; picture sleeve; T. Rex Wax Co. MARC 18

Albums

With Tyrannosaurus Rex

MY PEOPLE WERE FAIR AND HAD SKY IN THEIR HAIR . . .
BUT NOW THEY'RE CONTENT TO WEAR STARS ON THEIR
BROWS
July 1968; with lyric sheet; mono/stereo [S]LRZ 1003; No. 15

PROPHETS, SEERS & SAGES THE ANGELS OF THE AGES
October 1968; with lyric sheet; mono/stereo [S]LRZ 1005

UNICORN
May 1969; mono/stereo [S]LRZ 1007; No. 12

A BEARD OF STARS
March 1970; with lyric sheet; mono/stereo [S]LRZ 1013; No. 13

With T. Rex

T. REX
December 1970; semi-gatefold sleeve; Fly HIFLY 2; No. 13

ELECTRIC WARRIOR
September 1971; with illustrated inner sleeve and black-and-white poster;
HIFLY 6; No. 1

THE SLIDER
July 1972; with inner lyric sleeve; T. Rex Wax Co BLN 5001; No. 4

TANX
March 1973; illustrated inner sleeve and black-and-white poster; BLN 5002; No. 4

GREAT HITS
September 1973; with colour poster; BLN 5003; No. 32

ZINC ALLOY AND THE HIDDEN RIDERS OF TOMORROW/ A CREAMED CAGE IN AUGUST
February 1974; inner lyric sleeve and gatefold cover; BLNA 7751; No. 12

BOLAN'S ZIP GUN
as Marc Bolan & T. Rex; February 1975; inner sleeve and die-cut cover; BLNA 7752

FUTURISTIC DRAGON
January 1976; inner lyric sleeve; BLN 5004; No. 50

DANDY IN THE UNDERWORLD
February 1977; inner sleeve and die-cut cover; BLN 5005; No. 26

Miscellaneous Vinyl Releases

45s

Marc Bolan as Toby Tyler
The Road I'm On (Gloria)
March 1990; Archive Jive TOBY 1
A one-sided collectable now eclipsed by various CD releases.

Jasper C. Debussy/Hippy Gumbo/The Perfumed Garden Of Gulliver Smith
August 1974; picture sleeve; Track 2094 013

Return Of The Electric Warrior EP: Sing Me A Song/Endless Sleep/The Lilac Hand Of Menthol Dan
March 1981; picture sleeve; Rarn MBFS 001

The two rare cuts on the above two releases, 'Perfumed Garden' and 'Lilac Hand', have since been made available on Sanctuary's expanded edition of *The Beginning Of Doves* (a collection of demos from 1966–67 originally released in June 1974; Track 2410 201). Many of these demos reappeared alongside the previously unheard 'I'm Weird' and 'Horrible Breath (You Scare Me To Death)' on *You Scare Me To Death* (October 1981; with booklet; Cherry Red ERED 20), albeit with instrumentation added posthumously.

John's Children

The best vinyl entrée into the wayward world of John's Children is *A Midsummer Night's Scene* (1987; inner sleeve; Bam Caruso KIRI 095), which includes the three Bolan-era singles, plus the band's other singles. The same label also released a 12″ edition of 'Midsummer Night's Scene' which included non-Bolan versions of Marc's 'Jasper C. Debussy' (retitled 'Casbah Candy') and 'Hippy Gumbo'.

Two John's Children mini-albums, *Playing With Themselves Vols. 1 & 2* (Zinc Alloy Records MLP 9001/2; 1990/91) include several Bolan-era performances, including a complete instrumental take of 'Sally Was An Angel' (the version that finds Bolan sharing verses with Andy Ellison remains unreleased).

A radio-friendly re-recording of 'Desdemona' (with a keyboard overdub and the offending lyric altered to "Why do you have to lie") turned up on *Marc: The Words And Music Of Marc Bolan, 1947–1977* (April 1978; 2-LPs, gatefold sleeve; Cube HIFLD 1). Meanwhile, Andy Ellison's 'You Can't Do That' solo 45 (SNB SNB-3308; May 1968) features 'Cornflake Zoo' (a Bolan song but not titled by him) on the B-side, with an audible Bolan backing vocal line and guitar part.

Tyrannosaurus Rex

The Beginning Of Doves includes the duo's earliest sessions, taped for Simon Napier-Bell, and the expanded CD version also features 'Sleepy Maurice', which survived on acetate for almost 25 years before appearing on a limited edition single release in November 1991 (picture sleeve plus insert; Tyrannosaurus Rex Records TYR 001).

Across The Airwaves (February 1982; Cube/Dakota ICS 1004) is a collection of recordings made for BBC Radio, and includes 11 Tyrannosaurus Rex recordings. Six are with Steve Took, including two from the duo's first session appearance late in 1967; and all five from the first electric session with Mickey Finn from November 1969.

Fly cashed in on Bolan's new found popularity in 1971 with *The Best Of T. Rex* (March 1971; Fly TON 2; No. 21) which features two previously unreleased Tyrannosaurus Rex outtakes from spring 1969, 'Once Upon The Seas Of Abyssinia' (29 April) and 'Blessed Wild Apple Girl' (28 May).

Another May 1969 outtake, 'Demon Queen', turned up on the flip of the Bolan's Best + 1 7″ (August 1977; Cube ANT 1); and two first album outtakes, 'Rock Me' (alias 'Puckish Pan') and 'Lunacy's Back' surfaced on the 'Mellow Love' 12″ (January 1982; Marc On Wax SBOLAN 13).

Miscellaneous Releases

Oh Baby/Universal Love
credited to Dib Cochran & The Earwigs; August 1970; Bell 1121

Blackjack/Squint Eyed Mangle
credited to Big Carrot; August 1973; EMI EMI 2047

Sunken Rags (acoustic version) appears on the *Glastonbury Fayre* album; July 1972; 3-LPs, fold-out sleeve, with booklet and inserts; Revelation REV 1/2/3

Bolan's session/guest appearances

Beware: Bolanic myth making has distinctly muddied this area!

As Tony Visconti has stated, the rumoured Bolan/Bowie sessions are little more than wishful thinking, at least during those years prior to the mid-Seventies. Only 'The Prettiest Star' (March 1970; Mercury MF 1135) can be confirmed as a genuine collaboration that made it on to vinyl.

Bolan sang a brief line on Marsha Hunt's version of 'My World Is Empty Without You' which appeared alongside three Bolan originals (none of which feature him) on her *Woman Child* album (November 1971; Track 2410 101).

As Bolan increasingly frequented the Superstar circuit, he invariably ended up at several big-name recording sessions. One of these was for Alice Cooper, though rumours that he played on 'Hello Hurray' and 'Slick Black Limousine' remain unconfirmed.

The friendship with Ringo Starr led to the *Born To Boogie* film but little else. Marc contributed the title and the inspiration for Ringo's T. Rex-like 'Back Off Boogaloo' 45, and played guitar on one song, 'Have You Seen My Baby?' (alias 'Hold On'), on the *Ringo* album

(November 1973; gatefold sleeve and lyric booklet, Apple PCTC 252; No. 7).

Marc's recently confirmed session with ELO in April 1973 gets its official seal of approval on a new remastered edition of the band's 1973 *ELO II* album (Harvest). Marc's guitar-playing can be heard on 'Ma Ma Ma Belle', 'Dreaming Of 4000' and a previously unknown track, 'Everyone's Born To Die'.

One further collaboration, with Ike and Tina Turner, came in the midst of his American adventures. Marc played guitar on the second side of the 'Sexy Ida' (parts one and two) single (June 1974; United Artists UP 35726).

Around ten tracks were completed for the aborted Pat Hall solo album during the winter of 1973–74, with Bolan producing and playing guitar. Some of the backing tracks were salvaged and utilised for Gloria Jones' Bolan-produced *Vixen* album (December 1976; EMI EMC 3159), for which he contributes guitar parts throughout. He also overdubbed an additional lead line on the single version of 'Go Now'/'Drive Me Crazy (Disco Lady)' (February 1977; EMI EMI 2570).

Marc made two notable guest appearances on guitar during the last months of his life – on 'If I Just Can Get Through Tonight' from Alfalfa's *Alfalfa* (April 1977; EMI EMC 3213); and on 'Amerika The Brave' which turned up on Steve Harley's *Hobo With A Grin* (July 1978; EMI EMC 3254).

NOTABLE POSTHUMOUS T. REX RELEASES

Dozens of unreleased T. Rex recordings have appeared since 1977, scattered across a bewildering number of releases. Between 1982 and 1991, the chief outlet for these was Marc On Wax, the record company arm of the Marc Bolan Fan Club. One of the label's most significant coups was the nearest thing to a *Born To Boogie* soundtrack album in 1991 (2-LPs, with 16-page photo-booklet; gatefold sleeve; Marc On Wax MARC LP 514). This featured live material from the film – suitably doctored at the time by Marc and Visconti – together with the Tea Party sequence and several of the humorous sketches. *T. Rex In Concert* (August 1981; gatefold sleeve; Marc On Wax ABOLAN 1) is a poor-quality document of scrappy performances from the autumn 1971 and spring 1972 British tours. *T. Rextasy* (May 1983; LP + 12"; gatefold sleeve; early copies with a free poster; Marc On Wax ABOLAN 5) is a little better soundwise, though it does include some wild mixing and overdubbed bass parts.

The first major posthumous release was *Marc: The Words And Music Of Marc Bolan, 1947–1977*. Compiled by Tony Visconti, it documents the 1967–1971 era, and included 'The Children Of Rarn Suite', complete with sympathetic overdubs by the producer. The suite later reappeared in the form of a 10″ mini-LP (June 1982; with 12-page booklet; Marc On Wax ABOLAN 2), with the bonus of the original unadorned demo tape on the other side of the disc.

Another early rarity to surface was an acoustic outtake from the 1970 *T. Rex* album, 'One Inch Rock', together with the instrumental title track on the 'Deep Summer' 12″ (July 1982; Rarn MBFS RAP 2).

Two studio albums featuring 1972–1977-era outtakes appeared during the mid-Eighties. *Dance In The Midnight* (October 1983; double gatefold sleeve; Marc MARCL 501) and *Billy Super Duper* (August 1984; inner sleeve; Marc ABOLAN 4) offered welcome glimpses into the archive, but some unwelcome overdubs undermined the venture. (Incidentally, *Billy Super Duper* was not the same as Bolan's unrealised 1975 project.)

Rather more successful was Marc On Wax's *Rarities* series, which delivered four volumes of raw, untampered archive material, offering an important glimpse into the T. Rex archive, albeit with little theme or annotation.

The Marc Shows (1989; gatefold sleeve; Marc On Wax MARCL 513) features a selection of re-recorded hits and rock'n'roll covers taped for Granada Television's *Marc* show in summer 1977.

A double set, *Till Dawn* (November 1985; 2-LPs, gatefold sleeve; Marc On Wax MARCL 509), boasts one disc of acoustic versions of material from *Electric Warrior* and *The Slider* taped for American radio in 1972 together with an album of remixed material. More radio material turned up on *Honey Don't* (March 1990; with plastic outer sleeve; The Tyrannosaurus Rex Appreciation Society TS 14971). Three extracts of poetry recorded for *Top Gear* in 1968 and 1969, sat uneasily alongside material that otherwise dated from the T. Rex era. The sound quality on the US radio sessions, two recorded during the spring 1971 T. Rex tour (work-in-progress for *Electric Warrior*, plus a version of Carl Perkins' 'Honey Don't' and a jam called 'I Love The Way'), was poor. A third session, dating from September 12, 1972 and recorded for WBCN Radio in Boston, includes unique versions of 'The Slider' and 'Left Hand Luke And The Beggar Boys'.

Note: Many of these posthumous vinyl releases have been eclipsed on

CD, which invariably come with better packaging and upgraded sound quality.

Two further albums are worthy of mention. The budget-price *Solid Gold T. Rex* (June 1979; EMI NUT 5) was the compilation Marc had been working on at the time of his death; while *The Unobtainable T. Rex* (September 1980; EMI NUT 28) pulled together virtually all the single material that had yet to find its way onto album (bar 'Laser Love').

Interview Discs

There are several 7″ interview discs. The first (BINT 1) came with early copies of *Marc: The Words And Music*, which included excerpts from a 1973 conversation with Stevie Dixon, backed by tributes from Steve Harley, Jennifer Sharp and John Peel recorded in 1977. The free 7″ flexi (Lyntone LYN 10086) that accompanied the first 20,000 copies of the 'You Scare Me To Death' single, included an interview with Marc conducted by *Melody Maker*'s Chris Welch.

The earliest spoken-word recordings were the extracts from a convivial chat with John Peel, which originally appeared on a Blue Thumb promotional 45 pressed to publicise the 1969 US tour. The three extracts subsequently turned up on the 'Sleepy Maurice' 45.

In 1971, Marc spoke to radio DJ Michael Cuscuna, and the best bits were pressed up for a Warner Brothers promotional album (PRO 511) as *The Electric Warrior Interview*. A year later, the religious broadcasting service *What's It All About?* manufactured a promo-only pressing of a 7″ interview single.

Since 1977, *Where's The Champagne?* (March 1982; picture disc; Rhino RNDF 252) and *Marc Bolan – The Interview* (June 1982; What Records W12 2401), dating from 1971 and 1969 respectively, have appeared. Also look out for the excellent Australian *20th Century Boy* triple album (1981; fold-out sleeve with inserts; EMI MARC 1) which, as well as providing the only vinyl-era overview of Marc's career from 1965–1977, also includes interview extracts at the end of each side. A poor quality interview picture disc, recorded in the States in 1972, has appeared on the Baktabak label.

CD RELEASES

Note: The following list is intended to provide a guide to the best of what's available. If it's not here it's probably not worth bothering with.

Pre-Rex

Marc Bolan as Toby Tyler

The Maximum Sound Session (Zinc Alloy Records ZAR CD 9006; 1993) includes the entire two-track recordings from the original Toby Tyler master tape, plus one finished mix of each song. The sound quality of these multiple takes of 'The Road I'm On (Gloria)' and 'Blowin' In The Wind' are perfect; the performances, though historically crucial, are rather less so. Different mixes of the two songs appear on a CD single, 'Blowin' In The Wind' (Archive Jive ZAR CDS 9005; 1993).

Marc Bolan

The Beginning Of Doves (Sanctuary CMRCD 491; 2002)
A comprehensive and well-presented repackage of Bolan's 1966 and 1967 demos recorded for Track/Simon Napier-Bell. This vastly expanded edition (37 tracks including many outtakes/alternate versions) of the original 1974 album boasts great sound quality, detailed sleeve-notes, a well-illustrated booklet and a slipcase.

John's Children

The Complete John's Children (New Millennium Communications) contains everything you need. It includes the band's five singles, the two Zinc Alloy mini-albums of outtakes, the Radio 1 session, an outtake of 'Hippy Gumbo' that features Bolan plus three Andy Ellison solo recordings.

Tyrannosaurus Rex

All four Tyrannosaurus Rex albums are currently available on CD, though both sound quality and packaging leave much to be desired.

The good news is that *My People Were Fair And Had Sky In Their Hair . . . But Now They're Content To Wear Stars On Their Brows* (A&M

541 009-2), *Prophets, Seers & Sages The Angels Of The Ages* (A&M 541 010-2), *Unicorn* (A&M 541 012-2) and *A Beard Of Stars* (A&M 541 003-2) are likely to be upgraded in 2003.

Meanwhile, for a fine-sounding introduction to Tyrannosaurus Rex seek out the now deleted *Last Of The Great Underground Groups: The Definitive Tyrannosaurus Rex* (Sequel NEX CD 250).

For the live Tyrannosaurus Rex experience, try *Tyrannosaurus Rex: BBC Radio 1 Live In Concert* (Windsong WINCD 032), taped in January 1970. *Midnight Court At The Lyceum* (New Millennium Communications PILOT 28), recorded with Steve Peregrine Took in April 1969, provides a distinctly lo-fi alternative.

T. Rex

The début T. Rex album (A&M 541 011-2) is awaiting an upgrade. After 30 years, *Electric Warrior* was finally afforded a decent repackage in 2001 (A&M 493 113-2) with bonus tracks, and a booklet featuring sleeve-notes and rare photos from Tony Visconti, who also remastered the set. For a second alternate view, try the neatly packaged *Electric Warrior Sessions* (Burning Airlines PILOT 04).

The post 1971 material has, since 1992, been given a significant over-haul. All six original albums are available, each with bonus tracks culled from relevant singles, sleeve-notes and memorabilia-strewn booklets and 20-bit remastering.

The Slider (Edsel EDCD 390), *Tanx* (EDCD 391), *Zinc Alloy And The Hidden Riders Of Tomorrow/A Creamed Cage In August* (EDCD 392), *Bolan's Zip Gun* (EDCD 393), *Futuristic Dragon* (EDCD 394) and *Dandy In The Underworld* (EDCD 395) have also been repackaged as 2-CD sets together with their twin from Edsel's Alternate series. These – *Rabbit Fighter: The Alternate Slider* (Edsel EDCD 403), *Left Hand Luke: The Alternate Tanx* (EDCD 410), *Change: The Alternate Zinc Alloy* (EDCD 440), *Precious Star: The Alternate Zip Gun* (EDCD 443), *Dazzling Raiment: The Alternate Futuristic Dragon* (EDCD 522) and *Prince Of Players: The Alternate Dandy* (EDCD 523) mirror each album by utilising a plethora of outtakes and alternate versions.

The same label has released eight volumes of *Marc Bolan & T. Rex: Unchained*, which provide a comprehensive, fascinating – and just some-times exasperating – raid on the Bolan tape archive. This 'for fans only' series has since been deleted, though some of the better material can be found on *Messing With The Mystic: Unissued Songs 1972–1977* (Edsel EDCD 404) and *Best Of Unchained* (Edsel NEST CD 907).

Edsel have also released the original US-only album, *Light Of Love* (EDCD 413), on CD.

COMPILATIONS

The TV-advertised *Marc Bolan & T. Rex: The Essential Collection* (Universal Music TV 525 961-2) is an obvious starting-place, although the 20-track *Hits! The Very Best Of T. Rex* set, budget price and remastered, is a decent cheap alternative.

For the bigger picture, go straight to the 4-CD *Marc Bolan & T. Rex: 20th Century Superstar* (Universal) box set. It's the first truly comprehensive career summary, and takes in all aspects of Bolan's career – from the earliest demos through John's Children, spin-off 45s, many stray rarities and outtakes, unreleased songs and never-before-heard alternate takes in pristine quality. The booklet includes a 10,000-word essay, and a feast of illustrations (including memorabilia), while all the material has been newly remastered. For a wider view on the 1972–1977 era, head for the 3-CD *A Wizard, A True Star: Marc Bolan & T. Rex 1972–77* box set (Edsel FBOOK 17), a mix of hits, album tracks, outtakes, alternate versions and assorted rarities, spiced with interview segments.

The original 1973 *Great Hits* set provided the basis for two singles compilations, *Great Hits: 1972–1977 – The A Sides* (EDCD 401) and *Great Hits: 1972–1977 – The B Sides* (EDCD 402), both now packaged together as *The T. Rex Wax Co. Singles: A's And B's 1972–77* (Edsel MEDCD 714).

Miscellaneous Releases

Two volumes document T. Rex's regular ventures into the BBC studios. *Tyrannosaurus Rex & T. Rex: A BBC History* (Band Of Joy BOJCD 016) covers the years 1967–1971, while *T. Rex – The BBC Recordings 1970–1976* (New Millennium Communications PILOT 17) surveys the Seventies.

Two non-Edsel collections from the 1972–1977 period are worthy of investigation. *Bump'n'Grind* (Thunderwing TECI 24004) essentially compiles extended and alternate versions of single material, while Shadowhead

(TECI 24055) features more of the same. Be aware that some of the original unmixed tapes have been necessarily remixed for these releases.

Marc Bolan Presents Sister Pat Hall (Edsel EDCD 449) pieces together Pat's aborted, Bolan-produced solo album and throws in a bunch of outtakes, as well as the Big Carrot single.

Live T. Rex albums are generally aimed at connoisseurs. The tape sources are less than perfect for *Live 1977* (Edsel EDCD 530), though the bonus disc, recorded at the Agora Club in Cleveland, Ohio, in November 1974, is a ghoulish delight. *T. Rex Live At The Boston Gliderdrome 1972* (Diamondstar Productions LATBG 02), seeks to document T. Rextasy at its height, but once again, the sound quality leaves much to be desired. European television recordings from 1971 and 1973 provide the material for *Uncaged* (Burning Airlines PILOT 73), which also includes two blurry video performances and sleeve-notes by Bill Legend.

Marc: Songs From The Granada TV Series (Edsel EDCD 545) includes 15 songs taped at the end of his life and broadcast during the *Marc* shows in August and September 1977. Unfortunately, the recordings have necessarily been taken from television footage; consequently, the sound is thin.

Acknowledgements

I'd like to thank the following people who agreed to be interviewed, either for the original book or for this new revised and enlarged biography: Keith Altham, Mick Box, Joe Boyd, Pete Brown, Jeff Dexter, Andy Ellison, Harry and Sandy Feld, Gary Glitter, Mick Gray, Jack Green, Jeff Griffin, Bob Harris, John Hewlett, Dave Hill, Gloria Jones, Janie Jones, Vic Keary, Mike Leander, Bill Legend, Donovan Leitch, Gered Mankowitz, Mike McGrath, Colin Miles, Simon Napier-Bell, John Pearse, John Peel, Frances Perrone, David Platz, Mike Pruskin, Keith Reid, Mick Rock, Pete Sanders, Tony Secunda, Clive Selwood, Captain Sensible, Helen Shapiro, Jerry Shirley, Susan Singer, Danny Thompson, Chris Townson, George Underwood, Tony Visconti, Rick Wakeman, Allan Warren, Mick Wayne, David Wedgbury, plus two close friends of Steve Peregrine Took who prefer to remain unnamed.

Several of the above-named have since died (although for stylistic reasons, original interview material is kept in the present tense throughout the book). Also no longer around are June Bolan and Richard Jones, both of whom answered my questions in an informal, non-interview situation without ever quite consenting to a full grilling.

This heavily revamped biography has benefited greatly from the input of Martin Barden, whose time, knowledge and enthusiasm has been a constant source of inspiration. I am grateful to him on several counts: for opening the door to Gloria Jones and Mick Gray, for encouraging me to develop one or two important aspects that had been shortchanged in the 1992 biography (not least Marc's convoluted financial affairs), for his diplomacy in curbing some of my wilder excesses while proof-reading the book and for allowing me to draw on his interview with Riggs O'Hara. I know he doesn't always agree with my take on Marc Bolan's life and work – and certainly doesn't share my tolerance for the early Tyrannosaurus Rex material – but that has only made his input more invaluable.

Cliff McClenehan, who wrestled with the original script back in 1992, is now a Bolan chronicler in his own right. I am grateful for the many conversations I've shared with him over the years, and for his attention to detail that has since been put to good use in his own *Marc Bolan 1947–1977: A Chronology*. Other keepers of the flame who have assisted in some way include Ros Davies, Paul Johnson (of The Bolan Society), Uwe Klee, Caron Thomas and John Willans.

From Marc's own family, I am indebted once again to his brother Harry and his wife Sandy for permission to use photographs from the family archives; and to Marc's son Rolan, who I hope will understand the need to pursue the truth rather more rigorously this time round.

Others who have contributed to the book (sometimes in obscure ways) include Acid Mothers Temple (the best band in the world right now), Debbie Bennett at CBC PR, Chuck Berry for the chapter headings, Joe Black at Universal Music, Penny 'Britney' Brignell, Rob Caiger, Andy Davis and all the staff at *Record Collector*, Fred Dellar, Peter "Are you sure he's more important than Dylan?" Doggett, Pat Gilbert, Paul Trynka and all the staff at *Mojo* (not least for their patience), Val Jennings at Demon Records, Trevor ("Whatever happened to the Breadwinner album?") King, Mark and Lard for their spirit-raisingly brilliant radio show, Claudia Pinto, John "Weller!" Reed, Carlton Sandercock at New Millennium Communications, the Smersh Bar in Ravey Street, Bob Stanley, the mighty Lucy ("Can I interview Nick Cave for you?") Williams and Jo Kendall at *Kerrang!*, and the amazing Lois 'Little Miss Understood' Wilson, Simon McEwan, Lora "What exactly are we doing on the floor?" Findlay, Tom Bryant, Carol Briggs, Dani Golfieri, David Brolan, Ruth "Not bloody Bolan again!" Dodson and everyone else who helped make *Mojo Collections* such a pleasure to work on.

Chris Charlesworth, the editor at Omnibus Press, commissioned me to update the original book when we bumped into each other at a record fair at Wembley in October, 2001. He didn't expect or deserve such hideously fluctuating deadlines. I'd like to thank him for his flexibility, encouragement and for publishing my first (not very good) book back in 1988. I am also grateful to Andy ("Drink, dear boy?") Neill (co-editor), Helen Donlon (publicity), Steve Behan (picture research) and Johnny Rogan (for expert proofreading and indexing).

I would also like to thank the many journalists who have unknowingly contributed to this book through their original interviews, critiques and reviews. . . . And Roy Wright for the magnificent 1968 photo.

On a personal level, I'd first like to mention two women whose contributions to the book weren't – for different yet entirely understandable reasons – always as positive as they could have been. But we're still talking

. . . So, a passionate embrace to my partner Zulema 'Woman On The Verge Of A Nervous Breakdown' Gonzalez, from whom I was forced to extricate myself for lengthy periods in order to write this book to my satisfaction. And an affectionate farewell to Fiona Bleach who lived through the Bolan story the first time round. Long may you enjoy the considerable charms of D. Von-Stropp in your new rustic bolt-hole.

Much love to Erika and Ben in Wales, to Norman, Julie-Anne, Kirsty and Sophie in Bournemouth, y muchos besos para Concha y Victor en Madrid. Fraternal greetings, too, go out to Simon ("You're not still listening to that shit, are you?") Lamdin and Dave Chapman, Pete ("The original vinyl junkie") McConnell, Mike ("Elton was better") Channing, Chris Fraser and Vanessa Clarke and everyone else whose conversations and various enthusiasms have no doubt left some mark on this book.

Thanks to Essex Music and the Marc Bolan Estate for permission to use extracts from copyrighted material.

Honorable mentions to those who made contributions to the original 1992 biography: Nina Antonia, Marc Arscott, John and Shan Bramley, Alan Clayson, Steve Cook, Nigel Cross, Jed Dmochowski, Hannah Griffiths, Helen Gummer, Pat Hehir, Mike Heron, Kevin Howlett, Paul Johnson, Malcolm Jones, Uwe Klee, Faebhean Kwest, John Platt, Dave Rimmer, Danny Secunda, Nikki Sudden, Mike Torry, John Tracy and Dave Williams.

Source Notes & Bibliography

I consulted a wide range of sources while researching this book, both during 1991–92 and on and off since then, culminating in the second extensive trawl for new material in the early months of 2002.

The bulk of the interview material in the book stems from conversations conducted with the author. I have used the present tense throughout the book when drawing on these first-hand sources.

I am also indebted to the writers and publishers of other material I've read, digested and occasionally quoted from during the course of writing this book.

Books – Marc Bolan and Glam Rock

Bolan, Marc. *The Warlock Of Love* (Lupus Music, 1969). The best-selling poetry book during the early Seventies; a hippie era relic that has since been re-published by The Bolan Society.

Bolan, Marc. *The Krakenmist* (The Tyrannosaurus Rex Appreciation Society, 1995)

Bolan, Marc. *The Caged Thrush* (The Tyrannosaurus Rex Appreciation Society, 1995)

Bolan, Marc. *Pictures Of Purple People* (The Bolan Society, 1996)

Bramley, John & Shan. *Marc Bolan: The Illustrated Discography* (Omnibus Press, 1983). The first serious attempt to compile a worldwide listing of record releases.

Bramley, John & Shan. *Marc Bolan: The Legendary Years* (1992). Nicely illustrated.

Dicks, Ted (ed.). *Marc Bolan . . . A Tribute* (Omnibus Press/Essex Music, 1978). An oral history put together in the immediate aftermath of Bolan's death. Also includes sheet music to several songs.

du Noyer, Paul. *Marc Bolan: Virgin Modern Icons* (Virgin, 1999). Slim, stylish thumbnail history.

Hoskyns, Barney. *Glam! Bowie, Bolan And The Glitter Revolution* (Faber, 1998). Sharp, intelligent, literate introduction to the genre – slim but impeccably informed.

McLenehan, Cliff. *Marc Bolan: 1947–1977 – A Chronology* (Zinc Alloy Books, 1999). This impressive piece of research, a virtual day-by-day account, is being updated for a new edition published by Helter Skelter Books.

Paytress, Mark. *20th Century Boy: The Marc Bolan Story* (Sidgwick & Jackson, 1992). First formal, hardback biography now rendered obsolete by this current edition.

Sinclair, Paul. *Electric Warrior: The Marc Bolan Story* (Omnibus Press, 1982). Enthusiastic, old-school scissors-and-paste biography.

Sukita. *T. Rex: Photographs by Sukita* (Colour Field, 1999). Lavish shots by noted Japanese photographer.

Thompson, Dave. *Children Of The Revolution! – Gum Into Glam 1967–76*, (self-published). An authoritative, history-from-below account of the links between Sixties bubblegum and Glam Rock in its myriad manifestations.

Thompson, Dave. *John's Children* (Babylon Books, 1988). Pioneering biography that helped restore the reputation of the cult band that deserve to be more than a footnote in pop history.

Tremlett, George. *The Marc Bolan Story* (Futura, 1975). Pocket-sized biography by the master of the Seventies' quickie pop paperback.

Welch, Chris, & Napier-Bell, Simon. *Marc Bolan: Born To Boogie* (Eel Pie, 1982). Fairly detailed account, with good photographic material, by two music industry associates who knew Bolan reasonably well.

Willans, John (alias Danielz) & Thomas, Caron. *Wilderness Of The Mind* (Xanadu, 1992). Episodic account that focuses on certain periods of Bolan's life. It includes some fine illustrative material. Still available in Japan via Parco Publishing.

Williams, Dave, *Marc Bolan: The Motivator* (Silver Surfer, 1985). Encyclopaedic fact book from one of Marc's many superfans.

General books on rock music and culture, art and social history

Barnes, Richard. *Mods!*, (Eel Pie, 1979)

Bennett, Mercer, Woolacott (eds). *Popular Culture & Social Relations* (Open University, 1986)

Buckley, David. *Strange Fascination: David Bowie – The Definitive Story* (Virgin, 1999)

Campbell, Colin. *The Romantic Ethic & The Spirit Of Modern Consumerism* (Basil Blackwell, 1987)

Chambers, Iain. *Popular Culture: The Metropolitan Experience* (Methuen, 1986)

Chambers, Iain. *Urban Rhythms: Pop Music & Popular Culture* (Macmillan, 1985)

Cohen, Stanley. *Folk Devils & Moral Panics* (MacGibbon & Kee, 1972)

Cutler, Chris. *File Under Popular: Theoretical And Critical Writings* (November Books, 1985)

Dyer, Richard. *Stars* (BFI, 1979)

Frith, Simon (ed.). *Facing The Music* (Mandarin, 1990)

Frith, Simon. *Music For Pleasure* (Polity, 1988)

Frith, Simon & Goodwin, Andrew (eds.). *On Record: Rock, Pop & The Written Word*, (Routledge, 1990)

Frith, Simon & Horne, Howard. *Art Into Pop* (Methuen, 1987)

Gibran, Jean & Kahlil. *Kahlil Gibran: His Life And World* (New York Graphic Society, 1974)

Gibran, Kahlil. *The Prophet* (William Heinemann, 1976)

Gillett, Charlie. *The Sound Of The City* (Souvenir Press, 1983)

Green, Jonathon. *Days In The Life: Voices From The English Underground 1961–1971* (William Heinemann, 1989)

Harvey, David. *The Condition Of Postmodernity* (Blackwell, 1989)

Hebdige, Dick. *Subculture: The Meaning Of Style* (Methuen, 1979)

Hewison, Robert. *Too Much: Art & Society In The Sixties – 1960–75* (Methuen, 1986)

Hoggart, Richard. *The Uses Of Literacy* (Chatto & Windus, 1957)

Hunt, Marsha. *Real Life* (Chatto & Windus, 1986)

Lacan, Jacques. *The Four Fundamental Concepts Of Psychoanalysis* (Hogarth Press, 1977)

Laing, RD. *The Divided Self* (Pelican, 1965)

Leigh, Spencer. *Stars In My Eyes* (Raven Books, 1980)

Mabey, Richard. *The Pop Process* (Hutchinson Educational, 1969)

Manlove, CN. *Modern Fantasy* (Cambridge University Press, 1975)

McAuley, Ian. *Guide To Ethnic London* (Michael Haag, 1987)

McRobbie, Angela (ed.). *Zoot Suits And Second-Hand Dresses: An Anthology Of Fashion & Music* (Macmillan, 1989)

Melly, George. *Revolt Into Style: The Pop Arts In Britain* (Penguin, 1970)

Napier-Bell, Simon. *You Don't Have To Say You Love Me* (New English Library, 1982)

Neville, Richard. *Playpower* (Jonathan Cape, 1970)

Pitt, Kenneth. *David Bowie: The Pitt Report* (Design, 1983)

Platt, John. *London's Rock Routes* (Fourth Estate, 1985)

Rogan, Johnny. *Starmakers & Svengalis* (Queen Anne Press, 1988)

Savage, Jon. *England's Dreaming* (Faber & Faber, 1991)

Schaffner, Nicholas. *Saucerful Of Secrets: The Pink Floyd Odyssey* (Sidgwick & Jackson, 1991)

Shapiro, Helen. *Walking Back To Happiness* (HarperCollins, 1993)

Shaw, Arnold. *The Rock Revolution* (Collier-Macmillan, 1969)

Street, John. *Rebel Rock: The Politics Of Popular Music* (Blackwell, 1986)

Swinfen, Ann. *In Defence Of Fantasy* (Routledge & Kegan Paul, 1984)

Thompson, Dave. *David Bowie: Moonage Daydream* (Plexus, 1987)

Tobler, John & Grundy, Stuart. *The Record Producers* (BBC Books, 1982)

Tolkien, JRR. *The Lord Of The Rings* (Allen & Unwin, 1968)

Wade, Michael. *Voxpop: Profiles Of The Pop Process* (Harrap, 1972)

Wicke, Peter. *Rock Music: Culture, Aesthetics, Sociology* (Cambridge Press, 1990)

Several essays merit specific mention:

Cross, Nigel. *Beautiful Dreamer – A Tribute To Steve Took* (from *Rockerilla*, May–June 1991)

Fowler, Peter. *Skins Rule* (from *Rock File*, Gillett, Charlie (ed.), New English Library, 1972)

Hebdige, Dick. *Towards A Cartography Of Taste 1935–1962* (from *Popular Culture: Past And Present*, Waites, Bennett, Martin, (eds), Croom Helm, 1982)

Marwick, Arthur. *A Social History Of Britain 1945–83* (from *Introduction To Contemporary Cultural Studies*, David Punter (ed.), Longman, 1986)

Shaar Murray, Charles. *Hello. I'm Marc Bolan. I'm A Superstar. You'd Better Believe It* (from *Shots From The Hip*, Penguin, 1991)

Various. *King Of The Mountain Cometh: A Tribute To Marc Bolan* (1991)

I am also indebted to Martin Barden, Alan Betrock and Andy Gardiner who all conducted interviews that have proved useful in the preparation of this book.

Newsapers & Magazines

The pop and underground press: *Beat Instrumental, Billboard, Circus, Cream, Creem, Disc & Music Echo, Gandalf's Garden, International Times, Look-In, Melody Maker, New Musical Express, Mojo, Music Now!, Music Scene, Popswop, Record Collector, Record Mirror & Disc, Record Mirror, Rolling Stone, Sounds, Superstar* and *Zigzag.*

Other magazines and newspapers: *Challenge, Daily Mirror, Diana, Chicago Tribune, Evening Standard, Jackie, LA Times, New York Times, She, The Observer, The Sun, Sunday Mirror, Sunday Pictorial, Toronto Star, Town, The Weekly News* and *New Left Review.*

Other sources

I am grateful to staff at the BBC, Demon Records (Val Jennings), Essex Music (Ken Finnes) and Universal Music (Joe Black) for their co-operation in helping me exhume long-lost information during the course of my research.

Fan Clubs and websites

The original T. Rex fan club closed down during Marc's period of exile during the mid-Seventies.

In the aftermath of Bolan's death, a new 'Official' Marc Bolan Fan Club was established in 1978. In the absence of any interest from EMI Records, it won the right to release Bolan's music. The T. Rex albums were repackaged in new sleeves, and a number of previously unissued recordings were made available. But the repackaging – and, by the mid-Eighties, the remixing – of Bolan's work didn't always meet with approval and many questions were raised, not least why such an important rock catalogue was not being overseen by a major record company.

The battles between rival Bolan factions reached an ugly head in 1992 when Marc's star was again in the ascendant. The situation cooled considerably when the Bolan Estate decided instead to license the master-tapes to specialist reissue label Demon Records. However, such is the fractious nature of the Bolan fan network that many rival fanzines and internet sites have since emerged to keep the long-running disputes alive.

Seeking to rise above them all, at least in terms of its dedication to sourcing (and publishing) rare and previously unseen manuscripts and photos, is The Bolan Society. It publishes a regular magazine, *Rumblings*, and is a recommended first port of call, particularly for those with a bias towards the Tyrannosaurus Rex era. Contact: The Bolan Society, PO Box 297, Newhaven, E. Sussex BN9 9NX. They have a website – www.marcbolansociety.co.uk.

The old 'Official' Marc Bolan Fan Club has since been taken over by Chris and Anna-Marie Bromham, with the assistance of Bolan veteran Barrie Smith. However, in order to stay afloat, the organisation has recently been selling off Bolan master-tapes to fans.

That Marc Bolan masters now exist in all four corners of the world, and in a variety of hands, is a discredit to Bolan's legacy. If unchecked, this will make it virtually impossible for compilers to document his work properly in the future. It has also led to widespread bootlegging and remixing of Marc's material, which only confuses an already dense, bewildering marketplace. However, many fans are now realising that the absence of any active involvement by the Bolan Estate has been the real cause of this extraordinary situation. It is a situation that needs addressing before Bolan's legacy crumbles into complete disrepair.

Apart from typing 'Marc' and 'Bolan' into a search engine, your first port of call on the internet should be: http://www.thegroover.com/t-rex/TillDawn/tomb.html, which provides a clear and comprehensive guide to what happens and where.

For information on Steve Peregrine Took, contact Shire News c/o Susan Hibbard, 10 Spring Grove, Loughton, Essex IG10 4QB.

Index

Single releases are in roman type and albums are in italics

A Beard Of Stars (Tyrannosaurus Rex), 154–155, 157–158, 160, 162, 169–170
A Beard Of Stars (Tyrannosaurus Rex), 155
A Certain Girl (K-Doe, Ernie), 30
A Clockwork Orange (Anthony Burgess), 275, 298
A Hard Day's Night (film), 75
A Sound Of Thunder (short story) (Ray Bradbury), 95
A Teenager In Love (Dion), 40, 303
A Teenager In Love (Frankie Lymon & The Teenagers), 303
A Teenager In Love (Marty Wilde), 303
A Whiter Shade Of Pale (Procul Harum), 103
A-Jaes, The, 79
Abba, 270
Adam & The Ants, 227
Adler, Larry, 39
Afghan Woman (Tyrannosaurus Rex), 107
Ain't That A Shame (Fats Domino), 255
Aladdin Sane (David Bowie), 146n.
Alfalfa, 329
Alice Cooper (see Cooper, Alice)
All Alone (T. Rex), 302
All Shook Up (Elvis Presley), 175
All The Young Dudes (David Bowie), 274
All The Young Dudes (Mott The Hoople), 219
All You Need Is Love (Beatles), 143, 211
Allan, Andy, 329
Allan, Elkan, 329
Alley Oop (Hollywood Argyles), 259
Altham, Keith, 58, 116, 121, 171, 197, 199, 244, 248–249, 293, 297–298, 319, 324, 326
Amanda (Shagrat), 193
Anarchy In The UK (Sex Pistols), 317, 320
Anderson, Miller, 309–311, 319
Angel, Randolph, 262
Angels, The, 312
Another Day (Paul McCartney/Wings), 174
Another Side Of Bob Dylan (Bob Dylan), 36–37
Arden, Don, 50, 72
Arrows, The, 311
Astronomy Domine (Pink Floyd), 193
Atkins, Elsie (grandmother), 3, 6, 8
Atkins, Henry Leonard (grandfather), 3

Atkins, Phyllis Winifred (see Phyllis Feld)
Atomic Rooster, 225
Avalon, Frankie, 29
Ayers, Virginia, 223

Baby Baby (Tyrannosaurus Rex), 163
Baby Boomerang (T. Rex), 306
Baby Jump (Mungo Jerry), 174
Baby Lemonade (Syd Barrett), 124
Bacharach, Burt, 51
Back Door, 250–251
Back Off Boogaloo (Ringo Starr), 239
Baez, Joan, 36, 44, 55
Ballad Of Davy Crockett (Bill Hayes), 12
Ballard, Hank, & The Midnighters, 30
Band, The, 143
Bang A Gong (Get It On) (see Get It On)
Barker, Geoff, 305
Barnes, Richard, 17
Barnett, Angie (see Angie Bowie)
Barnsley, Peter, 23, 25
Barrett, Syd, 9, 79, 83, 86, 100, 123–124, 127, 130, 231, 281, 313n., 319
Bartholomew, Stan, 20
Barton, Geoff, 302
Bassey, Shirley, 286
Bay City Rollers, The, 266, 269, 286, 311, 320
Bayldon, Geoffrey, 169, 212
Beach Boys, The, 51, 66, 127, 133, 146, 196, 306
Beatles, The, 20, 31–32, 35, 37–38, 51, 66–67, 73, 75, 85, 91, 101–102, 120, 125, 133, 141, 143, 158, 173–175, 184, 186, 188, 196–197, 203–204, 210–212, 217, 219, 224, 230, 239, 249, 265, 306
Beck, Jeff, 64, 76, 156
Beefheart, Captain, 79, 92, 124, 132, 136
Beggars Banquet (Rolling Stones), 237
Bell, Thom, 256
Belle Isle (Bob Dylan), 159–160
Beltane Walk (T. Rex), 169
Bennett, Gordon, 72
Bergman, Ingmar, 297
Berry, Chuck, 182, 184–186, 190, 208, 272
Berry, Dave, 35, 52
Best, George, 212

Betrock, Alan, 271, 275
Beyond The Risin' Sun (Marc Bolan), 53, 55
Beyond The Risin' Sun (Sylvie Varten), 149*n.*
Beyond The Risin' Sun (Tyrannosaurus Rex), 96
Bidwell, Dave, 193
Big Brother & The Holding Company, 88
Big Carrot, 238, 243, 254
Bilgiorri, Alfred, 20, 22
Billet, Valerie, 229
Billy Super Duper (abandoned punk opera), 288, 298, 302
Billy Super Duper (T. Rex), 288, 298, 317
Black And Blue (Rolling Stones), 256
Black And White Incident (Marc Bolan), 64
Black, Cilla, 233
Black Country Rock (David Bowie), 159, 304
Black Night (Deep Purple), 214
Black Oak Arkansas, 275
Black Sabbath, 187, 198
Blackburn, Tony, 165
Blackhill Enterprises, 110–111, 113–114, 132, 191
Blackjack (Big Carrot), 254
Blackwell, Chris, 166
Blackwood, Derek, 118–119
Blake, John, 247
Blake, William, 109, 119, 130
Blakely, Alan, 173
Blakely, Mike, 173
Blonde On Blonde (Bob Dylan), 66, 77
Blow Monkeys, The, 285
Blowin' In The Wind (Bob Dylan), 38–39
Blowin' In The Wind (Mark Feld), 39–40, 44, 46, 53
Blue Moon (Bob Dylan), 160
Blue Oyster Cult, 274–275
Blue Suede Shoes (Elvis Presley), 12, 303
Blues Project, The, 90
Bob Dylan (Bob Dylan), 39
Bogart, Neil, 271
Bohan, Mark, 49
Bolam, James, 46, 49
Bolan Boogie (Tyrannosaurus Rex), 214, 221
Bolan, June (see June Child)
Bolan, Marc (Mark Feld), 1–2, 5–71, 73–103, 105–333
   aloofness from friends/associates, 80–81, 115, 182–183, 191–192, 248, 285, 322
   America, failure to break into, 176–177, 201, 204–207, 222–223, 225, 249–251, 274–277, 291
   androgynous image, 42, 47–48, 50–51, 65–66, 321
   Bill Legend, departure from T. Rex, 256–257
   Bill Legend, recruitment of, 172–173
   birth, 5

Bob Dylan, influence of, 36–39, 50–51, 53–55, 57, 59, 77, 91, 94, 97, 120, 123, 159–160, 184–185
brother, relationship with, 6–7, 9–10, 29
carnivore conversion, 248–249, 315
cinema, love of, 7–9, 15
CND/Ban The Bomb March appearance, 44
crucifixion of cats story, 46–47
David Bowie, rivalry with, 27, 128, 145–149, 156–157, 159, 218–219, 232–233, 259, 263–264, 274–275, 289, 300, 304–305, 323–325
death, 328, 331–332
Decca Records recordings, 52–54, 57–58, 63
drug/alcohol use, 91, 99, 162–163, 202, 207, 209, 227, 229–230, 236, 242, 244, 247, 252, 258, 261, 265, 277–282, 287–288, 299–300, 308, 313, 323, 329–330
Düsseldorf/Ludwigshafen, incendiary live debacle, 68–70, 82
early groups/collaborations, 13–14
Elvis Presley fixation, 1, 10–12, 14, 36, 58, 91, 181, 189, 239, 303, 305, 320
EMI/Columbia audition, 41–42
family history, 2–5
fantasy interests, 7–9, 55, 93, 118–119
fashion interests, 16–25, 27–28, 31, 34–35, 40, 43, 57
financial affairs, 194–197, 220, 222, 244–247, 256, 307, 318
funeral, 332–333
Gloria Jones, relationship and influence, 237–238, 243, 249, 252–256, 265, 278–280, 283, 287, 294, 307, 311–312
guitar, first/early purchases of, 11–12, 35–36
Helen Shapiro, friendship with, 12–13, 15, 21, 30, 50, 56
hippie image, 93–95, 98, 106, 108, 158, 181, 187, 191, 292
Jeff Dexter, early adventures with, 21–24, 28, 31
John Peel friendship, 90–91, 97, 102–103, 108, 110, 113, 120, 122, 125–126, 129, 131, 138, 153, 182–183, 191–192
John's Children, involvement with, 68–71, 74–89, 92
June Child, break-up of relationship, 246–247, 249–250, 252, 282–283, 307
June Child, marriage to, 151
June Child, relationship with, 113–114, 126, 132, 191, 322
Marsha Hunt, relationship with, 149–150
Mickey Finn, firing of, 285–286
Mickey Finn, recruitment of, 141–142
mod culture affliations, 17–25, 28–29, 31, 34, 40, 43
modelling career, 35
narcissism and ego inflation, 1, 16, 19–20, 23, 28–29, 37–38, 58, 64–65, 79–80,

87–88, 112–113, 116, 135, 202, 210, 213, 247–248, 251, 281, 293–294, 319
Paris, legendary visit, 46–48, 54, 58
plagiarism claim against, 305–306
pop star, diminishing powers as, 265–266, 290–291, 296, 301, 304
punk, reaction and relevance to, 312–315, 319–321
recording début, 38–39, 43–44
reinvention of image and fabrications 1–2, 7, 9, 14, 17–18, 19, 23–24, 29, 32, 37, 40–42, 44–50, 56, 58, 62, 64–65, 87, 91, 93–95, 98, 112–113, 116, 125, 144, 170–171, 187–188, 191–192, 226, 315–316, 326
Riggs O'Hara, influence of, 45–48, 66
Rolan Bolan, birth of, 296
Romanticism, flirtation with, 33–34, 37, 41, 51, 95, 115, 266
schooling, 8–9
sexuality, 42–43, 47–48, 65–66, 131–132, 178, 297, 307, 321
Simon Napier-Bell, involvement with, 62–67, 76–77, 82, 84, 87–89, 95–99
Steve Currie, recruitment of, 168
Steve Took, deterioration of friendship with, 127, 134–136, 140
suburbs, move to, 26–27, 33
Syd Barrett, fascination with, 83, 100, 124, 231, 281, 319
T. Rex, abbreviated name, 165, 171
T. Rex, fan mania, 203–204, 215, 224, 228, 230, 260
Theresa Whipman, relationship with, 50–51, 61, 65, 111–112, 114
Toby Tyler pseudonym, 44–45, 48
Tolkien, influence of, 60, 93, 99, 116, 118–120, 123
Town magazine, teenage appearance in, 23–26
Tyrannosaurus Rex, formation, 92–93, 96
violence towards women, 247, 278, 280
weight problems, 41, 234, 259–261, 265, 277, 284, 287, 291, 295, 313
Wizard/black magic story, 45–47, 54, 58
writings (poetry, plays and prose), 59–60, 63, 65, 92, 102–103, 118, 122–124, 126, 132, 169, 177, 180, 301–302
Bolan, Rolan, 246, 296, 298, 308–309, 311, 318, 323
Bolan's Zip Gun (T. Rex), 273–274, 286, 301, 306
Bombs Out Of London (T. Rex), 297
Bono, Sonny, 51, 54, 57, 63
Boo! I Said Freeze (Shagrat), 193
Booker T & The MGs, 71
Boomtown Rats, 320
Borg, Bjorn, 283
Born To Boogie (film), 203, 230–231, 241

Born To Boogie (T. Rex), 227, 234, 250
Bowie, Angie, 148, 297
Bowie, David, 27, 37, 40, 51, 62, 109–110, 127–128, 133, 145–149, 155–157, 159, 186, 214–219, 232–233, 240, 248, 253–254, 258–259, 263, 268–270, 274–275, 284, 289–290, 296, 299–300, 303–306, 310, 313*n.*, 319–320, 323–325, 327, 332
Bowie, Zowie, 296
Box, Mick, 205
Boy George, 207
Boyd, Joe, 99–102, 253
Bradbury, Ray, 95, 258
Brain Police (T. Rex), 288
Brando, Marlon, 61
Bridget The Midget (Ray Stevens), 174
Bringing It All Back Home (Bob Dylan), 53–54
Broken Hearted Blues (T. Rex), 234
Brotherhood Of Man, The, 332
Brown, Arthur, 124
Brown, Joe, 161
Brown, Pete, 123, 211
Brown, Vicki, 233
Bruce, Tommy, 161
Brummell, Beau, 16–17
Buckley, David, 258
Buick Mackane (T. Rex), 214, 232
Burgess, John, 41
Burton, Humphrey, 207
Burton, James, 122, 153, 164
Burton, Richard, 212
But She's Mine (John's Children), 75–76
Butler, Annabel, 126
Buzzcocks, The, 317
By The Light Of A Magical Moon (Tyrannosaurus Rex), 153–154, 161–162
Bye Bye Love (Everly Brothers), 13
Byrds, The, 56, 66, 136, 139

C'mon Everybody (Eddie Cochran), 173
Cadilac (T. Rex), 191*n.*, 206
Cagney, James, 97, 99
Caiger, Rob, 239
Caine, Marti, 311
Callas, Maria, 331
Cambridge, John, 156, 163
Campbell, Sandy, 244
Candy (film), 211
Captain Sensible, 313, 316, 320
Carniverous Circus Part II (Mick Farren), 192
Caron, Sandra, 45
Carpenters, The, 198, 216, 240
Carr, Robert, 8
Carr, Roy, 185–186, 284
Carroll, Peter, 207, 244–245
Carsmile Smith & The Old One (T. Rex), 243
Cartland, Ben, 88, 96
Casbah Candy (John's Children), 78

Casey, Howie, 233, 260*n*.
Cash, Johnny, 143
Cassidy, David, 217, 240
Casual Agent (T. Rex), 302, 304
Cat Black (John's Children), 77, 79
Cat Black (Marc Bolan), 64, 262
Catblack (The Wizard's Hat) (Tyrannosaurus
    Rex), 129–130
Catch My Soul (musical), 150
Catch The Wind (Donovan), 44
Celebrate Summer (T. Rex), 325
Chadbourne, Eugene, 276
Chambers, Iain, 179–180, 219
Chandler, Chas, 195, 225
Chandler, Gene, 190
Change (T. Rex), 254, 264
Changes (David Bowie), 264
Chapman, Roger, 152
Chapter 24 (Pink Floyd), 100
Chariot Choogle (T. Rex), 232
Chariots Of Silk (Tyrannosaurus Rex),
    129–130
Charles, Ray, 14, 224, 255
Charles, Tina, 307
Charlie (Marc Bolan), 64
Chase, 204
Chateau In Virginia Waters (Tyrannosaurus
    Rex), 101, 106
Cheech & Chong, 210
Chicken Shack, 121, 193
Chiffons, The, 305
Child, June (wife), 83, 91, 100, 110–111,
    113–115, 122, 126, 128, 130–133, 135,
    138*n*., 139, 144–146, 148–151, 153, 162,
    164, 169, 173, 178, 187, 191–192, 202,
    205, 207, 212–213, 215, 221, 230,
    244–247, 249–253, 257, 265, 282–283,
    285, 307, 311, 321–322
Child Star (Tyrannosaurus Rex), 101–102, 106,
    109–110
Children Of The Revolution (T. Rex), 212,
    214, 220, 222, 226–227, 325
Christian, Charlie, 184
Christmas Bop (T. Rex), 298
Chrome Star (T. Rex), 301–302
Churchill, Winston, 5, 183
City Port (Marc Bolan & Gloria Jones), 314
City Port (Pat Hall), 255
Clapton, Eric, 37, 79, 84, 133, 153, 205
Clark, Dave, 219
Clarke, Steve, 282
Clayton, Lucie, 35
Clayton, Merry, 237
Clean Up Woman (Betty Wright), 255
Cleave, Maureen, 50, 55
Clinton, George, 269
Coasters, The, 14
Cobb, Ed, 237
Cochran, Dib, & The Earwigs, 163–164

Cochran, Eddie, 2, 15, 45, 88, 97, 164, 166,
    173, 186
Cocker, Joe, 166, 223–224, 260
Cockney Rebel, 275
Cogan, Alma, 45
Cohen, Leonard, 122–123, 143
Cohn, Nik, 22–23
Cold Turkey (John Lennon/Plastic Ono Band),
    158–159
Collins, Burt, 189
Colosseum, 185
Come And Play With Me In The Garden
    (John's Children), 86
Conesuala (T. Rex), 300
Conn, Leslie, 51, 62, 109
Coon, Caroline, 314
Cooper, Alice, 216–217, 239, 262, 319, 322
Cordell, Denny, 103–106, 147, 195, 224
Corea, Chick, 319
Cornflake Zoo (John's Children), 79
Cosmic Dancer (T. Rex), 177, 188, 190,
    205–206
Country Joe & The Fish, 137
Coville, Chris, 86
Coxhill, Gordon, 240
Crampsie, Henry Storey, 5
Crane, Vincent, 225
Cream, 109, 123, 292
Creedence Clearwater Revival, 133
Crickets, The, 13
Cromelin, Richard, 222
Crompton, Michael, Dr, 229
Cross, Nigel, 192
Cry Baby (Gloria Jones), 255, 308
Currie, Hazel, 168
Currie, Steve, 168, 173, 202, 205, 209, 220,
    250, 256, 267, 279–280, 288, 299,
    309–310
Curved Air, 192
Cuscana, Michael, 200–201
Cutler, Ivor, 192

Daddy Rolling Stone (John's Children), 84
Dali, Salvador, 297
Damned, 313–317, 332
Dandy In The Underworld (T. Rex), 313–314,
    316–317
Dandy In The Underworld (T. Rex), 317, 319
Dandy In The Underworld (television
    programme), 215
Darling, Silver, 192
Dave Dee, Dozy, Beaky, Mick & Tich, 79
David, Hal, 51
Davies, Ray, 55, 139, 159, 272
Davies, Ros, 326
Davis, Billie, 52
Davis, Hal, 237
Dawn, 186–187
Dawn Storm (T. Rex), 301–302

Dawset, Chris, 71

Days In The Life (book) (Jonathon Green), 34, 115, 162

De Sykes, Stephanie, 320

De Witt, Barbara, 324

Dean, James, 40–41, 62, 136

Debora (Marc Bolan & David Bowie), 324

Debora (T. Rex), 299, 315, 326

Debora (Tyrannosaurus Rex), 106–107, 116, 153, 161, 221

Deep Purple, 187, 198, 214

Delaney & Bonnie, 237

Delilah (Tom Jones), 107

Demon Queen (T. Rex), 325

Depth Charge (T. Rex), 288

Desdemona (John's Children), 76–79, 82–86, 89

Desdemona (Marsha Hunt), 149

Deviants, The, 140, 192

Dexter, Jeff, 21–23, 25–26, 28–29, 31, 42–43, 45, 47, 57, 98–99, 110, 114, 141–142, 151, 162, 179, 231, 244, 261, 292, 301, 303, 305, 310, 316, 318, 320–324, 329–330

Diamond Dogs (David Bowie), 258, 274–275

Dickens, Charles, 62

Dicks, Ted, 242, 246, 279, 330

Dillon, Barry, 179

Dines, Peter 'Dino', 270, 288, 299, 309, 311, 315

Dion, 39–40

Disney, Walt, 44–45, 96

Do I Love Thee (Marc Bolan), 267

Do You Remember (Tyrannosaurus Rex), 134

Do You Wanna Dance (Bobby Freeman), 296

Do You Wanna Dance (Cliff Richard), 296

Do You Wanna Dance (T. Rex), 296

Doggett, Bill, 14

Domino, Fats, 15, 255

Donovan, 36, 39, 43, 52, 55–57, 77, 94, 122–123, 137, 148, 289

Don't Be Cruel (Elvis Presley), 13

Don't Look Back (film), 184

Don't Shoot Me I'm Only The Piano Player (Elton John), 240

Doobie Brothers, The, 223

Dore, Gustave, 109

Dorset, Ray, 158–159

Dove (Tyrannosaurus Rex), 153–155

Dr John, 67, 149

Dragon's Ear (Tyrannosaurus Rex), 155

Drake, Omah, 223

Dreaming Of 4000 (Electric Light Orchestra), 239

Dreamy Lady (T. Rex Disco Party), 295–296, 299, 302, 320

Drifters, The (UK), 14

Drifters, The (US), 14–15, 255

Drive Me Crazy (Disco Lady) (Gloria Jones), 308

Drive-In Saturday (David Bowie), 233

Dudgeon, Gus, 148–149

Duke Of Earl (Gene Chandler), 190

Dunbar, Aynsley, 132, 136–137

Duncan, Lesley, 145, 226

Dunn, Clive, 168, 310

Dwarfish Trumpet Blues (Tyrannosaurus Rex), 101–102, 106

Dylan, Bob, 36–39, 43–44, 48, 50, 52–53, 55, 57–59, 61, 63, 66, 76–77, 91, 94, 97, 102, 120–123, 125, 136, 143, 148, 157–160, 184–185, 195, 198, 208, 210, 213–214, 218, 283, 319

Dynamite (Cliff Richard), 31

Dynamo (T. Rex), 288

East, Ken, 104

Eastern Spell (Marc Bolan), 64

Eckstine, Billy, 63

Economides, Jim, 51–53, 57–58, 62

Eddie & The Hot Rods, 320

Eddy, Duane, 30

Edison Lighthouse, 163

Edmunds, Dave, 174

Edwards, Scott, 256

Effervescing Elephant (Syd Barrett), 124

EG Management, 167

Electric Light Orchestra, 239–240

Electric Slim & The Factory Hen (T. Rex), 234–235

Electric Warrior (T. Rex), 177–178, 187–190, 193, 195, 197, 200, 203–204, 209, 214–216, 220, 234, 272

Elemental Child (Tyrannosaurus Rex), 152–154, 162, 169, 176

Elenore (Turtles), 139

11.15 (Jam) (Marc Bolan), 267

Elliott, Rambling Jack, 36

Ellison, Andy, 69, 71–74, 77–81, 83*n*., 84–85

Ellison, Donald, 307

ELO (see Electric Light Orchestra)

ELO 2 (Electric Light Orchestra), 240

ELP (see Emerson, Lake & Palmer)

Emerson, Lake & Palmer, 187

Endless Sleep (Marc Bolan), 320

Endless Sleep (Marty Wilde), 320

English, Michael, 141

Eno, 272

Enthoven, David, 161, 194–195, 244

Entire Sioux Nation, The, 193

Epics, The, 173

Epstein, Brian, 73

Ernie (Benny Hill), 200

Essex, David, 286, 294

Evans, Allen, 110

Everett, Betty, 42, 46

Everly Brothers, The, 13, 17

Everyone's Born To Die (Electric Light Orchestra), 239
Exile On Main Street (Rolling Stones), 235, 263–264
Expresso Bongo (film), 15

Fabian, 29
Faces, The, 185, 192
Fairytale (Donovan), 55
Faith, Adam, 14–15, 24
Faithfull, Marianne, 52
Fallon, B.P., 167, 187, 213, 248
Family, 152, 187
Farren, Mick, 192–193
Farthingale, Hermione, 128, 147
Faulkner, Marcia, 194
Feld, Arthur (uncle), 29
Feld, Betsie, 3, 5
Feld, Harry Leonard (brother), 4, 6–11, 14–16, 20, 22, 26, 28–30, 34–35, 42, 47, 49, 308
Feld, Henry (grandfather), 2–3, 8, 11
Feld, Mark (see Bolan, Marc)
Feld, Mark (uncle), 5
Feld, Phyllis (mother), 3–4, 6–7, 9–11, 19, 26, 34–35, 62, 151, 245, 293, 308, 323
Feld, Simeon (Sid) (father), 3–4, 6, 8, 11–12, 26, 29, 77, 151, 245, 293, 308, 323
Fellini, Federico, 312
Fenton, Paul, 260*n.*
Fenwick, Mark, 195
Ferry, Bryan, 306
Few, The, 71
Fields, Melvyn, 13
Fields, Vanetta, 235
Fifield, Bill (see Bill Legend)
Finn, Mickey, 141–142, 144, 151–152, 154–155, 158, 165, 167, 170, 172–173, 188, 199, 202, 206–207, 209, 212, 245, 249, 252, 260–261, 267, 272, 274, 276, 284–286, 309, 321, 326
Fist Heart Mighty Dawn Dart (Tyrannosaurus Rex), 154
Fleetwood Mac, 121, 163, 294
Flo & Eddie, 141, 178, 182, 190, 209, 239, 243, 281, 289
Flowers, Herbie, 310–311, 324, 329
Flowers In The Rain (Move), 104, 194
Fog On The Tyne (Lindisfarne), 198
Four Tops, 223, 238
Fox, 305
Frame, Pete, 185
Frank, Clive, 288
Franklin, Aretha, 235
Free, 167
Freeman, Alan, 144
Freeman, Bobby, 296
From A Buick Six (Bob Dylan), 58
Frowning Atahuallpa (My Inca Love) (Tyrannosaurus Rex), 107, 109

Fuller, Jesse, 60
Funky London Childhood (T. Rex), 297, 309, 317
Fury, Billy, 15, 173
Future Man Buick (abandoned project), 302
Futuristic Dragon (T. Rex), 282, 298–299, 301–303

Gabrels, Reeves, 27
Galaxy (T. Rex), 264
Gallagher, Rory, 185
Gamble, Kenny, 256
Garbo, Greta, 297
Gardiner, Andy, 299, 304, 308
Gardner, Beverly, 223
Garland, Judy, 243
Gass, 145
Gates Of Eden (Bob Dylan), 53
Gaydon, John, 161
Gaye, Marvin, 223, 238
Generation X, 313, 320–321
Get Down And Get With It (Slade), 195
Get It On (Gloria Jones), 307–308
Get It On (T. Rex), 178, 182–185, 190, 195, 204, 206, 210, 212, 251, 307, 314–315
Get It On In The Morning (Chase), 204
Get Together (Youngbloods), 143
Ghetto Baby (Pat Hall), 274*n.*, 308
Gibran, Kahlil, 119–120, 130
Gilmour, Dave, 133
Ginsberg, Allen, 34
Girl (T. Rex), 206, 234
Glam Rock (book) Dave Thompson, 218
Glitter Band, The, 273
Glitter, Gary, 216–219, 226–227, 240, 253, 260, 266, 294, 311, 332
Go Go Girl (John's Children), 78
Go Now (Gloria Jones), 307
Go Now (Moody Blues), 103
God (John Lennon/Plastic Ono Band), 188
God Save The Queen (Sex Pistols), 320
Goldman, Albert, 43
Goldsboro, Bobby, 107
Goldstein, Gerry, 20
Goldstein, Henry, Rabbi, 333
Gonzalez, 307, 310
Good, Jack, 15, 150
Good, John, 278
Good Vibrations (Beach Boys), 66
Gooner, Louie, 71
Gould, Stephen, 12–13, 30
Graham, Kenneth, 100
Grainger, Stewart, 16
Grand Funk Railroad, 211
Grandad (Clive Dunn), 168, 310
Grass, Gunter, 77
Grateful Dead, The, 92, 139, 273
Gray, Mick, 202, 207, 215, 221–222, 224–225, 227, 229–231, 233, 238, 242–244,

246–253, 257–258, 261, 270–271,
278–285, 287–290, 299–300, 305*n*., 317,
321–322
Great Hits (T. Rex), 257, 325
Great Horse (Tyrannosaurus Rex), 155
Grech, Rick, 239
Green, Barry, 41
Green, Ed, 256, 281
Green, Jack, 238, 250–251, 256, 260–261, 281
Green, Jonathon, 34, 115, 162
Green, Peter, 294
Green Onions (Booker T & The MGs), 71
Greenwood, Bernie, 162
Griffin, Jeff, 192
Groove A Little (T. Rex), 317
Groovin' With Mr Bloe (Mr Bloe), 163
GTOs, The, 150
Guthrie, Woody, 36, 53

Hadden, Sid, 42
Hair (musical), 149–150
Haley, Bill, 12, 45
Hall, Eric, 20, 321, 330
Hall, Pat, 238, 243, 249, 251, 254–256,
259–260, 263–264, 267–268, 274, 308,
314
Hamp, Johnny, 324
Hang-Ups (T. Rex), 315, 323
Happenings Ten Years Time Ago (Yardbirds),
64
Happy Together (Turtles), 139
Hapshash & The Coloured Coat, 110, 141
Hard On Love (fanzine), 326
Hard On Love (Tyrannosaurus Rex), 221, 268
Hargreaves, Alan, 297
Harley, Steve, 275, 312, 321–322, 327–328,
332
Harper, Roy, 36, 132
Harris, Bob, 110, 183, 186–187, 192, 198, 200,
210, 213
Harrison, George, 32, 174, 198, 213, 305
Harrison, Wilbert, 30
Hartley, Keef, 309
Harty, Russell, 311
Have You Seen My Baby (Ringo Starr), 239
Hawkwind, 127, 174, 198, 329
Hayes, Bill, 12
Hayman, Martin, 290
Heart Throb, 320
Heartbreak Hotel (Elvis Presley), 13, 175, 305
Heavy Metal Kids, The, 296
Heckman, Don, 206
Heider, Wally, 178
Hendrix, Jimi, 67, 79, 92, 107, 109, 133, 143,
153, 157, 175, 186, 190–191, 205, 239,
243, 261, 292, 303
Heroes (David Bowie), 324
Heroes And Villains (Beach Boys), 146
Heron, Mike, 101

Heskell, Peta, 309
Hesse, Herman, 120
Hewlett, John, 69–74, 77–78, 80–81, 83, 86
Hey Jude (Beatles), 174–175
High (Gloria Jones), 254–255, 308
High (Pat Hall), 255
Highway Knees (T. Rex), 234
Highway 61 Revisited (Bob Dylan), 58
Highways (Marc Bolan), 57
Highways (Tyrannosaurus Rex), 96–97,
101–102
Hill, Benny, 200
Hill, Dave, 225
Hill, Roy, 255
Hippy Gumbo (John's Children), 78,
Hippy Gumbo (Marc Bolan), 64, 66–67, 71,
90, 97, 149, 158
Hippy Gumbo (Tyrannosaurus Rex), 106
Hogan, Carl, 184
Hoggart, Richard, 7
Holder, Noddy, 225
Hollies, The, 107
Hollingworth, Roy, 167
Holloway, Brenda, 237
Holloway, Danny, 85
Holloway, Patrice, 237
Holly, Buddy, 13, 45, 209, 303
Hollywood Argyles, The, 259
Holton, Gary, 296
Holy Holy (David Bowie), 159
Holzman, Jac, 121
Honey (Bobby Goldsboro), 107
Honey Don't (Carl Perkins), 305
Honky Chateau (Elton John), 208
Honky Tonk (Bill Doggett), 14
Hooker, John Lee, 55, 297
Hope You Enjoy The Show (T. Rex), 243
Hopkin, Mary, 253, 332
Hopkins, Nicky, 71
Horrible Breath (Marc Bolan), 64
Horses (Patti Smith), 306
Hoskyns, Barney, 180
Hot Love (T. Rex), 172–175, 177–180, 183,
185, 212, 305
Hot Rod Mama (John's Children), 78, 82*n*.,
84–85, 96
Hot Rod Mama (Marc Bolan), 64
Hot Rod Mama (Tyrannosaurus Rex), 96, 102,
109, 149, 153, 161, 174
Hot Rod Pappa (Marsha Hunt), 149
Hound Dog (Elvis Presley), 11, 13
Howard, Tony, 221, 223, 227, 238, 244–246,
249, 257, 261, 285, 290, 305, 318, 320,
324, 329–330, 332
Howlin' Wolf, 189, 303*n*.
Huff, Leon, 256
Hughes, Howard, 293
Human, All Too Human (Nietzsche), 1
Humble Pie, 133, 176

Hunky Dory (David Bowie), 218
Hunt, Marsha, 149–150
Hunter, Ian, 240
Hunter, Russell, 228
Hurst, Mike, 57
Hyland, Brian, 35
Hynde, Chrissie, 268
Hype, The, 155–156

I Believe (T. Rex), 297
I Can't Explain (Who), 75
(I Can't Get No) Satisfaction (Rolling Stones), 227
I Hear You Knocking (Dave Edmunds), 174
I Love To Boogie (T. Rex), 305–306, 309, 320
I Really Love You Babe (T. Rex), 304
I Want To Hold Your Hand (Beatles), 211
I Wish It Could Be Christmas Everyday (Wizzard), 298
I'm A Fool For You Girl (T. Rex), 316
I'm Weird (Marc Bolan), 64
I'm Your Hoochie Coochie Man (Dion), 40
Idle Race, The, 124
Idol, Billy, 321
If I Were Your Woman (Gladys Knight & The Pips), 238
Iggy & The Stooges, 218, 292
Iggy Pop, 204, 231, 313*n*., 319–320
Iles, Jan, 284–285
In The Heat Of The Morning (David Bowie), 304
In The Summertime (Mungo Jerry), 158–159
Incredible String Band, The, 99–101, 127, 139, 161
Interstellar Overdrive (Pink Floyd), 153
Interstellar Soul (T. Rex), 243, 264
Is It Love (T. Rex), 166, 169
Iscariot (Tyrannosaurus Rex), 130, 159
Isley Brothers, The, 303
It Don't Come Easy (Ringo Starr), 211
It's A Beautiful Day, 139
It's My City (T. Rex), 297
It's Only Make Believe (Conway Twitty), 298
Itchycoo Park (Small Faces), 210

Jackson, Colm, 326
Jackson, Michael, 217
Jackson 5, The, 223, 237
Jagged Time Lapse (John's Children), 82*n*., 84
Jagger, Mick, 73, 181, 184, 204–205, 210, 218, 240, 297
Jailhouse Rock (Elvis Presley), 175
Jam, The, 320
James, Dick, 51
Jasmine 49 (Marc Bolan), 64
Jason B. Sad (T. Rex), 316–317
Jasper C. Debussy (John's Children), 96
Jasper C. Debussy (Marc Bolan), 71, 75–76, 78, 87

Jasper C. Debussy (Tyrannosaurus Rex), 96, 116
Jeepster (T. Rex), 177, 189–190, 199–200, 206, 210, 212, 238, 250, 277, 303*n*., 314, 325
Jefferson Airplane, 97, 139, 143
Jenner, Pete, 110, 191
Jennifer Eccles (Hollies), 107
Jethro Tull, 132–133
Jewel (Tyrannosaurus Rex), 162, 166, 169, 176
Jitterbug Love (T. Rex), 227, 255, 325–326
Joanna (Scott Walker), 107
Jobriath, 150, 237
John, Elton, 40, 198–199, 207–208, 212, 216, 240, 286, 288, 321–322, 332
John Lennon/Plastic Ono Band (John Lennon/Plastic Ono Band), 188
John Wesley Harding (Bob Dylan), 143
John's Children, 67–71, 73–89, 92–94, 99, 102, 121, 155, 321
Johnny B. Goode (Chuck Berry), 303, 317
Johnson, Derek, 54, 116, 133, 174
Johnson, James, 226, 231
Johnson, Lonnie, 262
Jones, Allan, 301, 314
Jones, Brian, 30, 199
Jones, Gloria, 150, 223, 237–238, 243–245, 249, 251–256, 259–261, 263–271, 274–284, 287–290, 293–294, 296, 298–299, 303–304, 307–314, 316, 321–323, 325, 327–332
Jones, Janie, 56
Jones, John Paul, 58, 71*n*.
Jones, Malcolm, 166
Jones, Peter, 116, 183
Jones, Richard, 256, 268, 279–282, 287, 301, 329–331
Jones, Steve, 319
Jones, Tom, 52, 107
Joplin, Janis, 88, 92, 139, 157
Junior's Eyes, 228
Juniper Suction (Tyrannosaurus Rex), 117, 124
Jupiter Liar (T. Rex), 302
Just Seven Numbers (Can Straighten Out My Life) (Four Tops), 238
Just What You Want, Just What You'll Get (John's Children), 75

K-Doe, Ernie, 30
Kansas City (Wilbert Harrison), 30
Karma Man (David Bowie), 147–148, 304
Katz, David, 189
Kauffman, Martin, 17–18
Kaylan, Howard, 139–141, 175, 178
Keary, Vic, 39, 44
Keep On Truckin' (Pat Hall), 255
Kelly, Grace (Princess Grace), 283
Kendricks, Eddie, 255
Kennedy, Robert, 108
Kent, Nick, 230–231

Kerr, Richard, 104
Khan, Chaka, 308
Kidd, Johnny, 14, 31
Kim, Andy, 282
King, Andrew, 110, 132, 244
King, Carole, 198
King, Clydie, 234
King, Jonathan, 57
King Crimson, 133
King Kong (Kinks), 159
King Of The Mountain Cometh (T. Rex), 174
King Of The Rumbling Spires (Tyrannosaurus Rex), 133–134, 155, 174
Kinks, The, 54–55, 71, 139, 159
Kirby, Fred, 138
Kirsch, David, 61–62
Kiss, 275
Klein, Allen, 212
Knight (Tyrannosaurus Rex), 107
Knight, Gladys, & The Pips, 223, 237–238
Knock Three Times (Dawn), 187
Kristina, Sonja, 192
Kydd, Sam, 38

Labelle, 255
Lacan, Jacques, 112
Lady Madonna (Beatles), 325
Lady Stardust (David Bowie), 218
Ladybirds, The, 52, 57
Laine, Denny, 98
Laine, Frankie, 19
Laing, R.D., 112
Lalena (Donovan), 289
Lambert, Kit, 69–70, 78–79, 82, 99, 101, 149, 165–166, 221*n*., 268
Laser Love (T. Rex), 310, 312
Lea, Jim, 225
Leander, Mike, 52–54, 57–58, 216
Led Zeppelin, 58, 133, 187, 212, 251, 270, 318–319
Lee, Alvin, 153
Lee, Arthur, 193
Lee, Brenda, 35
Lee, Christopher, 127
Lee, Jackie, 174
Lee, Stan, 297
Left Hand Luke (T. Rex), 235
Legend, 173
Legend, Bill (Bill Fifield), 172–173, 176–178, 182, 190, 205, 220, 241, 243, 250, 256–257, 309
Leigh, Spencer, 22
Lemarr, Hedy, 186–187, 211
Lennon, John, 30*n*, 32, 36, 66, 105, 120, 143, 159–160, 175, 181, 188, 198, 210, 212, 218, 254, 261, 279, 282
Lenoir, Phil, 193
Let Me Sleep Beside You (David Bowie), 147
Let's Dance (Chris Montez), 320

Let's Dance (T. Rex), 320
Lettermen, The, 51
Lewis, C.S., 55, 60, 99, 109, 127
Lewis, Jerry Lee, 15, 143
Lewis, Linda, 332
Liberace, 216
Life Is Strange (T. Rex), 234
Life's A Gas (Marc Bolan & Cilla Black), 233
Life's A Gas (T. Rex), 188, 234, 299
Life's An Elevator (T. Rex), 310
Light Of Love (T. Rex), 270–271, 273
Light Of Love (T. Rex), 272–274, 276, 286
Lightning Raiders, The, 329
Like A Rolling Stone (Bob Dylan), 184
Lindisfarne, 185, 198
Liquid Gang (T. Rex), 243, 264
Listen To The Music (Doobie Brothers), 223
Little Queenie (Chuck Berry), 182, 184, 190
Little Richard, 35, 175, 212, 303
Live Peace In Toronto (John Lennon/Plastic Ono Band), 159
Liverpool Scene, The, 90
Living Doll (Cliff Richard), 31
Lofty Skies (Tyrannosaurus Rex), 155
Logan, Nick, 175, 183, 197
Lola (Kinks), 55
London Boys (T. Rex), 297, 302–303, 306, 309
London Bye Ta Ta (David Bowie), 145
Long Tall Sally (Little Richard), 175
Love, 136, 193
Love Me Do (Beatles), 32
Lovin' Spoonful, The, 66
Lulu, 52
Lumley, Joanna, 311
Lunacy's Back (John's Children), 78, 96
Lunacy's Back (Tyrannosaurus Rex), 96, 106
Lutton, Davey, 260*n*., 267, 288, 299, 309–310
Lymon, Frankie, 161, 303
Lynn, Vera, 320
Lynne, Jeff, 240, 322
Lyons, Patrick Francis, 5

Ma-Ma-Ma-Belle (Electric Light Orchestra), 239
MacColl, Ewan, 95
MacDougall, Ian, 222
Mack, Lonnie, 161
Mad Dogs And Englishmen, 224
Mad Donna (T. Rex), 234
Madman (Marc Bolan & David Bowie), 327
Maggie May (Rod Stewart), 198
Mahavishnu Orchestra, The, 289
Mamas & The Papas, The, 66
Mambo Sun (T. Rex), 177, 190, 197, 300*n*.
Manfred Mann, 104
Mansfield, Jayne, 1
Mansfield, Mike, 294–295, 309–310, 320, 329
Marc (television programme), 320–323, 329
Marley, Bob, & The Wailers, 307

Marsh, Dave, 138, 161
Marshall, John, 284
Martin, George, 101
Martyn, John, 36
Matilda Mother (Pink Floyd), 100
Mayall, John, 297
McCartney, Linda, 313
McCartney, Paul, 30n, 32, 36, 66, 174, 181,
    199, 218, 313
McClelland, Geoff, 71, 73, 75–77
McCracklin, Jimmy, 169
McCullin, Donald, 23, 25
McDonald, Ian, 189
McGrath, Mike, 40
McLaughlin, John, 289
McPhatter, Clyde, 255
McTell, Ralph, 36
Meek, Joe, 31, 41
Melanie, 131
Mellow Yellow (Donovan), 94
Melly, George, 54
Melody (Rolling Stones), 256
Melvin, Harold, & The Blue Notes, 256
Memory Of A Free Festival (David Bowie),
    159, 304
Mendelsohn, John, 217
Metal Guru (T. Rex), 209–211
Meteors, The, 168
Metropolis (T. Rex), 288
Metzger, Gustav, 69, 81
Michael, John, 43
Midnight (T. Rex), 239
Midsummer Night's Scene (John's Children),
    77–78, 85–86
Miles, Colin, 325–326
Milligan, Mick, 114
Miss Mercy, 151
Misty Mist (Marc Bolan), 57
Misty Mist (Tyrannosaurus Rex), 96, 102
Mitchell, Joni, 143
Mixtures, The, 116
Mona The Carniverous Circus (Mick Farren), 192
Monkees, The, 74, 92, 107, 222
Monolith (T. Rex), 177, 190, 325
Montez, Chris, 320
Moody Blues, The, 51, 103, 167, 234
Moon, Keith, 70, 82, 239, 279, 297, 332
Moore, Scotty, 153
Morrison, Bryan, 126, 132, 136
Morrison, Van, 50
Morrissey, 215, 272
Mott The Hoople, 219, 232, 240
Mountain, 176, 260
Move It (Cliff Richard), 14, 183
Move, The, 81, 103–104, 106, 124, 166,
    194–195
Mr Tambourine Man (Bob Dylan), 184
Mud, 286, 320
Mungo Jerry, 116, 158–159, 163, 174

Murphy, Audie, 8, 10
Murphy, Kieron 'Spud', 187
Murray, Charles Shaar, 203, 211, 214, 228, 306
Murray The K, 195
Music From Big Pink (Band), 143
Mustang Ford (John's Children), 82n., 86
Mustang Ford (Marc Bolan), 64, 78
Mustang Ford (Tyrannosaurus Rex), 107, 109
My Baby Left Me (Elvis Presley), 189
My Mistake (Was To Love You) (Diana Ross
    & Marvin Gaye), 238
*My People Were Fair And Had Sky In Their Hair
    . . . But Now They're Content To Wear
    Stars On Their Brows* (Tyrannosaurus
    Rex), 106–109, 111, 117, 132, 301
My Sweet Lord (George Harrison), 174, 305
My World Is Empty Without You (Marsha
    Hunt), 149
Myron (painting) (Gore Vidal), 312
Myskow, Nina, 186–187

Nameless Wildness (T. Rex), 243, 264
Napier-Bell, Simon, 48, 62–67, 70–79, 81–82,
    84–89, 92, 95–99, 135, 147, 158, 221,
    244, 261, 268
Nashville Skyline (Bob Dylan), 143
Nashville Teens, The, 50–51
Nelson, Ricky, 122, 153, 164
Nessim, Barbara, 178
New Rose (Damned), 317
New Seekers, The, 198
New York City (T. Rex), 282, 289, 293, 296,
    299, 309
New York Dolls, The, 272
Newman, Randy, 198, 239
Newman, Tony, 310–311, 324
Nice, The, 133
Nietzsche, Fredrich, 1
Nijinsky Hind (Tyrannosaurus Rex), 130
Nilsson, 239, 248, 279, 322
Niven, David, 284, 298
No No No (Richard Jones), 256
No Particular Place To Go (Chuck Berry),
    184n.
Norman, Tony, 126, 160, 167
Not The Sort Of Girl (You'd Take To Bed)
    (John's Children), 79
Nureyev, Rudolph, 326

O'Dowd, George (see Boy George)
O'Halloran, Mickey, 136, 209, 215, 260,
    276–277, 294, 322
O'Hara, Riggs, 45–49, 62, 115, 312
O'Jays, The, 256
O'Leary, Alphi, 215, 221, 322
O'Rourke, Steve, 136
Observations (Marc Bolan), 64–65
Obsession (film), 284, 298
Ochs, Phil, 53

Oh Baby (Dib Cochran & The Earwigs), 163
Oh Boy (Buddy Holly), 303
Oldham, Andrew Loog, 50, 73, 194
On The Third Day (Electric Light Orchestra),
    239
One Fine Day (Chiffons), 305
One Inch Rock (T. Rex), 300
One Inch Rock (Tyrannosaurus Rex), 96–97,
    116, 161–162, 169, 173, 201, 289
Ono, Yoko, 159, 174, 210
Orbison, Roy, 30
Organ Blues (T. Rex), 304
Organ Blues (Tyrannosaurus Rex), 161
Orgasm (John's Children), 75, 85
Orlando, Tony, 186
Ormsby-Gore, Alice, 145, 151, 153
Osmond, Donny, 217
Osmond, Little Jimmy, 240
Osmonds, The, 181
Othello (play) (William Shakespeare), 79
Over The Flats (Marc Bolan), 27

Page, Jimmy, 64, 181
Pain And Love (T. Rex), 323
Painless Persuasion v. The Meathawk Immacu-
    late (T. Rex), 264
Palmer, Mark, 141
Pan's People, 185
Parker, Charlie, 53
Parker, Ray, Jr, 256, 281
Parkinson, Michael, 23
Parliament, 320
Parry, Dick, 260*n.*
Party (Elvis Presley), 212
Pavilions Of Sun (Tyrannosaurus Rex), 153,
    155, 162
Paxton, Tom, 44, 253
Peacock, Steve, 238
Pearls, The, 282
Peel, John, 90–91, 97–98, 101–103, 107–110,
    113, 115–117, 120, 122, 124–126,
    129–133, 136, 138, 141, 144, 147,
    152–153, 169, 172, 182–183, 191–192,
    248, 259, 328
Peel, Sheila, 117, 122, 132
Peppermint Flipstick (Shagrat), 193
Peppers, 282
Perkins, Carl, 15, 36, 143, 305
Perrone, Francis, 10, 12, 19, 22, 25–26
Pet Sounds (Beach Boys), 66, 146
Peter, Paul & Mary, 39
Petticoat Lane (T. Rex), 297
Pewter Suitor (Tyrannosaurus Rex), 128, 134
Phil Spector's Christmas Album (Phil Spector/
    Various Artistes), 237
Phillips, Gregory, 38
Phillips, Kate, 273
Phillips, Sam, 177
Piccadilly Line, The, 98

Pickettywitch, 163
Pictures Of Purple People (Marc Bolan), 64
Pictures Of Purple People (Tyrannosaurus
    Rex), 102–103
Pictures Of Purple People (play) (Marc Bolan), 60,
    65, 102–103
Pierce, Webb, 305–306
Pink Fairies, The, 127, 140, 144, 192–193, 228
Pink Floyd, The, 79, 83, 92, 99–100, 107,
    109–111, 127, 132–133, 136–137, 153,
    174, 193, 203, 243, 270, 319, 332
Pipkins, The, 163
Pitt, Kenneth, 51, 62, 127–128, 145, 147
Plastic Man (Kinks), 159
Plastic Ono Band, 158–159, 174, 188
Platz, David, 99, 104–106, 132, 134, 163–166,
    194–197, 200, 207, 228, 244
Pollock, Jason, 53
Porter, Bobbye Hall, 281
Powell, Aubrey, 187
Powell, Don, 225
Powell, Enoch, 320
Power Of Love (Richard Jones), 256
Power To All Our Friends (Cliff Richard), 240
Precious Star (T. Rex), 273
Prelude (Tyrannosaurus Rex), 155
Presley, Elvis, 1, 10–14, 25, 36, 45, 52, 58, 76,
    91, 136, 141, 143, 152–153, 175, 179,
    181, 189, 199, 209, 212, 217, 230, 239,
    260–261, 265, 269, 303, 320, 324, 328
Preston, Billy, 237, 256, 319
Pretty Things, The, 127, 132, 140, 192
Price, Vincent, 127
Princess Margaret, 311
Proby, P.J., 52
Procul Harum, 20, 102, 104, 106, 166, 195
Prophets, Seers & Sages The Angels Of The Ages
    (Tyrannosaurus Rex), 48, 117–119, 121,
    127
Pruskin, Mike, 49–53, 55–56, 60–62, 71
Puckish Pan (Tyrannosaurus Rex), 106

Quant, Mary, 42
Quatro, Suzi, 240, 268
Queen, 318
Quicksilver Messenger Service, 193
Quintessence, 185

R Is For Rocket (book) (Ray Bradbury), 95
Rabbit Fighter (T. Rex), 214
Radio Stars, 321
Rainier, Prince, 283
Rains, Claude, 9
Ramone, Joey, 325
Rattles, The, 69
Raven, Paul, 216
Ray, Johnnie, 32
Real Life (book) (Marsha Hunt), 150
Reality (Marc Bolan), 57–58

Rebel Rock (book) (John Street), 184
Redding, Otis, 190, 296
Reed, Lou, 240, 306, 313n., 319
Reeves, Martha, 237
Rehger, Bob, 223
Reid, John, 321
Reid, Keith, 20, 77, 103
Remember Thomas A'Beckett (John's
  Children), 82n., 86
Richard, Cliff, 14–15, 24, 29–31, 33, 36,
  38–39, 45, 48, 52, 63, 76, 183, 240, 296,
  332
Richards, Keith, 231, 264
Ride A White Swan (T. Rex), 162, 164–166,
  168–175, 179, 191–192, 236, 299, 310,
  325, 327
Ringo (Ringo Starr), 239
Rings Of Fortune (Marc Bolan), 57
Rings Of Fortune (Tyrannosaurus Rex), 96–97
Rinpoche, Chime, 115, 214
Rip It Up (Little Richard), 303
Rip Off (T. Rex), 189–190
Rite Of Spring (Stravinsky), 96
Rivers, Sylvester, 256
Rock & Roll (Parts 1 & 2) (Gary Glitter), 216
Rock 'n' Roll (John Lennon), 210
Rock Around The Clock (Bill Haley & His
  Comets), 12, 143
Rock Me (Tyrannosaurus Rex), 106
Rock, Mick, 233
Rodgers, Jimmie, 36
Rods, The, 320
Roeg, Nic, 284
Rogan, Johnny, 194
Rollin' Bolan (television programme), 306, 309,
  330
Rollin' Danny (Gene Vincent), 84
Rolling Stones, The, 30, 35, 50–51, 64, 73, 91,
  120, 125, 132n., 141, 182, 194, 196, 199,
  205, 210, 212, 217, 227, 233, 235, 237,
  243, 249, 256, 263–264, 266, 310, 320,
  325
Romany Soup (Tyrannosaurus Rex), 130
Ronettes, The, 35, 150
Ronson, Mick, 146n., 156, 163
Rooney, Dave, 326
Root Of Star (T. Rex), 169
Rosetta Stone, 320
Ross, Diana, 223, 238
Rotten, Johnny, 306
Rowe, Dick, 51–52
Roxon, Lillian, 232
Roxy Music, 240, 251
Rubettes, The, 269
Rudge, Peter, 243
Ruffell, Betsie (see Betsie Feld)
Rumble, The, 168
Runaround Sue (Dion), 40, 129
Rupert (Jackie Lee), 174

Russell, Rosalind, 214, 263
Ryan, Barry, 128

Sailors Of The Highway (Gloria Jones), 308
Sailors Of The Highway (T. Rex), 200, 255
Saint Laurent, Yves, 49
Saint-Marie, Buffy, 63
Salamanda Palaganda (Tyrannosaurus Rex),
  117–118
Sally Was An Angel (John's Children), 78, 96
Sally Was An Angel (Tyrannosaurus Rex), 96
Salt Of The Earth (Rolling Stones), 237
Samwell-Smith, Paul, 64
San Francisco Bay Blues (Jesse Fuller), 60
San Francisco Poet (Marc Bolan), 58
Sanctified (T. Rex), 302
Sanctified Sisters, The, 223
Sanders, Pete, 114, 130–132, 141–142, 151,
  157–158, 165, 170, 190–191, 248
Sanders, Rick, 117
Sanderson, Duncan, 228
Santana, 139
Sara Crazy Child (John's Children), 78, 86,
  96–97
Sara Crazy Child (Tyrannosaurus Rex), 96
Sassoon, Vidal, 299
Savage Beethoven (Gloria Jones), 308
Savalas, Telly, 297
Savoy Brown, 309
Sawyer, Pam, 237, 308
Scenescoff (Tyrannosaurus Rex), 102
School Day (Chuck Berry), 184n.
School's Out (Alice Cooper), 217
Schwab, Coco, 324
Scott, Tyrone, 299
Secunda, Chelita, 180, 191, 194–195, 199, 207,
  212, 230, 244–246
Secunda, Tony, 194–197, 205–208, 212,
  220–221, 228, 244–245
See Emily Play (Pink Floyd), 83n.
See My Baby Jive (Wizzard), 239
See You Later Alligator (Bill Haley & His
  Comets), 12, 65
Seeger, Pete, 36
Self Portrait (Bob Dylan), 159–160
Selwood, Clive, 131, 248
Serious Charge (film), 15
Sex Pistols, The, 306, 313, 317, 320
Sgt. Pepper's Lonely Hearts Club Band (Beatles),
  85, 143, 200, 275
Shadows, The, 155
Shagrat, 193
Shang-A-Lang (television programme), 311
Shangri-Las, The, 306
Shankar, Ravi, 89
Shapiro, Helen, 2, 12–15, 21, 30, 42, 50, 56
Share My Love (Grace Jones), 254
Sharp, Jennifer, 330
Shaw, Adrian, 329

She Loves You (Beatles), 32
She Was Born To Be My Unicorn
   (Tyrannosaurus Rex), 130
She'd Rather Be With Me (Turtles), 139
Sheller, Martin, 71
Shirelles, The, 189
Shirley, Jerry, 176
Shock Rock (T. Rex), 234
Showaddywaddy, 269, 320
Showdown (Electric Light Orchestra), 240
Silence, The, 71–72
Silent Night (Phil Spector), 237
Silly Boy Blue (David Bowie), 148
Simmonds, Michael, 21, 23–25, 28
Simon, Paul, 206
Sims, Judith, 251
Sinatra, Frank, 12, 32, 320
Singer, Glenn, 13, 30
Singer, Susan, 13, 21, 30, 42
Sioux, Siouxsie, 295, 320–321
Siouxsie & The Banshees, 320
(Sittin' On) The Dock Of The Bay (Otis
   Redding), 296
Skweeze Me Pleeze Me (Slade), 239
Slade, 195, 207, 216–217, 225, 232, 239, 266
Slater, Eve, 244
Sleepy La Beef, 189–190
Sleepy Maurice (Tyrannosaurus Rex), 96
Slik, 305
Slim, Memphis, 30
Small Faces, The, 72, 210
Smashed Blocked (John's Children), 74–75,
   82n., 85
Smiley Smile (Beach Boys), 146
Smith, Bessie, 63
Smith, Hurricane, 186
Smith, Ian, 108
Smith, John, 178
Smith, Patti, 306
Smith, Robin, 308, 318
Smith, Tony, 178
Smokestack Lightning (Silence), 71
So Long Dad (Manfred Mann), 104
Soft Machine, The, 192
Solid Baby (T. Rex), 273, 306
Solid Gold Easy Action (T. Rex), 220, 227,
   232, 325
Solomon, Phil, 50
Something Else (Eddie Cochran), 88
Song For A Soldier (Marc Bolan), 57–58
Sonny & Cher, 66
Soul Love (David Bowie), 218
Sound Pit (T. Rex), 264
Southern, Terry, 227
Space Boss (T. Rex), 273
Space Oddity (David Bowie), 128, 145, 146,
   148, 214, 219, 304
Spaceball Ricochet (T. Rex), 205–206, 208,
   214

Sparks, Steve, 34, 115
Spector, Phil, 129–130, 146, 154, 208, 210,
   237, 298
Spedding, Chris, 309
Spiral Scratch EP (Buzzcocks), 317
Spruill, Stephanie, 223
Squint Eye Mangle (Big Carrot), 254
St John, Barry, 233
St John, Bridget, 192, 248
Stacey Grove (Marsha Hunt), 149
Stacey Grove (Tyrannosaurus Rex), 118
Stairway To Heaven (Led Zeppelin), 187
Stamp, Chris, 69, 165–166
Stamping Ground (film), 161
Standing Next To You (Marc Bolan & David
   Bowie), 324
Stapleton, Doug, 215
Stardust, Alvin, 263, 269, 313, 332
*Starmakers & Svengalis: The History Of British Pop
   Management* (book) (Johnny Rogan), 194
Starman (David Bowie), 217
Starr, Ringo, 32, 186, 202–203, 211–213, 227,
   230, 239, 279, 283, 321–322
Steel Abortion (Shagrat), 193
Steele, Tommy, 14
Stephen, John, 24, 27, 43
Stevens, Cat, 57, 99, 143, 198, 303
Stevens, John, 60
Stevens, Ray, 174
Stevenson, Ray, 102, 128, 132
Stewart, Al, 36
Stewart, Rod, 192, 198, 207, 216, 240, 249,
   332
Strange Orchestras (Tyrannosaurus Rex),
   106–107, 110
Street Fighting Man (Rolling Stones), 120
Street, John, 184
Streisand, Barbra, 65
Subterranean Homesick Blues (Bob Dylan),
   184, 214
Sue & Sunny, 145, 233
Sugar, Peter, 21, 23–25, 28
Sullivan, Big Jim, 71n.
Summer Deep (T. Rex), 152, 169
Summer Holiday (film), 31
Summertime Blues (Eddie Cochran), 166, 173
Summertime Blues (T. Rex), 206
Suneye (T. Rex), 169
Sunken Rags (T. Rex), 227, 255
Sunshine, 250
Sunshine Superman (Donovan), 94
Supersonic (television programme), 294–296,
   306, 309–311, 319
Supremes, The, 149, 237, 273
Susie & The Hula Hoops, 13, 30
Sutch, Screaming Lord, 31
Swanson, Gloria, 281, 290
Sweet, The, 216–218, 240, 262, 294
Swinging Blue Jeans, The, 35

T. Rex (T. Rex), 168–169, 177, 188, 269

T. Rex, 1, 71, 90, 93, 116, 163, 165, 167–180, 182–183, 185–189, 193, 195, 197–200, 202–207, 211–213, 215, 218–234, 237–239, 241–245, 247, 249, 251–252, 254–261, 263–264, 267–270, 272–275, 278–279, 281–282, 285–288, 290–291, 297–302, 304–305, 307–312, 314–315, 317–319, 322, 326, 329, 332

Tainted Love (Gloria Jones), 237, 307

Tanner, Stewart, 173

Tanx (T. Rex), 224–225, 233–235, 238, 250, 263

Tarantula (book) (Bob Dylan), 185

Taste, 167

Taylor, Elizabeth, 212

Taylor, Hound Dog, 169

Taylor, Ian, 244

Taylor, James, 143, 187, 198

Taylor, Mick, 310

Taylor, Tim, 193

Taylor's Boogie (Hound Dog Taylor), 169

Teddy Bears, The, 314

Teen Riot Structure (T. Rex), 317

Teenage Boogie (Webb Pierce), 305–306

Teenage Dream (T. Rex), 236, 259, 262–263, 276–277, 289, 317

Teenage Lament '74 (Alice Cooper), 262

Teenage Rampage (Sweet), 262

Teenbeats, The, 173

Telegram Sam (T. Rex), 203, 208, 224, 250, 277

Tell Me (Pat Hall), 255

Tell Me Now (Gloria Jones), 308

Tell Me What He Said (Helen Shapiro), 30

Temple, John, 35

Ten Years After, 161, 167, 186–187

Tenement Lady (T. Rex), 227, 234

Tennyson, Alfred, Lord, 119

That'll Be The Day (Buddy Holly/Crickets), 13, 209

That's The Bag I'm In (Marc Bolan), 53

Thatcher, Margaret, 240

The Avengers (Superbad) (T. Rex), 243, 264

The Beginning Of Doves (Marc Bolan/ Tyrannosaurus Rex), 96, 221, 268

The Beginning Of Doves (Tyrannosaurus Rex), 96

The Best Of T. Rex (T. Rex), 178

The Children Of Ram (abandoned album) (T. Rex), 168–169, 177, 200–201, 241, 248, 268–269, 288, 298

The Children Of Rarn (T. Rex), 169

The Cry Of Love (Jimi Hendrix), 190

The Divided Self (book) (R.D. Laing), 112

The 5000 Spirits Or The Layers Of The Onion (Incredible String Band), 101

The Freewheelin' Bob Dylan (Bob Dylan), 39

The Gnome (Pink Floyd), 100

The Groover (T. Rex), 238–239, 243, 250

The Hobbit (book), (J.R.R. Tolkien), 120

The Jean Genie (David Bowie), 232

The King Of Stamford Hill (David Bowie), 27

The Kraken (poem) (Tennyson), 119

The Kraken Wakes (book) (John Wyndham), 119

The Krakenmist (poem) (Marc Bolan), 119

The Leopards Featuring Gardenia And The Mighty Slug (T. Rex), 264

The Lilac Hand Of Menthol Dan (Marc Bolan/ John's Children), 87–88

The London Opera (abandoned project), 288, 302

The Lord Of The Rings (book) (J.R.R. Tolkien), 93, 99, 118, 120, 193

The Love I Thought I'd Found (John's Children), 74

The Magic Christian (film), 211

The Man Who Fell To Earth (film), 284

The Man Who Sold The World (David Bowie), 156–157, 159

The Man Who Sold The World (David Bowie), 232

The Motivator (T. Rex), 190

The Perfumed Garden Of Gulliver Smith (Marc Bolan), 64

The Perfumed Garden Of Gulliver Smith (Mark Feld), 39

The Perfumed Garden Of Gulliver Smith (John's Children), 78, 84

The Pilgrim's Tale (Tyrannosaurus Rex), 130

The Piper At The Gates Of Dawn (Pink Floyd), 100

The Prettiest Star (David Bowie), 145–149

The Prophet (book) (Kahlil Gilbran), 119

The Rise And Fall Of Ziggy Stardust And The Spiders From Mars (David Bowie), 217–218, 232, 258

The Road I'm On (Gloria) (Mark Feld), 39–40

The Sacred Squall Of Now (Reeves Gabrel), 27

The Scarecrow (Pink Floyd), 83*n*., 100

The Scenescof Dynasty (Tyrannosaurus Rex), 118–119, 134, 197, 302

The Slider (T. Rex), 207, 209, 214–215, 221–222, 224–226, 233, 246, 250, 257, 263, 301, 306, 316

The Slider (T. Rex), 212–214

The Soul Of My Suit (T. Rex), 288, 309, 315, 317, 325

The Sparrow Is The Sign (Twink), 192

The Star Spangled Banner (Jimi Hendrix), 143

The Street & Babe Shadow (T. Rex), 234

The Third Degree (John's Children), 78–79, 82*n*.

The Third Degree (Marc Bolan), 51, 58, 63

The Times They Are A-Changin' (Bob Dylan), 36

The Tin Drum (book) (Gunter Grass), 77

The Twist (Hank Ballard & The Midnighters), 30
The Uses Of Literacy (book) (Richard Hoggart), 8
The Walk (Jimmy McCracklin), 169, 214
The Wanderer (Dion), 40
The Warlock Of Love (poetry book) (Marc Bolan), 122–124, 126, 132
The Wicker Man (film), 284
The Wind In The Willows (book) (Kenneth Graham), 138
The Witch (Rattles), 69
The Wizard (In The Woods) (Marc Bolan), 51
The Wizard (Marc Bolan), 52–56, 58, 62, 97
The Wizard (T. Rex), 169
The Wizard (Tyrannosaurus Rex), 153, 162
The Woodland Bop (Tyrannosaurus Rex), 155
Them, 50–51
There Goes My Baby (Drifters), 15
Think Pink (Twink), 192
Think Zinc (T. Rex), 273
Third Ear Band, The, 110
Thomas, Caron, 272
Thompson, Danny, 101, 253, 328
Thompson, Dave, 218
Three Dog Night, 249–250
Three Little Piggies (Twink), 192
Thurmond, Wally, 268
Til Dawn (T. Rex), 273–274
Tillman, Julia, 223
Ting A Ling (David Bowie), 304
To Know Him Is To Love Him (Marc Bolan & Gloria Jones), 314
To Know Him Is To Love Him (Teddy Bears), 314
Token Of My Love (T. Rex), 273, 277
Tolkien, J.R.R., 60, 93, 98–99, 116, 118–120, 193
Tommy (Who), 187, 200
Tony & Siegrid, 103
Too Much Monkey Business (Chuck Berry), 184
Took, Steve Peregrine (Steve Porter), 88, 92–93, 95–96, 98, 100, 102, 105, 110, 113, 117, 122, 126–130, 133–137, 139–141, 144–145, 148, 150, 153, 155, 158, 161, 163, 165, 183, 192–193, 227–229, 296, 309, 326
Town (magazine), 16–17, 23, 26, 35
Townshend, Pete, 55, 69, 75, 78–79, 81–82, 84, 133, 186, 303
Townson, Chris, 68–73, 75, 79–80, 82–84, 86–87, 321
Traffic, 124
Travis, Dave Lee, 165, 167
Trelawny Lawn (Tyrannosaurus Rex), 118
Tremeloes, The, 173
Truck On (Tyke) (T. Rex), 257, 259–260
Truth, 30*n.*

Tumbling Dice (Rolling Stones), 210
Turner, Ike & Tina, 237
Turner, Mickey, 20
Turner, Steve, 172, 197, 200, 226
Turner, Tina, 303
Turtle Soup (Turtles), 139
Turtles, The, 74, 139
Tutti Frutti (Little Richard), 212
20th Century Boy (T. Rex), 233, 238, 319–320
Twiggy, 311
Twink, 144, 192
Twinkle, 52
Twist And Shout (Isley Brothers), 303
Twitty, Conway, 298
2468 (Jackson 5), 237
200 Motels (film), 211
Tyler, Toby (see Marc Bolan)
Tyrannosaurus Rex, 1, 48, 88, 90–92, 95–104, 106–111, 113, 116–117, 119, 121–122, 126–129, 131–142, 144–145, 150, 152–154, 156, 158, 160–165, 167–169, 171–172, 174–175, 177, 183, 187, 192–193, 195, 211, 221, 228, 248, 253, 259, 273, 277, 282, 289, 292, 296, 317

Ulmer, Gary, 272, 281
Underwood, George, 108–109, 114, 147, 301
Unicorn (Tyrannosaurus Rex), 129–130, 133–134, 149, 154, 159, 211
Union Gap, The, 107
Universal Love (Dib Cochran & The Earwigs), 163
Uriah Heep, 205, 282

Valenti, Dino, 193
Valentine, Penny, 148, 178–179, 195
Valentino, Rudolph, 310
Valleri (Monkees), 107
Valli, Frankie, 312
Varley, Paul, 311
Varten, Sylvie, 149*n.*
Vegetables (Beach Boys), 146
Velvet Underground, The, 84, 218, 292
Venus Loon (T. Rex), 259, 264
Vicious, Sid, 320
Vidal, Gore, 312
Video Drama (Marc Bolan), 267
Vincent, Gene, 84, 97, 141
Visconti, Tony, 90, 103–107, 110, 115, 120, 128–129, 133, 135, 139, 142, 145–149, 153–156, 159, 163–165, 167, 169, 172–174, 177–180, 182, 188–190, 197, 200, 203, 208–210, 212, 214, 220, 224–225, 239, 242–243, 245, 247, 253, 257–258, 262–263, 272, 274, 280–281, 301, 305, 332
Visons Of Domino (T. Rex), 317
Vixen (Gloria Jones), 255, 307
Volman, Mark, 139–141, 175

Wakeman, Rick, 163, 189, 303
Walk On Gilded Splinters (Marsha Hunt), 149
Walker, Scott, 57, 107
Walker, Sid, 208
Walker, T-Bone, 184
Walkin' Back To Happiness (Helen Shapiro), 30
Wallis, Larry, 193
War, 262
War Heroes (Jimi Hendrix), 239*n*.
Warhol, Andy, 208, 258, 290
Warlord Of The Royal Crocodiles
    (Tyrannosaurus Rex), 128
Warren, Allan, 37–38, 40–47, 61, 106
Waters, Roger, 124
Watts, Michael, 213, 218
Waymouth, Nigel, 141–142
Wayne, Carl, 124
Wayne, John, 264
Wayne, Mick, 228
We Can Be Together (Jefferson Airplane), 143
Weaver, Blue, 189
Wedgbury, David, 56
Weedon, Bert, 37, 161
Weilder Of Words (Tyrannosaurus Rex), 109
Weisman, John, 205
Welch, Chris, 128, 131, 133–134, 144, 167,
    170, 172, 183, 187, 197, 273
Welles, Orson, 297, 312
Wesley, Mark, 267
West, Keith, 124
West, Leslie, 260, 319–320
When I Was A Child (Pat Hall), 255
Where Did Our Love Go (Supremes), 273
Whipman, Theresa 'Terry', 50–51, 61, 65, 77,
    82, 92, 96, 111–114, 119
White, Barry, 281
White Plains, 163
White, Trevor, 79
Who, The, 69, 71–73, 75, 81–82, 84, 243, 249,
    318
Whyton, Wally, 37
Width Of A Circle (David Bowie), 156
Wild Eyed Boy From Freecloud (David
    Bowie), 304
Wild Honey (Beach Boys), 146
Wilde, Marty, 15, 35, 161, 303, 320
Wilderness Of The Mind (poetry collection)
    (Marc Bolan), 301
Will You Love Me Tomorrow (Shirelles), 189
Willans, John, 272
Williams, Binky, 237
Williams, Richard, 213
Wills, Viola, 223
Wilson, Brian, 231

Wilson, Harold, 60, 194
Wilson, William, Inspector, 331
Wind Quartets (Tyrannosaurus Rex), 161
Windstorm (Gloria Jones), 321
Winter, Johnny, 176
Witches Brew (Janie Jones), 56
With A Little Help From My Friends (Beatles),
    224
With A Little Help From My Friends (Joe
    Cocker), 224
Witherspoon, Jimmy, 30
Wizzard, 239–240
Woman Child (Marsha Hunt), 149
Wombles, The, 270
Wonder, Stevie, 282
Wood, Chris, 124
Wood, Roy, 194, 268, 297–298, 303, 322
Woodland Rock (T. Rex), 172, 175
Woodland Story (Marc Bolan), 108, 131
Worth, Sue, 151, 285
Wray, Link, 161
Wright, Betty, 255
Wright, Edna, 237
Wyndham, John, 119
Wynette, Tammy, 286

Yardbirds, The, 30, 64, 73, 76
Yellow River (Christie), 163
Yes, 187
You Can't Do That (John's Children), 79
You Damaged The Soul Of My Suit (T. Rex),
    282
You Don't Know (Helen Shapiro), 30
You Got The Power (Marc Bolan), 64
You'll Be Mine (Howlin' Wolf), 189
You're No Good (Betty Everett), 42, 46
You're No Good (Mark Feld), 42, 46
You're No Good (Swinging Blue Jeans), 42
Young Americans (David Bowie), 274*n*.
Young Girl (Union Gap), 107
Young, Muriel, 37, 320, 329
Young, Neil, 143, 264
Youngbloods, The, 143

Zappa, Frank, 92, 150, 157, 211
Zinc Alloy And The Hidden Raiders Of
    Tomorrow, 241, 259, 263
*Zinc Alloy And The Hidden Riders Of Tomorrow/
    A Creamed Cage In August* (T. Rex), 253,
    257–259, 262–264, 267, 271, 316
Zip Gun Boogie (T. Rex), 277, 282, 286
Zodiacs, The, 173
Zombies, The, 51
ZZ Top, 275

About The Author

Most likely conceived to the sound of Perry Como's 'Magic Moments', Mark Paytress was born in Bournemouth in February 1959. The first pop story he remembers is Dusty quitting The Springfields (in September 1963), his first 45 The Rolling Stones' '(I Can't Get No) Satisfaction' and first brush with celebrity a personal letter from the *Thank Your Lucky Stars* girl Janice "Oi'll give it foive!" Nicholls. Encouraged by melody-mad parents, a succession of language student lodgers and a family friend who kindly passed on all his pop weeklies, he dedicated himself to studying the fortunes of his favourite pop singles and spending his pocket-money on records by The Move and The Herd.

Some time during 1968, a kindly hippie next door named Mick introduced him to a world where long-haired men wore fur coats and played their records on hand-painted machines with two speakers (stereo!). Laughing at his mention of Dave Dee, Dozy, Beaky, Mick & Tich, Mick nevertheless placated him with a scratchy copy of The Pink Floyd's 'See Emily Play', an earful of the Floyd's *The Piper At The Gates Of Dawn* and this odd song about a girl called 'Debora'. It was by Tyrannosaurus Rex and its wobbly voiced singer was Marc Bolan.

After Bolan broke big in the early Seventies, the teenaged Mark turned his back on the new decade and dedicated himself instead to reviving the Summer of Love single-handedly. He failed all his exams, preferring instead to 'play' along to Cream and Jimi Hendrix records in front of his bedroom mirror. And he began to greet every stranger with the words: "Have *you* heard *Trout Mask Replica*?"

Accepting punk rock's invitation to rejoin the real world, he chopped off his hair, joined a band and waited for the *NME* to come knocking. It didn't, so he started writing; in March 1986 he had his first feature (on The Fall) published in a rock magazine. He's been writing about rock ever since for a variety of music and lifestyle publications. He has had books published on The Rolling Stones, Nirvana and David Bowie, once wrote an impenetrable Cultural Studies postgraduate thesis on 'The Concept Of Dystopia In Industrial Music' and, in 1992, completed a Marc Bolan biography, which provides the basis for this latest book.

A freelance writer who has a regular home editing *Mojo Collections* for *Mojo* magazine, his hobbies include speaking Spanish badly and dancing like Joe Cocker at parties.